The Rise of Blockchain Applications in Customer Experience

Mohammed Majeed
Tamale Technical University, Ghana

Kwame Simpe Ofori
International University of Grand Bassam, Cote D'Ivoire

George Kofi Amoako
Ghana Communication Technology University, Ghana

Abdul-Raheed Alolo
Tamale Technical University, Ghana

Gideon Awini
Business School, University of Ghana, Ghana

A volume in the Advances in Marketing, Customer Relationship Management, and E-Services (AMCRMES) Book Series

IGI Global
PUBLISHER of TIMELY KNOWLEDGE

Published in the United States of America by
IGI Global
Business Science Reference (an imprint of IGI Global)
701 E. Chocolate Avenue
Hershey PA, USA 17033
Tel: 717-533-8845
Fax: 717-533-8661
E-mail: cust@igi-global.com
Web site: http://www.igi-global.com

Library of Congress Cataloging-in-Publication Data

Names: Majeed, Mohammed, 1982- editor. | Ofori, Kwame, 1983- editor. | Amoako, George Kofi, 1965- editor. | Alolo, Abdul-Raheed Akeji, 1972- editor. | Awini, Gideon, 1987- editor.
Title: The rise of blockchain applications in customer experience / edited by Mohammed Majeed, Kwame Simpe Ofori, George Kofi Amoako, Abdul-Raheed Alolo, and Gideon Awini
Description: Hershey, PA : Business Science Reference, [2023] | Includes bibliographical references and index. | Summary: "The Rise of Blockchain Applications in Customer Experience provides an overview of how blockchain influences consumers and considers the key characteristics of blockchain models for institutional success. Covering key topics such as online customer experiences, customer satisfaction, and consumer behavior, this premier reference source is ideal for business owners, managers, policymakers, scholars, researchers, academicians, practitioners, instructors, and students"-- Provided by publisher.
Identifiers: LCCN 2023002186 (print) | LCCN 2023002187 (ebook) | ISBN 9781668476499 (hardcover) | ISBN 9781668476505 (paperback) | ISBN 9781668476512 (ebook)
Subjects: LCSH: Consumers' preferences--Technological innovations. | Consumers--Attitudes--Technological innovations. | Blockchains (Databases)
Classification: LCC HF5415.32 .R56 2023 (print) | LCC HF5415.32 (ebook) | DDC 658.8/34--dc23/eng/20230127
LC record available at https://lccn.loc.gov/2023002186
LC ebook record available at https://lccn.loc.gov/2023002187

This book is published in the IGI Global book series Advances in Marketing, Customer Relationship Management, and E-Services (AMCRMES) (ISSN: 2327-5502; eISSN: 2327-5529)

British Cataloguing in Publication Data
A Cataloguing in Publication record for this book is available from the British Library.
All work contributed to this book is new, previously-unpublished material.
The views expressed in this book are those of the authors, but not necessarily of the publisher.
For electronic access to this publication, please contact: eresources@igi-global.com.

Advances in Marketing, Customer Relationship Management, and E-Services (AMCRMES) Book Series

ISSN:2327-5502
EISSN:2327-5529

Editor-in-Chief: Eldon Y. Li, National Chengchi University, Taiwan & California Polytechnic State University, USA

MISSION

Business processes, services, and communications are important factors in the management of good customer relationship, which is the foundation of any well organized business. Technology continues to play a vital role in the organization and automation of business processes for marketing, sales, and customer service. These features aid in the attraction of new clients and maintaining existing relationships.

The Advances in Marketing, Customer Relationship Management, and E-Services (AMCRMES) Book Series addresses success factors for customer relationship management, marketing, and electronic services and its performance outcomes. This collection of reference source covers aspects of consumer behavior and marketing business strategies aiming towards researchers, scholars, and practitioners in the fields of marketing management.

COVERAGE

- Social Networking and Marketing
- CRM in financial services
- Ethical Considerations in E-Marketing
- CRM strategies
- Text Mining and Marketing
- Cases on Electronic Services
- Electronic Services
- B2B marketing
- Relationship Marketing
- Data mining and marketing

IGI Global is currently accepting manuscripts for publication within this series. To submit a proposal for a volume in this series, please contact our Acquisition Editors at Acquisitions@igi-global.com or visit: http://www.igi-global.com/publish/.

The Advances in Marketing, Customer Relationship Management, and E-Services (AMCRMES) Book Series (ISSN 2327-5502) is published by IGI Global, 701 E. Chocolate Avenue, Hershey, PA 17033-1240, USA, www.igi-global.com. This series is composed of titles available for purchase individually; each title is edited to be contextually exclusive from any other title within the series. For pricing and ordering information please visit http://www.igi-global.com/book-series/advances-marketing-customer-relationship-management/37150. Postmaster: Send all address changes to above address.

Titles in this Series

For a list of additional titles in this series, please visit:
http://www.igi-global.com/book-series/advances-marketing-customer-relationship-management/37150

Effective Digital Marketing for Improving Society Behavior Toward DEI and SDGs
Inês Veiga Pereira (Accounting and Business School, Polytechnic of Porto, Portugal) Paulo Botelho Pires (Centre for Organizational and Social Studies, Polytechnic of Porto, Portugal) and José Duarte Santos (Accounting and Business School, Polytechnic of Porto, Portugal)
Business Science Reference • © 2023 • 320pp • H/C (ISBN: 9781668489840) • US $240.00

Sustainable Marketing, Branding, and Reputation Management Strategies for a Greener Future
Reason Masengu (Middle East College, Oman) Stanilas Bigirimana (Africa University, Zimbabwe) Option Takunda Chiwaridzo (University of Science and Technology, Beijing, China) Ruzive Bensson (Modern College of Business and Science, Oman) and Christina Blossom (Middle East College, Oman)
Business Science Reference • © 2023 • 670pp • H/C (ISBN: 9798369300190) • US $250.00

Origin and Branding in International Market Entry Processes
Carlos Francisco e Silva (Universidade Europeia, Portugal)
Business Science Reference • © 2023 • 298pp • H/C (ISBN: 9781668466131) • US $250.00

The Role of Brands in an Era of Over-Information
Ricardo Fontes Correia (Polytechnic Institute of Bragança, Portugal) Dominyka Venciūtė (ISM University of Management and Economics, Lithuania) and Bruno Miguel Sousa (Polytechnic Institute of Cávado and Ave, Portugal)
Business Science Reference • © 2023 • 257pp • H/C (ISBN: 9781668483510) • US $250.00

Influences of Social Media on Consumer Decision-Making Processes in the Food and Grocery Industry
Theodore Tarnanidis (International Hellenic University, Greece) Maro Vlachopoulou (University of Macedonia, Greece) and Jason Papathanasiou (University of Macedonia, Greece)
Business Science Reference • © 2023 • 317pp • H/C (ISBN: 9781668488683) • US $250.00

IGI Global
PUBLISHER of TIMELY KNOWLEDGE

701 East Chocolate Avenue, Hershey, PA 17033, USA
Tel: 717-533-8845 x100 • Fax: 717-533-8661
E-Mail: cust@igi-global.com • www.igi-global.com

Table of Contents

Detailed Table of Contents

Blockchain technology's introduction to social media marketing is an influential force to transform security and build trust in a social media platform, thus encouraging greater consumer engagement. This chapter explores the economic benefits of combining blockchain and social media marketing, and how this creates a powerful synergy to address consumer behaviour, through a process of a systematic and thematic content analysis of 30 selected peer-reviewed literature as well as 11 pieces of grey literature (which included social media site posts and blogs) published between 2012 and 2021. The implementation of blockchain technology has the potential to bring about a strategic transformation by inculcating a change in the customer's behaviour towards the organisation. The information in this chapter will provide compelling support that organisations can increase their consumer as well as influencer numbers online and successfully entice high traffic to their home page by implementing blockchain technology in their social media marketing campaigns.

Blockchain is a transparent, encrypted, distributed database. It is utilised effectively by financial instruments, e-government, supply networks, and others. This paper examines emergency uses for the Blockchain. There needs to be a sound information system for managing and controlling disasters, making decisions, and creating a conceptual model from disaster and blockchain literature. This chapter discusses parties exchanging and storing data on one platform. This study proposes a system model for pre-, during-, and post-disaster user scenarios. The methodology asserts holistic disaster resolution.

Technological entrepreneurship has considerably aided the commercialization of internet technology by transferring it to the web; internet technology has changed traditional buying practices. The idea of blockchain technology was created when digital signatures were first used in the 1990s to confirm that signed documents had not been altered. The chapter comes to a conclusion by emphasizing the crucial role that blockchains serve in maintaining a safe and decentralized record of transactions. The innovation of a blockchain resides in its capacity to establish trust without the involvement of a reliable third party and to ensure the safety and integrity of a record of data.

COVID-19's phenomenal effect has expedited the adoption of digital technologies over several years, indicating that several of these breakthroughs are here to stay. Several enabling technologies are currently being implemented as major solutions for improving and responding to the pandemic's numerous issues, with blockchain being one of the preferred solution options. Blockchain can be used to re-structure processes, resulting in most effective operational and business models (e.g., democratising quality cancer detection with advanced artificial intelligence based

Preface

Welcome to *The Rise of Blockchain Applications in Customer Experience*, a comprehensive reference book exploring the transformative power of blockchain technology in the realm of consumer behavior, loyalty, satisfaction, and more. This book is the result of a collaborative effort by a team of passionate and dedicated editors: Mohammed Majeed, Kwame Simpe Ofori, George Kofi Amoako, Abdul-Raheed Alolo, and Gideon Awini.

Blockchain, the ingenious technology behind cryptocurrencies like Bitcoin, has become a disruptive force with far-reaching implications for businesses and industries. While numerous scholarly publications have delved into the impact of distributed ledger technology on organizations, one crucial stakeholder has been conspicuously absent from the conversation - the consumer. This reference book aims to fill that void by shedding light on the profound influence of blockchain on customer experiences.

In the pages of this book, we embark on a journey to demystify the blockchain and its role as the operating system underpinning Bitcoin. Our exploration leads us to a deeper understanding of the blockchain as a decentralized shared ledger that utilizes chronological, encrypted, and chained blocks to store verified and synchronized data over firm-to-customer (F2C) networks.

The significance of this work lies in its potential to lay a solid foundation for future scholars, offering insights into the critical research areas that elucidate how blockchain impacts the contemporary consumer. We delve into customer experiences, loyalty, customer relationship management (CRM), customer care, satisfaction, and the word of mouth, among other vital aspects. Our ultimate goal is to empower marketers, businesses, academics and institutions to harness blockchain's capabilities and deploy them effectively in this fiercely competitive era.

The target audience for this book encompasses a diverse group of individuals and professionals, including consultants seeking strategic insights, academic scholars pushing the boundaries of knowledge, postgraduate and graduate students eager to grasp the latest developments, researchers in search of cutting-edge research material, IT professionals navigating the tech landscape, and customer-oriented institutions such as banks and data managers keen on enhancing their customer interactions.

Within these pages, you will discover a rich tapestry of topics that explores the intersection of blockchain and customer experience. Our selected chapters delve into areas such as customer order management, the future of customer experience, the synergy between blockchain and the Internet of Things, and the economics of customer satisfaction in a blockchain-driven world.

Chapter 1 sets the stage by examining the transformative power of blockchain technology in the context of social media marketing. By conducting a systematic analysis of a wide range of literature, including peer-reviewed sources and grey literature spanning almost a decade, the authors unveil the economic benefits of fusing blockchain and social media marketing. The chapter showcases how this fusion can drive consumer behavior, enhance trust, and ultimately lead to increased consumer and influencer engagement online.

Chapter 2 ventures into the exciting domain of the Internet of Things (IoT) and explores the recent buzz surrounding the integration of blockchain technology. This comprehensive analysis delves into the inherent challenges of IoT, such as decentralization, interoperability, privacy, and security, and examines how blockchain can address these issues. The chapter introduces the innovative concept of Blockchain for 5G Beyond IoT (BCoT) and highlights its potential applications across various industries.

Healthcare takes center stage in Chapter 3 as it undergoes a remarkable transformation through blockchain technology. The chapter explores how blockchain can create a secure data management platform, granting patients ownership over their medical records. It also examines the role of blockchain in fostering trust among healthcare stakeholders and standardizing its implementation on a global scale, with a nod to sustainability principles.

Chapter 4 delves deeper into the challenges faced by healthcare data management systems, including issues of transparency, traceability, privacy, and security. It shines a light on the potential of blockchain technology to revolutionize healthcare data management, offering innovative solutions and advancements for the industry.

Chapter 5 explores the profound impact of blockchain on the world of business-to-consumer (B2C) commerce. By promoting security, transparency, and fast payment processing, blockchain empowers businesses to engage with customers more effectively. The findings suggest that blockchain is poised to become a globally recognized tool in future government operations.

Chapter 6 takes a closer look at how blockchain technology is revolutionizing the e-commerce industry. By potentially eliminating the need for intermediaries and central authorities in permissionless blockchains, blockchain has the power to reorganize the way businesses and customers exchange information and value in the electronic commerce sector.

Chapter 7 dives into the world of Initial Coin Offerings (ICOs) and their potential as an alternative financing option for start-ups. Through a systematic review and bibliometric analysis, it explores the current understanding of ICOs, fractional ownership of digital assets, and the associated opportunities and challenges. The chapter emphasizes the impact of regulatory frameworks on the ICO market and offers valuable insights into this evolving field.

Chapter 8 explores the uncharted territory of using blockchain for emergency management. The chapter delves into the need for a robust information system to manage and control disasters, emphasizing data exchange and storage on a single platform. It proposes a system model for addressing pre-, during-, and post-disaster scenarios, laying the groundwork for holistic disaster resolution.

Chapter 9 delves into the pivotal role of blockchain technology in the evolution of internet technology and technological entrepreneurship. It traces the origins of blockchain and its innovative capacity to establish trust without the involvement of third parties. The chapter highlights blockchain's role in securing and decentralizing transaction records.

Chapter 10 reflects on the accelerated adoption of digital technologies due to the impact of COVID-19. It explores the potential of blockchain in restructuring processes and creating effective operational and business models. The chapter stresses the importance of a structured decision-making process and good business logic when implementing blockchain, highlighting the technology's role as a means to an end.

Chapter 11 uncovers the myriad ways in which blockchain is transforming the student experience. Through smart contracts, data analysis, transparency, and innovative credentialing, blockchain enriches the student (customer) experience and introduces novel possibilities in education, assessment, and progress tracking.

Chapter 12 focuses on the growing importance of cyber ethics, safety, and security in education, particularly in the context of social networks and increasing social network users. It includes guidelines for protecting personal information and highlights the need for increased awareness and security measures in the ever-evolving digital landscape.

Chapter 13 delves into the potential of blockchain technology in education. It examines the obstacles and challenges blockchain faces in the educational sector, such as funding, security, scalability, and awareness. The chapter emphasizes the need for a structured approach to harnessing the potential of blockchain in education.

Chapter 14 uncovers the unique challenges and opportunities associated with integrating blockchain into healthcare. The authors categorize blockchain into various forms and highlight the obstacles, including interconnectivity, security, standardization, and patient mistrust. This chapter emphasizes the importance of exploring blockchain's integration in healthcare despite the challenges.

The final chapter explores the dynamic interplay between blockchain technology and the emerging concept of the Metaverse. It examines how these technologies can enhance customer interactions, offering immersive previews and secure payment options. The chapter provides valuable managerial and practical insights for businesses navigating the ever-evolving landscape of customer interactions.

Together, these chapters form a comprehensive exploration of the multifaceted influence of blockchain technology on customer experiences and behaviors across diverse sectors.

We invite you to embark on this enlightening journey through the world of blockchain and customer experience. Whether you are an industry expert, an academic visionary, or a curious mind eager to explore the possibilities, this reference book is your gateway to a deeper understanding of the transformative potential of blockchain technology in shaping the consumer landscape.

As editors, we extend our heartfelt gratitude to all the contributors who have shared their expertise and insights, making this book a reality. We hope that this collection of knowledge will inspire further research and innovation, helping businesses and consumers alike unlock the true potential of blockchain in customer experience.

Mohammed Majeed
Tamale Technical University, Ghana

Kwame Simpe Ofori
International University of Grand Bassam, Côte d'Ivoire

George Kofi Amoako
Ghana Communication Technology University, Ghana

Abdul-Raheed Alolo
Tamale Technical University, Ghana

Gideon Awini
Business School, University of Ghana, Ghana

Chapter 1
Understanding Blockchain's Role in Social Media Marketing:
A Review of Academic Literature and Social Media Discussions

Ashish Prithviraj Ramlakan
Victoria University, Australia

Sardar M. N. Islam
Victoria University, Australia

Ruchi Gupta
University of Delhi, India

Yuan Miao
Victoria University, Australia

ABSTRACT

Blockchain technology's introduction to social media marketing is an influential force to transform security and build trust in a social media platform, thus encouraging greater consumer engagement. This chapter explores the economic benefits of combining blockchain and social media marketing, and how this creates a powerful synergy to address consumer behaviour, through a process of a systematic and thematic content analysis of 30 selected peer-reviewed literature as well as 11 pieces of grey literature (which included social media site posts and blogs) published between 2012 and 2021. The implementation of blockchain technology has the potential to bring about a strategic transformation by inculcating a change in the customer's behaviour towards the organisation. The information in this chapter will provide compelling support that organisations can increase their consumer as well as influencer numbers online and successfully entice high traffic to their home page by implementing blockchain technology in their social media marketing campaigns.

DOI: 10.4018/978-1-6684-7649-9.ch001

1. INTRODUCTION_

Social media platforms like Facebook, Twitter, Pinterest, and LinkedIn solicit participant interaction by enticing reactions through memes, emojis, comments and likes (emotions) (Burns, K.S. 2017). These reactions are referred to (in marketing) as customer engagement (de Oliveira Santini, F.et. al 2020). Businesses using social media as a means to market, may be able generate a similar customer reaction, and this reaction may eventuate as a purchase or a favourable influence, thus prompting others to engage and purchase. The potential opportunities presented by social media engagement for businesses are profound.

The concept of blockchain involves the fact that it enables the storage of data on several decentralised servers. These servers are at different locations instead of one centralised site (Buterin, V. 2013). Each computer in the server network receives a copy of the unalterable data (Swan, M. 2015). This serves as a means to build trust between parties, and thus enables greater transparency and security during interactions between the parties.

The accelerated growth in social media has impacted the traditional classical methods of marketing and social interaction. This has presented challenges to both industry and consumers. At the forefront is cyber-security (Swan, M. et.al 2017). The development of blockchain technology maybe a powerful force in helping to transform security in social media marketing. Thus, this chapter seeks to discuss how the incorporation of blockchain technology in small and medium sized businesses, maybe a powerful force in helping to transform security in social media marketing.

The chapter aims to answer the following questions:

Question 1: What research has been carried out on blockchain incorporation in social media marketing?
Question 2: What are the benefits that the implementation of blockchain can bring to social media marketing?
Question 3: What are the challenges that the implementation of blockchain in social media marketing pose to both the consumer and the marketer?

The chapter undertakes qualitative research by using social media marketing data, generated by content analysis from existing peer reviewed literature and grey literature. Most businesses may have already reached out to customers in their defined markets by using existing social media platforms (Edosomwan, S et.al. 2011) like Facebook, Twitter, LinkedIn, and other sites. These social platforms offer services to the customers while at the same time collecting their personal data. This personal data is shared/sold (Harvey, C. R. et.al, 2018a) to potential advertisers. These advertisers utilise the data by targeting their marketing directly to the newly acquired customer list. This financially benefits the social media platform as this platform once again acts as an intermediary.

2. LITERATURE REVIEW

There has been an increase in academic interest in social marketing. This interest is propelled by the popularization of such sites such as Facebook, Twitter and Pinterest (Al Tawara & Gide, 2017). This has become more apparent to academia that these platforms play an integral part in the lives of individuals. Together with the internet, social media is beginning to suggest a re-think of identity, presentation and impression management (Godey et al., 2016).

For most of the multinational companies, marketing is essential for achieving development and growth both in the domestic and international markets. According to Tafesse and Wien (2018), digitization (which encompasses social media) is gaining increasing prominence in the process which enables marketers to connect with their customers. These companies gather market data from both within their organization and external commercial sources and apply this to develop a marketing platform on social media. Without this data, these companies are not able to develop or even survive amidst foreign markets competition (Fraccastoro et al., 2021). Similarly domestic companies including small and medium businesses may also, in most cases, not have sufficient financial muscle to proceed with digitization. They have to spend time and effort to develop these through established platforms like Facebook, Twitter etcetera. As such the implementation of the marketing data in the social media platform needs to become their focal point and in most cases this is sometimes uncharted, unsafe and unrewarding territory (Burns, 2017).

Bala and Verma (2018) state "The consumer is searching more on internet to find the best deal from the sellers …as compared to traditional or conventional advertising methods". They further acknowledge that it is generally agreed that we all are connected through What's App and Facebook (or other social apps) and the increasing use of social media is creating new opportunities for digital marketers to attract the customers through this digital platform. The authors conclude that successful marketing means engaging with users on a daily basis, at least four to five times a day, and this can be help branding and drive sales.

According to Constantinides (2014), social media now has a defining role ''as customer empowerment agents". One of the conclusions made by the author is that "marketers can utilize the social media domain to their own advantage and regain some control over the marketing process". However very little is being said about cyber security.

Blockchain technology is one of the promising technologies which has contributed to the revolutionization of the modern internet (McPhee & Ljutic, 2017). Soni (2021), in the publication entitled "Are Block chain based digital networks the future of social media", writes "Blockchain-based digital networks can be the future of social media primarily because of security. The majority of the masses who use social media platforms stay concerned about the security of the valuable data they are uploading."

Blockchain technology is described as "a decentralised and distributed ledger in which transactions are logged and added in a chronological order with the goal of creating permanent and tamperproof records" (Treiblmaier, 2018). This decentralised platform not only enables peer to peer transactions that eliminates the need for middlemen but it also validates the information by a process of encryption and records this permanently. A few researchers suggest that it can improve social media marketing and address certain issues, such as personal information safety, improve safety of online social media marketing and financial transactions (Casino et al., 2019; Choi et al., 2020; Dutra et al., 2018; Li & Glass, 2020; Stallone et al., 2021).

Previous researchers have introduced a few integrations of blockchain and social media with the application of the disruptive business models, and the Internet of Things (IoT)(Harvey et al., 2018a; Sümer, 2020), or by applying case studies (Upadhyay, 2019) or literature survey methods(Lamberton & Stephen, 2016; Liu et al., 2021b; McPhee & Ljutic, 2017; Purva et al., 2019), and social media survey analytics (Mnif et al., 2021; Purva et al., 2019). These studies presented some benefits, such as improving traceability efficiency, improving consumer transparency, while there are also challenges, including scalability, lack of understanding, and an immature (new) technology (Liu et al., 2021b; Purva et al., 2019).

There is minimal published literature that explores this subject in a systematic manner, especially with a consumer and social media marketers focus (Choi et al., 2020; Liu et al., 2021b; Mnif et al., 2021; Rahman, 2021; Tee & Murugesan, 2018; Upadhyay, 2019). Therefore, this research aims to fill this gap. This chapter aims to explore how the introduction of blockchain technology in social media marketing can aid the personal security issues, and thus improve consumer confidence when using social media.

Many authors agree that Blockchain is a complicated process that is likely only to be fully understood by a small number of persons(Casino et al., 2019; Hughes et al., 2019; Karafiloski & Mishev, 2017). But due to the popularity and rapid development of social media, it is essential that businesses understand why it is rapidly going to become a key constituent of our future digital world (Swan & De Filippi, 2017).

2.1 History and Background

A person or a group of persons working under the pseudonym Satoshi Nakamoto released a white paper that established the model for a blockchain (Nakamoto, 2008). In 2009 Nakamoto implemented the first blockchain as the public ledger for transactions made using bitcoin. It was called Bitcoin v 0.1(Nakamoto, 2009).

In 2014 Blockchain technology was being separated from the currency and its potential for other financial, interorganisational transactions was starting to be explored. Blockchain 2.0 (Hazratjee, 2015) was born, this was referring to applications beyond currency.

Ethereum is the second-largest blockchain project in the world (Kim et al., 2018). The Ethereum blockchain system (Oliva et al., 2020) introduced computer programs into the blocks, representing financial instruments such as bonds. These become known as smart contracts. Social media marketing platforms and the concept of blockchain marketing is discussed below.

In recent years, there has been elevated academic interest in relation to social media marketing(Appel et al., 2020). This interest is propelled by the popularization of such sites such as Facebook, Twitter and Pinterest (Al Tawara & Gide, 2017). Together with the internet, social media is beginning to suggest a re-think of identity, presentation and impression management (Godey et al., 2016).

Iankova et al. (2019), in their discussion conclude that social media platforms "facilitate one-to-one and one-to-many communications", this implies an opportunity to "embed direct communications with members". The authors speculate that the relationship… "is an important factor in the perception of effectiveness, and value it may bring". Iankova et al (2019), go on to speculate that users may be "concerned about the risks" of social media.

Bala and Verma (2018) state "the consumer is searching more on the internet to find the best deal from the sellers …as compared to traditional or conventional advertising methods". They further acknowledge that it is generally agreed that we all are connected through What's App and Facebook (or other social apps). Due to the increased use of social media, this has presented new challenges for social media marketers to appeal to the customers through this digital platform. The authors conclude that successful marketing means engaging with users on a daily basis, at least four to five times a day, and this can be help branding and driving sales.

However according to Constantinides (2014) "Social Media has changed the power structures in the marketplace… and this points to a "major power migration taking place" and the "emergence of a new breed of powerful and sophisticated customer", which is... very difficult to influence, persuade and retain. He also said that social media now has a defining "role as customer empowerment agents". One of the conclusions made by the author is that "marketers can utilize the social media domain to their own advantage and regain some control over the marketing process."

2.2 The Concept of Utilising Blockchain Technology in Social Media Marketing

The idea of blockchain began in 2008 as a type of technology that supported the Bitcoin protocol – a peer to peer payment network that utilised a cryptographic protocol to authenticate a trade without the use of third parties (Swan, 2015). By creating a decentralised and tamper-proof environment, Blockchain is understood to enhance security, data integrity and transparency of the transfer of information or assets (Nowiński & Kozma, 2017).

Halabi-Echeverry et al. (2020) define blockchain as "a technology that consists of linking several repositories, in the past centralised for diverse purposes, to become a decentralised unit capable of accomplishing unified goals pursued by Inter-Organisational Systems (IOS)".

Liu et al. (2020) describe blockchain as "an important strategic technology" that "can solve a series of supply chain problems, such as traceability. Liu et. al., (2021a), further describe blockchain as having "no single user controls" and the information "can be inspected by anyone". But in-order to reap the full benefits of Blockchain, an organization must both understand its strategic implications and overcome its implementation challenges (Davidson et al., 2016). For a small to medium sized organization, that means finding the funds, organizing the right talent, and demonstrating success to stakeholders. And, ultimately, it means defining a Blockchain marketing campaign implementation (Harvey et al., 2018a) by the outcomes the social media can deliver. That is essential in any successful deployment of the technology.

According to Soni, (2021), in the publication "Are Block chain based digital networks the future of social media", he writes "Blockchain-based digital networks can be the future of social media primarily because of security. The majority of the mass who use social media platforms stay concerned about the security of the valuable data they are uploading."

This is expanded upon by Jothikumar and Baby (2021) where the authors list 7 key benefits of Blockchain for business. However, the authors list "improves data protection" as number 1, and "allows for data verification and immutability" as number 2 respectively. Blockchain's revolutionary technology is being recognised as cutting-edge, as this enables a safer platform for social interaction. This is due to blockchains' ability to enable distrusting entities to exchange information and interact with each other, thus not having to rely on a trusted third party (Nakamoto, 2008) .

2.2.1 Blockchain Flow Diagram Decision-Making Process

The use of an open or permissioned blockchain is a feasible decision when multiple "mutually mistrusting entities" want to collaborate and change the circumstances under which they operate. This is also applicable if the entities do not agree to use an online trusted third party service provider (Wüst & Gervais, 2018).

Below is a flow diagram that typifies the decision-making process.

Figure 1. A flow diagram illustrating the decision-making process
Source: Wüst and Gervais (2018)

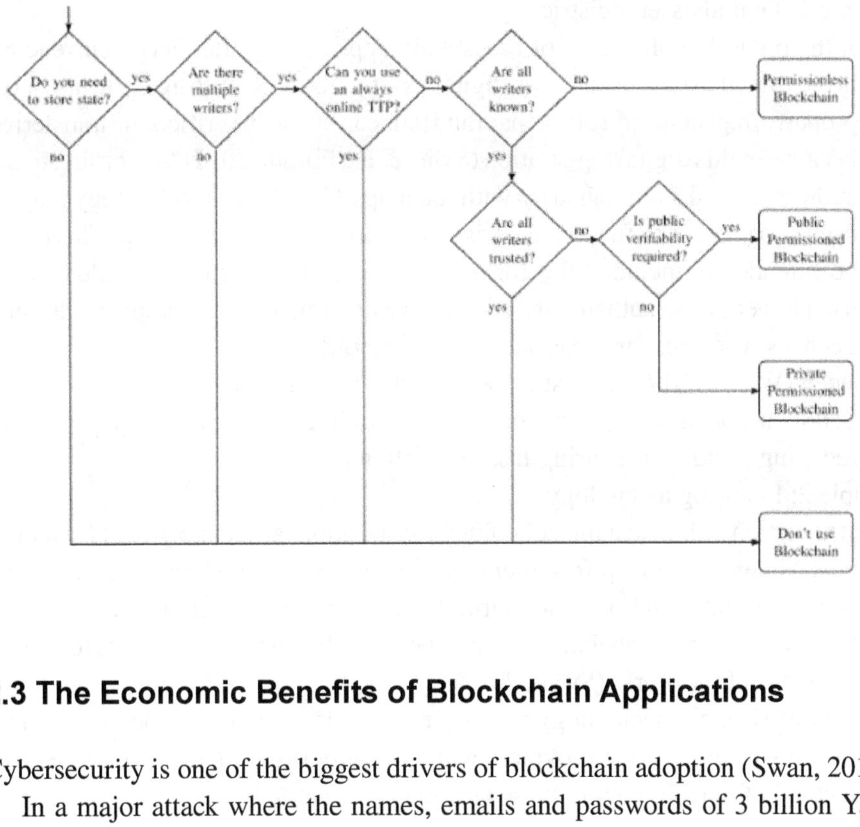

2.3 The Economic Benefits of Blockchain Applications

Cybersecurity is one of the biggest drivers of blockchain adoption (Swan, 2017).

In a major attack where the names, emails and passwords of 3 billion Yahoo user accounts were stolen Larson (2017), underlines the urgent need for better cybersecurity. Centralised databases provide an attractive target for hackers, whereas decentralised storage records are protected by cryptographic signatures which dramatically improve network cybersecurity.

Blockchains are called "trustless" as they eliminate having to trust a third-party institution such as Yahoo with personal data. Blockchains are also referred to as smart networks as they can confirm and transfer value directly without using a third-party intermediary. The trust is placed in the computational smart network system, removing the dependence on third party software, and this smart network could help create the next generation cybersecurity solutions.

2.4 Examples of Applications Demonstrating the Economic Benefits of Blockchain and Social Media Marketing

Listed below are some of the more common applications that demonstrate the economic benefits of combining blockchain with social media marketing.

Example 1: Digital asset registries

One of the biggest applications of blockchain applications after cryptocurrencies, is the digital asset registries. A digital asset registry is a listing of the asset (or property) registered to a blockchain and thus can be easily verified and transferred because of this digital registration (Swan & De Filippi, 2017). According to the authors, digital asset registries with the help of blockchain technology may be used as a process to file, relocate and authenticate asset ownership. This could be extended to include titles for cars, homes and properties. It could also be used to verify the authenticity of sensitive documents e.g., passports, driver's licences, voter registrations and medical records.

In Sweden (Wong, 2017), it is estimated that the government could save over USD $106 million in tax payers money by eliminating additional paper work, reducing fraud and ensuring fast transaction times.

Example 2: Leapfrog technology

The introduction of blockchain technology for the application into global financing is considered as a leap frog moment. This where e-wallet banking apps take over the traditional brick and mortar banking system, effectively reaching out to the two billion "unbanked" people (people who do not have access to formal banking) of the world (Swan, 2017).

This kind of financial technology may have the added benefit of opening up new markets to the service providers who currently do not have a cost-effective method of reaching out to these customers (Swan, 2017).

3. METHODOLOGY

This study has utilised a structured, systematic review and thematic content analysis of the selected literature as well as social media site posts and blogs to answer the research questions. There are numerous publications on blockchain and others on social media marketing; however, none of them have a specific focus on implementing blockchain in social media marketing (Antoniadis et al., 2019; Choi et al., 2020; Hacioglu, 2020; Harvey et al., 2018a, 2018b; Rejeb et al., 2020; Shen & Bissell, 2013; Shen et al., 2020). These papers provided the foundation for this research. Fink (2019) defined a literature review as "a systematic, explicit, and reproducible design for identifying, evaluating, and interpreting the existing body of recorded work". Tranfield et al. (2003) also suggested that a literature review could be used "to map and assess the existing intellectual territory", and "to specify a research question" to "develop the existing knowledge base". This research study adopts a content-analysis-based literature review method to analyse the literature on the application of blockchain technology in social media marketing.

3.1 The Six-Stage Data Refinement Process

A six-stage refinement process (Durach et al. (2017) was utilised. These are listed below:

a) define research questions,
b) set inclusion and exclusion criteria,
c) determine searching databases,
d) apply criteria,
e) synthesize relevant literatures, and
f) report findings.

The keywords used in this study were: blockchain, social media marketing, trust, and consumer behaviour. By using these keywords, the research articles and technical papers about blockchain technology and its applications in social media marketing could be located and the content reviewed. Science Direct, Scopus, Ebsco, and IEEEXplore were the four online databases that were applied to search for the relevant academic literature, as these four databases have a wide range of resources, and they have been extensively used in social media, marketing, and blockchain technology research. Peer-reviewed journal articles are generally favoured because they are seen as a way of identifying quality-controlled publications (Bornmann, 2011). However, in this study, other resources, such as conference papers, grey papers, such as newspaper articles, and third-party reports such as social media sites posts and blogs that could provide relevant insight, were also considered due to the early stages of blockchain adoption together with social media marketing and the limited published articles. The initial search in the four databases and the grey literature sources produced a total of 103 papers and articles. The guidelines as per Page et al. (2021) is called the Preferred Reporting Items for Systematic reviews and Meta-Analyses (PRISMA) were used. This method was utilised to enable the unbiased reporting of the literature. In the figure 2 (see below) the flow diagram for new systematic reviews which included searches of databases, registers and other sources was used as a template for reporting the process.

PRISMA Flow Diagram The flow diagram depicts the flow of information through the different phases of a systematic review. It maps out the number of records identified, included, and excluded, and the reasons for exclusions.

Figure 2. PRISMA 2020 flow diagram for new systematic reviews which included searches of databases, registers, and other sources
Source: Page et al. (2021)

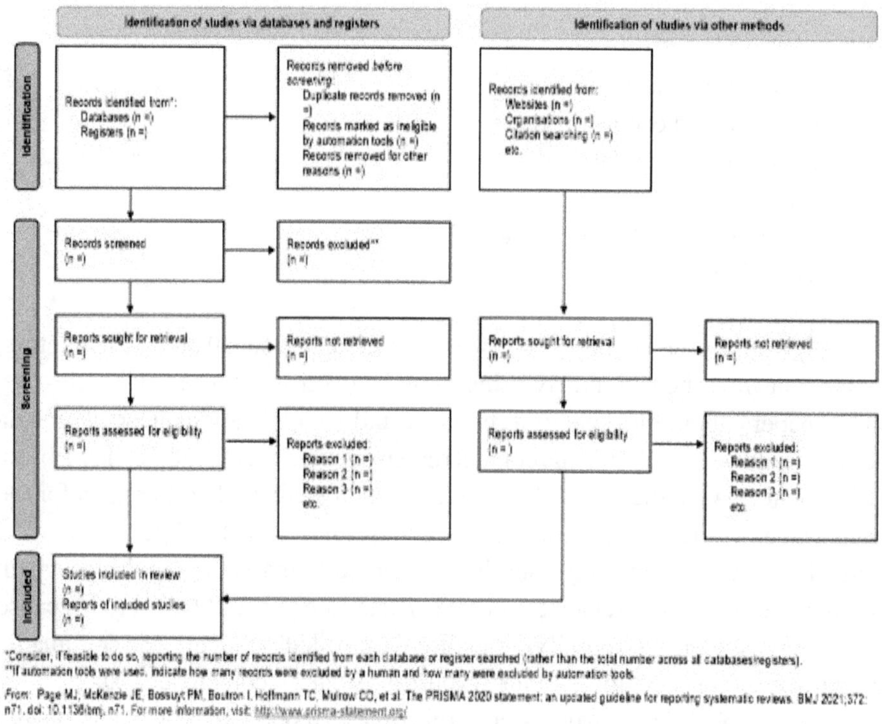

Any duplicated papers were removed and then the inclusion and exclusion criteria adapted from Zimmerman et al. (2020) were applied. Refer to Table 1- below for criteria used for this project.

Table 1. Inclusion and exclusion criteria

Inclusion	Exclusion
Published in English	Published in other languages
Papers and social media posts focussed on social media marketing	Papers and social media posts focussed on other marketing technologies
Published dates from 2005 to 2021	Published before 2005, and post 2021
Papers and social media posts with a focus on blockchain technology	Papers and social media posts focussed on other technologies
Peer review/conference papers and grey literature (including books, social media posts, and blogs, vlogs, and newspaper articles)	Technical and business news
Business management focus	Systems and technique focus
Selected years 2015 to 2021 of grey literature focussing on social media, marketing, and blockchain (including books, vlogs, blogs, social media posts, and newspaper articles)	Excluded all grey literature before the year 2015 and post 2021

This reduced the number of useful papers and grey literature (including social media posts and blogs) to 78 in the preliminary sifting process (Figure 3).

3.2 The Stepped Sifting Process

Figure 3. showing stepped sifting process until a final combined tally of 41 peer-reviewed and grey literature (including social media posts and blogs) is reached

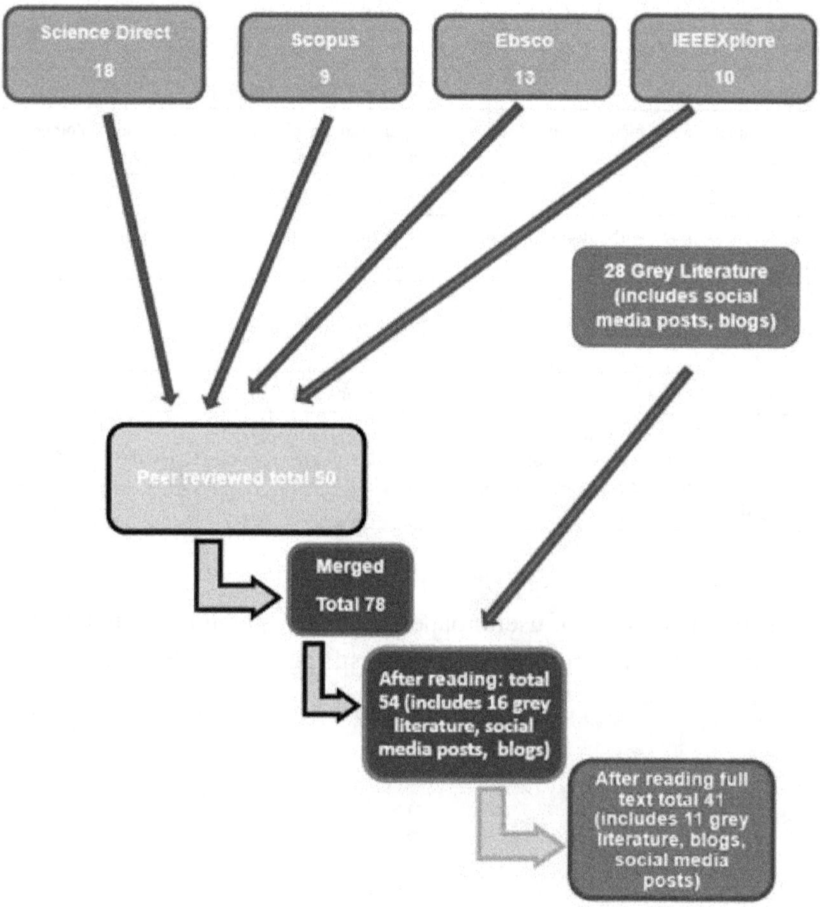

As a continuation of the refinement selection process, the abstracts or summaries of the 54 articles (both peer-reviewed and grey literature including social media sites and blogs) were read (as shown in the penultimate stage in Figure 3). These were further categorized and evaluated using the systematic review and thematic content analysis method, which is an objective research method that has been used to quantify phenomena, documents, or communications as described by Seuring and Gold (2012). This process enabled the further reduction to a final quantity of 41 articles (which included 11 grey literature articles, social media posts, and blogs).

These 41 articles are listed in Table 2, numbered 1 to 41 together with the corresponding citation and database source. The full reference is listed in the reference section.

Table 2. List of all 41 articles including 11 grey pieces of literature (as well as social media posts and blogs) used in this content analysis study

Number	Author/s and Year	Database Source
1	(Albayati et al., 2020)	Science Direct
2	(Alves et al., 2016)	Ebsco
3	(Cell, 2020)	blog
4	(Casey & Vigna, 2018)	Ebsco
5	(Casino et al., 2019)	Science Direct
6	(Choi et al., 2020)	Science Direct
7	(Conick, 2017)	Ebsco
8	(Constantinides, 2014)	Science Direct
9	(de Oliveira Santini et al., 2020)	Ebsco
10	(Dutra et al., 2018)	Scopus
11	(Fraccastoro et al., 2021)	Science Direct
12	(Godey et al., 2016)	Science Direct
13	(Guidi & Michienzi, 2020)	IEEEXplore
14	(Hughes et al., 2019)	Scopus
15	(Iankova et al., 2019)	Science Direct
16	(Jain et al., 2021)	Science Direct
17	(Järvinen et al., 2012)	Ebsco
18	(Jothikumar & Baby, 2021)	Grey Literature - journal
19	(Lai & To, 2015)	Ebsco
20	(Li & Glass, 2020)	Grey literature - journal
21	(Michael 2021)	Social media post
22	(Menon & Mady, 2021)	Ebsco
23	(Moore et al., 2013)	Scopus
24	(Oh & Park, 2012)	Scopus
25	(Park, 2021)	Grey literature dissertation
26	(Parsons, 2013)	Scopus
27	(Pärssinen et al., 2018)	Scopus
28	(Peck, 2017)	IEEEXplore
29	(Poongodi et al., 2020)	Grey literature-journal

Continued on following page

Table 2. Continued

Number	Author/s and Year	Database Source
30	(Rahman, 2021)	Grey literature - journal
31	(Reyna et al., 2018)	Science Direct
32	(Sarosa, 2012)	Science Direct
33	(Shen et al., 2020)	Science Direct
34	(Stallone et al., 2021)	Science Direct
35	(Sprinkl, 27 Feb 2019)	Blog
36	(Swan & De Filippi, 2017)	Ebsco
37	(Tandon et al., 2021)	Science Direct
38	(Tee & Murugesan, 2018)	IEEEXplore
39	(Venkatraman et al., 2020)	Grey literature-journal
40	(Wintermeyer, 2021)	Blog
41	(Zakharenkov, 2021)	Social media post

Table 3 provides the first insight into these 41 articles by listing the year of publication and the different databases the papers were sourced from. The earliest selected papers were released in 2012 (3 papers out of 41), 2 out of 41 were released in 2013, and one in 2014. From 2017 to 2021 a total of 32 out of 41 articles were published. This represents a total of 78% of 41 papers. This time trend analysis shows that blockchain and social media marketing is fairly young of age and that there has been increasing interest in this technology in the last 5 years.

Table 3. Timeline analysis of total 41 articles including 11 pieces of grey literature (including social media posts and blogs) used in this content analysis study

Year	Science Direct	Scopus	Ebsco	IEEEXplore	Grey Literature
2012	1	1	1		
2013		11			
2014	1				
2015			1		
2016	1		1		
2017			11	1	
2018	1	11	1	1	
2019	11	1			1
2020	111		1	1	1111
2021	1111		1		111111
TOTALS	**13**	**6**	**8**	**3**	**11**

While the prior analysis sheds some descriptive light on blockchain and social media marketing at a high level, it fails to inform the reader as to how much how specific topics have been discussed and how they have evolved. The information also does not advise as to whether newer research work has built on earlier work in ways that advance the understanding of the topic.

3.3 Use of Six Priori Themes

A theme is (also known as coding) a recurring idea, subject, or topic that appears in published literature. A theme can demonstrate what the particular paper is about and can it be helpful to the reader or researcher to form patterns of analysis. A theme can consist of one or more words. It is imperative that studious reading of the paper is required to appreciate where the theme is present or applicable.

There are many different ways of coding qualitative data. One way is the frequently used method called Nvivo coding. This is where the participant's spoken words become the data which is coded based on the keyword or phrase used by the participant.

Another method is referred to as priori coding, in which the researcher has defined codes before beginning to analyze the data. In this study, the themes were identified in advance, referred to as 'priori' themes.

The six themes include:

a) Innovation and Entrepreneurship
b) Capital Market and Risk
c) Consumer behaviour and Value
d) Strategic foresight and creativity
e) New forms of organising and ways of working
f) Research Gap

There are some inherent limitations to the use of the priori method for research. The first is, because the research may focus exclusively on the data to try and fit the priori themes, hence the research may overlook material that does not relate to them. Another limitation of the priori method is that the research may fail to recognise when a priori theme is not suitable to be the best way of coding the data.

A list of these priori themes and the author's definitions of them are given in Table 4.

Table 4. Shows the coding scheme used in this research and the definitions of these codes

Code (Theme)	Definition
a) Innovation and Entrepreneurship	To apply prior and new information to construct new concepts or understanding
b) Capital Market and Risk	To evaluate the information for its ability to fulfill the market need and the reliability of the source itself
c) Consumer behaviour and Value	To disseminate information to others who have an information need or as a way of sharing results of the information process
d) Strategic foresight and creativity	To construct a strategy to locate and access needed information or identify ways to fulfill the information needed
e) New forms of organising and ways of working	To use information effectively to fulfill the information needed
f) Research Gap	To recognize the need for information for a particular problem and the resources needed to fulfill the information need

NVivo software was used to interpret the coded data gathered during the research process. NVivo is a software program used to analyse correlations and overlaps of the different themes. NVivo enabled the organisation and analysis of non-numerical and unstructured data. The software also enabled the classification, sorting, and arranging of the information; examining of the relationships in the data; and combined analysis with linking, shaping, searching, and modelling. The NVivo program also enabled the identification of any trends and cross-examined the information in a multitude of ways using its various functions.

All 41 articles were categorized by the six themes used in this study. By listing and dividing the papers as per Table 5, the brief content and highlights of every paper can be shown more clearly.

The number of an article (see Table 2 for citation) depicting the different priori themes that they contain are listed below.

Table 5. Showing the 41 articles and the priori themes that they contained

Number	Theme a	Theme b	Theme c	Theme d	Theme e	Theme f
1				✓		
2		✓		✓		
3		✓		✓		
4					✓	
5	✓	✓		✓	✓	
6		✓		✓	✓	✓
7	✓	✓			✓	✓
8			✓			
9			✓		✓	✓
10					✓	
11			✓			
12			✓			
13					✓	
14	✓	✓	✓			
15			✓		✓	
16		✓			✓	
17				✓		
18	✓				✓	
19				✓	✓	✓
20	✓	✓			✓	
21	✓	✓				
22			✓			
23	✓			✓		
24	✓	✓	✓	✓	✓	✓
25			✓		✓	
26			✓			
27	✓			✓		
28			✓			
29	✓			✓		
30		✓				
31		✓		✓	✓	
32	✓			✓	✓	
33			✓			
34		✓			✓	
35					✓	
36					✓	
37					✓	
38		✓			✓	
39			✓			

Continued on following page

Table 5. Continued

Number	Theme a	Theme b	Theme c	Theme d	Theme e	Theme f
40			✓	✓	✓	
41					✓	✓

4. RESULTS

The main findings, which are derived from the systematic analysis and thematic content analysis have been divided into 6 main themes. These themes are: a) Innovation and Entrepreneurship, b) Capital Market and Risk, c) Consumer behaviour and Value, d) Strategic foresight and creativity, e) New forms of organising and ways of working, and lastly, f) Research Gaps. The codes derived using NVivo software associated with each of these themes are presented below.

4.1 Innovation and Entrepreneurship (Theme A)_

The definition of this theme was listed in Table 4 as "to apply prior and new information to construct new concepts or understanding". As per Table 5, this theme (numbered as 'a' in the table) was found to be present in 11 of the 41 articles (including grey literature, social media posts and blogs). NVivo was used and identified 5 codes that are associated with the theme of innovation and entrepreneurship. Each of these codes is discussed below.

4.1.1 Innovation Decision Process

Hughes et al. (2019) presented a Model of the Innovation Decision Process (MIDP) that describes uncertainty during innovation and outlines the 5 stages encountered during the innovation-decision process. These are:

1) Knowledge - where a decision-maker finds out about a possible innovation.
2) Persuasion - a positive or negative view is formed on the innovation.
3) Decision - where the innovation is rejected or accepted.
4) Implementation - the new idea is developed further or purchased.
5) Confirmation - does the innovation deliver what was expected?

Figure 4. Model of the innovation decision process (MIDP)
Source: Hughes et al. (2019)

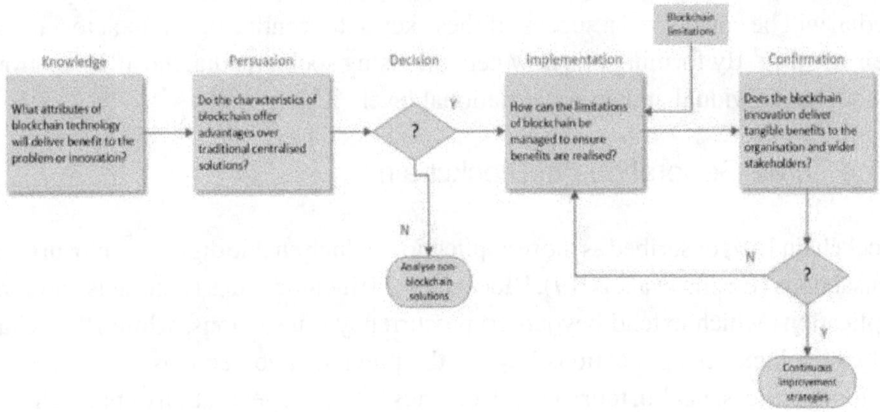

By following the processes in Figure 4, an organisation can establish key decision points and where they need to reflect on the decisions made at each step. The framework enables the company to determine if blockchain is best suited for the organisation and whether the technology can be applied.

4.1.2 Blockchain Integrity Verification

According to Casino et al. (2019), blockchain integrity verification applications can store information and transactions during the creation, and throughout the lifetime of the product or service. The possible service applications for individuals and organisations include:

(i) protecting the original identity or information and preventing fakes,
(ii) safeguarding/assurance against duplication; and
(iii) intellectual property (IP) management.

This is particularly important in all organisations to ensure the financial viability and longevity of the business.

4.1.3 Actor Network Theory (ANT)

In a paper by Sarosa (2012), the author describes how Indonesian small and medium enterprises (SMEs) adopted social media networks to support their businesses by using the Actor Network Theory (ANT) to help explain the incorporation process. Sarosa (2012) demonstrated that key persons (referred to as key actors) who try to impose their view on other persons (actors) by building a network through social media, will be considered a success if these key actors entice the other actors to join their network. By forming this new network using social media, the alliance grows at both an individual and an organisational level.

4.1.4 Three Generations of Blockchain

Blockchain 1.0 is described as those applications which enable digital cryptocurrency transactions (Casino et al., 2019). Blockchain 2.0 includes smart contracts and some applications which extend beyond cryptocurrency transactions, while Blockchain 3.0 which includes applications beyond the previous two versions and extends to the food services, health, tourism and logistics. The next generation of blockchain is going to be the Blockchain 4.0 era. This is where tokens such as NFTs (non-fungible tokens) become more prevalent in conducting transactions.

4.1.5 eWord of Mouth (eWOM)

Social media success in advertising is associated with the powerful influence of e- word of mouth (eWOM) (also known as influencers) . Godey et al. (2016) attribute this to research that showed that eWOM has higher credibility, empathy and customer- focused market information on the internet. Influencers have the peculiar task of endorsing products, companies and individuals through social media. They are supposed to have expert knowledge or be well connected thus have great social influence in their field or product.

4.2 Capital Market and Risk (Theme B)

The definition of this theme (b) was listed in Table 4 as "To evaluate the information for its ability to fulfill the market need and the reliability of the source itself". As per Table 5, this theme (numbered as 'b' in the table) was found to be present in 14 of the 41 articles (including grey literature, social media posts and blogs). NVivo was used and identified 4 codes that are associated with the theme of capital market and risk. Each of these codes is discussed below.

4.2.1 Web 2.0

According to Constantinides (2014), Web 2.0 is described as "enabling technologies" as this supports the sharing of information, knowledge and promotes networking. This in effect forms the foundation of modern social media (Constantinides, 2014). These application sites include blogs, and microblogs such as Twitter, social networking sites such as Facebook and LinkedIn, collaborative sites such as Wikipedia and content community sites like YouTube.

4.2.2 Blockchain and Security

Currently, the largest platforms like Facebook and LinkedIn are centralised organisations. These platforms collate the data from all the visitors to their platforms, and this collated data is sold to advertisers (Jain et al., 2021). The data is stored by these platforms in a centralised database. When these databases are compromised, the data which is stored all in one place, can be hacked or siphoned for "other" unlawful purposes. Many incidents have occured over the years, but one of the major ones was that of Facebook and the data breach of 540 million users (Jain et al., 2021). Jain et al. (2021) describe a decentralised (blockchain-based) platform where all the user data is stored and encrypted in a decentralised manner. This process makes it easier to identify scammers (Jain et al., 2021), as their details can be checked by all users instead of by centralised checkers.

4.2.3 Blockchain Supported Social Media

Digital marketing has dramatically changed due to the presence of blockchain technology as marketers can now interact with their target audience and thus manage their digital marketing campaigns accordingly (Rahman, 2021). Rahman (2021) also reports that Facebook is planning to integrate a cryptocurrency into its social media platform. This highlights the fact that the social media marketing platform will evolve with the introduction of blockchain.

Blockchain supported social networks offers the following benefits (Rahman, 2021);

i) User's data is protected
ii) User has control over the content
iii) Improved privacy and security
iv) Freedom of speech
v) The ability to engage safely in crowdfunding
vi) A better and safer payment method
vii) The ability to verify truth from fake content

Due to these benefits and the welcomed solution to privacy and security, the transition to blockchain-based social media networks seems a logical step.

4.2.4 Challenges of the Implementation of Blockchain

The key idea of blockchain technology is supposedly simple, but its implementation poses several challenges (Reyna et al., 2018). These include:

a) Storage capacity and scalability – in this technology, the chain is always growing (Reyna et al., 2018) requiring more resources (such as computational power).
b) Security weakness and threats – as the blockchain grows, it becomes more vulnerable to security threats. (Reyna et al., 2018).
c) Smart contracts according to Reyna et al. (2018), may be subject to hacking which adds costs to maintain security
d) Legal issues – a central legislative authority is absent (Reyna et al., 2018) especially when dealing with the internet, social media, and cryptocurrency. This creates volatility, lack of consensus, and risk.

4.3 Consumer Behaviour and Value (Theme C)

The definition of theme (c) was listed in Table 4 as "To disseminate information to others who need it, or as a way of sharing results of the information". As per Table 5, this theme (numbered as 'c' in the table) was found to be present in 14 of the 41 articles (including grey literature, social media posts and blogs). NVivo was used and identified 4 codes that are associated with the theme of consumer behaviour and value. Each of these codes is discussed below.

4.3.1 Consumer Engagement in Social Media

Customer engagement in social media comprises three sequential stages (de Oliveira Santini et al., 2020). These include:

1) the relationship formation stage: during which trust and promise form the basis for customer satisfaction and positive encounters, then follows;
2) the customer engagement stage: this results after trust is developed, the customer then experiences satisfaction from the purchase or encounter and positive emotions are developed. The third and final stage is;
3) closing of sale and /or customer referral stage: this directly contributes to the generation of a sale or the customer promoting the organisation or product to others, thus acknowledging the positive encounter with this organisation. This positive feedback undoubtedly enhances customer engagements, resulting in growth in the number of social media influencers (eWOM).

As can be seen from the above sequential stages, when customers enjoy emotional bonding relationships with organisations, they become engaged (de Oliveira Santini et al., 2020). These positive online customer engagements generate value to organisations in the form of sales, brand building, online consumption, and recommendations to others on social media.

4.3.2 Experience

Experience, according to Albayati et al. (2020), refers to "the level of customer's knowledge and experience that supports their use of new technologies". Thus a high level of experience implies a high level of trust, hence a favourable customer behaviour to use/try a new software or platform. This is where the use of blockchain technology can be used to support the development of trust.

4.3.3 Positive Emotions

Consumer emotions are a state of mind arising from the cognitive and interactive assessment of activities (de Oliveira Santini et al., 2020). Positive emotions include agreeable gestures, feeling of happiness, and this leads to positive outcome expectations. Thus positive emotions positively affect consumer engagement (de Oliveira Santini et al., 2020).

4.3.4 External Constructs Affecting Blockchain Adoption

Figure 5. External constructs affecting blockchain technology adoption
Source: Albayati et al. (2020)

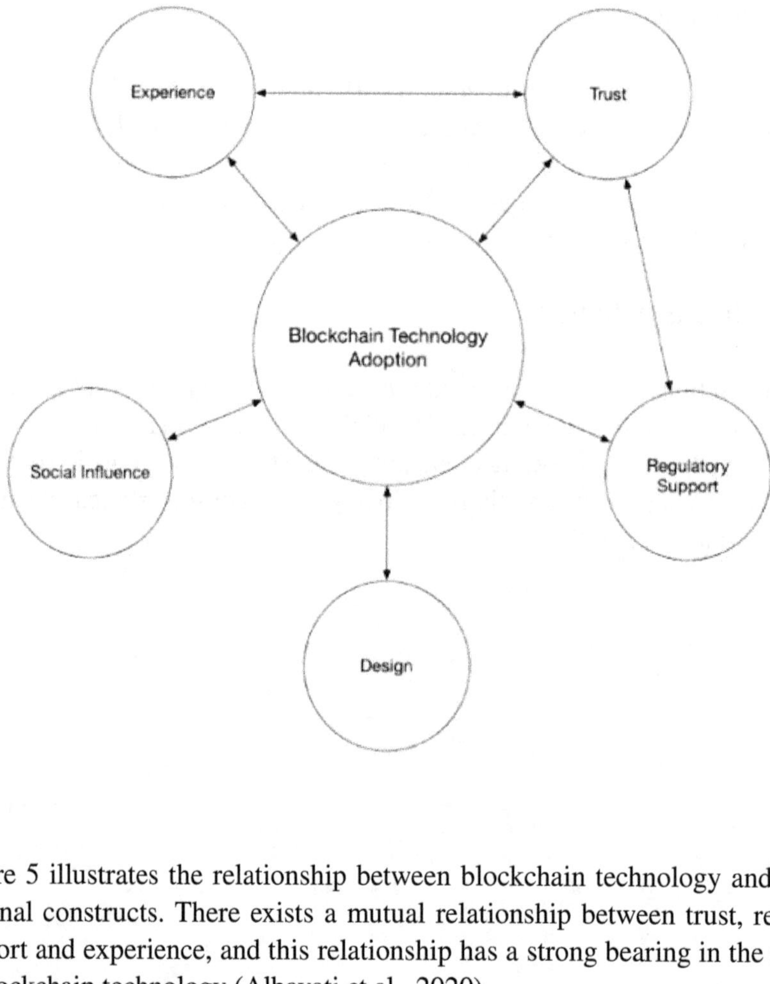

Figure 5 illustrates the relationship between blockchain technology and the five external constructs. There exists a mutual relationship between trust, regulatory support and experience, and this relationship has a strong bearing in the adoption of blockchain technology (Albayati et al., 2020).

A definition of each of the constructs are:

a) Trust: refers to the level of comfort and confidence when using technologies, this is the main element needed to maintain a relationship with the customer
b) Regulatory support: refers to the legal framework established by governments to ensure compliance, increase trust and facilitate the use of blockchain applications (such as cryptocurrencies)

c) Experience: refers to the level of the customer's knowledge and experience that supports their use of the new technologies(for example blockchain). Experience can motivate adoption and increase trust.

d) Social influence: refers to individual norms and values which directly influence one's perception and how they react to a situation or new technology. Social factors could affect blockchain adoption.

e) Design: refers to "experiencing technological aspects" of the software such as the ease of navigation, appearance, and layout. In the case of blockchain adoption, the application's design could influence the technology's acceptance and usability.

4.4 Strategic Foresight and Creativity (Theme D)

The definition of this theme (d) was listed in Table 4 as "To construct a strategy to locate and access needed information or identify ways to fulfill the information needed". As per Table 5, this theme (numbered as 'd' in the table) was found to be present in 14 of the 41 articles (including grey literature, social media posts and blogs). NVivo was used and identified 5 codes that are associated with the theme of strategic foresight and creativity. Each of these codes is discussed below.

4.4.1 The Influence of Social Media

For advertisers, social media allows them to 'talk to' (or interact with) their customers in a way, unlike traditional media. Similarly, this platform also allows consumers to respond or 'talk' directly to the advertiser (Parsons, 2013). Given this tremendous tool of direct communication with the consumer, companies are hurriedly trying to figure out how best to utilise social media to reach the millions of consumers who use it on a daily basis. These companies understand that this connection with the potential consumer may influence their future purchase decisions (Parsons, 2013) and therefore they want to capitalise on this. Thus social media marketing has been dominated by a focus on interactions between businesses and consumers (Iankova et al., 2019).

4.4.2 Social Media Marketing B2B and B2C

The B2B and some B2C companies utilise social media to enable search engine optimization and in so doing drive traffic to their home/landing pages. The sites utilise innovative tools to provide novel ways to attract and keep the conversations active with the existing customer base (Järvinen et al., 2012) According to Iankova et al. (2019), B2B and B2C relationship lifecycles need to be constantly stimulated and managed using social media platforms. Organisations are looking at new ways to engage with their users and this often forms a large part of a company's marketing strategy (Iankova et al., 2019).

4.4.3 Data Management Using Blockchain Technology

Data management has been enhanced using blockchain technology since all the transactions and operations can be verified and audited (Casino et al., 2019). As mentioned in a blog by Cell (2020), Vitalik Buterin was one of the developers who felt that the blockchain technology supporting Bitcoin had not reached its pinnacle of development concerning data management and safety. He then went on to develop the technology that supports the cryptocurrency Ethereum.

4.4.4 Timestamping

Timestamping is the allocation of a digital time record on the blockchain ledger at that specific instant that the record was created (Dutra et al., 2018). The timestamp does not track when ownership of an item changes but it helps to determine that the creator owned the asset at a specific point in time. This timestamp ability in blockchain technology has proven invaluable in the media and entertainment industry to show ownership of songs, protect intellectual property such as digital art and register proof of copyright quickly and inexpensively (Dutra et al., 2018), so that the creators can protect their creations from unauthorised use on the internet.

4.4.5 Trust

Trust refers to the level of comfort, confidence and security (Albayati et al., 2020) that consumers have when using technologies.Trust is one of the external factors that influence people to either embrace or reject new technology. Consumer trust also has a direct significant effect on internet purchases and confidence towards internet usage (Albayati et al., 2020). Trust is critical in e-commerce and banks create the image of being strong and secure – hence removes the perception of the bank being a high-risk institution, and this helps consumers overcome the insecurity. This then encourages the consumer to feel safe when interacting with the bank over a new medium like internet banking. If trust can be improved through the incorporation of blockchain technology, then this will have a significant and positive influence on the consumers attitude toward cryptocurrency transactions (Albayati et al., 2020).

4.5 New Forms of Organising and Ways of Working (Theme E)

The definition of this theme (e) was listed in Table 4 as "To use information effectively to fulfill the information needed". As per Table 5, this theme (numbered as 'e' in the table) was found to be present in 23 of the 41 articles (including grey literature, social media posts and blogs). NVivo had been used and identified 4 codes that are associated with the theme of "new forms of organising and ways of working". Each of these codes is discussed below.

4.5.1 The Features of the Social Networking Platform

The features of the social networking platform enable the formation of relationships among people who share similar interests and activities (Poongodi et al., 2020). The authors describe the four types of platforms as:

a) The social network where friends get together (non-internet based)
b) Distributed social network where social network users get connected through the internet
c) Non-social interpersonal linking eg in an office work environment
d) Social navigation to search on specific resources for example chatting with someone in a pub (unplanned event)

The popularity of social networking through the internet can be seen through the high user engagement and increased number of people spending more time on sites like Facebook, Twitter and Youtube (Poongodi et al., 2020).

4.5.2 How Blockchain Helps Social Media

Companies that incorporated blockchain technology in social media marketing grew the most (Stallone et al., 2021). The authors further state that companies that are trying to "revolutionise their advertising campaigns drive the focus" to incorporate blockchain technology.

Blockchain can influence digital marketing in several ways and an important trait is that of online data privacy. Companies through their marketing campaigns collect profiles for every customer based on the visited sites, searches made, products purchased and other criteria that they may use (Jothikumar & Baby, 2021). According to the authors Jothikumar and Baby (2021), blockchain signifies innovation and modernisation to organisations. The authors also state that businesses need to fully grasp what the technology is and what it has the potential to do as "it will be a key constituent of our future lives".

4.5.3 How Is Blockchain Changing Social Media?

Blockchain technology is changing social media and social media advertising by rewarding the users through its peer-to-peer payments (Wintermeyer, 2021). This allows the users to generate income for their content while simultaneously earning by doing other activities such as watching adverts online. It is this very form of incentive that attracts customers away from traditional social media platforms and steers them towards blockchain-enhanced social media platforms (Wintermeyer, 2021).

4.5.4 How Is Blockchain Impacting Digital Marketing?

In the field of digital marketing (Menon & Mady, 2021), blockchain can increase the effectiveness in verifying the transfer and payment of assets/money between sellers and buyers by the fast verification of the seller's and customer's identities, the utilisation of smart contracts and the introduction of tokens (a form of online payment). This is an example of cost and time-saving. Blockchain technology will also provide transparency in recording and sharing information thus increasing trust in the social media platform (Menon & Mady, 2021).

4.6 Research Gap (Theme F)

The definition of this theme (f) was listed in Table 4 as "To recognize the need for information for a particular problem and the resources needed to fulfill the information need". As per table 5, this theme (numbered as 'f' in the table) was found to be present in 23 of the 41 articles (including grey literature, social media posts and blogs). NVivo was used and identified 4 codes that are associated with the theme of "research gap". Each of these codes is discussed below.

4.6.1 Relationships

According to the customer engagement theory (de Oliveira Santini et al., 2020), a relationship is formed based on trust and commitment, satisfaction, and positive emotions. These will stimulate customer engagement. Further research needs to be done to determine the extent of the relationship in the case of social media and to test whether this relationship is long lasting if positive emotions and customer satisfaction is maintained for the duration of the relationship.

4.6.2 Satisfaction

Customers tend to show satisfaction by posting their enthusiasm and pleasure on social media in the form of feedback reviews, blogs, vlogs, and emojis (de Oliveira Santini et al., 2020). An interesting question for future study is whether the level of customer satisfaction is directly proportional to customer engagement.

4.6.3 Social Influence

The social influence factor (particularly influencers) has been considered as the most successful of all the internet services (Albayati et al., 2020). It is unique in that the user displays a high level of trust for the technology. There is an equal level of trust of the user with the social influencers to provide solutions, thus enabling a purchase.

4.6.4 Scalability Blockchain

Scalability of a blockchain refers to the number of nodes able to participate in a blockchain (Pärssinen et al., 2018).

5. DISCUSSION

In this section, the findings from the qualitative data collected are analysed. The analysis and discussion aim to gain a deeper understanding of the relationship between blockchain technology incorporation and social media marketing; thus, the goal was to answer the research questions of this chapter, including highlighting implications to businesses, managers, policymakers and researchers. In order to answer the research questions, this discussion section has been divided into three parts answering each of the research questions in turn. The priori themes will be used to answer the research questions, and the coding associated with these themes will be used to further substantiate the results.

5.1 Research Question One: What Research Has Been Carried Out on Blockchain Incorporation in Social Media Marketing?

From the empirical findings, the study found that themes a and b related to this research question.

As per table 5, the themes (numbered as 'a' and 'b' in the table) were found to be present in a total of 25 of the 41 articles (including grey literature, social media posts and blogs). NVivo had identified a total of 9 codes that are associated with the two themes.

These can be outlined as Model of the Innovation Decision Process (MIDP), intellectual property protection, Actor Network Theory (ANT), blockchain security, e- Word of Mouth (eWOM), and social media marketing. Some of the findings suggest that blockchain can enhance the freshness of data, increase the rate of collection and processing of data, and hence, enables data to be collected in real-time.

This aligns with Constantinides (2014) description of "enabling technologies", as social media supports the sharing of information, knowledge and promotes networking.

The data demonstrated that the success in advertising is directly associated with e word of mouth (also known as influencers), (Godey et al., 2016). The influencers have the capacity to either direct traffic to or away from the site promoting the products or service. This is supported by Sarosa (2012) in the Actor Network Theory where key persons (which he refers to as key actors) impose their view on other persons (actors) to entice them to join the network or participate in the activity. As the alliance grows the networks also grows. In effect the key actors are the influencers.

As the network continues to grow, the data security becomes a concern since most of the largest platforms like Facebook and LinkedIn are centralised organisations (Jain et al., 2021). According to Jain et al. (2021), this data can be compromised . A blockchain based platform enables all the data to be stored and encrypted in a decentralised manner which improves security (Jain et al., 2021). Similarly the incorporation of blockchain in social media marketing (Rahman, 2021) offers data protection, content management, improved privacy and security (including the ability to verify if the content is fake) .

In addition, Liu et al. (2021b) described blockchain as "an important strategic technology" whose trusted ledger has "no single user control and therefore can be inspected by anyone".

One of the codes described in the results section is the evolution of blockchain technology from Blockchain 1.0, through to Blockchain 2.0. It is currently in the Blockchain 3.0 phase (Casino et al., 2019), and is now on the cusp of entering the Blockchain 4.0 era. Casino et al. (2019) explain that this progression leads to the increase in the credibility of the data and as such social media users demonstrate an increase in trust. Smart tokens and NFT have become more prevalent in the management of transactions (Casino et al., 2019) . It is through this blockchain supported social media network, that enable the use of smart tokens and NFTs to offer a better and safer payment system method (Rahman, 2021).

Despite the accolades that the implementation of blockchain technology affords there are also some challenges that this technology poses (Reyna et al., 2018).

These include storage capacity, security weaknesses and threats such as hacking and legislative issues (Reyna et al., 2018).

The picture that emerges from the analysis of the results is that research into blockchain incorporation in social media marketing is still in its infancy, and improved privacy as well as security which is intrinsic to blockchain technology, is lagging in social media. Therefore, this poses several opportunities for researchers to study this gap in the knowledge.

The study has established a link between innovation (new technology) and the reliability of its ability to fulfil the consumers need. What is striking is that the largest social media platforms like Facebook and LinkedIn are only now putting in plans to transition to a blockchain based (decentralised) platform to store data in an encrypted manner. However, each social media platform tends to have an understanding that by incorporating blockchain technology, it will lead to an increased volume of on-line traffic, and this, from a digital marketing context is arguably a positive result.

This demonstrates that the introduction of blockchain technology in social media marketing promotes consumer confidence as personal data is being safely stored.

5.2 Research Question Two: What Are the Benefits That the Implementation of Blockchain Can Bring to Social Media Marketing?

From the empirical findings, the study concluded that themes c and e relate to this research question.

As per Table 5, the themes (numbered as 'c' and 'e' in the table) were found to be present in a total of 37 of the 41 articles (including grey literature, social media posts and blogs). NVivo identified a total of 8 codes that are associated with the two themes.

These codes included consumer engagement in social media, experience and positivity, external constructs affecting blockchain adoption, and the impact of blockchain on social media marketing. de Oliveira Santini et al. (2020) highlighted that all customers enjoy an emotional relationship with organisations, once trust and positive encounters are experienced. This demonstrates to businesses and managers alike, that the positivity leads to a positive consumer engagement. Such trust, driven by the adoption of blockchain technology (Albayati et al., 2020), can also lead to high traffic and thus more customers visiting the internet / social media marketing site. This is further supported by Poongodi et al. (2020) when the authors list that the popularity of social networking through the internet can be seen through high user engagement and increased number of people going to sites like Facebook and Twitter. These social network platforms are characterised by the formation of relationships where people share similar interests (Poongodi et al., 2020).

It was shown by Stallone et al. (2021) that companies that incorporated blockchain technology in social media marketing grew the most. This is supported by Wintermeyer (2021) when the author states that blockchain technology incorporated social media systems advertise by rewarding the users through peer to peer payments. This form of rewards attracts the customers and steers them away from traditional social media platforms (Wintermeyer, 2021). Furthermore, blockchain enables safe payments and transfers of assets between sellers and buyers (Menon & Mady, 2021). Thus, the economic benefits of the synergy provides an increase in revenue to business after the implementation of blockchain in social media marketing. Furthermore, the analysis conducted on the 8 codes of the two themes (c and e) demonstrated an enhanced level of utilisation of blockchain incorporated social media marketing. Companies, marketers and consumers alike gain valuable advantages by utilising peer to peer payments, the safe transfer of personal information as this is encrypted, the introduction of tokens as a form of online payment and the use of smart contracts.

The study indicates that there is a strong relationship between the incorporation of blockchain technology and social media marketing. This is supported by the increased growth reported by companies that utilize blockchain technology, the increased number of users engaging via the social media platform and the reportedly increased level in trust due to customer satisfaction and positive encounters. These results also confirm the association between the two themes namely c (consumer behaviour and value) and theme e (new forms of organising and ways of working), which together, further support the aim of this study which is that the implementation of blockchain technology can improve customer engagement when using social media marketing. This was demonstrated by the positive online customer engagements, the growth of the social media influencers (eWOM), the increased popularity of social networking and the increasing trust in blockchain supported social media platforms.

5.3 Research Question Three: What Are the Challenges That the Implementation of Blockchain in Social Media Marketing Pose to Both the Consumer and the Marketer?

From the empirical findings, the study has identified that themes d and f related to this research question.

As per Table 5, the themes (numbered as 'd' and 'f' in the table) were found to be present in a total of 20 of the 41 articles (including grey literature, social media posts and blogs). NVivo had identified a total of 9 codes that are associated with the two themes.

These codes included the focus of businesses as they haste to dominate social media marketing and capture the attention of more consumers, by optimising their landing pages to engage users, hence providing enhanced data management using blockchain, timestamping, and the increase in trust making the consumer feel safe when interacting over the internet.

The study found that companies are increasingly starting to realise the power of direct interaction with their customers (Parsons, 2013). As a result of this, according to Iankova et al. (2019), the emphasis from business has been to tailor their social media marketing campaigns to capitalise on the high volume of consumers who use social media on a daily basis.

A recurrent challenge for business is to find novel ways to attract and direct traffic to their home page. The next challenge is keeping the communication active so as to maintain the existing customer's interest (Järvinen et al., 2012).

Blockchain technology allowed for more accurate and truthful data and hence enhanced data management (Casino et al., 2019). However according to Cell (2020), the founder of Ethereum was concerned about data management and safety and thus went on to develop the technology further.

The interdependence of some of the concepts like time stamping and trust, highlights the influence that blockchain has on both the marketer's and the consumer's confidence when using online platforms. Timestamps has the additional benefit of verifying ownership of assets, documents and intellectual property at a specific point in time.

The study's findings demonstrate to policymakers that blockchain is a promising technology that has the potential to revolutionise social media marketing, improve consumer confidence and improve data security. As the technology is still at its infancy stage, the technology is yet to be fully understood and accepted by business. The study has found that social media marketers and consumers are familiar with the concept of blockchain and in general have a positive attitude to blockchain adoption. However there is still a lack of understanding of blockchain and its implementation in social media (Albayati et al., 2020).

5.4 A Summary of the Discussion Points

The analysis of the findings suggests that the incorporation of blockchain technology can influence social media marketing in several ways. For instance, the findings suggest that this can positively influence the organisation's knowledge of their customers as well as how companies collect, process data and utilise this data for marketing purposes. Similarly, blockchain incorporation can also have a negative influence on the impact of social media marketing. This negative influence is based on the premise that the customer is not developing the level of trust in the company or social media platform. This means that the customer does not share their personal information or other data as required by the company's marketing platform. The findings of this study strongly concur that the incorporation of blockchain technology in social media marketing has the ability to lead to enhanced customer engagement and growth in the number of customers visiting the web site or landing page since blockchain promotes an increased level of trust and customer satisfaction. Another favourable feature is that blockchain has the ability to encrypt data thus removing fraud within social media marketing, hence providing marketers with trustworthy and reliable data. Also, the consequences of the incorporation of blockchain will improve consumer confidence through the improved security measures that they experience while they are using the social media marketing platforms.

6. CONCLUSION

The aim of this chapter was to explore how the introduction of blockchain technology in social media marketing can aid the personal security issues, and thus improve consumer confidence when using social media.

There is consensus in the data that blockchain brings promising benefits to social media marketing. From an improved level of trust because personal data is protected, through to an enhanced data verification using data encryption, and a higher customer engagement as a result of developed trust, blockchain is found to be able to bring about a dependable platform which is quickly gaining credibility in areas other than cryptocurrency such as logistics, finance and marketing.

Despite the success demonstrated and the increased attention from both industry and academics, blockchain is still in its infancy. This limitation results in a lack of understanding and poses some challenges when the technology is to be adopted by business in their social media marketing campaigns. Another limitation of the study was the use of the priori themes for research. This maybe because the chapter had focussed exclusively on the data to try and fit the priori themes, hence the chapter may have overlooked material that does not relate to them. Despite these limitations, based on the findings of this study, the six priori themes and their supporting codes provided substantial insight into blockchain supported social media. The study demonstrated the transformative effect of blockchain on social media marketing as customers developed a relationship with the organisation. This led to customer trust and further enhanced customer engagement which included sharing of their personal details with the organisation. These positive online interactions created value to both the customer and the organisation alike. By providing a platform for the safe sharing of information and transacting, this positive experience prompted customers to share their experiences with others using the social media platforms. They in effect become social media influencers as they encouraged others to either purchase the product or experience the same positive encounter that they had experienced. After completing a positive encounter, the consumers agreed that they have more confidence, trust and satisfaction in the blockchain led social media marketing platform. This positive experience resulted in increased growth and popularity of the social media platforms as more customers visited these online platforms.

7. LIMITATIONS OF THE STUDY

The main limitation of this study would be the fact that the research was limited to 4 databases (which included 30 peer reviewed journal articles), as well as 11 grey literatures (which included blogs and social media posts). Therefore, complementary analysis including other databases would be necessary to confirm this study's conclusions.

This study was based on the review of a total 41 articles (including 11 grey literature, blogs and social media posts), which, because of the small sample size, might not be enough to prevent research bias.

A third limitation was that there was minimal prior research literature available on this topic as the application of blockchain in the field of social media marketing is in its infancy. This meant that the researchers had to focus on the most contemporary and evolving research problems or narrow the research problem to identify related literature and grey literature.

8. RECOMMENDATIONS FOR FUTURE RESEARCH

This study opens up several directions for future research. First, the study sample size can be expanded to include Australian companies. Second, this study focused only on using a systematic thematic analysis method; therefore, another study can examine the topic using the mixed methods approach consisting of both qualitative and quantitative data. The results obtained from these mixed methods of study may lead to a better understanding of the impact of blockchain incorporation in social media marketing.

Third, this study used cross-sectional data. Future studies can investigate the topic of this research by using longitudinal data. The benefit of using longitudinal data is that it would allow for the statistical analysis of the data which may provide a different view or concept to the topic.

9. REFERENCES

Al Tawara, A., & Gide, E. (2017). A Comprehensive Literature Review on the Adoption of Social Media Marketing in SME Retailors in Jordan. *International Journal of Business and Management Studies.*

Albayati, H., Kim, S. K., & Rho, J. J. (2020). Accepting financial transactions using blockchain technology and cryptocurrency: A customer perspective approach. *Technology in Society*, *62*, 101320. doi:10.1016/j.techsoc.2020.101320

Alves, H., Fernandes, C., & Raposo, M. (2016). Social media marketing: A literature review and implications. *Psychology and Marketing*, *33*(12), 1029–1038. doi:10.1002/mar.20936

Antoniadis, I., Kontsas, S., & Spinthiropoulos, K. (2019). Blockchain applications in marketing. *The Proceedings of 7th ICCMI*. Research Gate.

Appel, G., Grewal, L., Hadi, R., & Stephen, A. T. (2020). The future of social media in marketing. *Journal of the Academy of Marketing Science*, *48*(1), 79–95. doi:10.100711747-019-00695-1 PMID:32431463

Bala, M., & Verma, D. (2018). A critical review of digital marketing. *International Journal of Management, IT & Engineering*, *8*(10), 321–339.

Bornmann, L. (2011). Scientific peer review. *Annual Review of Information Science & Technology*, *45*(1), 197–245. doi:10.1002/aris.2011.1440450112

Burns, K. S. (2017). *Social Media: A Reference Handbook* [Online Non-fiction Electronic document]. ABC-CLIO, LLC. https://search.ebscohost.com/login.aspx?direct=true&AuthType=shib&db=cat06414a&AN=vic.b3962456&site=eds-live&custid=s1145751 https://ebookcentral.proquest.com/lib/vu/detail.action?docID=4819121

Buterin, V. (2013). *Ethereum white paper: A next-generation smart contract and decentralized application platform.* The Blockchain. http://www. the-blockchain.com/docs/Ethereum white papera next generation smart contract and decentralized application platform-vitalik-buterin. pdf

Casey, M. J., & Vigna, P. (2018). In blockchain we trust. *MIT's Technology Review*, *121*(3), 10–16.

Casino, F., Dasaklis, T. K., & Patsakis, C. (2019). A systematic literature review of blockchain-based applications: Current status, classification and open issues. *Telematics and Informatics*, *36*, 55–81. doi:10.1016/j.tele.2018.11.006

Cell, E. (2020). *The future of blockchain and social media.* Socially Powered. https://sociallypowered.com/episodes/the-importance-of-blockchain-the-future-of-social-media/

Choi, T.-M., Guo, S., & Luo, S. (2020). When blockchain meets social-media: Will the result benefit social media analytics for supply chain operations management? *Transportation Research Part E, Logistics and Transportation Review, 135*, 101860. doi:10.1016/j.tre.2020.101860

Chris, A. (2004). The long tail. *Wired, 12*(10), 170–177.

Conick, H. (2017). What marketers need to know about blockchain. *Marketing News, 51*(10), 12–14.

Constantinides, E. (2014). Foundations of social media marketing. *Procedia: Social and Behavioral Sciences, 148*, 40–57. doi:10.1016/j.sbspro.2014.07.016

DavidsonS.De FilippiP.PottsJ. (2016). Economics of blockchain. SSRN 2744751.

de Oliveira Santini, F., Ladeira, W. J., Pinto, D. C., Herter, M. M., Sampaio, C. H., & Babin, B. J. (2020). Customer engagement in social media: A framework and meta-analysis. *Journal of the Academy of Marketing Science, 48*(6), 1211–1228. doi:10.100711747-020-00731-5

Durach, C. F., Kembro, J., & Wieland, A. (2017). A new paradigm for systematic literature reviews in supply chain management. *The Journal of Supply Chain Management, 53*(4), 67–85. doi:10.1111/jscm.12145

Dutra, A., Tumasjan, A., & Welpe, I. M. (2018). Blockchain is changing how media and entertainment companies compete. *MIT Sloan Management Review, 60*(1), 39–45.

Edosomwan, S., Prakasan, S. K., Kouame, D., Watson, J., & Seymour, T. (2011, July). 2011). The History of Social Media and its Impact on Business. *The Journal of Applied Management and Entrepreneurship, 16*(3), 79–91. https://www.proquest.com/scholarly-journals/history-social-media-impact-on-business/docview/889143980/se-2?accountid=14844

Fink, A. (2019). *Conducting research literature reviews: From the internet to paper.* Sage publications.

Fraccastoro, S., Gabrielsson, M., & Pullins, E. B. (2021). The integrated use of social media, digital, and traditional communication tools in the B2B sales process of international SMEs. *International Business Review, 30*(4), 101776. doi:10.1016/j.ibusrev.2020.101776

Godey, B., Manthiou, A., Pederzoli, D., Rokka, J., Aiello, G., Donvito, R., & Singh, R. (2016). Social media marketing efforts of luxury brands: Influence on brand equity and consumer behavior. *Journal of Business Research*, *69*(12), 5833–5841. doi:10.1016/j.jbusres.2016.04.181

Guidi, B., & Michienzi, A. (2020). Users and Bots behaviour analysis in Blockchain Social Media. *2020 Seventh International Conference on Social Networks Analysis, Management and Security (SNAMS)*. https://search.ebscohost.com/login.aspx?direct=true&AuthType=shib&db=edseee&AN=edseee.9336553&site=eds-live&custid=s1145751

Hacioglu, U. (2020). *Digital business strategies in blockchain ecosystems*. Springer International Publishing. doi:10.1007/978-3-030-29739-8

Halabi-Echeverry, A. X., Nino-Vergara, H. L., Obregon-Neira, N., & Islam, S. M. N. (2020). Blockchain for data sharing in the rational use of coastlines and seaport demands in inter-organizational networks: Development of a new intelligent decision support system. *2020 5th International Conference on Innovative Technologies in Intelligent Systems and Industrial Applications (CITISIA)*. Research Gate.

HarveyC. R.MoormanC.ToledoM. (2018). How blockchain will change marketing as we know it. SSRN 3257511. doi:10.2139/ssrn.3257511

Hazratjee, S. (2015). Bitcoin: The Trade of Digital Signatures. *T. Marshall L. Rev.*, *41*, 55.

Hughes, L., Dwivedi, Y. K., Misra, S. K., Rana, N. P., Raghavan, V., & Akella, V. (2019). Blockchain research, practice and policy: Applications, benefits, limitations, emerging research themes and research agenda. *International Journal of Information Management*, *49*, 114–129. doi:10.1016/j.ijinfomgt.2019.02.005

Iankova, S., Davies, I., Archer-Brown, C., Marder, B., & Yau, A. (2019). A comparison of social media marketing between B2B, B2C and mixed business models. *Industrial Marketing Management*, *81*, 169–179. doi:10.1016/j.indmarman.2018.01.001

Jain, D., Dash, M. K., Kumar, A., & Luthra, S. (2021). How is blockchain used in marketing: A review and research agenda. *International Journal of Information Management Data Insights*, *1*(2), 100044. doi:10.1016/j.jjimei.2021.100044

Järvinen, J., Tollinen, A., Karjaluoto, H., & Jayawardhena, C. (2012, Fall). Digital and social media marketing usage in B2B industrial section. *Marketing Management Journal, 22*(2), 102-117. https://search.ebscohost.com/login.aspx?direct=true&AuthType=shib&db=bth&AN=87023191&site=eds-live&custid=s1145751

Jothikumar, B., & Baby, N. (2021, February). Blockchain Digital Marketing. *International Journal of Advanced Research in Science*, *2*(1).

Karafiloski, E., & Mishev, A. (2017). Blockchain solutions for big data challenges: A literature review. *IEEE EUROCON 2017-17th International Conference on Smart Technologies*. IEEE.

Kim, S. K., Ma, Z., Murali, S., Mason, J., Miller, A., & Bailey, M. (2018). Measuring ethereum network peers. *Proceedings of the Internet Measurement Conference 2018*. IEEE.

Lai, L., & To, W. M. (2015). Content analysis of social media: A grounded theory approach. *Journal of Electronic Commerce Research*, *16*, 138–152.

Lamberton, C., & Stephen, A. T. (2016). A thematic exploration of digital, social media, and mobile marketing: Research evolution from 2000 to 2015 and an agenda for future inquiry. *Journal of Marketing*, *80*(6), 146–172. doi:10.1509/jm.15.0415

Larson, S. (2017). Every single Yahoo account was hacked-3 billion in all. *CNN Business*.

Li, S., & Glass, R. (2020). Understanding blockchain through social media. *Issues in Information Systems*, *21*(4).

Liu, L., Zhang, W., & Han, C. (2021a). A survey for the application of blockchain technology in the media. *Peer-to-Peer Networking and Applications*, *14*(5), 3143–3165. doi:10.100712083-021-01168-5

Liu, L., Zhang, W., & Han, C. (2021b). A survey for the application of blockchain technology in the media. *Peer-to-Peer Networking and Applications*, *14*(5), 1–23. doi:10.100712083-021-01168-5

McPhee, C., & Ljutic, A. (2017). Blockchain. *Technology Innovation Management Review*, *7*(10), 3–5. doi:10.22215/timreview/1108

Menon, M., & Mady, A. (2021). Blockchain: A non-technical primer for marketing academics. *Marketing Education Review*, 1–19. doi:10.1080/10528008.2021.1943445

Michael, B. (2021). *How blockchain technology is changing social media?* Academic Press.

Mnif, E., Mouakhar, K., & Jarboui, A. (2021). Blockchain technology awareness on social media: Insights from twitter analytics. *The Journal of High Technology Management Research*, *32*(2), 100416. doi.org/10.1016/j.hitech.2021.100416

Moore, J. N., Hopkins, C. D., & Raymond, M. A. (2013). Utilization of relationship-oriented social media in the selling process: A comparison of consumer (B2C) and industrial (B2B) salespeople. *Journal of Internet Commerce, 12*(1), 48–75. doi:10.1080/15332861.2013.763694

Nakamoto, S. (2008). Bitcoin: A peer-to-peer electronic cash system. *Decentralized Business Review*, 21260.

Nakamoto, S. (2009). Bitcoin v0. 1 released. *The Mail Archive, 9*.

Nowiński, W., & Kozma, M. (2017). How can blockchain technology disrupt the existing business models? *Entrepreneurial Business and Economics Review, 5*(3), 173–188. doi:10.15678/EBER.2017.050309

Oh, I., & Park, G.-S. (2012). From B2C to B2B: Selling Korean pop music in the age of new social media. *Korea Observer, 43*(3), 365–397.

Oliva, G. A., Hassan, A. E., & Jiang, Z. M. J. (2020). An exploratory study of smart contracts in the Ethereum blockchain platform. *Empirical Software Engineering, 25*(3), 1864–1904. doi:10.100710664-019-09796-5

Page, M. J., McKenzie, J. E., Bossuyt, P. M., Boutron, I., Hoffmann, T. C., Mulrow, C. D., Shamseer, L., Tetzlaff, J. M., Akl, E. A., & Brennan, S. E. (2021). The PRISMA 2020 statement: An updated guideline for reporting systematic reviews. *BMJ (Clinical Research Ed.)*, 372. PMID:33782057

Park, S. (2021). *Data rights in the 21st century: exploring the boundaries of empowerment in blockchain social media settings.* Academic Press.

Parsons, A. (2013). Using social media to reach consumers: A content analysis of official facebook pages. *Academy of Marketing Studies Journal, 17*(2), 27–36. https://search.ebscohost.com/login.aspx?direct=true&AuthType=shib&db=edselc&AN=edselc.2-52.0-84891108093&site=eds-live&custid=s1145751

Pärssinen, M., Kotila, M., Rumin, R. C., Phansalkar, A., & Manner, J. (2018). Is blockchain ready to revolutionize online advertising? *IEEE Access : Practical Innovations, Open Solutions, 6*, 54884–54899. doi:10.1109/ACCESS.2018.2872694

Peck, M. E. (2017). Blockchain world-Do you need a blockchain? This chart will tell you if the technology can solve your problem. *IEEE Spectrum, 54*(10), 38–60. doi:10.1109/MSPEC.2017.8048838

Poongodi, T., Sujatha, R., Sumathi, D., Suresh, P., & Balamurugan, B. (2020). Blockchain in social networking. *Cryptocurrencies and Blockchain Technology Applications*, 55-76.

Purva, G., Arpan Kumar, K., & Marijn, J. (2019). Diffusion of blockchain technology: Insights from academic literature and social media analytics. *Journal of Enterprise Information Management*, *32*(5), 735–757. doi:10.1108/JEIM-06-2018-0132

Rahman, K. T. (2021). Applications of Blockchain Technology for Digital Marketing: A Systematic Review. *Blockchain Technology and Applications for Digital Marketing*, 16-31.

Rejeb, A., Keogh, J. G., & Treiblmaier, H. (2020). How blockchain technology can benefit marketing: Six pending research areas. *Frontiers in Blockchain*, *3*, 3. doi:10.3389/fbloc.2020.00003

Reyna, A., Martín, C., Chen, J., Soler, E., & Díaz, M. (2018). On blockchain and its integration with IoT. Challenges and opportunities. *Future Generation Computer Systems*, *88*, 173–190. doi:10.1016/j.future.2018.05.046

Sarosa, S. (2012). Adoption of social media networks by Indonesian SME: A case study. *Procedia Economics and Finance*, *4*, 244–254. doi:10.1016/S2212-5671(12)00339-5

Seuring, S., & Gold, S. (2012). Conducting content-analysis based literature reviews in supply chain management. *Supply Chain Management*, *17*(5), 544–555. doi:10.1108/13598541211258609

Shen, B., & Bissell, K. (2013). Social media, social me: A content analysis of beauty companies' use of Facebook in marketing and branding. *Journal of Promotion Management*, *19*(5), 629–651. doi:10.1080/10496491.2013.829160

Shen, C., Luong, T., Ho, J., & Djailani, I. (2020). Social media marketing of IT service companies: Analysis using a concept-linking mining approach. *Industrial Marketing Management*, *90*, 593–604. doi:10.1016/j.indmarman.2019.11.014

Soni, B. (2021, Feb). Are Blockchain based digital networks the future of social media. *The European Business Review*. https://www.europeanbusinessreview.com/are-blockchain-based-digital-networks-the-future-of-social-media/

Sprinkl. (2019). *The future of blockchain in Marketing*. Sprinkl. https://www.sprinklr.com/blog/blockchain-cryptocurrency-marketing/

Stallone, V., Wetzels, M., & Klaas, M. (2021). Applications of Blockchain Technology in marketing systematic review of marketing technology companies. *Blockchain: Research and Applications*, 100023. doi.org/10.1016/j.bcra.2021.100023

Sümer, S. I. (2020). A New Marketing Trend in the Digital Age: Social Media Marketing. In *Digital Business Strategies in Blockchain Ecosystems* (pp. 133–151). Springer. doi:10.1007/978-3-030-29739-8_7

Swan, M. (2015). *Blockchain: Blueprint for a new economy*. O'Reilly Media, Inc.

Swan, M. (2017, October). Anticipating the Economic Benefits of Blockchain. *Technology Innovation Management Review*, *7*(10), 6–13. doi:10.22215/timreview/1109

Swan, M., & De Filippi, P. (2017). Toward a philosophy of blockchain: A symposium: Introduction. *Metaphilosophy*, *48*(5), 603–619. doi:10.1111/meta.12270

Szabo, N. (2008). *Bit gold*. Website/Blog.

Tafesse, W., & Wien, A. (2018). Implementing social media marketing strategically: An empirical assessment. *Journal of Marketing Management*, *34*(9/10), 732–749. doi:10.1080/0267257X.2018.1482365

Tandon, A., Kaur, P., Mäntymäki, M., & Dhir, A. (2021). Blockchain applications in management: A bibliometric analysis and literature review. *Technological Forecasting and Social Change*, *166*, 120649. doi:10.1016/j.techfore.2021.120649

Tee, W. J., & Murugesan, R. K. (2018). Trust network, blockchain and evolution in social media to build trust and prevent fake news. *2018 Fourth International Conference on Advances in Computing, Communication & Automation (ICACCA)*.

Tranfield, D., Denyer, D., & Smart, P. (2003). Towards a methodology for developing evidence-informed management knowledge by means of systematic review. *British Journal of Management*, *14*(3), 207–222.

Upadhyay, N. (2019). *Transforming social media business models through blockchain* [Bibliographies Online Non-fiction Electronic document]. Emerald Publishing Limited. https://search.ebscohost.com/login.aspx?direct=true&AuthType=shib&db=cat06414a&AN=vic.b6372525&site=eds-live&custid=s1145751 https://go.openathens.net/redirector/vu.edu.au?url=https://doi.org/10.1108/9781838672997

Venkatraman, V., Timpone, R., Garcia-Garcia, M., Godard, O., Baldo, D., Schoeller, M., Strong, C., & Ansons, T. (2020). *Disrupting System 1 Thinking: Better Science for Smarter Marketing*. Insights Festival Esomar.

Wintermeyer, L. (2021). *Can SoFi -Social Media DeFi- Topple Facebook and Twitter?* Forbes Blog. https://www.forbes.com/sites/lawrencewintermeyer/2021/12/16/can-sofisocial-media-defitopple-facebook-and-twitter/?sh=28a28511c8dd

Wong, J. I. (2017). Sweden's blockchain-powered land registry is inching towards reality. *Quartz Daily Brief, 3.*

Wüst, K., & Gervais, A. (2018). Do you need a blockchain? *2018 Crypto Valley Conference on Blockchain Technology (CVCBT).*

Zakharenkov, A. (2021). *Blockchain social media Eliminates Centralized control and brings benefits.* Pixelplex.

Zarrella, D. (2009). *The social media marketing book.* O'Reilly Media, Inc.

Zimmerman, M., Balling, C., Chelminski, I., & Dalrymple, K. (2020). Applying the inclusion/exclusion criteria in placebo-controlled studies to a clinical sample: A comparison of medications. *Journal of Affective Disorders*, *260*, 483–488. doi:10.1016/j.jad.2019.09.012 PMID:31539683

ADDITIONAL READING

Caldarelli, G., & Ellul, J. (2021). Trusted Academic Transcripts on the Blockchain: A Systematic Literature Review. *Applied Sciences (Basel, Switzerland)*, *11*(4), 1842. doi:10.3390/app11041842

Fleischmann, M., & Ivens, B. (2019). Exploring the role of trust in blockchain adoption: an inductive approach. *Proceedings of the 52nd Hawaii international conference on system sciences.* IEEE. 10.24251/HICSS.2019.820

Treiblmaier, H. (2018). The impact of the blockchain on the supply chain: A theory-based research framework and a call for action. *Supply Chain Management*, *23*(6), 545–559. doi:10.1108/SCM-01-2018-0029

Xu, M., Chen, X., & Kou, G. (2019). 2019/07/04). A systematic review of blockchain. *Financial Innovation*, *5*(1), 27. doi:10.118640854-019-0147-z

Chapter 2
Does Blockchain and Internet of Things (BCoT) Help in Managing Customer Data?

Gideon Awini
Tamale Technical University, Ghana

Alhassan Abdul-Rasheed Alolo Akeji
https://orcid.org/0000-0001-6358-0063
Tamale Technical University, Ghana

Mohammed Majeed
https://orcid.org/0000-0001-9804-5335
Tamale Technical University, Ghana

Kobby Mensah
https://orcid.org/0000-0001-7444-7989
University of Ghana, Ghana

ABSTRACT

The internet of things (IoT) is transforming the established sector into a smart sector with "data-driven decision making." IoT's inherent characteristics, however, provide a variety of difficulties, including decentralization, weak interoperability, privacy concerns, and security flaws. Blockchain technology offers possibilities for overcoming IoT issues. In the realm of the internet of things, the introduction of blockchain has recently sparked a lot of attention. The existing blockchain system, however, has a number of non-trivial issues that prohibit it from serving as a general foundation for extensive IoT services and applications. This study provides a comprehensive

DOI: 10.4018/978-1-6684-7649-9.ch002

analysis of BCoT and explores the lessons learned from this novel paradigm. In particular, the authors first briefly describe the IoT and its difficulties. Then, they provide an introduction to blockchain technology. Next, they focused on describing the IoT and blockchain convergence and outlining the BCoT architecture proposal. They talk about BCoT's industrial uses and the problems of adopting "blockchain for 5G beyond IoT."

1. INTRODUCTION

In the age of digital transformation, the confluence of two revolutionary technologies, blockchain and the Internet of Things (IoT), has given rise to a new paradigm: blockchain and the Internet of Things (BCoT). As businesses grapple with the challenges of managing vast amounts of customer data, ensuring its security, authenticity, and accessibility become paramount. The traditional centralised systems, while efficient, often fall short in guaranteeing data integrity and protection against breaches. Enter BCoT, a synergy that promises not only enhanced security through decentralised ledgers but also real-time, transparent data exchanges through interconnected devices. But does this fusion truly offer a panacea for the challenges of customer data management? Blockchain and the Internet of Things (IoT) have the potential to work together to create a more customer experience-driven approach to business. The combination of these technologies can provide companies with a secure and transparent way to track and manage customer data, interactions, and transactions. One way this can be achieved is by using blockchain to secure the data generated by IoT devices. IoT devices generate vast amounts of data, often including sensitive customer information, which can be vulnerable to cyberattacks. By using blockchain, this data can be securely stored and accessed only by authorized parties, providing customers with greater confidence in the security of their information. Another way that blockchain and IoT can work together is by enabling more personalized customer experiences. Blockchain can be used to create secure and transparent records of customer interactions, such as purchases and service requests, which can then be used to personalize future interactions with that customer. For example, a smart home system could use blockchain to track a customer's preferences and habits, enabling it to automatically adjust settings to suit their preferences. Overall, the combination of blockchain and IoT has the potential to create a more customer-centric approach to business, with greater transparency, security, and personalization. However, the implementation of these technologies must be carefully managed to ensure customer privacy and data security are maintained.

Interestingly, both industry and academia have shown a lot of interest in the Internet of Things (IoT) (Chen et al., 2018). IoT, which uses ubiquitous connectivity, widely dispersed sensors, and broad accessibility, has the ability to create new interactions between devices and devices, much like the old Internet, which has had considerable success connecting people. The number of IoT devices will sharply increase in the coming years due to the development of IoT. In 2021, it's predicted that there will be 26 billion IoT devices (Kaushik & Bagga, 2020). The era of the internet of things will replace the era of the internet of information. IoT will benefit a wide range of applications because of the development of wearable technology, the growth of wireless networks, and the decreasing cost of embedded computers. Traditional applications like smart healthcare, the "smart grid," "smart manufacturing," "smart transportation," and "smart agriculture" have seen a number of creative waves. The extremely centralized architecture, which has issues with single points of failure (SPOF), data privacy, dependability, robustness, etc., severely restricts the existing IoT. Now, one of the most logical candidates to handle the aforementioned IoT concerns is blockchain (Novo, 2018). Blockchain facilitates the creation of decentralized applications, serves as a decentralized public ledger for transactions, and controls peer-to-peer communication in multi-peer systems. Blockchain depends on the use of encryption, and people communicate with one another in a verifiable way. So, it makes sense to apply the success of blockchain to IoT beyond the financial sector.

Nevertheless, the existing blockchain system has a number of non-trivial issues that prevent it from serving as a general foundation for extensive IoT services and applications. The scalability issue is one of the most difficult drawbacks (Qiu et al., 2019). For instance, although Ethereum can process 15 transactions per second (TPS), Bitcoin can only process 7 TPS (Yao et al., 2019). As an example, a miniature smart factory needs more than 5000 TPS capability, with a peak of 59,000 TPS. These capabilities are much below what is needed for the IoT. (Li et al., 2018). The difficulty has spurred the need to boost blockchain throughput in order to enhance scalability.

Recently, a number of initiatives and studies—including EOS, Zilliqa, and Plasma—have been put out to increase the scalability of blockchain. Nevertheless, they only employ one consensus process as the most appropriate one, disregarding the conditions of various users. For instance, Zilliqa is powered by the "Practical Byzantine Fault Tolerance (PBFT) protocol," while Plasma employs the democracy-as-proof-of-stake (dPoS) consensus process. The "quality of service" (QoS) requirements for blockchain-enabled IoT vary greatly. For instance, reduced latency is necessary for real-time transmission of time-sensitive IoT applications (Corcoran & Datta, 2016). While performing jobs that need lots of computing, robustness is more crucial than delay. Because different users have varied QoS requirements, it is impractical to utilize a single consensus process in the blockchain-enabled IoT.

The integration of blockchain with IoT (Internet of Things) has the potential to create a new paradigm of secure and decentralized systems that can revolutionize many industries. Blockchain is a distributed ledger technology that allows for secure and transparent transactions without the need for intermediaries. IoT refers to the interconnection of devices, sensors, and systems that enables them to collect and exchange data.

One of the main benefits of integrating blockchain with IoT is enhanced security. Blockchain's decentralized architecture makes it virtually impossible for hackers to tamper with the data being transmitted between IoT devices. This can be particularly important in applications where security is critical, such as smart homes, autonomous vehicles, and industrial control systems. Another benefit of integrating blockchain with IoT is increased transparency. Blockchain's distributed ledger allows for a transparent and auditable record of all transactions between IoT devices. This can be useful in supply chain management, where it is important to track the movement of goods from one point to another. In addition, the integration of blockchain with IoT can enable new business models and revenue streams. For example, by creating a decentralized marketplace for IoT devices and data, companies can monetize their IoT assets and create new revenue streams.

However, there are also challenges to the integration of blockchain with IoT. One of the main challenges is scalability, as blockchain can become slow and expensive when processing a large number of transactions. Another challenge is interoperability, as different IoT devices may use different protocols and standards, which can make it difficult to create a unified blockchain system. Overall, the integration of blockchain with IoT has the potential to create a new paradigm of secure, transparent, and decentralized systems that can transform many industries. However, it will require continued innovation and collaboration between blockchain and IoT developers to overcome the challenges and realize the full potential of this technology. Blockchain of Things (BCoT) is a concept that combines the decentralized and transparent nature of blockchain with the connectivity and data-sharing capabilities of the Internet of Things (IoT). Here are some of the key merits of BCoT: BCoT provides enhanced security for IoT devices by enabling a decentralized and tamper-proof system for data sharing. The distributed ledger technology of blockchain ensures that data is secure, and each transaction is validated through a consensus mechanism. BCoT ensures the integrity of data by providing a transparent system where data cannot be altered or deleted. The data recorded on the blockchain is immutable, and changes can only be made through a consensus mechanism. BCoT enables a decentralized system where IoT devices can communicate and transact with each other without the need for intermediaries. This eliminates the need for a central authority, reducing the risk of a single point of failure. BCoT can improve the efficiency of IoT devices by enabling automated transactions and reducing the need for human intervention. Smart contracts can be used to automate transactions between devices, reducing the time and cost of transactions. BCoT provides a common platform for IoT devices to communicate and transact with each other, regardless of their type, manufacturer, or protocol. This increases the interoperability of IoT devices, enabling a seamless exchange of data. BCoT provides a transparent and auditable system for tracking the origin and movement of IoT devices and data. This can be particularly useful in supply chain management, where it is important to track the movement of goods from one point to another.

Thus, Blockchain of Things (BCoT) can provide several benefits by combining the advantages of blockchain and IoT. It can create a secure, transparent, and efficient system for communication and transactions between IoT devices, enabling new business models and revenue streams.

In this research, we examine an IoT plan that uses blockchain technology and suggest an IoT permissioned blockchain that is service-oriented. The following is a summary of the paper's contributions. We suggest a "service-oriented permissioned blockchain" for the Internet of Things in order to enhance the functionality of the blockchain system and satisfy the requirements of various users. To meet the QoS needs of various users, various consensus techniques are deployed. The proposed blockchain may also dynamically distribute network capacity across IoT devices and choose block producers.

The remaining sections of the chapter are structured as follows: IoT overview is presented in Section II first. The introduction to blockchain technology follows in Part III. In Part IV, it is covered how blockchain and IoT have converged. The research issues around blockchain for 5G beyond networks are covered in Section V. The applications of BCoT are outlined in Section VI after that. In Section VII, unresolved research questions are covered. In Section VIII, the paper is finished.

2. BACKDROP OF INTERNET OF THINGS

The Internet of Things (IoT) is a concept that refers to the interconnection of devices, sensors, and systems through the internet, enabling them to collect and exchange data. IoT devices can be found in various domains such as healthcare, transportation, manufacturing, agriculture, and smart homes. The idea of IoT dates back to the early 1980s when the first internet-connected device, a toaster, was developed at Carnegie Mellon University. However, the term "Internet of Things" was first coined in 1999 by Kevin Ashton, a British entrepreneur, who used the term to describe a system where objects could be identified and tracked through the internet. Over the years, the development of wireless technologies, miniaturization of sensors, and the availability of low-cost hardware and software components have accelerated the growth of IoT. Today, billions of devices are connected to the internet, and the number is expected to grow to 25 billion by 2025. IoT has the potential to transform many industries by enabling new applications and services, improving efficiency, and enhancing customer experience. For example, in healthcare, IoT can be used to monitor patients remotely, providing real-time data to healthcare providers, improving patient outcomes and reducing costs. In manufacturing, IoT can be used to monitor machines and optimize production processes, reducing downtime and improving efficiency.

However, there are also concerns about the security and privacy implications of IoT, as the vast amounts of data generated by IoT devices can be vulnerable to cyber-attacks and misuse. As a result, efforts are being made to develop standards and protocols for secure and trustworthy IoT systems. Due to recent advancements in the "Internet of Things" (IoT) and "Big Data Analytics," the modern industrial sector is undergoing a paradigm shift from the traditional computer-aided industry to the "smart industry" (BDA). In this evolution, IoT is essential for bridging the gap between the actual industrial environment and the computing systems' cyberspace, and BDA can assist in sifting through the vast amounts of IoT data to find hidden insights that can be used to make wise judgments. IoT is essentially a network of intelligent things (or things) that offer a variety of industrial services. According to Figure 1, an IoT system typically consists of the following tiered sub-systems, from bottom to top.

Figure 1. IoT systems
Source: Adopted from Dai, Zheng and Zhang (2019)

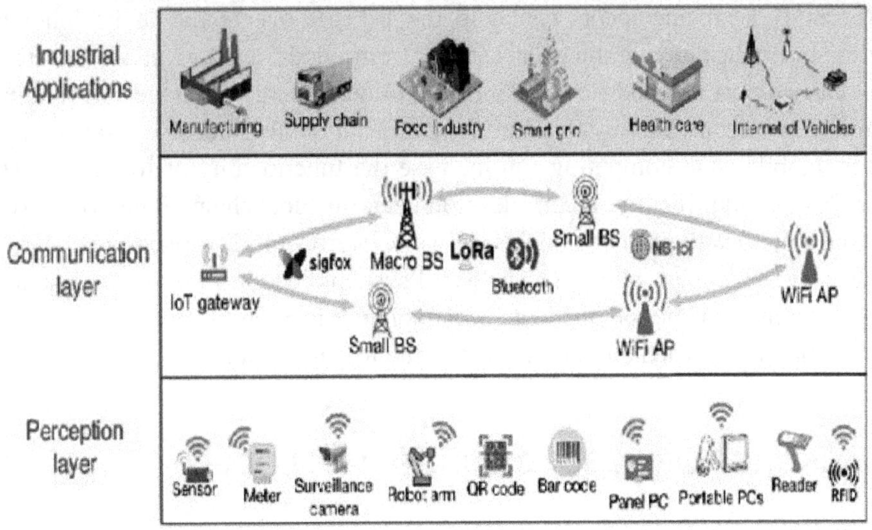

Research in the field of Internet of Things (IoT) presents various challenges that must be addressed in order to fully realize the potential of IoT. Here are some of the key challenges in IoT research: IoT devices generate vast amounts of data, which can be vulnerable to cyber-attacks and misuse. Ensuring the security and privacy of IoT devices and data is a major challenge, particularly given the wide range of devices and protocols used in IoT. The lack of interoperability and standardization among IoT devices can hinder their ability to communicate and share data. This can make it difficult to create a unified IoT system that can work seamlessly across different platforms and devices. The vast amounts of data generated by IoT devices require effective data management and analytics techniques to extract meaningful insights. This requires the development of new data processing and analytics tools that can handle the high volume, velocity, and variety of IoT data. Many IoT devices operate on limited battery power, making energy efficiency a critical challenge in IoT research. Developing energy-efficient devices and protocols is essential to enable the widespread adoption of IoT. As the number of IoT devices grows, scalability becomes an increasingly important challenge. Scaling IoT systems to handle large numbers of devices and data requires new approaches to computing and networking. IoT devices can generate sensitive data, raising concerns about trust and ethics. Ensuring that IoT devices are used in a responsible and ethical manner requires the development of ethical frameworks and guidelines for IoT research and deployment. Intuitively, addressing these challenges is critical to unlocking the full potential of IoT and enabling its widespread adoption in various industries. Continued research and innovation in these areas are essential to overcome these challenges and create a secure, interoperable, and scalable IoT ecosystem.

Recent ICT advancements can help the IoT get over some of its inherent constraints. For instance, ambient backscatter from aided communications (Lu et al., 2018) can support IoT nodes in obtaining additional energy from the surrounding environment. Meanwhile, by outsourcing computationally intensive tasks to edge servers, mobile edge computing can increase the functionality of IoT nodes (He et al., 2017). Additionally, recent developments in blockchain technology offer potential solutions to problems including weak interoperability, privacy concerns, and security flaws. Also, blockchain helps IoT systems become more heterogeneous. After providing a primer on blockchain technologies in Section III, we will address the potential that blockchain has brought to the IoT in Section IV.

3. BACKDROP OF BLOCKCHAIN TECHNOLOGIES

Blockchain technology is a decentralized and distributed ledger that allows data to be stored and shared securely across a network of computers. It was first introduced in

2008 by an anonymous person or group of people known as Satoshi Nakamoto, who used it as the underlying technology for the cryptocurrency, Bitcoin. The key feature of blockchain technology is that it allows for secure and transparent transactions without the need for a centralized intermediary or authority. Transactions are validated and recorded by a network of computers, known as nodes, and stored in blocks that are linked together in a chronological chain, forming a decentralized and tamper-proof record of all transactions. Since its inception, blockchain technology has evolved beyond its original application in cryptocurrency and has been applied to various domains, including finance, supply chain management, healthcare, and more. The use of blockchain technology has the potential to revolutionize these industries by enabling secure and transparent transactions, reducing the need for intermediaries, and increasing efficiency and trust. Some of the key benefits of blockchain technology include: Blockchain technology eliminates the need for a centralized authority or intermediary, reducing the risk of a single point of failure and increasing trust in transactions. Transactions on the blockchain are transparent and visible to all participants, allowing for greater accountability and reducing the risk of fraud. Blockchain technology provides a secure and tamper-proof system for transactions, ensuring the integrity of data and reducing the risk of cyber-attacks. Transactions on the blockchain can be processed quickly and efficiently, reducing the time and cost of transactions. Blockchain technology can increase trust among participants by providing a transparent and auditable system for transactions. Thus, blockchain technology has the potential to transform various industries by enabling secure, transparent, and efficient transactions. Continued research and innovation in this area will likely lead to further advancements and applications of blockchain technology in the future.

A distributed ledger that spans the whole blockchain system is what a blockchain essentially is (Zheng et al., 2018). A sample blockchain with several connected blocks in a row is shown in Figure 2. With the exception of the first block, every block in a blockchain has an inverted reference, which is simply the parent block's hash value, that links to the block that came before it (referred to as the parent block). As seen in Figure 2, block I for instance, contains the hash of block I, 1. The "genesis block," which has no parent block, is the very first block on a blockchain. A block structure specifically consists of the following data: block version (which displays the validation guidelines to adhere to), parent block hash, 3) A timestamp indicating the time in seconds as of the moment, 4) After starting at zero and going up for each hash computation, 5) The total volume of transactions, 6) Merkle Root, as depicted in the detailed view of Figure 2, which is the hash value of the root of a Merkel tree created by concatenating the hash values of each transaction in the block.

With each transaction that is completed, a blockchain expands. Every node in the network will take part in block validation whenever a new block is generated.

With the help of the inverted reference pointing to the parent block, a validated block will be immediately added to the end of the blockchain. The hash value of the tampered block differs greatly from that of the unaltered block, making any unauthorized changes to the previously-generated block simple to spot. Additionally, because the blockchain is dispersed throughout the whole network, other network nodes can immediately spot tampering activity.

Figure 2. Blockchain systems
Source: Adopted from Dai et al. (2019)

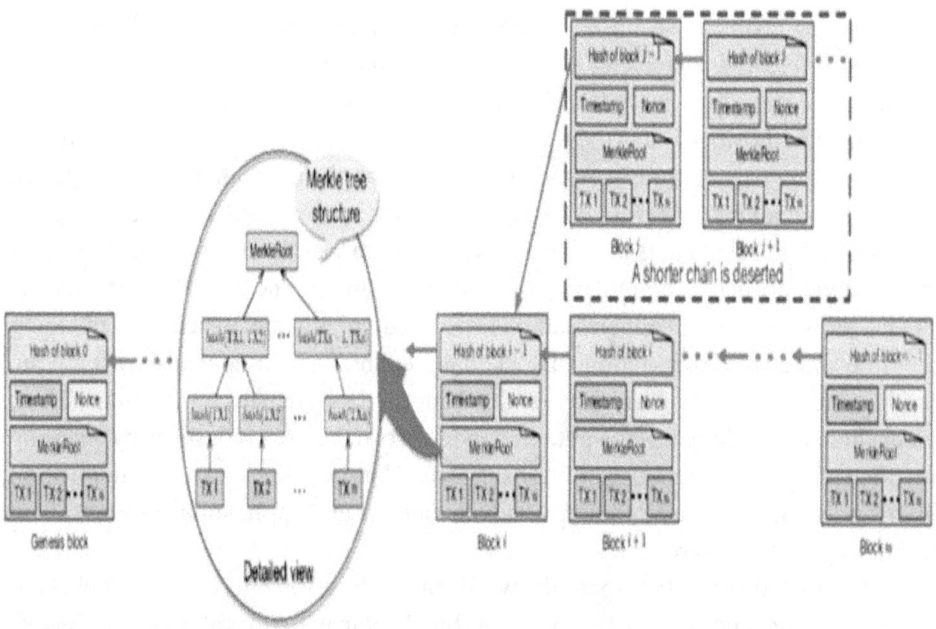

Blockchain technology has gained significant attention in recent years due to its potential to revolutionize various industries. However, there are several key challenges in Blockchain research that need to be addressed in order to fully realize its potential. Some of these challenges include: One of the primary challenges facing Blockchain technology is scalability. Blockchains are designed to be decentralized, but as the number of transactions on the network increases, the network becomes congested, leading to slower transaction times and higher fees. Researchers are working on developing new consensus algorithms and scaling solutions to address this issue. Security is another major challenge in Blockchain research. While Blockchain is considered to be a secure technology, it is still vulnerable to attacks such as 51% attacks, Sybil attacks, and DDoS attacks. Researchers are working on developing new security protocols and encryption techniques to make Blockchains more secure. Blockchain technology is still in its early stages, and there are many different Blockchain platforms and protocols that are not compatible with each other. This lack of interoperability makes it difficult for different Blockchain networks to communicate and share data. Researchers are working on developing standard protocols and interoperability solutions to address this issue. While Blockchain technology is designed to be transparent, there are instances where privacy is required. For example, in financial transactions, users may not want their personal information to be visible on the Blockchain. Researchers are working on developing new privacy-enhancing techniques, such as zero-knowledge proofs and ring signatures, to address this issue. Another challenge in Blockchain research is governance. Blockchains are designed to be decentralized, but there needs to be some form of governance to ensure that the network is functioning properly and to resolve disputes. Researchers are working on developing new governance models and mechanisms to address this issue.

Likewise, Blockchain research is a rapidly evolving field, and researchers are working on developing new solutions to address these challenges and improve the scalability, security, interoperability, privacy, and governance of Blockchain technology. That notwithstanding, one of the key benefits of using Blockchain technology is its ability to guarantee data integrity. Blockchain achieves this through a combination of cryptographic techniques and consensus algorithms that make it difficult for anyone to tamper with the data stored on the Blockchain. The basic idea behind data integrity in Blockchain is that once data is added to the Blockchain, it becomes part of an immutable, tamper-proof ledger that cannot be altered without the consensus of the network. This is achieved through the use of cryptographic hashing, which generates a unique digital fingerprint for each block of data added to the Blockchain. Each block also contains a reference to the previous block, creating a chain of blocks that makes it difficult to alter any previous transactions without altering the entire chain.

Furthermore, because Blockchains are decentralized, with multiple nodes verifying transactions and maintaining a copy of the ledger, any attempt to tamper with the data would require a majority of the nodes to collude, making it extremely difficult to execute successfully. This makes it virtually impossible to corrupt or alter data on the Blockchain without detection. In addendum, some Blockchains also implement smart contracts, which are self-executing contracts with the terms of the agreement between buyer and seller being directly written into lines of code. Smart contracts can be used to automatically enforce the rules and regulations governing the use of data on the Blockchain, further ensuring data integrity. All-encompassing, Blockchain technology provides a robust solution for ensuring data integrity, making it a valuable tool for industries that require secure and tamper-proof record-keeping. The working flow of Blockchains can be broken down into several steps: The first step in the Blockchain working flow is data entry. This involves adding new transactions or data to the Blockchain. Transactions can include things like financial transactions, contracts, or any other type of data that needs to be securely recorded. Once a transaction is entered into the Blockchain, it needs to be verified by the network. This involves using consensus algorithms to ensure that the transaction is legitimate and that the data is correct. Verification is typically done by a network of nodes or computers that are connected to the Blockchain. Once a transaction is verified, it is added to a block. Blocks are a collection of transactions that have been verified by the network. Each block has a unique digital signature, or hash, that identifies it and links it to the previous block, creating a chain of blocks. Mining is the process of creating new blocks on the Blockchain. Mining involves solving complex mathematical problems that require a significant amount of computational power. Miners who successfully solve these problems are rewarded with new cryptocurrency, which incentivizes them to continue mining and securing the network. Consensus is the process by which the network agrees on the state of the Blockchain. Consensus algorithms ensure that all nodes on the network have the same copy of the Blockchain and that all transactions are valid. Once a block is mined, it needs to be validated by the network. Validation involves verifying that the new block contains only valid transactions and that the digital signature is correct. Once a block is validated, it is added to the Blockchain. The new block is linked to the previous block in the chain, creating a new link in the Blockchain. The process of adding new transactions to the Blockchain, verifying them, and adding them to the Blockchain continues in a continuous cycle. Generally, the working flow of Blockchains is a complex and sophisticated process that relies on consensus algorithms, cryptography, and incentivization to ensure the integrity and security of the network. Figure 3 shows the workflow of blockchain.

Figure 3. Workflow of blockchain technology

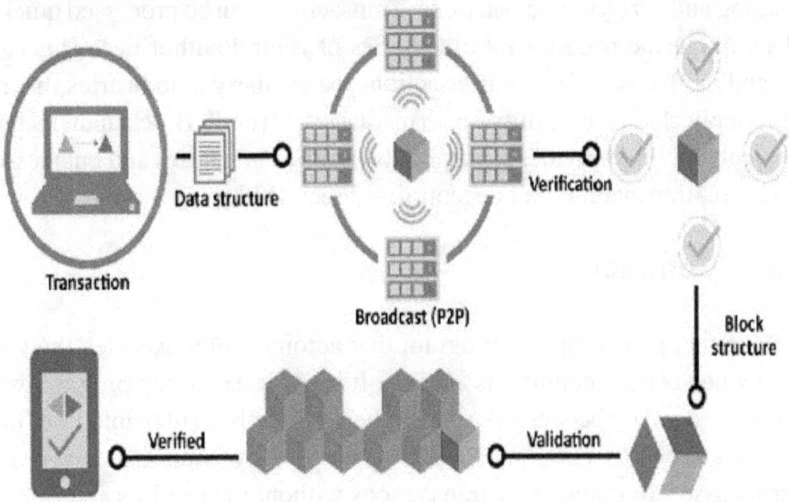

3.1 Characteristics of Blockchain Technologies

Blockchain technology is a revolutionary concept that has the potential to transform various industries by providing secure, transparent, and decentralized record-keeping systems. The following are some of the key characteristics of Blockchain technologies: One of the key characteristics of Blockchain technology is its decentralized nature. Unlike traditional systems, which rely on a central authority to validate and verify transactions, Blockchains are maintained by a network of nodes that work together to validate transactions and maintain the integrity of the ledger. Another important characteristic of Blockchain technology is its immutability. Once data is added to the Blockchain, it cannot be altered or deleted without the consensus of the network. This makes Blockchains an ideal solution for record-keeping and data storage, as it provides a tamper-proof and transparent system that can be audited and verified. Blockchains are transparent systems, which means that all transactions on the network are visible to all participants. This provides a high degree of transparency, as users can see exactly what is happening on the network and verify the authenticity of transactions. Blockchain technology is designed to be secure, using cryptography to protect against attacks and ensure the integrity of the data stored on the Blockchain. Transactions on the Blockchain are verified by the network, making it difficult for malicious actors to tamper with the data or corrupt the system. Blockchains rely on consensus algorithms to ensure that all participants on the network agree on the state of the ledger. This helps to prevent double-spending and other types of fraudulent activity, as all transactions must be verified by the network before they are added to the Blockchain. Finally, Blockchain technology is designed to be an efficient system for managing and verifying transactions. Transactions can be processed quickly and securely, without the need for intermediaries or central authorities. This can lead to faster and more cost-effective transactions, particularly in industries that rely on complex supply chains or multiple intermediaries. Overall, Blockchain technology is a powerful tool that provides a range of benefits to industries and businesses that require secure, transparent, and decentralized record-keeping systems.

3.2 Smart Contract

A smart contract is a computer program that automatically executes the terms of a contract when certain conditions are met. It is a self-executing program with the terms of the agreement between the parties being directly written into lines of code. Smart contracts are often used in Blockchain technology to automate the process of transferring assets or completing transactions without the need for intermediaries. They can be used to automate a wide range of processes, from financial transactions to supply chain management. Smart contracts are designed to be tamper-proof and self-executing, ensuring that the terms of the contract are enforced automatically and transparently. Once a smart contract is deployed to a Blockchain network, it cannot be altered or deleted without the consensus of the network. Smart contracts are typically written in a programming language that is specifically designed for the purpose of creating smart contracts, such as Solidity for the Ethereum network. These programming languages include a range of features that enable developers to create complex smart contracts that can automate a wide range of processes.

In summary, smart contracts are an innovative and powerful tool that has the potential to transform a wide range of industries by providing a transparent, secure, and automated way of executing contracts and transactions.

The life cycle of a smart contract typically involves the following stages:

1. Design: The first stage of the life cycle is the design stage, where the requirements and specifications of the smart contract are defined. This includes identifying the parties involved, the terms and conditions of the contract, and the conditions under which the contract will execute.
2. Development: The next stage is the development stage, where the smart contract is coded using a programming language such as Solidity. During this stage, the contract is tested to ensure that it operates as intended.
3. Deployment: Once the smart contract is developed and tested, it is deployed to the Blockchain network. The contract becomes available to all parties on the network, and can be executed when certain conditions are met.

4. Execution: The smart contract executes automatically when the conditions specified in the contract are met. For example, if the contract is a payment contract, it will automatically transfer the funds when the specified conditions are met.
5. Monitoring: During the execution stage, the smart contract is monitored to ensure that it operates correctly and that the conditions are being met. Any errors or issues that arise during the execution stage are addressed and resolved.
6. Completion: Once the contract has executed, it is considered complete. The parties involved in the contract can review the transaction and ensure that the terms of the contract have been met.
7. Maintenance: After the completion of the contract, it may need to be maintained to ensure that it continues to operate correctly. This may involve updating the contract to reflect changes in the underlying business process or technology.

The life cycle of a smart contract involves several stages, from design to maintenance. By automating the execution of contracts and transactions, smart contracts provide a transparent, secure, and efficient way to conduct business on Blockchain networks. Figure 4 below depicts the lifecycle of smart contracts.

Figure 4. Lifecycle of smart contract

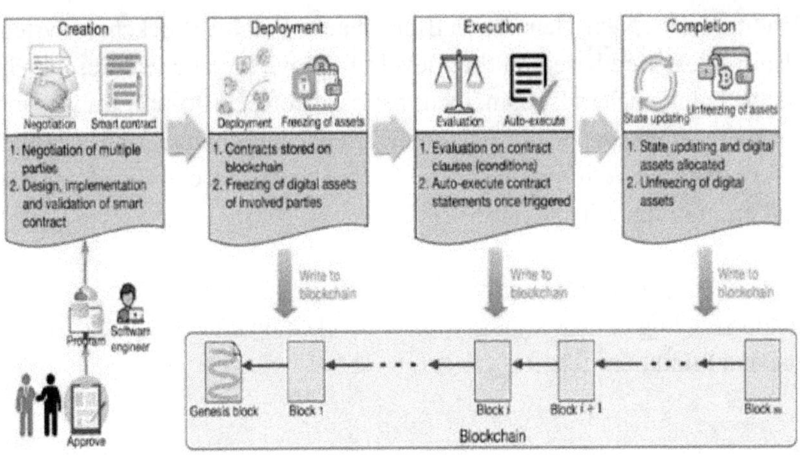

3.3 Taxonomy of Blockchain Systems

There are several ways to classify or categorize Blockchain systems, but the following are some common taxonomies of Blockchain systems:

1. Public vs. Private Blockchains: The first and most common classification of Blockchain systems is based on their accessibility. Public Blockchains are open to anyone and allow anyone to participate in the network, whereas Private Blockchains are restricted to a certain group of users, usually within an organization or consortium.
2. Permissioned vs. Permissionless Blockchains: Another way to classify Blockchain systems is based on their governance model. Permissioned Blockchains have a set of predefined rules and regulations, and access to the network is granted only to authorized users, while permissionless Blockchains have no such restrictions and anyone can join and participate.
3. Proof of Work (PoW) vs. Proof of Stake (PoS): Blockchain systems can also be categorized based on their consensus mechanism. Proof of Work Blockchains require users to solve complex mathematical problems to validate transactions and add new blocks to the chain, while Proof of Stake Blockchains rely on users staking their own coins or tokens to validate transactions and earn rewards.
4. Native vs. Interoperable Blockchains: Native Blockchains are standalone networks that have their own protocols and infrastructure, while Interoperable Blockchains allow for seamless communication and exchange of data and assets between different Blockchain networks.
5. Traditional vs. Next-Generation Blockchains: Finally, Blockchain systems can also be classified based on their level of innovation and features. Traditional Blockchains, such as Bitcoin, focus primarily on peer-to-peer transactions and currency exchange, while next-generation Blockchains, such as Ethereum, offer advanced features such as smart contracts, decentralized applications, and programmability.

In conclusion, these taxonomy of Blockchain systems can help to provide a better understanding of the various types of Blockchain networks and their features, benefits, and limitations.

4. CONVERGENCE OF BLOCKCHAIN AND IoT

The convergence of Blockchain and the Internet of Things (IoT) is a promising development that has the potential to revolutionize various industries. The combination of these two technologies can provide new solutions for data management, security, and automation.

The key benefits of the convergence of Blockchain and IoT are as follows:

1. Decentralization: Blockchain provides a decentralized infrastructure for managing data, which is highly beneficial for IoT applications where data is generated and exchanged by various devices. Decentralization eliminates the need for a central authority or intermediary, providing a more efficient and secure data exchange.
2. Data security: Blockchain's security features, such as cryptographic encryption and distributed ledgers, can provide an additional layer of security for IoT devices and networks. The decentralized nature of Blockchain also makes it more difficult for hackers to manipulate or compromise the data.
3. Automation: Smart contracts, which are built on Blockchain technology, can be used to automate various processes in IoT networks, such as data exchange, payments, and supply chain management. This can reduce the need for human intervention and improve efficiency.
4. Improved data management: The combination of Blockchain and IoT can provide a more efficient and secure way to manage data generated by IoT devices. The decentralized nature of Blockchain can ensure that the data is stored securely and can be easily accessed by authorized parties.
5. Transparency: Blockchain's distributed ledger technology can provide a transparent and auditable record of all transactions and data exchange in IoT networks. This can improve accountability and trust among parties involved in the network.

Instantaneously, the convergence of Blockchain and IoT has the potential to create new opportunities for innovation and disruption across various industries, from supply chain management to healthcare and smart cities. However, there are also challenges to be addressed, such as scalability, interoperability, and regulatory compliance, before the full potential of this convergence can be realized.

4.1 Overview of BCoT Architecture

BCoT (Blockchain of Things) architecture is a combination of Blockchain and IoT (Internet of Things) technologies. The aim of BCoT is to create a secure and decentralized infrastructure for managing data and devices in IoT networks. The architecture of BCoT consists of three layers:

1. The Perception Layer: This layer comprises IoT devices, sensors, and gateways that collect and transmit data. The data is encrypted and securely stored on the Blockchain.
2. The Network Layer: This layer includes nodes that participate in the Blockchain network, including miners, validators, and smart contracts. The Blockchain provides a decentralized infrastructure for managing the data and devices in the IoT network, as well as executing smart contracts.
3. The Application Layer: This layer includes the applications and services that utilize the data and devices in the IoT network. The applications can interact with the Blockchain network using APIs and SDKs, and can execute smart contracts to automate various processes.

The key features of BCoT architecture include:

1. Decentralization: BCoT architecture provides a decentralized infrastructure for managing data and devices in IoT networks. This eliminates the need for a central authority or intermediary, providing a more efficient and secure data exchange.
2. Security: BCoT architecture provides a high level of security for IoT networks by leveraging Blockchain's security features, such as cryptographic encryption and distributed ledgers.
3. Interoperability: BCoT architecture supports interoperability between different Blockchain networks and IoT devices, enabling seamless communication and exchange of data and assets.
4. Automation: BCoT architecture enables the automation of various processes in IoT networks, such as data exchange, payments, and supply chain management, through the use of smart contracts.

Inclusive, BCoT architecture provides a promising solution for creating secure, decentralized, and interoperable IoT networks. However, there are still challenges to be addressed, such as scalability, standardization, and regulatory compliance, before BCoT can be widely adopted in various industries. The figure 5 below shows the hybrid of Blockchain and IoT.

Figure 5. BCoT architecture

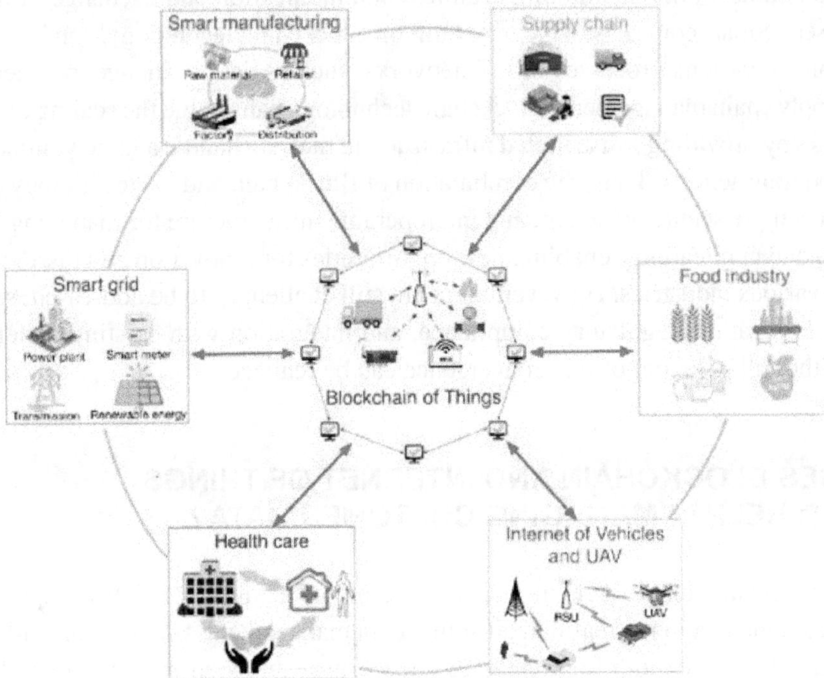

5. BLOCKCHAIN FOR 5G BEYOND IN IoT

Blockchain for 5G beyond in IoT refers to the use of Blockchain technology in conjunction with 5G networks to enhance the capabilities and security of IoT (Internet of Things) devices and applications. 5G is the latest mobile network technology that promises faster speeds, lower latency, and higher reliability compared to its predecessors, which can greatly benefit IoT devices and applications. However, 5G networks also introduce new security and privacy risks, as the volume and complexity of data generated by IoT devices increase. Blockchain technology can provide a solution to these challenges by enabling secure and decentralized data management and communication between IoT devices in 5G networks. The combination of Blockchain and 5G can provide the following benefits: Blockchain technology can provide a high level of security and privacy for IoT devices and applications in 5G networks by enabling secure data storage and transmission, as well as identity management. Blockchain technology can eliminate the need for central intermediaries in 5G networks, providing a more efficient and secure data exchange between IoT devices. Blockchain technology can enable interoperability between different IoT devices and networks, facilitating seamless communication and exchange of data and assets. Smart contracts, which are built on Blockchain technology, can be used to automate various processes in IoT networks, such as data exchange, payments, and supply chain management. Blockchain technology can enable the scaling of IoT networks by providing a distributed infrastructure that can handle a large volume of data and transactions. Thus, the combination of Blockchain and 5G technology can provide a more secure, efficient, and interoperable infrastructure for managing IoT devices and applications, enabling new opportunities for innovation and disruption across various industries. However, there are still challenges to be addressed, such as standardization, regulatory compliance, and integration with existing systems, before the full potential of this convergence can be realized.

6. DOES BLOCKCHAIN AND INTERNET OF THINGS (BCoT) HELP IN MANAGING CUSTOMER DATA?

The convergence of blockchain and the Internet of Things (BCoT) has sparked significant interest in the realm of customer data management. Blockchain, with its immutable ledger system, offers unparalleled security features, ensuring that once data is recorded, it cannot be altered without consensus. This characteristic is pivotal in maintaining the integrity of customer data, especially in an era where data breaches and cyberattacks are rampant. On the other hand, the Internet of Things (IoT) has revolutionised data collection, with countless devices continuously generating and transmitting data. This vast influx of data, while valuable, poses challenges in terms of storage, analysis, and security. Integrating blockchain with IoT can address these challenges. For instance, with BCoT, data from IoT devices can be stored securely on the blockchain, ensuring its authenticity and reducing the risk of tampering. Furthermore, the decentralised nature of blockchain can eliminate the need for intermediaries in data transactions, leading to more streamlined and transparent processes. This can be particularly beneficial for businesses that rely on multi-party transactions, where data integrity and transparency are paramount. However, while the benefits of BCoT in managing customer data are evident, its implementation is not without challenges. Concerns regarding scalability, interoperability, and energy consumption need to be addressed for widespread adoption. Moreover, as with any emerging technology, there's a learning curve involved, necessitating investments in training and infrastructure. Thus, the fusion of blockchain and IoT, forming BCoT, has the potential to redefine customer data management. By ensuring data security, authenticity, and transparency, BCoT can pave the way for more trustworthy and efficient data-driven decision-making processes in businesses. However, its successful implementation requires a holistic approach, considering both its advantages and inherent challenges. Figure 6.0 shows a conceptual framework for how the hybrid of blockchain and IoTs leads to the management of customer data.

Figure 6. Conceptual framework

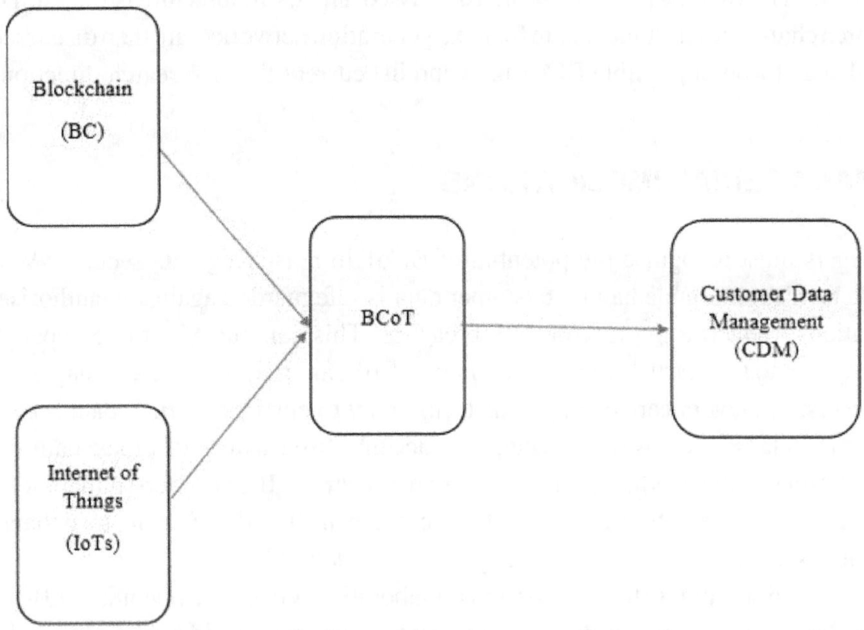

7. CONCLUSION

In the evolving landscape of digital transformation, the integration of Blockchain and the Internet of Things (BCoT) presents a promising avenue for enhancing customer data management. Blockchain's decentralized nature ensures data integrity and security, while the Internet of Things facilitates real-time data collection from a myriad of interconnected devices. Together, as BCoT, they offer a robust framework that can address the challenges of data breaches, unauthorized access, and data inconsistency. By leveraging the strengths of both technologies, businesses can not only ensure the safety and authenticity of customer data but also derive actionable insights from it. As industries continue to recognize the potential of BCoT, it is anticipated that its adoption will revolutionize customer data management, fostering trust and enhancing customer experiences in the digital age. The existing Internet of Things (IoT) systems are dealing with a variety of issues, such as "heterogeneity, poor interoperability, resource limitations, privacy concerns, and security vulnerabilities." Blockchain technologies have recently emerged, essentially providing a solution to the problems with improved interoperability, privacy, security, traceability, and reliability. In this article, we look into how blockchain might be combined with IoT. The combination of "blockchain and IoT" is known as BCoT. We offer a thorough analysis of BCoT. We begin by briefly introducing blockchain technology and the internet of things in particular. The BCoT's potential is then discussed, and its architecture is shown. The research challenges in "blockchain for next-generation networks" are then discussed. We also go through possible BCoT uses and list current BCoT research directions.

8. MANAGERIAL IMPLICATIONS

Managers must recognise the potential of BCoT in bolstering data security. With blockchain's immutable nature, customer data is safeguarded against unauthorised alterations, reducing the risk of data breaches. This can enhance the company's reputation and foster trust among customers. BCoT can streamline data management processes. Managers can leverage this technology to ensure real-time data access, reducing delays in decision-making. The decentralised nature of blockchain can also eliminate intermediaries, leading to cost savings. BCoT offers unparalleled transparency in data transactions. Managers can utilise this feature to enhance accountability in operations, ensuring that all stakeholders have a clear view of data transactions and fostering trust and collaboration. Given the potential of BCoT in revolutionising customer data management, managers should consider strategic investments in this technology. This includes infrastructure development, training programmes, and partnerships with BCoT experts. With increasing concerns about data privacy and regulations like General Data Protection Regulation (GDPR) coming into play, BCoT can assist managers in ensuring compliance. The transparent and secure nature of blockchain can aid in adhering to data protection regulations, reducing legal risks. While BCoT offers numerous benefits, managers must be aware of the interoperability challenges it might pose, especially when integrating with legacy systems. Strategic planning and phased implementation can mitigate these challenges. The successful implementation of BCoT requires a skilled workforce. Managers should invest in training programmes to equip employees with the necessary skills to navigate and leverage BCoT for optimal benefits. While BCoT can lead to cost savings in the long run, its initial implementation might require significant investment. Managers need to conduct a thorough cost-benefit analysis to ensure that the investment in BCoT aligns with the company's strategic goals. Given the transformative nature of BCoT, managers should engage with all stakeholders, including customers, employees, and partners, to ensure smooth adoption. Transparent communication about the benefits and challenges of BCoT can foster collaboration and reduce resistance to change. The realm of BCoT is rapidly evolving. Managers should establish mechanisms for continuous monitoring of BCoT trends and advancements to ensure that the company remains at the forefront of customer data management innovations.

9. LIMITATIONS

While the integration of blockchain and the Internet of Things (BCoT) presents promising advancements in managing customer data, several limitations should be acknowledged: Both blockchain and IoT are relatively nascent technologies. Their full potential, especially when integrated, is yet to be realized. As such, there might be unforeseen challenges that arise as they evolve. Blockchains, especially public ones, can face scalability issues. As the number of IoT devices grows exponentially, the volume of data transactions can strain the blockchain networks. While blockchain offers enhanced security, the permanent nature of its ledger means that once data is recorded, it cannot be altered. This can pose challenges, especially in light of regulations like GDPR, where users have the right to modify or delete their personal data. Integrating blockchain with IoT requires a deep understanding of both technologies. Organisations might face challenges in terms of finding the right expertise and resources for successful implementation. Blockchain, particularly proof-of-work-based systems, can be energy-intensive. With millions of IoT devices transmitting data, energy consumption can be significant. There are multiple blockchain platforms and IoT standards. Ensuring seamless interoperability between different systems and standards can be challenging. Setting up, maintaining, and scaling blockchain systems, especially in integration with vast IoT networks, can be costly for organisations.

REFERENCES

Chen, L., Zhao, N., Chen, Y., Yu, F. R., & Wei, G. (2018). Over-the-air computation for IoT networks: Computing multiple functions with antenna arrays. *IEEE Internet of Things Journal*, *5*(6), 5296–5306. doi:10.1109/JIOT.2018.2843321

Corcoran, P., & Datta, S. K. (2016). Mobile-edge computing and the Internet of Things for consumers: Extending cloud computing and services to the edge of the network. *IEEE Consumer Electronics Magazine*, *5*(4), 73–74. doi:10.1109/MCE.2016.2590099

Dai, H. N., Zheng, Z., & Zhang, Y. (2019). Blockchain for Internet of Things: A survey. *IEEE Internet of Things Journal*, *6*(5), 8076–8094. doi:10.1109/JIOT.2019.2920987

He, J., Wei, J., Chen, K., Tang, Z., Zhou, Y., & Zhang, Y. (2017). Multitier fog computing with large-scale IoT data analytics for smart cities. *IEEE Internet of Things Journal*, *5*(2), 677–686. doi:10.1109/JIOT.2017.2724845

Kaushik, N., & Bagga, T. (2020, March). Internet of Things (IOT): Implications in Society. *Proceedings of the International Conference on Innovative Computing & Communications (ICICC)*. SSRN. 10.2139srn.3563104

Li, X., Li, D., Wan, J., Liu, C., & Imran, M. (2018). Adaptive transmission optimization in SDN-based industrial Internet of Things with edge computing. *IEEE Internet of Things Journal*, *5*(3), 1351–1360. doi:10.1109/JIOT.2018.2797187

Lu, X., Niyato, D., Jiang, H., Kim, D. I., Xiao, Y., & Han, Z. (2018). Ambient backscatter assisted wireless powered communications. *IEEE Wireless Communications*, *25*(2), 170–177. doi:10.1109/MWC.2017.1600398

Novo, O. (2018). Blockchain meets IoT: An architecture for scalable access management in IoT. *IEEE Internet of Things Journal*, *5*(2), 1184–1195. doi:10.1109/JIOT.2018.2812239

Qiu, C., Yao, H., Yu, F. R., Jiang, C., & Guo, S. (2019). A service-oriented permissioned blockchain for the Internet of Things. *IEEE Transactions on Services Computing*, *13*(2), 203–215. doi:10.1109/TSC.2019.2948870

Yao, H., Mai, T., Wang, J., Ji, Z., Jiang, C., & Qian, Y. (2019). Resource trading in blockchain-based industrial Internet of Things. *IEEE Transactions on Industrial Informatics*, *15*(6), 3602–3609. doi:10.1109/TII.2019.2902563

Zheng, Z., Xie, S., Dai, H. N., Chen, X., & Wang, H. (2018). Blockchain challenges and opportunities: A survey. *International Journal of Web and Grid Services*, *14*(4), 352–375. doi:10.1504/IJWGS.2018.095647

Chapter 3
Blockchain Application for Healthcare Data Management and Patient Experience

Amin Ayarnah
https://orcid.org/0000-0003-3348-0832
University of Ghana, Ghana

Raphael Odoom
https://orcid.org/0000-0001-7765-0851
University of Ghana, Ghana

Kobby Mensah
https://orcid.org/0000-0001-7444-7989
University of Ghana, Ghana

Noel Nutsugah
University of Media, Arts, and Communication, Accra, Ghana

ABSTRACT

Blockchain technology is transforming the healthcare sector in light of data management and patient experience. It can be used in building a more secure data management platform that allows patients to retain ownership over their medical records. Permitted healthcare practitioners can also monitor patients' medical histories, view their most recent prescriptions, and provide prognoses with excellent patient experience. Ultimately, healthcare policymakers responsible for the regulation of innovation should create a favourable environment that will spur the building of blockchain digital solutions with the propensity of providing a single protocol of trust among healthcare stakeholders. This will standardise the implementation of blockchain in the global healthcare space. Green-oriented organisations should also join the conversation on how blockchains are designed, especially ensuring that blockchain is built with sustainability principles.

DOI: 10.4018/978-1-6684-7649-9.ch003

INTRODUCTION

Smart technologies, including blockchain technology, artificial intelligence (AI), metaverse, cloud computing, internet of things (IoT), cyber security, machine learning (ML), virtual reality (VR), and augmented reality (AR), have revolutionised the financial, manufacturing, supply chain, and healthcare sectors. (Zaabar et al., 2021; Ayarnah et al., 2023). The healthcare industry sector is concentrating its efforts on utilizing emerging technology to improve the intelligence and effectiveness of healthcare systems. According to Statista (2022), market revenue for medical technology is anticipated to reach US$579.40 billion this year.

The global healthcare industry is a clinical realm that regularly generates, accesses, and disseminates enormous amounts of data. The sensitive nature of healthcare data suggests the need to use secured platforms that allows traceability and consensus. Thus, both patients and providers of healthcare services continue to have serious concerns about the security and privacy of electronic health records (EHRs).

For instance, the healthcare industry in the United States experienced more than 340 data intrusion incidents in 2022. This shows a huge increase from 2005 when the industry reported only 16 data breaches nationwide. Fast forward 398 data breaches were recorded in 2019 (Statista, 2023). Sensitive health information is revealed as a result of these healthcare system breaches. This data comprises both common details, such as the patient's gender and date of birth, as well as particular details about the particular service offered, like the procedure carried out, the care plan, and other notes. This data is typically maintained in centralized databases, which introduces security flaws and encourages cyberattacks.

Personal health records (PHRs) are crucial medical records that help improve patient safety, healthcare services, and experiences. (Kim et al., 2022). Medical professionals may effectively diagnose and treat patients, as well as eliminate needless lab or test procedures, thanks to data and information. (Abel et al., 2017). Following current practice, a patient must sign a paper-based agreement that details the sort of data that will be shared, who it will be shared to and how will it be properly secured to reduce data breaches. However, the majority of this data sharing is still a time-consuming manual procedure, and it frequently takes days for the records to become accessible. Thus, resulting in significant delays in patient care and a negative patient experience (Dubovitskaya et al., 2020).

Blockchain technology has been the subject of certain studies in the healthcare industry. Patient-centred platforms, such OmniPHR, MedRec Solve.Care, Medicalchain, and FHIRChain, are utilised to transform the sharing of patient health data. (Roehrs et al., 2017; Zhang et al., 2018). When it comes to managing patient data in the healthcare industry, a convenient, secure, and mutually agreeable method is needed because data are dispersed among healthcare stakeholders like hospitals, health insurance companies, health research institutions, and ambulatory healthcare facilities. There is relatively little research that focuses on the patient experience, although several studies have proposed how blockchain technology could be used in healthcare data management. (Tanwar et al., 2020; Miyachi & Mackey, 2022).

Due to the relatively high potential of the technology and, on the other hand, the relatively limited research on blockchain technology, healthcare data management, and patient experience is the focus of this book chapter in the healthcare sector. This chapter aims to examine the healthcare industry, explain what blockchain is, and the use cases of blockchain technology in patient data management to enhance patient experience The final step will be to address the recommendations needed to implement blockchain technology in healthcare data management to enhance patient experience.

LITERATURE

Healthcare

Modular IT solutions existed in the 1970s when healthcare provision first began. This era is referred to as Healthcare 1.0. Due to a lack of resources, healthcare systems at this time were constrained and did not integrate with digital systems. In a similar vein, networked electronic devices did not yet include bio-medical machines that could be integrated. During this time, healthcare institutions frequently employed paper-based prescriptions and reporting, which increased operational expenses and time.

From 1991 until 2005, there was a period known as "Healthcare 2.0." During this time, healthcare systems as we know them now were developed by fusing health and information technologies. This phase saw the introduction of digital tracking, which gave clinicians access to imaging equipment for analysing patients' health. At the same time, social media was being introduced, and new user-enabled technologies started to appear in the healthcare sector. In order to enable ubiquitous access for both the patient and the healthcare professional, healthcare providers started to develop online communities for information and knowledge sharing, store information on cloud servers, and allow access to papers and patient records via mobile devices. However, critics raised concerns about false information and not knowing how much data to collect from patients.

Healthcare 3.0, which enabled user-customisation of how patient healthcare records were presented, was introduced at the same time as the idea of Web 3.0. User interfaces were more streamlined and tailored, enabling optimum and unique experiences. Along with wearable and implanted technologies, electronic healthcare records (EHRs) were also made available, allowing for the constant, real-time monitoring of patients' medical conditions. In a similar vein, EHR systems started to appear that integrated standalone, non-networked systems, such as social media channels, to store patient information. This made it easier to share health data between physicians or across networked channels, such as social media, when using EHR systems. Additionally, there was improved interaction and communication between patients and healthcare professionals. (Vora et al., 2018).

The Healthcare 4.0 era, which began in 2016, has now ended. This period was inspired by the idea of Industry 4.0, where high-tech and high-touch systems are being implemented. Blockchains are being built to allow real-time access to patients' clinical data using cloud computing, fog computing, edge computing, big data analytics, AI, and machine learning. This era's primary goal is to advance virtualization so that customised medical services can be provided in real-time. The current emphasis is on cooperation, coherence, and convergence, which can improve the predictability and personalisation of healthcare.

Blockchain Technology

One of the most significant inventions of the twenty-first century is blockchain technology. It improves trackability and visibility throughout the supply chain of numerous businesses in addition to providing operational and regulatory verification efficiencies (Attaran, 2022). Blockchain is a decentralised, immutable database that makes asset tracking and transaction recording in a corporate network easier. A blockchain is composed of a growing number of documents, or "blocks," that are securely joined together using encryption. Each block contains a timestamp, a cryptographic hash of the block before it, and transaction data. The timestamp demonstrates that the transaction data existed when the block was generated.

Consensus protocol, hash cryptography, immutable ledger, distributed P2P networking, and mining is some of the technical functions blockchain technology offers to businesses or users.

Table 1. Techniques and services of blockchain

Consensus protocol	Her specific users possess individual rights to access and validate transactions on the blockchain network.
Hash cryptography	A blockchain adds transactions using the SHA256 algorithm. This consensus algorithm possesses sixty-four characters and was created by the United States National Security Agency (NSA). This is used to verify the validity of data.
Immutable ledger	All transactions are append-only on the blockchain network. They are not modifiable in the shared ledger.
Distributed P2P network	Transactions on the blockchain ledger are distributed to all users and new transactions are also made known to all participants in the network.
Mining	Blocks of nonce values are used by miners to generate hash values for the network. For the reward to be achieved and obtained, fast computing speed is highly required.

Source: Ghosh *et al.* (2023)

The Kinds of Blockchain Explained

Public, private, or consortium blockchains are categories of blockchain, especially based on their purposes and requirements. (Chinaei et al., 2021; BelMannoubi et al., 2023).

Public Blockchain

Public blockchains are permissionless. Thus, anyone with access to the internet can join and participate in its networks (Kumar Sharma, 2022). This makes such blockchains self-governable as anyone can read, write and audit the network. Such blockchains are mostly used for mining and cryptocurrency exchange. The first illustration of such a blockchain is Bitcoin, which made transactions possible for everyone. Ethereum and Litcoin as some examples of public blockchains (Hassan et al., 2023).

Private Blockchain

A private blockchain, in comparison to a public blockchain, is a controlled blockchain that runs on a private network (Zarour et al., 2020; Wang et al., 2023). This type of blockchain is characteristically used internally. Private blockchains include Corda, Hyperledger Fabric, Ripple, and Corda.

Consortium Blockchain

The prospective firms for consortium blockchain (also known as federated blockchains) are companies that require both public and private blockchains. This kind of blockchain permits participants to have access to already chosen nodes for viewing, appending and also auditing from selected central authorities (Dib et al., 2018; Zhou et al., 2023). The decentralised nature of the control is maintained because there is no single authority overseeing it. Examples of such a blockchain include the IBM Food Trust, Contour, BankChain, and the Energy Web Foundation.

Table 2. Summary of blockchain types

Features	Public	Private	Consortium
Accessibility	Everyone	One Person/ Central Authority	At least one central authority
Who can join the network?	Everyone	Permissioned and known identities	Permissioned and known identities
Consensus mechanisms	Proof of Stake (PoS)/ Proof of Work (PoW)	Voting or multi-party consensus algorithm	Voting or multi-party consensus algorithm
Speed of transactions	Relatively slow	Relatively lighter and faster	Relatively lighter and faster
Decentralisation	Completely decentralised	Less decentralised	Less decentralised

Source: Kumar Sharma (2022)

Blockchain Industry Use Cases

The use cases for blockchain are expanding throughout the financial, health, insurance, agricultural, real estate, etc. sectors, even though it is still a relatively new technological invention. By 2027, up to 10% of the world's GDP may be stored and transferred via distributed ledger technology (DLT), according to the World Economic Forum (Ogée & Guinard, 2019). In Table 3, the authors provide an overview of blockchain application cases in the payment, healthcare, logistics, smart contracts, and blockchain credentialing & document management sectors.

Table 3. Brief blockchain use cases across sectors

Sector (s)	Firms	Uses
Credentialing and document management	Block.co, DocSafe	For credentialing and document management (i.e., certificates)
Payments	Banco Santander, HSBC, Barclays	Used for money transfers and international payments.
Blockchain smart contracts	Propy	For title registration services. Enforcing the terms of an agreement between two individual parties without the need for third-party verification or permission.
Logistics	DHL, FedEx, British Airways, Maersk	Tracking and recording data about global shipments.
Healthcare	MediLedger, ProCredEx, Akiri, Pfizer	Tracking the prescription drug supply chain. Validation of the legitimacy of drugs, and expiration dates
Insurance	AEGON, Prudential, MetLife, AIG	Automation of claims and verification of insurance coverage between companies and reinsurers

Source: Ayarnah et al. (2023)

Blockchain Technology Benefits

Below are some benefits of blockchain technology. Below are some of the advantages that come with blockchain technology.

Security

Blockchain technology has the power to radically transform how Personal Identifiable Information (PII), which is sensitive and private, is kept, shared, and viewed. By creating a record that cannot be changed and is end-to-end encrypted, blockchain helps to prevent fraud and illegal behaviour (Shrier et al., 2016; Verma et al., 2023). On the blockchain network, privacy concerns can be overcome by using permissions to limit access and anonymize personal data. Because data is protected and copied over a network of computers, hackers have a difficult time gaining access to it.

Transparency

Without blockchain, each business would have to manage its database. Blockchain makes use of a distributed ledger, which guarantees that data and transactions are recorded uniformly everywhere (Mohite & Kale, 2023). Since every network user who has the necessary permissions can view the same data at once, complete transparency is provided. Every transaction is permanently kept and has a time and date stamp. Parties on a blockchain may have access to the entire transaction history, which almost eliminates the potential for fraud (Hasan et al., 2022).

Traceability

A blockchain-based audit trail keeps track of an asset's provenance at every stage of its transition, recording its sources. This acts as evidence in sectors affected by fraud and counterfeiting, or if consumers are worried about environmental or human rights issues related to a product. Direct consumer communication of provenance information is now possible because of blockchain. Data can reveal supply chain faults and is traceable (Wang et al., 2022).

Efficiency and Speed

Traditional paper-intensive procedures take a long time and are susceptible to human mistakes. Transactions can be finished more quickly and effectively by automating these operations with blockchain. The blockchain provides the propensity to record documentation and transaction information, doing away with the requirement for paper trade (Malhotra et al., 2022). Thus, blockchain takes the duty of ledger reconciliation for clearing and settlement to proceed more quickly.

Automation

With "smart contracts," transactions can even be automated, enhancing the productivity and acceleration of completing transactions or agreements. The subsequent stage in the transaction or process is automatically started once pre-specified requirements are satisfied. According to Babkin et al. (2018), smart contracts lessen the need for human intervention and rely less on outside parties to confirm that a contract's provisions have been adhered to. When a consumer files an insurance claim, for example, and submits the required paperwork, the claim is automatically resolved and compensated with the assistance of the blockchain network.

The Healthcare Sector

According to Riley et al. (2019), healthcare simply refers to the diagnosis, treatment, and prevention of disease, illness, injury, and other physical and mental disabilities in humans. Practitioners in the fields of medicine, dentistry, nursing, pharmacy, and other care professionals are identified as providers of healthcare. The healthcare sector offers products and services for patients to get preventative and rehabilitative care. Table 4 classifies these sectors of the healthcare industry.

Table 4. Healthcare industry sectors

Healthcare services and facilities	o Hospitals o Nursing residential care facilities o Ambulatory healthcare services o Medical practitioners and healthcare professionals
Medical devices, equipment, and hospital supplies manufacturers	o In-vitro diagnostic substances o Irradiation apparatuses o Electro-medical and electrotherapeutic apparatuses
Medical insurance, medical services, and managed care	o Healthcare maintenance organisations (HMOs) o Medicare
Pharmaceuticals	o Over-the-counter (OTC) drugs and drug stores o Prescription and generic drugs o Biopharmaceutical drugs

Source: Sultz and Young (2006) and Laugesen *et al.* (2021)

An estimated $1 trillion of the $3 trillion healthcare industry is lost each year. As the prevalence of chronic diseases among the ageing population rises, care coordination is becoming more complicated. With the lack of standardised technological architecture to enable the secure transfer and administration of sensitive information among system stakeholders, healthcare records are currently fragmented (Haddad et al., 2022). This difficulty in sharing information between parties ultimately lowers the standard of care given to patients, resulting in a poor patient experience.

Then again, with the existence of dispersed data among numerous medical facilities, handling e-health/medical records (EHR/EMR) securely has become very tedious (Shahnaz et al., 2019). According to Sengupta et al. (2020), there is a growing number of cybersecurity assaults due to how the majority of current healthcare systems are centralised. This centralisation of patient data renders existing technological platforms susceptible to a single point of failure and information leakage. Moreso, the disclosure of sensitive information about patients could have negative effects on patient experience. This demonstrates that maintaining EHR/EMRs using current medical systems does not provide transparency, trustworthy traceability, immutability, audit, privacy, or security (Yue et al., 2016).

Blockchain and Healthcare Data Management

Blockchain technology can be used for medical data management systems that allow patients to maintain ownership of their records, remotely monitor this data, and exchange their medical records. The key advantages of applying blockchain in the management of healthcare data are concisely explained in Figure 1.

Figure 1. Benefits of using blockchain technology for healthcare data management
Source: Yaqoob et al. (2021)

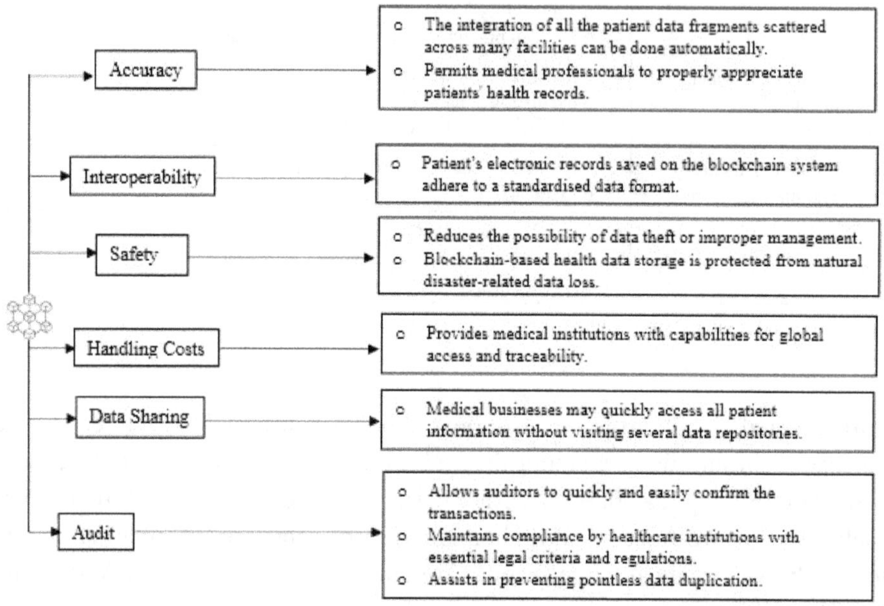

Accuracy of Healthcare Data

In commonplace, patients' medical records are dispersed among hospitals, clinics, and insurance companies (Li et al., 2020). More importantly, patients' medical records must be integrated to reduce data redundancies and ensure a holistic view of proper prognoses. Blockchain technology can assist healthcare institutions to store patient medical data (i.e., symptom data, treatment approach, facilities acquired, and payment information). This assists healthcare practitioners to treat patients well. Notedly, blockchains store only unchangeable, transparent, traceable, and secure data (Ahmad et al., 2021).

Interoperability of Healthcare Data

Interoperability is the capacity of diverse computer systems, applications, platforms or even digital products to exchange and collectively use information. Existing data management platforms are built using different clinical technologies, requirements, and functional capabilities (Fennelly et al., 2020). Thus, the ability to develop and exchange data in a single format is hampered by these aforementioned variances or incompatibilities. The transmission messages should be based on standardized coded data to enable interoperability between two EHR systems (Dagher et al., 2018). Using a blockchain-based healthcare system can get around this restriction. Every EHR/EMR saved on the blockchain system adheres to standardised data coding, making it simple for any healthcare provider to access and use.

Secured Healthcare Data

Over the last decade, numerous healthcare companies have been the target of cybersecurity assaults that could have been avoided. For the management of digital medical records, several healthcare companies use manual systems based on centralised infrastructure. Since these systems are now relatively antiquated, it is easy to modify them with malicious intent. Additionally, centralised systems are susceptible to failure hence medical records may be lost in the event fire outbreak or flood. According to Ghosh et al. (2023), healthcare firms should use the immutability and distribution nature of blockchain to reduce the danger of data theft or improper data management.

Handling Cost of Healthcare Data

One of the challenges in the current healthcare systems is high handling costs related to patient data retrieval and transfer. Delayance and high costs are recorded in collecting patients' medical records from healthcare facilities since they are mostly manual or unstructured (Andrew et al., 2023). Blockchain solutions can make it simple for healthcare businesses to digitise and access all of a patient's data without having to visit several locations where it was previously held (Kamruzzaman et al., 2022). Thus, reducing administrative costs.

Global Sharing of Healthcare Data

Before prescribing any drug for the proper management of a patient in some emergency medical situations, a complete understanding of the patient's prior medical history is required. (Ghosh et al., 2023). For instance, a patient with a serious illness who travels outside the country might need to see a doctor in the event of an emergency. The patient's prior medical history is often required for a medical expert to give better and higher-quality healthcare services in such a situation. However, most existing healthcare management systems use manual storage and processing methods, making it difficult to benefit from capabilities for global access and traceability (Jing et al., 2021). Blockchain technology can be leveraged to ensure medical data is readily accessible and distributed across key stakeholders in the global healthcare space.

Audit of Healthcare Data

Healthcare sectors are not immune from regulation, auditing, and compliance. Through rigorous and impartial evaluations, healthcare regulators ensure the auditing of healthcare facilities in determining how effective a healthcare compliance plan is. Nowadays, healthcare data management systems lack sophisticated functions in the coordination of the auditing process, rendering them susceptible to illegal changes and data breaches. Blockchain technology helps to demonstrate the reliability of recorded health data (Sharma et al., 2021).

Blockchain Technology and Patient Data Management

According to De Aguiar et al. (2020), the existence of inter-individual heterogeneity, similar patient techniques cannot typically be used because each patient is unique. To deliver individualised care, access to complete medical records is crucial. However, because the majority of modern medical systems can not guarantee trust, privacy, and security, sharing such documents within the medical community has become an extremely important issue (Tandon et al., 2020). Then again, patients are unable to fully profess ownership of their medical records. In addition, patients who are referred to different hospitals must engage in repetitive tests increasing diagnostic costs.

Besides, blockchain technology can aid in overcoming the aforementioned difficulties. As depicted in Figure 2, it saves data on a decentralised peer-to-peer network that is only reachable by the agreement of all parties on the blockchain platform. In Figure 2, a laboratory technician attaches a referral to a patient's e-health record in a block. This block contains the patient's medical data, the timestamp and the author (i.e., lab technician) who added the data. The block is sent to permitted parties in the patient's network, such as the patient, his/her family, and the general partitioner for further treatment. The final stage involves approval from parties to ensure validation or approval of the block creation process.

Such information can be moved across hospitals without fear of misuse since parties need to agree. Consequently, knowing a patient's prior medical history aids new doctors in better understanding the patient's condition and providing appropriate care. In addition, the blockchain infrastructure eliminates duplicated diagnostic tests resulting in reduced patient expenses. The blockchain network's numerous nodes hold each copy of the patient record, making it transparent and corrupt-free (Grover et al., 2021).

Figure 2. A simplified example of how blockchain can be used in patient record management
Source: Author

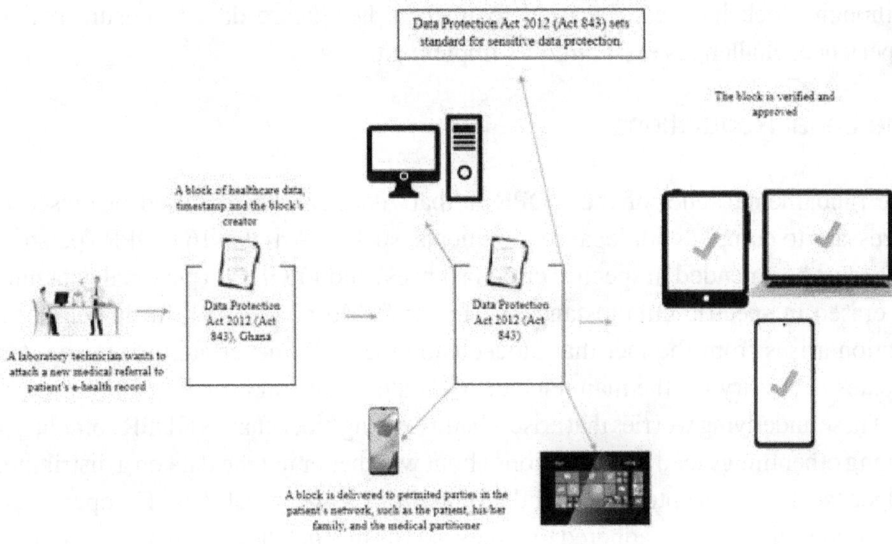

Blockchain Technology and Patient Experience

One of the most frequently used expressions, "patient experience," can refer to both the care that patients have received and their comments on that care. The term "patient experience" refers to "a patient's contact with the healthcare system in general, including the care they receive from health plans, physicians, nurses, and other staff members in hospitals, physician offices, and other healthcare facilities" (Agency for Healthcare Research and Quality, 2022).

In addition, the usage of blockchain can increase patient-centric interactions, which will improve the patient experience. Using blockchain-based platforms to increase security and consolidate patient data across many healthcare companies is one approach to accomplish this (Mahajan et al., 2022). Thus, blockchain-enabled data management solutions can enhance patient care.

For instance, tracking drugs and medical devices and managing medical data are made easier by ConsenSys' Ethereum blockchain platform. The applications allow patients to control who has access to their electronic health records (EHRs). Thus, empowering the patient. Patients can also monitor their medical histories, view their most recent prescriptions, and securely exchange their data with their doctors. According to Ray et al. (2020), this fosters better collaboration, builds patient trust, enhances patient access to reliable data, and personalises their experience.

Implementation Challenges of Blockchain Technology in Healthcare

Although blockchain can be used to manage healthcare data to ensure patient experience, challenges exist amid its implementation.

The Legal Regulations

The fundamental tenet of the GDPR is that "data can be modified or erased as necessary to comply with legal requirements, such as Articles 16 GDPR (personal data must be amended in specific circumstances) and 17 GDPR (personal data must be erased in specific circumstances)" (Finck & Moscon, 2019). In this case, the friction arises from the fact that blockchain essentially never authorises any data updates necessary for the maintenance of data integrity and trust.

These underlying worries that arise when assessing blockchain's GDPR compliance among other things lead to discussions about whether or not the data on a distributed ledger (such as encrypted, hashed data) qualifies as personal data. European data protection rules must be adhered to if the data fits the threshold for being considered personal data (Finck & Moscon, 2019).

Scalability

According to Alammary et al. (2019), the challenge of blockchain is "slow-speed blockchain transactions." The storage and acquisition of a sizable amount of student data imply the expansion of block sizes. Peer-to-peer verification is necessary because of the numerous data additions it allows for the validation and confirmation of each entry. In order to manage healthcare data and ensure patient experience in the healthcare sector, blockchain technology may need to be developed more slowly due to the growth of databases and transactions.

Data Security

Chowdhury et al. (2022) point out the pervasive assumption that data stored on blockchains are encrypted amid their insightful comparison of blockchains and databases. Although the parties to the transaction have digitally signed the data, it is not by default encrypted. According to Chowdhury et al. (2022), "It is an open ledger system, where anyone may join and validate any transaction in the network." Public key cryptography protects the participants' secrecy. Healthcare organisations are entreated to include additional privacy restrictions (i.e., using private blockchains).

The Market Adoption Challenge

The acceptance and implementation of blockchain technology are relatively slow at many healthcare institutions. There exists an inadequacy of confidence, a lack of necessary knowledge and skills and difficulty in handling patients' data on a blockchain platform. To ensure that blockchain-based healthcare solutions spread internationally and sustainably, the market acceptance problem must, in general, be overcome. However, there needs to be a perk for medical professionals to use the technology. To Attaran (2022), firms' ability to accurately quantify the impact of blockchains on the bottom line is increasingly difficult. Thus, reducing the adoption of blockchain among businesses.

CONCLUSION

In light of data management and patient experience, blockchain technology is revolutionizing the healthcare industry. (Zaabar et al., 2021). Market revenue for medical technology is anticipated to reach US$579.40 billion in 2023, according to Statista (2022). However, both consumers and providers of healthcare services continue to have serious concerns about the security and privacy of electronic health records (EHRs). With a total of 398 in 2019, this number grew to its greatest level ever (Statista, 2023). Patient experiences with healthcare delivery are negatively impacted as a result of these healthcare systems breaches that result in the leaking of sensitive health information of patients (Kim et al., 2022).

There is relatively little research that focuses on the patient experience, although several studies have proposed how blockchain technology could be used in healthcare data management (Tanwar et al., 2020; Miyachi & Mackey, 2022). Beyond issues of trust, blockchain offers additional business advantages like cost savings due to accelerated speed, efficiency, automation, and immediate traceability. Blockchain technology can be used in the administration of healthcare data in areas such as remote monitoring, mobile applications, and the access to and sharing of patient medical records. Blockchain technology can also be used in medical data management systems that give people ownership of their records. In order to better grasp the issue, treat the patient as necessary, and assure patient experience, blockchain data management solutions let new doctors learn about the prior patient history.

Additionally, the usage of blockchain can increase patient-centric interactions, which will improve the patient experience. Using blockchain-based platforms to increase security and consolidate patient data across many healthcare companies is one approach to accomplish this (Mahajan et al., 2022). The healthcare industry needs to address issues with blockchain implementation (i.e., novelty, inadequate skill set, lack of standardisation, unclear legal frameworks). Although blockchain in healthcare is still in its infancy, it has great potential for the sector.

PRACTICAL IMPLICATIONS

This book chapter demonstrates the potential for using blockchain use cases to manage patient experience and healthcare data. Stakeholders in the healthcare industry, including hospitals, nursing homes, and health maintenance organizations (HMOs), should fill knowledge gaps regarding blockchain technology. This book chapter will add to the existing literature on the use cases of blockchain in the global healthcare sector. It will again assist academics to pinpoint the healthcare system's most desirable and implementable blockchain applications. In addition, policymakers in areas of data protection and cyber security will appreciate the opportunities in preparing a legal or regulatory framework needed in the implementation of blockchain in the healthcare sector and other sectors.

FUTURE SCOPE OF WORK

Future studies should not only consider the application of blockchain in data management and patient experience but areas such as insurance or transaction settlement. Studies that seek to ascertain the use case of blockchain across the financial and agriculture sectors.

RECOMMENDATIONS

Healthcare regulators and institutions who are responsible for the regulation of technology should create a favourable environment that will spur the building of blockchain digital solutions with the propensity of providing a single protocol of trust among parties. This will standardise the utilisation of blockchain technology in healthcare data management and patient experience in the global healthcare space. Green-oriented organisations should also join the conversation on how blockchains are designed, especially ensuring that blockchain is built with sustainability principles.

REFERENCES

Abel, G. A., Mendonca, S. C., McPhail, S., Zhou, Y., Elliss-Brookes, L., & Lyratzopoulos, G. (2017). Emergency diagnosis of cancer and previous general practice consultations: Insights from linked patient survey data. *The British Journal of General Practice*, *67*(659), e377–e387. doi:10.3399/bjgp17X690869 PMID:28438775

Agency for Healthcare Research and Quality. (2022, August). *What Is Patient Experience?* AHRQ. https://www.ahrq.gov/cahps/about-cahps/patient-experience/index.html

Ahmad, R. W., Salah, K., Jayaraman, R., Yaqoob, I., Ellahham, S., & Omar, M. (2021). The role of blockchain technology in telehealth and telemedicine. *International Journal of Medical Informatics*, *148*, 104399. doi:10.1016/j.ijmedinf.2021.104399 PMID:33540131

Alammary, A., Alhazmi, S., Almasri, M., & Gillani, S. (2019). Blockchain-based applications in education: A systematic review. *Applied Sciences (Basel, Switzerland)*, *9*(12), 2400. doi:10.3390/app9122400

Andrew, J., Isravel, D. P., Sagayam, K. M., Bhushan, B., Sei, Y., & Eunice, J. (2023). Blockchain for healthcare systems: Architecture, security challenges, trends and future directions. *Journal of Network and Computer Applications*, 103633.

Attaran, M. (2022). Blockchain technology in healthcare: Challenges and opportunities. *International Journal of Healthcare Management*, *15*(1), 70–83. doi:10.1080/20479700.2020.1843887

Ayarnah, A., Mensah, K., & Odoom, R. (2023). *Exploring Blockchain Technology and Digital Certificates in the Education Sector*. Bentham Science. doi:10.2174/97898151247501230100 05

Azaria, A., Ekblaw, A., Vieira, T., & Lippman, A. (2016, August). Medrec: Using blockchain for medical data access and permission management. In *2016 2nd international conference on open and big data (OBD)* (pp. 25-30). IEEE.

Babkin, A. V., Burkaltseva, D. D., Betskov, A. V., Kilyaskhanov, H. S., Tyulin, A. S., & Kurianova, I. V. (2018). Automation digitalization blockchain: trends and implementation problems. *International Journal of Engineering and Technology (UAE)*, *7*(14), 254-260.

BelMannoubi, S., Touati, H., Hadded, M., Toumi, K., Shagdar, O., & Kamoun, F. (2023). A comprehensive survey on blockchain-based c-its applications: Classification, challenges, and open issues. *Vehicular Communications*, 100607.

Blockchain Platform for Digital Health Networks. (n.d.). *Solve Care*. Blockchain Platform for Digital Health Records. https://solve.care/

Chinaei, M. H., Gharakheili, H. H., & Sivaraman, V. (2021). Optimal Witnessing of Healthcare IoT Data Using Blockchain Logging Contract. *IEEE Internet of Things Journal*, *8*(12), 10117–10130. doi:10.1109/JIOT.2021.3051433

Chowdhury, S., Rodriguez-Espindola, O., Dey, P., & Budhwar, P. (2022). Blockchain technology adoption for managing risks in operations and supply chain management: Evidence from the UK. *Annals of Operations Research*, 1–36. PMID:35095153

Dagher, G. G., Mohler, J., Milojkovic, M., & Marella, P. B. (2018). Ancile: Privacy-preserving framework for access control and interoperability of electronic health records using blockchain technology. *Sustainable Cities and Society*, *39*, 283–297. doi:10.1016/j.scs.2018.02.014

De Aguiar, E. J., Faiçal, B. S., Krishnamachari, B., & Ueyama, J. (2020). A survey of blockchain-based strategies for healthcare. *ACM Computing Surveys*, *53*(2), 1–27. doi:10.1145/3376915

Dib, O., Brousmiche, K. L., Durand, A., Thea, E., & Hamida, E. B. (2018). Consortium blockchains: Overview, applications and challenges. *Int. J. Adv. Telecommun*, *11*(1), 51–64.

Dubovitskaya, A., Baig, F., Xu, Z., Shukla, R., Zambani, P. S., Swaminathan, A., Jahangir, M. M., Chowdhry, K., Lachhani, R., Idnani, N., Schumacher, M., Aberer, K., Stoller, S. D., Ryu, S., & Wang, F. (2020). ACTION-EHR: Patient-centric blockchain-based electronic health record data management for cancer care. *Journal of Medical Internet Research*, *22*(8), e13598. doi:10.2196/13598 PMID:32821064

Fennelly, O., Cunningham, C., Grogan, L., Cronin, H., O'Shea, C., Roche, M., Lawlor, F., & O'Hare, N. (2020). Successfully implementing a national electronic health record: A rapid umbrella review. *International Journal of Medical Informatics*, *144*, 104281. doi:10.1016/j.ijmedinf.2020.104281 PMID:33017724

Finck, M., & Moscon, V. (2019). Copyright law on blockchains: Between new forms of rights administration and digital rights management 2.0. *IIC; International Review of Industrial Property and Copyright Law*, *50*(1), 77–108. doi:10.100740319-018-00776-8

Ghosh, P. K., Chakraborty, A., Hasan, M., Rashid, K., & Siddique, A. H. (2023). Blockchain Application in Healthcare Systems: A Review. *Systems*, *11*(1), 38. doi:10.3390ystems11010038

Grover, B. A., Chaudhary, B., Rajput, N. K., & Dukiya, O. (2021). Blockchain and governance: theory, applications and challenges. *Blockchain for Business: How It Works and Creates Value*, 113-139.

Haddad, A., Habaebi, M. H., Islam, M. R., Hasbullah, N. F., & Zabidi, S. A. (2022). Systematic Review on AI-Blockchain Based E-Healthcare Records Management Systems. *IEEE Access : Practical Innovations, Open Solutions*, *10*, 94583–94615. doi:10.1109/ACCESS.2022.3201878

Hasan, M. K., Alkhalifah, A., Islam, S., Babiker, N. B., Habib, A. A., Aman, A. H. M., & Hossain, M. A. (2022). Blockchain technology on smart grid, energy trading, and big data: Security issues, challenges, and recommendations. *Wireless Communications and Mobile Computing*, *2022*, 1–26. doi:10.1155/2022/5617903

Hassan, H. S., Hassan, R., & Gbashi, E. K. (2023). E-voting System Based on Ethereum Blockchain Technology Using Ganache and Remix Environments. *Engineering and Technology Journal*, *41*(4), 1–16. doi:10.30684/etj.2023.135464.1273

Jing, N., Liu, Q., & Sugumaran, V. (2021). A blockchain-based code copyright management system. *Information Processing & Management*, *58*(3), 102518. doi:10.1016/j.ipm.2021.102518

Kamruzzaman, M. M., Yan, B., Sarker, M. N. I., Alruwaili, O., Wu, M., & Alrashdi, I. (2022). Blockchain and fog computing in IoT-driven healthcare services for smart cities. *Journal of Healthcare Engineering*, *2022*, 2022. doi:10.1155/2022/9957888 PMID:35126961

Kim, J. W., Kim, S. J., Cha, W. C., & Kim, T. (2022). A blockchain-applied personal health record application: Development and user experience. *Applied Sciences (Basel, Switzerland)*, *12*(4), 1847. doi:10.3390/app12041847

Kumar Sharma. (2022, October 12). *Types Of Blockchains Explained- Public Vs. Private Vs. Consortium*. Blockchain Council. https://www.blockchain-council.org/blockchain/types-of-blockchains-explained-public-vs-private-vs-consortium/#:~:text=Depending%20on%20the%20use%20and,(also%20known%20as%20federated)

Laugesen, K., Ludvigsson, J. F., Schmidt, M., Gissler, M., Valdimarsdottir, U. A., Lunde, A., & Sørensen, H. T. (2021). Nordic health registry-based research: A review of health care systems and key registries. *Clinical Epidemiology*, *13*, 533–554. doi:10.2147/CLEP.S314959 PMID:34321928

Li, X., Krumholz, H. M., Yip, W., Cheng, K. K., De Maeseneer, J., Meng, Q., Mossialos, E., Li, C., Lu, J., Su, M., Zhang, Q., Xu, D. R., Li, L., Normand, S.-L. T., Peto, R., Li, J., Wang, Z., Yan, H., Gao, R., & Hu, S. (2020). Quality of primary health care in China: Challenges and recommendations. *Lancet*, *395*(10239), 1802–1812. doi:10.1016/S0140-6736(20)30122-7 PMID:32505251

Mahajan, H. B., Rashid, A. S., Junnarkar, A. A., Uke, N., Deshpande, S. D., Futane, P. R., & Alhayani, B. (2022). Integration of Healthcare 4.0 and blockchain into secure cloud-based electronic health records systems. *Applied Nanoscience*, 1–14. PMID:35136707

Malhotra, D., Saini, P., & Singh, A. K. (2022). How blockchain can automate KYC: Systematic review. *Wireless Personal Communications*, *122*(2), 1987–2021. doi:10.100711277-021-08977-0

Miyachi, K., & Mackey, T. K. (2021). hOCBS: A privacy-preserving blockchain framework for healthcare data leveraging an on-chain and off-chain system design. *Information Processing & Management*, *58*(3), 102535. doi:10.1016/j.ipm.2021.102535

Mohite, J. S., & Kale, V. (2023, May). Blockchain Technology Based Supply Chain Management System. In *International Conference on Applications of Machine Intelligence and Data Analytics (ICAMIDA 2022)* (pp. 641-653). Atlantis Press. 10.2991/978-94-6463-136-4_55

Ogée & Guinard. (2019, August 19). *Blockchain is not a magic bullet for security. Can we trust it?* World Economic Forum. https://www.weforum.org/agenda/2019/08/blockchain-security-trust/

Ray, P. P., Dash, D., Salah, K., & Kumar, N. (2020). Blockchain for IoT-based healthcare: Background, consensus, platforms, and use cases. *IEEE Systems Journal*, *15*(1), 85–94. doi:10.1109/JSYST.2020.2963840

Riley, R. D., van der Windt, D., Croft, P., & Moons, K. G. (Eds.). (2019). *Prognosis research in healthcare: concepts, methods, and impact*. Oxford University Press. doi:10.1093/med/9780198796619.001.0001

Roehrs, A., Da Costa, C. A., & da Rosa Righi, R. (2017). OmniPHR: A distributed architecture model to integrate personal health records. *Journal of Biomedical Informatics*, *71*, 70–81. doi:10.1016/j.jbi.2017.05.012 PMID:28545835

Sengupta, J., Ruj, S., & Bit, S. D. (2020). A comprehensive survey on attacks, security issues and blockchain solutions for IoT and IIoT. *Journal of Network and Computer Applications*, *149*, 102481. doi:10.1016/j.jnca.2019.102481

Shahnaz, A., Qamar, U., & Khalid, A. (2019). Using blockchain for electronic health records. *IEEE Access : Practical Innovations, Open Solutions*, *7*, 147782–147795. doi:10.1109/ACCESS.2019.2946373

Sharma, A., Kaur, S., & Singh, M. (2021). A comprehensive review on blockchain and Internet of Things in healthcare. *Transactions on Emerging Telecommunications Technologies*, *32*(10), e4333. doi:10.1002/ett.4333

Shrier, D., Wu, W., & Pentland, A. (2016). Blockchain & infrastructure (identity, data security). *Massachusetts Institute of Technology-Connection Science*, *1*(3), 1–19.

Statista. (2022, December). Medical Technology – Worldwide. *Statista Market Forecast*. Statista. https://www.statista.com/outlook/hmo/medical-technology/worldwide

Statista. (2023, February 7). *Number of data compromises in the U.S. healthcare sector 2005-2022*. Statista. https://www.statista.com/statistics/798417/health-and-medical-data-compromises-united-states/

Sultz, H. A., & Young, K. M. (2006). *Health care, USA: Understanding its organization and delivery*. Jones & Bartlett Learning.

Tandon, A., Dhir, A., Islam, A. N., & Mäntymäki, M. (2020). Blockchain in healthcare: A systematic literature review, synthesizing framework and future research agenda. *Computers in Industry*, *122*, 103290. doi:10.1016/j.compind.2020.103290

Tanwar, S., Parekh, K., & Evans, R. (2020). Blockchain-based electronic healthcare record system for healthcare 4.0 applications. *Journal of Information Security and Applications*, *50*, 102407. doi:10.1016/j.jisa.2019.102407

Verma, A., Singh, A., Sethi, P., Jain, V., Chawla, C., Bhargava, A., & Gupta, A. (2023). Applications of Data Security and Blockchain in Smart City Identity Management. In *Handbook of Research on Data-Driven Mathematical Modeling in Smart Cities* (pp. 154–174). IGI Global. doi:10.4018/978-1-6684-6408-3.ch009

Vora, J., DevMurari, P., Tanwar, S., Tyagi, S., Kumar, N., & Obaidat, M. S. (2018, July). Blind signatures based secured e-healthcare system. In *2018 International conference on computer, information and telecommunication systems (CITS)* (pp. 1-5). IEEE.

Wang, L., He, Y., & Wu, Z. (2022). Design of a blockchain-enabled traceability system framework for food supply chains. *Foods*, *11*(5), 744. doi:10.3390/foods11050744 PMID:35267377

Wang, X., Jiang, P., Baker, T., Li, T., & Zhu, L. (2023). Enabling privacy and leakage resistance for dynamic blockchain-based access control systems. *Computer Standards & Interfaces*, *84*, 103690. doi:10.1016/j.csi.2022.103690

Yaqoob, I., Salah, K., Jayaraman, R., & Al-Hammadi, Y. (2021). Blockchain for healthcare data management: Opportunities, challenges, and future recommendations. *Neural Computing & Applications*, 1–16.

Yue, X., Wang, H., Jin, D., Li, M., & Jiang, W. (2016). Healthcare data gateways: Found healthcare intelligence on blockchain with novel privacy risk control. *Journal of Medical Systems*, *40*(10), 1–8. doi:10.100710916-016-0574-6 PMID:27565509

Zaabar, B., Cheikhrouhou, O., Jamil, F., Ammi, M., & Abid, M. (2021). HealthBlock: A secure blockchain-based healthcare data management system. *Computer Networks*, *200*, 108500. doi:10.1016/j.comnet.2021.108500

Zarour, M., Ansari, M. T. J., Alenezi, M., Sarkar, A. K., Faizan, M., Agrawal, A., Kumar, R., & Khan, R. A. (2020). Evaluating the impact of blockchain models for secure and trustworthy electronic healthcare records. *IEEE Access : Practical Innovations, Open Solutions*, *8*, 157959–157973. doi:10.1109/ACCESS.2020.3019829

Zhang, P., White, J., Schmidt, D. C., Lenz, G., & Rosenbloom, S. T. (2018). FHIRChain: Applying blockchain to securely and scalably share clinical data. *Computational and Structural Biotechnology Journal*, *16*, 267–278. doi:10.1016/j.csbj.2018.07.004 PMID:30108685

Zhou, J., Wang, N., Liu, A., Wang, W., & Du, X. (2023). CBCS: A Scalable Consortium Blockchain Architecture Based on World State Collaborative Storage. *Electronics (Basel)*, *12*(3), 735. doi:10.3390/electronics12030735

Chapter 4
Prospects and Challenges of Blockchain Technology in Managing Healthcare Data:
Evidence From Africa

Gideon Awini
Tamale Technical University, Ghana

ABSTRACT

In terms of data transparency, traceability, immutability, audit, data provenance, flexible access, trust, privacy, and security, healthcare data management systems face significant hurdles. Additionally, a significant portion of the existing healthcare data management systems are centralized, which could be dangerous in the event of a single point of failure. The handling of data in the healthcare sector has the potential to undergo a big transformation. Blockchain is an emerging, disruptive, decentralized technology. In this chapter, the authors explore how utilizing blockchain for healthcare data management systems might spur innovation and result in significant advancements.

1. INTRODUCTION

In an era where data integrity, security, and accessibility have become paramount, healthcare systems worldwide are seeking innovative solutions to manage patient information and optimise service delivery. Africa, with its diverse and rapidly evolving healthcare landscape, is no exception. Despite the continent's healthcare advancements, there remains a pressing need to address challenges related to data

DOI: 10.4018/978-1-6684-7649-9.ch004

fragmentation, security breaches, and inefficiencies in patient data management. Enter blockchain technology—a decentralised, immutable ledger system originally designed for digital currency transactions. Its potential applications in healthcare are vast, promising enhanced data security, traceability, and interoperability. However, like any burgeoning technology, blockchain comes with its own set of challenges, especially in the unique socio-economic and infrastructural context of Africa. Healthcare has undergone a shift thanks to the "internet of things" (IoT) paradigm's quick advancements. IoT-based medical devices can assist with the collection of priceless patient data, workflow automation, insight into disease symptoms and patterns, remote care, and increased patient control over their lives and treatments (Aazam et al., 2020; Ali et al., 2020; Tao et al., 2018). Hospital stays or readmission costs may be decreased with the aid of connected home health monitoring devices (Deloitte, 2023). Through warnings and trigger notifications, IoT-enabled medical devices can help with diagnosis before it gets serious. Additionally, they can reduce the frequency of hospital visits for standard health examinations (Awais et al., 2019; Zhu et al., 2019; Jiang et al., 2019; Ali et al., 2021). Changes in blood pressure, respiration, and other vital signs can be detected by sensors attached to various sections of a patient's medical equipment (Yaqoob et al., 2021). Due to the data being disseminated across numerous medical facilities, processing EHR and EMR in a safe manner has become quite difficult (Shahnaz et al., 2019). The majority of currently in-use healthcare systems are centralised, making them susceptible to single points of failure and data leakage (Global Blockchain in Healthcare report, 2022). A patient's private and sensitive information breach could have catastrophic repercussions (Sengupta et al., 2020). Some of the main problems in handling "electronic medical records" (EMR), like fraud and fake goods, could be resolved by blockchain technology (Deloitte, 2023). By 2025, it is predicted to result in savings of up to \$200–250 billion annually in expenditures associated with data breaches and fraud, counterfeit goods, and fraud (Global Blockchain in Healthcare report, 2022). Blockchain is an emerging technology that has the potential to help improve the efficiency of operations for managing healthcare data by delivering exceptional data efficiency and enforcing trust (Islam et al., 2019; Chukwu & Garg, 2020; Syed et al., 2019; Esposito et al., 2018; Al Omar et al., 2019). Decentralised storage, transparency, immutability, authentication, flexible data access, interconnection, and security are just a few of the many characteristics it offers. Figure 1 shows blockchain-enabled healthcare systems.

Figure 1. Blockchain-enabled healthcare systems
Source: Adopted from Global Blockchain in Healthcare Report (2022)

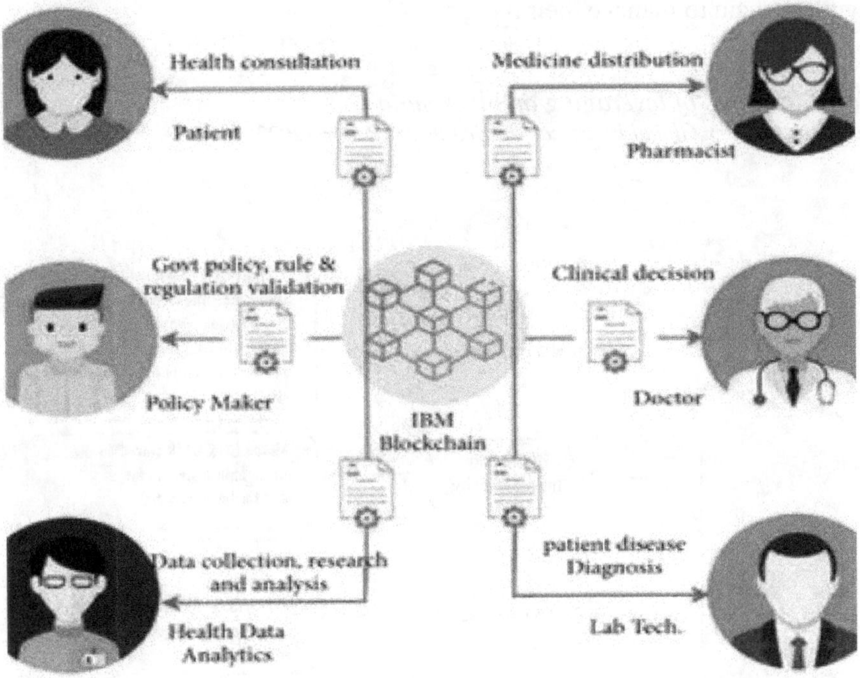

Blockchain technology employs the idea of "smart contracts," which establish terms and conditions that are accepted by all healthcare partners in the network and eliminate the need for a middleman (Zheng et al., 2020; Gupta et al., 2020). It lowers wasteful administrative expenses. "Peer-to-peer networks, public key cryptography, and consensus mechanisms make up the core three ideas of blockchain" (Salah et al., 2019). The three categories of public, private, and consortium blockchains are based on managing permission (Ali et al., 2018). Anyone with an Internet connection can take part in the consensus process on public blockchains. Public blockchains use proof-of-work or proof-of-stake systems to integrate incentives with encrypted digit verification. The identity of each participant is kept largely anonymous, yet the entire "public blockchain system" is transparent. The benefits of both "public and private blockchain networks" are combined in the consortium blockchain. Only specific organisations that want to improve communication with one another should use it. Healthcare firms can adopt any form of blockchain network, as each one has advantages and disadvantages that can be tailored to specific requirements or use-case situations. Other facets of the technology, including inherent characteristics, new business opportunities, and prospective difficulties, were not covered in earlier studies. Thus, Figure 2 illustrates the benefits that healthcare facilities can leverage using blockchain to manage their data.

Figure 2. Benefits of leveraging on blockchain
Source: Adopted from Global Blockchain in Healthcare Report (2022)

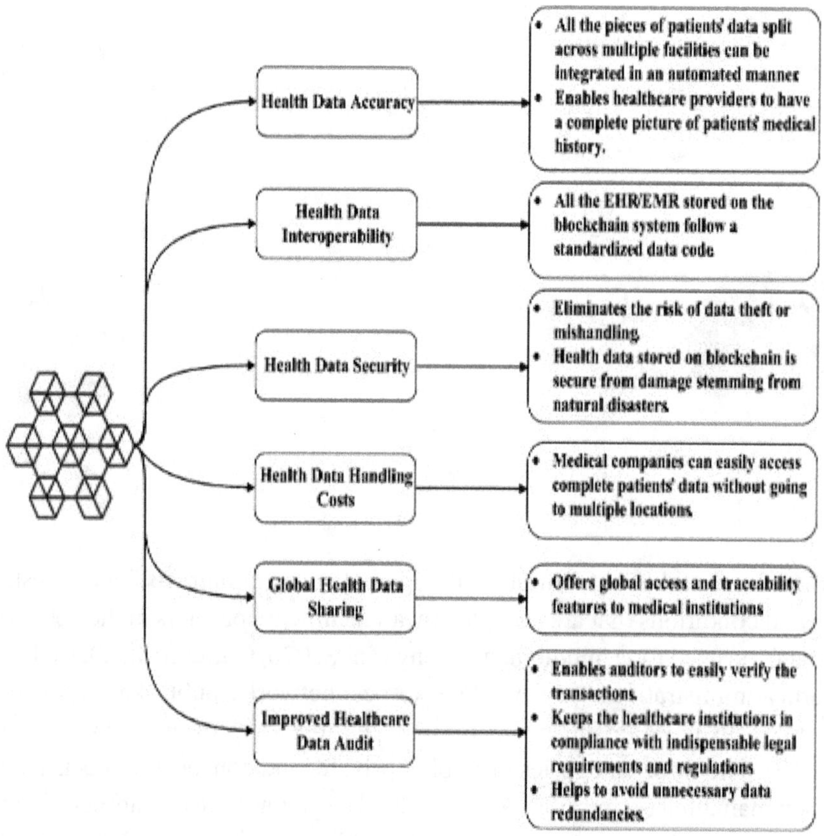

In a blockchain network, a block consists of four components: information, the current block's hash (identifying number), the previous block's hash, and the timestamp, which links each new block to its predecessor (Abu-Elezz et al., 2020). Blockchain technology comes in three basic architectural flavours: public (permission-less), private (permissioned), and hybrid blockchains. Anyone can join public blockchains because they are created to be open source. The most well-known technique used for public blockchains is called "Proof of Work" (PoW). Additionally, there is no control by any one person or institution because every transaction carried out on a public blockchain is totally transparent to everyone taking part. As opposed to hybrid blockchains, which are flexible and allow users to choose whether data should be made available to the public or kept private, private blockchains require participants to apply for permission to join the network, and all transactions are only accessible upon access granted by the authorised participants.

That said, blockchain technology has the potential to bring several benefits to the healthcare delivery system (Deloitte, 2023). One of the biggest advantages of blockchain technology is that it provides a secure and decentralised way of storing data. In the healthcare industry, this means that sensitive patient information can be stored in an immutable and tamper-proof manner, reducing the risk of data breaches and unauthorised access. Blockchain technology can help overcome the challenges of interoperability between different healthcare systems and organisations, enabling a secure and seamless exchange of patient data. It can help streamline the clinical trial process by providing a secure and transparent way to track the data and ensure its accuracy. It can improve transparency and trust in the healthcare system by enabling patients to access and control their own medical records and providing a secure and auditable trail of all transactions. Blockchain can help prevent fraud and counterfeiting in the healthcare industry by providing a secure and verifiable record of transactions, enabling quick and easy verification of the authenticity of drugs and medical devices. Thus, the use of blockchain in healthcare delivery has the potential to enhance data security, improve efficiency and collaboration, and increase transparency and trust, leading to better patient outcomes.

This manuscript delves into the promising prospects of blockchain technology in transforming Africa's healthcare data management and simultaneously highlights the potential obstacles that could impede its full-scale implementation.

2. BACKDROP AND CONVENTIONAL FACTS OF GHANA HEALTHCARE

The healthcare system in Ghana has been facing various challenges, including a shortage of healthcare workers, limited access to quality healthcare services, and a high burden of communicable and non-communicable diseases (Deloitte, 2023). Ghana faces a shortage of healthcare workers, including doctors, nurses, and other medical personnel. This shortage has resulted in a high patient-to-healthcare worker ratio, reducing the quality of care provided (WHO, 2023). Many rural and remote areas in Ghana lack access to quality healthcare services, resulting in high rates of preventable illnesses and deaths. Ghana is facing a high burden of both communicable and non-communicable diseases, including malaria, tuberculosis, HIV/AIDS, and chronic diseases such as diabetes and cardiovascular diseases. The healthcare infrastructure in Ghana is weak, with limited access to modern medical technology and equipment, which impacts the quality of care provided. Many people in Ghana face financial barriers to accessing quality healthcare services, including high out-of-pocket expenses and limited insurance coverage. Thus, the healthcare system in Ghana is facing significant challenges, including a shortage of healthcare workers, limited access to quality care, and a high burden of disease. Addressing these challenges is critical to improving the health and well-being of the population.

3. LITERATURE REVIEW

While blockchain technology applications are expanding quickly, knowledge of the actual technology and its potential is still far from ubiquitous, according to a recent survey by Deloitte (2023). This presents a barrier to further blockchain deployment and development, which has the potential to bring about significant social change, including advancements in the interchange of healthcare information (Deloitte, 2023). This technology approach primarily immutably stores digital data in a decentralised manner so that generated data, or meta-data, can be safely transferred between networks and users. Using cryptography, a list of records is connected together in a blockchain (Zhang et al., 2018). This design prevents data manipulation since, once recorded in a block, the data cannot be changed without also altering all subsequent blocks and necessitating network majority consent.

Since blockchain is a decentralised ledger system, it enables independent actors to work together inside the ecosystem, ensuring transparency and time-stamped recording of the information to improve processing speed, revenue creation, and security while lowering risk and costs (Deloitte, 2023). The blockchain employs a peer-to-peer (P2P) network, which contains numerous copies of the same data that are saved in different locations and on different devices, in contrast to conventional methods of storing information on one central point (see Deloitte, 2023). A peer enables the use of some computational resources (such as disc storage, network bandwidth, and processing power) by other participants without the requirement for server-centred centralization. These nodes enable the preservation, coordination, and security of commercial data flows by playing a variety of roles inside the network (Van Rijmenam & Ryan, 2018). By encoding data in a block, the blockchain's security is implemented utilizing cryptographic keys, a distributed network, and a network servicing protocol. By encoding data in a block, the blockchain's security is implemented utilising cryptographic keys, a distributed network, and a network servicing protocol. Once information (such as a transaction request) has been verified, meta-data is stored in a block and cannot be challenged, deleted, or changed without the network's consent and the knowledge of the individuals who originally produced the record. A block's behaviour does not alter when it is included in a chain of other blocks.

Smart contracts, also known as self-executing contracts, blockchain contracts, or digital contracts, are one of the uses of blockchain technology (Griggs et al., 2018; Zhang et al., 2018). A smart contract is a piece of software that can self-execute complicated instructions, which lowers the cost of signing contracts, keeping track of them, enforcing them, and processing payments. The use of smart contracts makes it possible to create advanced software that can function as autonomous agents. A distributed enterprise, like those found in hospital systems, could result from this arrangement since it eliminates agency and coordination costs. While the financial sector saw an early rise, implementations are ongoing in a variety of other industries, such as marketing (Kumar & Mallick, 2018) and supply chain (Zheng et al., 2017). For instance, blockchain implementations based on smart contracts are used in marketing, notably MarTech, to guarantee uniform promotion actions and prompt the initiation of promotional campaigns. This strategy may simplify the market environment, get rid of middlemen that add to costs, lessen the likelihood of fake traffic reports, and lower the risk of numerous ad requests (Sklaroff, 2017). Popular blockchain applications in the supply chain include, but are not limited to, smart contracts and globally searchable transaction databases. Blockchain technology can be used to ensure products are delivered on time and in good condition without middlemen, lowering costs, minimising waste, and fostering sustainability.

3.1 Blockchain and the Health Sector

According to the Global Blockchain in Healthcare report (2022), blockchain technology has the potential to transform various industries, including the health sector. Here are some of the ways blockchain could impact healthcare:

1. ***Secure patient data management:*** Blockchain technology offers a secure and decentralised way to store patient data. This eliminates the risk of data breaches and ensures that sensitive information is protected.
2. ***Improved data sharing:*** Blockchain can help to improve data sharing between healthcare providers, allowing for more coordinated and efficient patient care. This can result in improved patient outcomes and reduced medical errors.
3. ***Clinical trials management:*** Blockchain can help manage the complex process of clinical trials by providing secure and transparent tracking of patient data.

This can help to improve the accuracy and efficiency of clinical trials, ultimately leading to faster development and approval of new treatments.

4. ***Drug traceability:*** Blockchain can be used to track the supply chain of drugs from the manufacturer to the patient. This can help to ensure the authenticity and safety of drugs, reducing the risk of counterfeit medications.
5. ***Medical research and analysis:*** Blockchain can help to facilitate medical research by providing a secure and decentralized platform for storing and sharing data. This can lead to improved collaboration between researchers, leading to faster and more effective medical breakthroughs. Overall, the use of blockchain in healthcare has the potential to improve patient outcomes, reduce medical errors, and increase the efficiency of the healthcare system.

This said, the decentralised, open, and permissionless features of the blockchain could provide a special answer for the healthcare industry. A wider range of applications for the technology opens the way for wearables and the advancement of medical research, among other elements of healthcare. A recent survey by Deloitte demonstrates that the traditional industry is actively exploring new paths for the use of the blockchain to fulfil its vital needs. The healthcare sector has increased expectations for blockchain advancements (Deloitte, 2023). The blockchain's immutability is a crucial choice for healthcare data. It can protect clinical trial results, health records, and regulatory compliance. Blockchain is used to facilitate "real-time patient monitoring and medical interventions" through the use of smart contracts (Griggs et al., 2018). Such systems guarantee record security while enabling "Health Insurance Portability and Accountability Act" (HIPAA)-compliant access for patients and medical providers. Another use for blockchain is in the pharmaceutical supply chain and creating strategies to combat fake medicines. The use of smart contracts allows for the facilitation of the informed consent procedure as well as the improvement of identity management and data quality, despite the fact that the development of new pharmaceuticals involves significant costs connected to studies to evaluate the drug's safety and efficacy. Giving patients the ability to manage their own identity enables the informed consent process to be integrated while maintaining the privacy of each patient's personal health information.

4. BENEFITS OF BLOCKCHAIN IN THE HEALTH SECTOR

According to the Global Blockchain in Healthcare report (2022), blockchain technology has the potential to transform the healthcare industry in various ways. Here are some of the benefits of using blockchain in the health sector:

1. Security and privacy: Healthcare data is sensitive, and patient privacy must be protected. Blockchain technology provides a secure way of storing and sharing health records, ensuring that sensitive patient data is not compromised.
2. Data integrity: Blockchain is an immutable ledger that records every transaction or event. In healthcare, this means that all patient data is tamper-proof and cannot be altered or deleted. This ensures that all records are accurate, reliable, and transparent.
3. Interoperability: The healthcare industry has traditionally struggled with data interoperability due to the siloed nature of healthcare data. Blockchain technology can enable seamless data exchange between different healthcare organizations and providers, making it easier to share and access patient data across different systems.
4. Improved clinical trials: Blockchain can improve the efficiency and accuracy of clinical trials by enabling secure and transparent sharing of data between different organizations involved in the trials. This can help to reduce the time and cost of clinical trials, and improve the accuracy of the data collected.
5. Supply chain management: The use of blockchain can help to track and manage the supply chain of medical products and devices, ensuring that they are authentic and of high quality. This can help to reduce the incidence of counterfeit drugs and devices and ensure that patients receive safe and effective treatments.
6. Smart contracts: Smart contracts can be used to automate and streamline many healthcare processes, such as claims processing and payment, reducing the administrative burden on healthcare providers and improving efficiency.

In summary, the use of blockchain in the health sector can improve security, data integrity, interoperability, clinical trials, supply chain management, and the use of smart contracts. These benefits have the potential to transform the healthcare industry, improving the quality of care and reducing costs.

5. CHALLENGES OF BLOCKCHAIN IN THE HEALTH SECTOR

While blockchain technology has the potential to transform the healthcare industry, there are also several challenges that must be addressed before it can be widely adopted. Here are some of the key challenges of blockchain in the health sector:

While blockchain can facilitate data interoperability, it can also create interoperability issues if not implemented correctly. The lack of standardised data formats and the presence of different blockchain platforms can make it difficult to transfer data between different systems. Blockchain technology is currently limited in terms of scalability, and the size of the blockchain network can impact its performance.

Healthcare organisations generate large amounts of data, and the blockchain network must be able to handle this volume of data without compromising performance. Healthcare data is subject to strict regulations and compliance requirements, and blockchain technology must comply with these regulations. This can be challenging, given the decentralised nature of the blockchain network and the lack of a central authority that can be held accountable. While blockchain can improve data security, it can also raise concerns about data privacy. The immutable nature of the blockchain means that once data is recorded, it cannot be deleted, which can create privacy issues for sensitive patient data. Implementing blockchain technology in healthcare requires significant investment in infrastructure and resources, and integrating blockchain into existing healthcare systems can be challenging. The healthcare industry is traditionally slow to adopt new technologies, and it may take time for blockchain to gain widespread acceptance. That said, the challenges of blockchain in the health sector include interoperability, scalability, regulatory compliance, data privacy, and adoption and integration.

6. DISCUSSION AND CONCLUSION

Blockchain technology has emerged as a significant trend in information systems (IS) application development. Landscape knowledge development is therefore of utmost importance for creating understanding and enhancing design techniques. In order for "service providers and patients" to make educated clinical decisions, there are significant hurdles for information distribution and sharing in the healthcare industry. In this research, the researcher explored blockchain-based technologies and their possible uses for the healthcare sector.

As was already said, digitising data opens up new possibilities for studying medical trends and assessing the standard of treatment; additionally, as related technologies continue to advance, blockchain has the potential to provide a number of advantages for the "support service." Although records are digitalized, they are kept apart in locally centralised data storages, which severely limit future advancements. The use of blockchain technology enhances connectivity while ensuring the parties' security, privacy, and cost savings.

The implementation of blockchain technology in the health sector is undoubtedly a difficult and gradual process that must also overcome numerous challenges, including low digital literacy among the populace and pre-existing paper-based processes where all parties involved (including citizens) anticipate receiving a physical document as a result of the procedure. One of the psychological factors contributing to the technological transformation's delay is the fact that people frequently find it difficult to adapt to change, even when it is essential or beneficial. Although it is common to experience pain and anxiety when managing an invention that deviates from the norm and the familiar, the resistance to change shouldn't impede the unavoidable process of digitalization and process innovation.

The goal of the chapter was to provide a solid profile for blockchain in the following healthcare application areas, where provisions can be seen in terms of "smart contracts, data storage and exchange, physician credentialing, and peer-to-peer data exchange." They would be viewed as additional facets of the design of healthcare solutions and their innovations in order to satisfy organisational or contextual demands for information dissemination. Additionally, by employing a database containing "medical records" as individual patient information, blockchain-based medical records are expected to increase the accuracy of diagnoses, provide better-informed treatment options, and be a more cost-effective solution.

In order to highlight the rapid development of blockchain implementations in healthcare, which is being slowed down by the problems already outlined, it is necessary to conduct this study. This chapter describes the opportunities and difficulties that blockchain presents for the healthcare sector. The chapter's main concerns are data security and privacy. Coordination and data structure are additional difficulties. The chapter's conclusion points to future research directions that will encourage further innovations and developments in the design of health information systems (e.g., public healthcare decision support; Miah et al., 2017) or other problem domains, such as agricultural decision support systems (Miah, 2020), where blockchain can provide authenticated data dissemination methods.

With decentralisation, immutability, transparency, and traceability among its many useful sharing and storing properties, blockchain technology is gaining popularity for use in the healthcare industry. Scalability problems, interoperability, a lack of technical competence, security concerns, and authorization problems are some of the risks associated with using blockchain technology in the healthcare industry. While there is a lack of research advising healthcare organisations to use blockchain design types—public, private, and hybrid—it is crucial to provide data linked to distinctions between each blockchain design in future work.

Decentralisation in public administration will be a natural, inevitable, and revolutionary consequence of the application of this technology once a sufficient level of technological maturity is reached, as the researcher can affirm, and it has the potential to greatly expand the possible boundaries and scenarios of the development of public functions. Thus, it is essential to begin gaining the knowledge required to pressure governments to move in this direction and to implement the fundamental changes that all citizens require. In inference, blockchain technology has enormous potential, and the potential advantages are too significant to ignore. In fact, despite the fact that research into blockchain applications is still in its infancy, this technology has the potential to improve public integrity and boost citizens' faith in government institutions.

In conclusion, block chain technology has the potential to revolutionise healthcare delivery in developing countries. By providing secure, decentralised, and transparent platforms for data management, block chains can help overcome many of the challenges faced by healthcare systems in these regions, including data privacy, interoperability, and inefficiencies. However, the implementation of block chain technology in healthcare delivery requires careful consideration and planning, including the development of appropriate regulations, infrastructure, and stakeholder engagement. With the right approach, blockchain technology can be a powerful tool to improve healthcare outcomes in emerging countries and beyond.

7. RESEARCH AND PRACTICAL IMPLICATION

7.1 Research Implication

There are numerous gaps in the study on the application of "blockchain technologies" in healthcare. Few studies have made an effort to pinpoint blockchain assets "beyond privacy, security, and management" concerns. Also, as the data entered into the blockchain cannot be changed, a gap in the literature about the practical immutability features in electronic health records has been identified. For stakeholders considering implementing this technology in their healthcare systems, this can give rise to some legitimate concerns. Not only that, but there aren't many resources in the literature that analyse the advantages of the two types of designs—permissioned blockchains, which are private, and permissionless blockchains, which are public—in terms of their suitability for businesses.

Future studies could look into the direct advantages and risks of each "permissioned, permissionless, and hybrid blockchain" design as well as how effective they are in the healthcare industry. A future study might take into account a number of research gaps that were found in terms of blockchain usage regulations and authorization criteria, in addition to the societal acceptance of the technology within healthcare organizations. Further research should concentrate on other parts of the world, as the majority of the findings were based on advanced settings, allowing for more accurate interpretation for use globally and greater comprehension of blockchain technology applications in the healthcare sector.

7.2 Practical Implication

While deploying blockchain technologies, a variety of practical concerns must be taken into account. First, more research is required to determine how "blockchain technology" can help safeguard the accuracy of medical data. Second, more research has to be done on the security issues associated with blockchain deployment in healthcare organizations. Finding "technical talent that can implement, manage, and solve technical problems" related to blockchain technology is a major issue that has been raised in the literature.

REFERENCES

Aazam, M., Zeadally, S., & Harras, K. A. (2020). Health fog for smart healthcare. *IEEE Consumer Electronics Magazine*, *9*(2), 96–102. doi:10.1109/MCE.2019.2953749

Abu-Elezz, I., Hassan, A., Nazeemudeen, A., Househ, M., & Abd-Alrazaq, A. (2020). The benefits and threats of blockchain technology in healthcare: A scoping review. *International Journal of Medical Informatics*, *142*, 104246. doi:10.1016/j.ijmedinf.2020.104246 PMID:32828033

Al Omar, A., Bhuiyan, M. Z. A., Basu, A., Kiyomoto, S., & Rahman, M. S. (2019). Privacy-friendly platform for healthcare data in cloud based on blockchain environment. *Future Generation Computer Systems*, *95*, 511–521. doi:10.1016/j.future.2018.12.044

Ali, F., El-Sappagh, S., Islam, S. R., Ali, A., Attique, M., Imran, M., & Kwak, K. S. (2021). An intelligent healthcare monitoring framework using wearable sensors and social networking data. *Future Generation Computer Systems*, *114*, 23–43. doi:10.1016/j.future.2020.07.047

Ali, F., El-Sappagh, S., Islam, S. R., Kwak, D., Ali, A., Imran, M., & Kwak, K. S. (2020). A smart healthcare monitoring system for heart disease prediction based on ensemble deep learning and feature fusion. *Information Fusion*, *63*, 208–222. doi:10.1016/j.inffus.2020.06.008

Ali, M. S., Vecchio, M., Pincheira, M., Dolui, K., Antonelli, F., & Rehmani, M. H. (2018). Applications of blockchains in the Internet of Things: A comprehensive survey. *IEEE Communications Surveys and Tutorials*, *21*(2), 1676–1717. doi:10.1109/COMST.2018.2886932

Awais, M., Raza, M., Ali, K., Ali, Z., Irfan, M., Chughtai, O., Khan, I., Kim, S., & Ur Rehman, M. (2019). An Internet of Things based bed-egress alerting paradigm using wearable sensors in elderly care environment. *Sensors (Basel), 19*(11), 2498. doi:10.339019112498 PMID:31159252

Chukwu, E., & Garg, L. (2020). A systematic review of blockchain in healthcare: Frameworks, prototypes, and implementations. *IEEE Access : Practical Innovations, Open Solutions*, *8*, 21196–21214. doi:10.1109/ACCESS.2020.2969881

Esposito, C., De Santis, A., Tortora, G., Chang, H., & Choo, K. K. R. (2018). Blockchain: A panacea for healthcare cloud-based data security and privacy? *IEEE Cloud Computing*, *5*(1), 31–37. doi:10.1109/MCC.2018.011791712

Griggs, K. N., Ossipova, O., Kohlios, C. P., Baccarini, A. N., Howson, E. A., & Hayajneh, T. (2018). Healthcare blockchain system using smart contracts for secure automated remote patient monitoring. *Journal of Medical Systems*, *42*(7), 1–7. doi:10.100710916-018-0982-x PMID:29876661

Gupta, S., Malhotra, V., & Singh, S. N. (2020). Securing IoT-driven remote healthcare data through blockchain. In *Advances in data and information sciences* (pp. 47–56). Springer. doi:10.1007/978-981-15-0694-9_6

Islam, N., Faheem, Y., Din, I. U., Talha, M., Guizani, M., & Khalil, M. (2019). A blockchain-based fog computing framework for activity recognition as an application to e-Healthcare services. *Future Generation Computer Systems*, *100*, 569–578. doi:10.1016/j.future.2019.05.059

Jiang, L., Chen, L., Giannetsos, T., Luo, B., Liang, K., & Han, J. (2019). Toward practical privacy-preserving processing over encrypted data in IoT: An assistive healthcare use case. *IEEE Internet of Things Journal*, *6*(6), 10177–10190. doi:10.1109/JIOT.2019.2936532

Kumar, N. M., & Mallick, P. K. (2018). Blockchain technology for security issues and challenges in IoT. *Procedia Computer Science*, *132*, 1815–1823. doi:10.1016/j.procs.2018.05.140

Miah, M. (2020). Blockchain technology in peer-to-peer elearning: Opportunities and challenges. In *Proceedings of the EDSIG Conference ISSN* (Vol. 2473, p. 4901). Academic Press.

Miah, S. J., Hasan, J., & Gammack, J. G. (2017). On-cloud healthcare clinic: An e-health consultancy approach for remote communities in a developing country. *Telematics and Informatics*, *34*(1), 311–322. doi:10.1016/j.tele.2016.05.008

Salah, K., Rehman, M. H. U., Nizamuddin, N., & Al-Fuqaha, A. (2019). Blockchain for AI: Review and open research challenges. *IEEE Access : Practical Innovations, Open Solutions*, *7*, 10127–10149. doi:10.1109/ACCESS.2018.2890507

Sengupta, J., Ruj, S., & Bit, S. D. (2020). A comprehensive survey on attacks, security issues and blockchain solutions for IoT and IIoT. *Journal of Network and Computer Applications*, *149*, 102481. doi:10.1016/j.jnca.2019.102481

Shahnaz, A., Qamar, U., & Khalid, A. (2019). Using blockchain for electronic health records. *IEEE Access : Practical Innovations, Open Solutions*, *7*, 147782–147795. doi:10.1109/ACCESS.2019.2946373

Sklaroff, J. M. (2017). Smart contracts and the cost of inflexibility. *U. Pa. L. Rev.*, *166*, 263.

Syed, T. A., Alzahrani, A., Jan, S., Siddiqui, M. S., Nadeem, A., & Alghamdi, T. (2019). A comparative analysis of blockchain architecture and its applications: Problems and recommendations. *IEEE Access : Practical Innovations, Open Solutions*, *7*, 176838–176869. doi:10.1109/ACCESS.2019.2957660

Tao, H., Bhuiyan, M. Z. A., Abdalla, A. N., Hassan, M. M., Zain, J. M., & Hayajneh, T. (2018). Secured data collection with hardware-based ciphers for IoT-based healthcare. *IEEE Internet of Things Journal*, *6*(1), 410–420. doi:10.1109/JIOT.2018.2854714

Van Rijmenam, M., & Ryan, P. (2018). *Blockchain: Transforming your business and our world*. Routledge. doi:10.4324/9780429457715

Yaqoob, I., Salah, K., Jayaraman, R., & Al-Hammadi, Y. (2021). Blockchain for healthcare data management: Opportunities, challenges, and future recommendations. *Neural Computing & Applications*, 1–16.

Zhang, P., White, J., Schmidt, D. C., Lenz, G., & Rosenbloom, S. T. (2018). FHIRChain: Applying blockchain to securely and scalably share clinical data. *Computational and Structural Biotechnology Journal*, *16*, 267–278. doi:10.1016/j.csbj.2018.07.004 PMID:30108685

Zheng, Z., Xie, S., Dai, H., Chen, X., & Wang, H. (2017, June). *An overview of blockchain technology: Architecture, consensus, and future trends. In 2017 IEEE international congress on big data (BigData Congress)*. IEEE.

Zheng, Z., Xie, S., Dai, H. N., Chen, W., Chen, X., Weng, J., & Imran, M. (2020). An overview on smart contracts: Challenges, advances and platforms. *Future Generation Computer Systems*, *105*, 475–491. doi:10.1016/j.future.2019.12.019

Zhu, H., Wu, C. K., Koo, C. H., Tsang, Y. T., Liu, Y., Chi, H. R., & Tsang, K. F. (2019). Smart healthcare in the era of internet-of-things. *IEEE Consumer Electronics Magazine*, *8*(5), 26–30. doi:10.1109/MCE.2019.2923929

Chapter 5
Blockchain and Customer Engagement

Fatawu Alhassan
https://orcid.org/0000-0001-8257-7409
Tamale Technical University, Ghana

Stanley Cowther
Tamale Technical University, Ghana

Sussana Antwi-Boasiako
Accra Technical University, Ghana

Alamu Elizabeth Kehinde
Tamale Technical University, Ghana

Amodaah Deborah Apusiyine
Tamale Technical University, Ghana

ABSTRACT

Business-to-consumer (B2C) commerce has flourished as a result of the widespread availability of advanced e-commerce platforms integrated with mobile applications, which have also reformed organizational structures and revitalized the value-generating processes. This chapter seeks to provide literature into the effect of blockchain and customer engagement. Blockchain helps firms to deal with customers by fostering security, transparency, and fast payment. It was concluded that blockchain leads to customer engagement. In the future, governments are likely to use it, and it will be globally recognised.

DOI: 10.4018/978-1-6684-7649-9.ch005

INTRODUCTION

Bitcoin, the first cryptocurrency, was announced by its anonymous creator, Nakamoto, in a whitepaper in 2008 and implemented in 2009 (Zachariadis et al., 2019). It's interesting that Nakamoto doesn't call it a blockchain but rather "an electronic coin as a chain of digital signatures" (Frizzo-Barker et al., 2020 p. 2). Here, it's essential to stress that blockchain and Bitcoin are not interchangeable terms. Bitcoin is money built on top of the blockchain, which is a technology in and of itself. It's no secret that blockchain technology is revolutionizing the logistics industry. Blockchain, the underlying technology behind Bitcoin, has far-reaching implications for many industries. Several academic studies have set out to discover what impact distributed ledger technology will have on businesses and markets. From a technology perspective, the blockchain can be understood as a distributed shared ledger that employs time-stamped, encrypted blocks chained together to hold verified and synchronized information in a business-to-consumer (B2C) network. According to Schmidt & Wagner (2019), blockchain technology can be used for more than just financial transactions; it can also serve as a global system for recording, monitoring, and tracking all types of assets. By eliminating the requirement for third parties, consensus-based record validation not only lowers transaction costs but can also help businesses with governance decisions in their supply chain relationships (Schmidt & Wagner, 2019). At the same time, technological advancements have altered the nature of brand marketing, allowing for more extensive coverage and more specific targeting in an effort to boost credibility and commitment to the brand among consumers. The Internet has made it possible for businesses to expand into previously unreachable niches, establish whole new sales channels, and stimulate previously unanticipated demand (Rajeb et al., 2020). This adaptive approach to the marketplace makes use of cutting-edge tools to improve the precision with which it targets consumers.

There hasn't been a lot of research into blockchain, despite the fact that it's a promising new technology that has the potential to disrupt numerous sectors and usher in a technological revolution in the 21st century. Some firms and organizations implementing blockchain technology without a customer strategy could lead to poor customer management, which is a general IT problem. Some IT security managers don't have a plan to use blockchain applications' user-friendly advantages, and this is a real issue (Frizzo-Barker et al., 2020). However, the main stakeholder in these businesses and sectors, the consumers, is not well explained in the current study efforts (Dai et al., 2017). Using a digital wallet, customers can get their unused credits whenever it is most convenient for them. In return, advertisers can gain a more complete picture of their target audience through these data analytics (Weber, 2018). An efficient marketing plan relies heavily on collected client information for any organization. Blockchain provides novel approaches to working with this data, which will increase its commercial worth. Blockchain cuts away the middleman and establishes direct contact between businesses and customers, allowing the latter to glean trustworthy information that can be used to enhance services and products (Zachariadis et al., 2019). Because of this, more people will learn about the new product or service, and more people will buy it. Customers want a seamless transaction from beginning to end; therefore, after-sale service is a key factor in retaining them. Customers prefer online help resources over calling in to speak with support representatives, indicating a growing trend toward self-service (Cvitanovic, 2018). These transactions can be automated by blockchain via digital wallets if they are constructed and designed properly, providing a novel and satisfying experience for customers.

Although widespread implementation of blockchain technology has only begun, there are promising signs that it may quickly gain traction in the industry and dramatically alter the way consumers interact with businesses. Customers' expectations will shift as a result of the technology, which will allow for more personalized marketing campaigns (NanoMatriX, 2022). The most successful businesses of the future will be those that accept this technology and work actively to take advantage of the new possibilities it presents. If businesses can figure out how to use blockchain to boost client engagement, they'll reap huge rewards (Wong et al., 2020). With this development, blockchain has had a favorable effect on the ways in which businesses communicate with and interact with their clients (Cvitanovic, 2018). In this chapter, we'll try to give a high-level picture of the ways in which blockchain technology impacts customers' experiences as consumers and their buying habits. Adoption studies for blockchain applications are still in their infancy, and most of the available literature focuses on the advantages and disadvantages of blockchain technology once it has been put into practice (Kamble et al., 2019). This chapter seeks to address the dearth of literature on the effects of blockchain and customer engagement.

LITERATURE

Blockchain

The Blockchain protocol, which is the underlying technology of Bitcoin, has opened up a wealth of opportunities (Nguyen, 2016). Blockchain has numerous useful properties that can be applied to many different areas. Blockchain's two primary features are its decentralized nature and its immutability. Because it is dispersed among all participants, blockchain eliminates the need for a centralized database or ledger. It makes it possible for users to connect directly with one another, bypassing intermediaries (Gupta, 2018). Eliminating the middleman streamlines the process and reduces costs. In addition, once a transaction has been recorded, it cannot be altered in any way, which is known as immutability. When an update is necessary, a new transaction is generated and broadcast to all relevant networks. Once a transaction has been verified by the network, it cannot be altered by any other computer. Because of this, there is a great deal of confidence in the system's safety. Attaran and Gunasekaran (2019) use the term "blockchain" to describe a certain type of distributed, public, encrypted, and immutable digital ledger that can improve the reliability and efficacy of business networks (Weber, 2018). However, Knirsch et al. (2019) defined blockchain technology as a trustless and fully decentralized peer-to-peer storage system dispersed across all participants, also known as nodes in the blockchain system. A second definition comes from Dai et al. (2017), who see a blockchain as the underlying technical architecture of a distributed network that permits users to collectively maintain a trustworthy database in a decentralized fashion. The original purpose of blockchain technology was to ensure the safe storage and transfer of bitcoin transactions. Despite the fact that bitcoin has been the subject of much debate since its inception, the blockchain technology that underpins it has performed faultlessly in all of the financial and non-financial uses to which it has been put (Crosby et al., 2016). Researchers from a wide range of fields have concluded that blockchain technology will be the next big game changer (Crosby et al., 2016; Kshetri, 2018; Schmidt & Wagner, 2019).

Customer Engagement (CE)

CE is when a consumer actively participates in activities related to a brand (Kumar et al., 2019). No one saw the unprecedented level of internet participation in 2020 coming. Once the COVID-19 pandemic began, it immediately altered the ways in which we communicate with one another, whether we're talking about personal relationships or professional interactions (Kumar et al., 2019). The macro trend of digital transformation that has dominated the past decade has grown at a breathtaking clip. Out of the need to maintain communication despite geographic separation, innovative new solutions were developed. The lines between our digital and real-world selves blurred. The term "customer engagement" refers to the process of maintaining a long-term relationship with a customer that transcends a simple exchange of goods or services. It's when a business consistently and thoughtfully goes out of its way to satisfy its customers, earning their devotion (Murray, 2020). Roadside businesses have always relied on personal connections with their customers, but it's harder than ever to keep up such ties in the modern digital era (So et al., 2015). Technology has made it simpler to find and reach out to potential new customers, but it has become more challenging to keep existing ones (Kumar & Ramachandran, 2020). So et al. (2015) define customer engagement strategy as an effort to foster relationships between businesses and their clientele through a variety of channels of contact. In today's highly linked culture, companies that fail to actively involve their customers will quickly become extinct. As a result, it is imperative for a marketer to not only work toward increasing the brand's desirability, appeal, and preference in the eyes of the consumer but also to do whatever it takes to keep the customer engaged in and committed to the brand. The consumer makes an investment in the brand on multiple levels when they purchase, use, and consume the goods. The engagement we're referring to is the result of this kind of investment.

Maintaining a steady flow of cross-platform communication with clients is essential to establishing trust. In fact, most customers have inquiries not just before but even after making a purchase. By connecting with customers and taking their wants and needs into account across the whole customer journey, from discovery to purchase and beyond, you can create a successful engagement strategy. In the same vein, CE has been hailed as important in driving sales growth, referrals, competitive advantage, and stock returns (Pansari and Kumar, 2017). The impact of Facebook customer engagement on consumer trust and loyalty was evaluated. Researchers discovered that active participation can mitigate the impact of brand perception on customer loyalty (Hollebeek et al., 2021).

Blockchain and Customer Engagement

Companies and consumers alike can benefit from the democratizing effect of new technology since they are no longer limited by the resources of larger corporations and can instead afford to invest in cutting-edge tools and methods that were previously out of reach. It's also important to figure out how to keep repeat buyers as consumers. The use of blockchain technology could be investigated by companies to enable consumers to instantly share rewards points by linking content to a digital token associated with the customer's account (Wong et al., 2020). Blockchains take away the core, while other technologies only automate personnel on the perimeter executing menial chores. Since blockchain eliminates the need for a middleman, cab drivers may deal directly with customers (Tapscott & Tapscott, 2016).

Small businesses are increasingly spending money on technologies and platforms that charge a subscription fee because they see it as necessary to remain competitive in their industries (Rajeb et al., 2020). To combat these issues, blockchain technologies can serve as a useful instrument for connecting directly with one's target audience. Brands are fighting harder than ever to keep their customers loyal as the market becomes more saturated. Brands have been methodically gathering and retaining customer data, usually through loyalty programs, in an effort to increase customer retention (Cvitanovic, 2018). Using these methods, businesses can strengthen customer attachment to their brands, lower price sensitivity, spread positive word-of-mouth, and attract new clients (Uncles et al., 2003). And since customer loyalty programs have the potential to increase both sales and profitability, they can be quite useful to businesses. Brands can now reach a wider audience with their advertising campaigns, narrow in on specific customers, and speed up their response times for customer care requests thanks to this cutting-edge technology. Its pervasiveness and interactivity help businesses cut down on wasted time and money spent on advertising by cutting out middlemen. The information is kept in a secure location within the bank's computer network. The worlds of financial technology and customer engagement rarely collide. However, blockchain technology has the potential to radically alter the business landscape. It has the potential to affect and even revolutionize how businesses interact with their target demographic. That's much beyond the power it has to revolutionize financial transactions and the sector as a whole. Blockchain, surprisingly, has tremendous potential for improving service to customers. Those with limited resources can benefit from increased connectivity as a result. In addition, it can safeguard all types of business-customer interactions and give the impression that the company is open and honest. In a paradoxical and adaptable way, blockchain technology can move along a spectrum from a high degree of transparency, thanks to the decentralization of a public blockchain ledger that makes the data more available (Yli-Huumo et al., 2016), to a high degree of anonymity (Narayanan et al., 2016). Users can remain pseudonymous on Bitcoin and other blockchains due to the decentralized nature of the network and the security measures already in place.

Using blockchain technology, financial institutions may securely store consumer information in a shared ledger. (Gupta and Gupta, 2018). It streamlines processes and eliminates unnecessary labor (Gupta & Gupta 2018; Guo & Liang 2016). Block-based data storage guarantees the integrity of the records it contains. Once the information is saved, it can be accessed by many financial institutions. This was recently demonstrated by Guo and Liang (2016). As blockchain technology evolves, it has the potential to significantly alter how consumers interact with brands. However, successful adoption will rely heavily on how companies apply blockchain to reimagine consumer interactions (Wong et al., 2020). Blockchain technology presents an opportunity for business owners and marketers to roll out a suite of customer loyalty programs designed to attract and retain a growing customer base.

Brands can use customer loyalty programs to get people to open up and talk about their habits and preferences (i.e., points, cryptocurrency rewards, micropayments, and cash-back incentives). By using Blockchain technology, companies can forego storing customers' private information, which is normally necessary for conducting financial transactions. Since the information would not be stored in one place, companies wouldn't have to worry about keeping it safe, hygienic, or within the law (Gupta et al., 2021). Concerns about firms collecting too much personal information on customers would be eliminated. A new paradigm for boosting customer involvement and collaboration is revealed by blockchain technology. In this way, customers can reply to a company's advertising campaigns with genuine, third-party reviews of the company's products (Deighton & Kornfeld, 2008). A majority of nodes in a blockchain must agree on a transaction for it to be validated, making it a safe system. While this is often the case, it is not always the case. Since blockchain is always improving, so are the methods used to break into it. This approach, being computer-based, carries the same inherent dangers as any other technological implementation (Gupta et al., 2021).

For this reason, blockchains can serve as a single, reliable source of truth that can be used by many different institutions. They promote agreement and openness, which in turn guarantees that everyone is responsible for their actions and that agreements with other market participants and end users are kept. Thus, it's no surprise that more and more businesses with a focus on customers are using blockchain. Opportunities for blockchain-based record management extend far beyond the management of consumer identity records. The identity verification function built into blockchain will let businesses reach the appropriate people with hyper-specific advertisements.

Some institutions are considering using blockchain to keep track of medical records, payments, and communications between patients and doctors (Wong et al., 2020). The existence of blockchain-based databases ensures that this information can be encrypted and protected against tampering at the same time. Supply chain and monetary transaction use cases dominate current blockchain application leaders, per Gartner (2020). A lack of a single, overarching authority to serve as a coordinator in supply chains makes it common for multiple parties to engage in a complex web of interactions. Customers and businesses alike may see savings in transaction fees thanks to blockchain's decentralized ledger's elimination of middlemen (Hughes et al., 2019). In addition, global supply chain networks are adding complexity to the supply chain management process (Kouhizadeh et al., 2021). Efficiency, transparency, product tracing, smart contract administration, and data management are just a few of the areas where blockchain has the potential to enhance supply chain-related processes (Kamble et al., 2019). Companies will only be able to keep customers' money in the future if they can prove that the goods were delivered to them in accordance with the customer's blockchain record. This type of blockchain-facilitated process optimization may be seen as a competitive differentiator for businesses (Dutta et al., 2020). It can improve customer involvement along the way by reassuring consumers that they won't lose out if a product kit gets lost in the mail.

Recent developments in technology have made it easier to track customers' habits and preferences in order to design more targeted loyalty programs. Database management software, for instance, has enabled more nuanced and individual tracking of customers, ushering in a new era in loyalty marketing (Rajeb et al., 2020). Improved trade and custody services for securities are one area where blockchain can be put to use. A more streamlined and transparent real-time transaction is possible if all parties use the same blockchain platform (Gupta, 2018). Those who have paid for a service but not received it often feel cheated. Those unhappy customers are just the tip of the iceberg when it comes to problems with product shipping and delivery. Potential sales have been lost because these consumers are so put off by widespread criticism of a single brand that they refuse to give companies a chance to win them over. Such clients are easy to lose, as they quickly defect to a rival.

The Future of BC

Only time will tell how this turns out for everyone, but early indications are promising because of the blockchain's decentralized nature, high levels of security and transparency, and other desirable traits. In the future, advertisers will be able to easily track whether or not their ads reach their target audience, measure the success of their campaigns, and adapt their strategies accordingly thanks to this technology. Marketers can also utilize this information to ensure that the same consumer is not repeatedly exposed to the same ad. According to the previous discussions, the security of this technology would greatly improve if more people used it. Research in this area, as well as public education about the technology it enables, is crucial. Blockchain opens up an entire new era of engagement and trust, revolutionizing the way businesses connect to and touch with their clients, from authentic computation campaigns to altered frontline engagements. As more and more business is conducted online, electronic signatures are widely accepted as standard practice. In the not-too-distant future, many of the novel internet-based technologies and business practices made possible by Blockchains will likely become the norm. As these technologies advance to accommodate a wider variety of complicated transactions impacting not just financial assets but also cyberphysical infrastructure, policy and regulatory decision-makers are contemplating essential regulatory reforms. More efficient government operations are possible with the use of blockchain technology. Governments will use blockchain technology for its many benefits as they come to realize its potential for increasing efficiency and public confidence.

CONCLUSION

Disruptive innovations, such as blockchain and AI, are potent catalysts for change, altering not only the way a business operates but also its capabilities. Bitcoin's underlying technology is called "blockchain." Bitcoin transactions, and by extension, any other type of transaction, may be recorded and verified using blockchain technology. There has been consistent growth in blockchain's popularity among corporate users. Most companies should be able to handle this innovation with relative ease. Transparency, trust, security, and simplification in the purchasing process are just some of the ways in which blockchain technology alters the traditional business model, ultimately leading to greater consumer loyalty. Any given company is always on the lookout for ways to improve communication with its clientele. The goal is to provide easier and more customized service to customers. More and more companies today are exploring how blockchain technology may enhance their relationships with customers. To ensure that corporate decisions are based on the most recent information, blockchain streamlines data management to ensure that executives always have access to the most recent records.

Before the data from a blockchain can be made accessible to all authorized participants, it is time-stamped and the record of the transaction or occurrence is attached. This is a live event. Using this method, the data is protected from being altered without the knowledge of all parties involved. With this information permanently stored, an unbreakable chain of trust is established.

It's a malleable area for investment by companies for whom client involvement is of paramount importance. Existing digital marketing methods are being challenged by the rapid development of technology, which can make for a more open and pleasant user experience. Modern business is reimagining its relationship with its clientele. It's common for customer engagement and contentment to dwindle sometime in the long haul of the buyer's journey. However, it is now being strengthened as blockchain's influence grows. Customers are able to form stronger relationships with brands when they participate to this extent. In addition, it facilitates access to reliable analytics and data for businesses, reimagining the challenges of client interaction.

REFERENCES

Attaran, M., & Gunasekaran, A. (2019). *Applications of Blockchain Technology in Business: Challenges and Opportunities.* Springer International Publishing. doi:10.1007/978-3-030-27798-7

Crosby, M., Nachiappan, P., Verma, S., & Kalyanaraman, V. (2016). BlockChain Technology: Beyond Bitcoin. *Applied Innovation Review Issue*, (2), 6–19.

Cvitanovic, P. L. (2018). New technologies in marketing as competitive advantage. *2018 ENTRENOVA Conference Proceedings (Split: ECONSTOR),* (pp. 294–302). EconStor.

Deighton, J., & Kornfeld, L. (2008). *Digital Interactivity: Unanticipated Consequences for Markets, Marketing, and Consumers*. Harvard Business School. http://weigend.com/files/teaching/ tsinghua/readings/DeightonKornfeldHBS2007.pdf

Dutta, P., Choi, T.-M., Somani, S., & Butala, R. (2020). Blockchain technology in supply chain operations: Applications, challenges and research opportunities. *Transportation Research Part E, Logistics and Transportation Review*, *142*, 102067. doi:10.1016/j.tre.2020.102067 PMID:33013183

Frizzo-Barker, J., Chow-White, P. A., Adams, P. R., Mentanko, J., Ha, D., & Green, S. (2020). Blockchain as a disruptive technology for business: A systematic review. *International Journal of Information Management*, *51*, 102029. doi:10.1016/j.ijinfomgt.2019.10.014

Gartner. (2020, July 13). *Hype Cycle for Blockchain Technologies, 2020*. Gartner. https://www.gartner.com/en/documents/3987450/hype-cycle-for-blockchaintechnologies-2020

Gupta, A., & Gupta, S. (2018). Blockchain technology: Application in Indian banking sector. *Delhi Business Review, 19*(2), 75-84. https://search.proquest.com/docview/2247499893?accountid=10007

Gupta, M. (2018). *Blockchain for dummies* (3rd ed.). John Wiley & Sons.

Hollebeek, L. D., Sharma, T. G., Pandey, R., Sanyal, P., & Clark, M. K. (2021) Fifteen years of customer engagement research: a bibliometric and network analysis. *Journal of Product & Brand Management*. https://centaur.reading.ac.uk/98973/ doi:10.1108/JPBM-01-2021-3301

Kamble, S., Gunasekaran, A., & Arha, H. (2019). Understanding the Blockchain technology adoption in supply chains-Indian context. *International Journal of Production Research*, *57*(7), 2009–2033. doi:10.1080/00207543.2018.1518610

Kamble, S., Gunasekaran, A., & Sharma, R. (2020). Modeling the blockchain enabled traceability in agriculture supply chain. *International Journal of Information Management*, *52*, 101967. doi:10.1016/j.ijinfomgt.2019.05.023

Kouhizadeh, M., Saberi, S., & Sarkis, J. (2021). Blockchain technology and the sustainable supply chain: Theoretically exploring adoption barriers. *International Journal of Production Economics*, *231*, 107831. doi:10.1016/j.ijpe.2020.107831

Kshetri, N. (2018). 1 Blockchain's roles in meeting key supply chain management objectives. *International Journal of Information Management*, *39*, 80–89. doi:10.1016/j.ijinfomgt.2017.12.005

Kumar, V., & Pansari, A. (2016). Competitive advantage through engagement. *JMR, Journal of Marketing Research, 53*(4), 497–514. doi:10.1509/jmr.15.0044

Kumar, V., Rajan, B., Gupta, S., & Dalla Pozza, I. (2019). Customer engagement in service. *Journal of the Academy of Marketing Science, 47*(1), 138–160. doi:10.100711747-017-0565-2

Kumar, V., & Ramachandran, D. (2020). (in press). Developing firms' growth approaches as a multidimensional decision to enhance key stakeholders' wellbeing. *International Journal of Research in Marketing*. doi:10.1016/j.ijresmar.2020.09.004

Murray, C. (2020). *What is Customer Engagement? Definition, Benefits, and Strategies for Success*. Outreach. https://www.outreach.io/blog/what-is-customer-engagement

Nakamoto, S. (2008). *Bitcoin: A Peer-to-Peer Electronic Cash System*. Bitcoin. https://bitcoin.org/bitcoin.pdf

NanoMatriX. (2022). *The Future of Customer Engagement with Blockchain*. NanoMatriX. https://www.nanomatrixsecure.com/the-future-of-customer-engagement-with-blockchain/

Narayanan, A., Bonneau, J., Felten, E., Miller, A., & Goldfeder, S. (2016). *Bitcoin and Cryptocurrency Technologies: A Comprehensive Introduction*. Princeton University Press.

Pansari, A., & Kumar, V. (2018). Customer engagement marketing. In R. Palmatier, V. Kumar, & C. Harmeling (Eds.), *Customer Engagement Marketing* (pp. 1–27). Springer. doi:10.1007/978-3-319-61985-9_1

Rejeb, A., Keogh, J. G., & Treiblmaier, H. (2020). How Blockchain Technology Can Benefit Marketing. *Six Pending Research Areas. Front. Blockchain, 3*, 3. doi:10.3389/fbloc.2020.00003

Schmidt, C. G., & Wagner, S. M. (2019). Blockchain and supply chain relations: A transaction cost theory perspective. *Journal of Purchasing and Supply Management, 25*(4), 100552. doi:10.1016/j.pursup.2019.100552

So, K., King, C., & Sparks, B. (2015). Customer Engagement with Tourism Brands: Scale Development and Validation. *Journal of Hospitality & Tourism Research (Washington, D.C.)*, 304–329.

Tapscott, D., & Tapscott, A. (2016). *Blockchain Revolution: How the technology behind Bitcoin is changing money, business, and the world*. Penguin.

Tapscott, D., & Tapscott, A. (2017). How Blockchain Will Change Organizations. *MIT Sloan Management Review*, *58*(2), 10–13.

Uncles, M. D., Dowling, G. R., & Hammond, K. (2003). Customer loyalty and customer loyalty programs. *Journal of Consumer Marketing*, *20*(4), 294–316. doi:10.1108/07363760310483676

Yli-Huumo, J., Ko, D., Choi, S., Park, S., & Smolander, K. (2016). Where Is Current Research on Blockchain Technology?-A Systematic Review. *PLoS One*, *11*(10), e0163477–e0163477. doi:10.1371/journal.pone.0163477 PMID:27695049

Zachariadis, M., Hileman, G., & Scott, S. V. (2019). Governance and control in distributed ledgers: Understanding the challenges facing blockchain technology in financial services. *Information and Organization*, *29*(2), 105–117. doi:10.1016/j.infoandorg.2019.03.001

Chapter 6
Constructing an E-Commerce Model Using the Framework of Blockchain

Chabi Gupta
https://orcid.org/0000-0002-1927-4349
Christ University, Bengaluru, India

ABSTRACT

Blockchain technology is gaining immense popularity in the realm of online e-commerce, advertising, and consumerism. This study aims to develop a model that comprehends how blockchain can act as a significant disruptor for various functions and applications related to e-commerce. The research explores the possibility that this technological advancement has the potential to revolutionize the core operations of e-commerce industry by providing trade connections devoid of trust or need for specialized intermediaries or central authority in case of permission less blockchains. Furthermore, it could facilitate equitable access to immutable data across supply chains which may result in a major reorganization pertaining to information and value exchanged between businesses involved in electronic commerce and their customers.

INTRODUCTION

The blockchain is a kind of distributed ledger technology that protects data so that it is impossible to manipulate it in any way. Because of this, it is exceptionally trustworthy for commercial use. Honestly, it's fairly comparable to how data is now stored by online retailers like Amazon and eBay. But with the distributed ledger technology

DOI: 10.4018/978-1-6684-7649-9.ch006

known as blockchain, the data is kept safely by each individual user. This indicates that there is no one place where all of the information can be kept at the same time. It is dispersed throughout. This indicates that anybody, at any moment, may access the information that is stored on the blockchain. The blockchain is most recognised for its role as the foundation of cryptocurrencies, but it also has a wide variety of other applications, many of which are applicable to online shopping (see Frey et al., 2016). The blockchain is a very remarkable technology that is gradually beginning to make its way into widespread use. Blockchain technology was first developed to serve as the foundation of the digital currency Bitcoin; however, it has since been accepted as a way of transforming whole sectors in addition to enhancing a broad variety of other fields and businesses (Jiang & Chen, 2021). In fact, the blockchain is currently being used as a tool to improve almost every facet of our lives, including but not limited to banking, healthcare, and online shopping. The blockchain is a decentralised data structure designed to securely, transparently, and verifiably record transactions. It is often referred to as a ledger system that is used to record various transactions. Typically, a blockchain is used to verify digital data. It operates by recording a hash of each transaction that is encrypted. Each block in the blockchain includes a hash of the block that came before it. This establishes a timestamp system that enables anybody to demonstrate the presence of information at a certain moment. A key benefit of blockchain is that it is hard to alter data once it has been recorded. It cannot be corrupted. This is one of the blockchain applications that the majority of people can comprehend and enjoy. Using blockchain technology, they can easily and transparently confirm that the item they're purchasing is what it claims to be (Kim & Kim, 2020). This implies that manufacturers and dealers cannot replace a lesser or more costly product for the one ordered. It also implies that one cannot return or get a replacement for a "fake" good. If the goods match what they bought, they will get them for sure. The blockchain is a decentralised ledger that may be used to record digital data. There are no gatekeepers since the ledger is decentralised, which makes the data more reliable. One can easily have authority over their own data. They have control over who can access their data, and no one can alter it. The blockchain is especially effective for supply chain management because it enables information to be transmitted along the supply chain without being altered or seen by outside parties (Lahkani et al., 2020). This implies that the blockchain may be used to guarantee that the items are obtained ethically, a problem that is crucial to many online businesses.

It is common knowledge that the internet purchasing experience is flawed. When a consumer makes a purchase on Amazon, for instance, they essentially believe that Amazon is their only option for that specific good. There is no assurance that they will get the goods, that they will match their prescribed specifications, or that they will be dispatched on time. However, due to blockchain, the online buying experience may soon be extraordinary. The blockchain is a digital ledger that may record transactions between two parties quickly, inexpensively, verifiably, and permanently (Kumar et al., 2020). By using this technology, consumers might determine precisely where their things are coming from, when they will arrive, and how much they will cost. In 2008, the blockchain was created with the aim of authenticating bitcoin transactions. The blockchain's underlying technology is no longer exclusive to bitcoin transactions. A blockchain is a distributed digital log of transactions that is stored on several computers. The blockchain is designed to be safe and is in the form of an open, distributed ledger that may record transactions between two parties in a post-verifiable, permanent, and efficient way (Li et al., 2020). Everyone on the network has access to the distributed ledger. It is the enabling technology for bitcoin and cryptocurrencies.

The concern of not knowing who consumers are purchasing from is one of the most frequent issues we hear about e-commerce. "Is this individual or organisation legitimate?" "Can I truly put my credit card information in their hands?" What plans do they have for my information? The good news is that there is a method to make e-commerce easier, safer, and more reliable for both customers and sellers. The blockchain is an online ledger that can be used to monitor transactions in a secure manner. The blockchain is the technology behind cryptocurrencies such as bitcoin, but it can also be used to monitor tangible items such as clothes that consumers purchase online (Liao & Shao, 2021). Companies such as Amazon, UPS, and FedEx are already using this rapid and dependable technology. Therefore, the aim of this chapter is to consider constructing an e-commerce model using the framework of blockchain.

LITERATURE REVIEW

Liu and Li (2020), advocated through their research that the blockchain system can enhance the business model of e-commerce, increase operational effectiveness, facilitate cross-border payments, and maintain the security of financial payments by using the technologies of distributed ledgers, consensus mechanisms, identification, smart contracts, and encryption algorithms, amongst others. A well-distributed digital storage system, timeseries and secure protocol data, astute execution of contracts, security, and privacy protection are some of the attributes that are found on a professional services platform that is built on blockchain technology. These features can also be discovered on a business process outsourcing launch pad that has been built on blockchain technology (Kumar et al., 2020). Ryan (2017) constructed a model for trustworthy systems using blockchain technology, such as those used in e-commerce. As consumers are taking a risk transacting online, additional measures of safety and security of transactions can make them purchase much more than their budgeted expenditure. The use of blockchain technology has the potential to increase the openness of financial dealings, improve the adaptability of system operations, and automate procedures. (Li et al., 2020) advocated that this will have a substantial influence on the business models of finance, accounting, and payment systems, banking, data storage, e-commerce, energy, and other related industries.

E-commerce that is based on the trending Internet of Things (IoT) is a fairly new kind of business model that operates via the use of autonomous transaction management on IoT devices (Jiang et al., 2021). The management system that is being used for e-commerce based on IoT models must be independent, neutral, easy, timely, and legitimate. Since blockchain is a cutting-edge technology that is capable of effectively controlling a decentralised network, e-commerce businesses use it to create a decentralised system for managing IoT e-commerce transactions. A consensus method is used to effectively negotiate the contents of the distributed ledger. Cryptographic algorithms and digital signatures are used inside the distributed ledger to guarantee the authenticity of e-commerce transactions (Treiblmaier et al., 2021).

Sector statistics can be employed to prove that blockchain is one of the most promising technologies that can improve online commerce (Lahkani, 2020). Some of the worries that have influenced people's willingness to do business online include ethical sourcing, product safety, and counterfeit goods (Jiang et al. 2019). E-commerce businesses study the usage of a blockchain-based method to ensure authenticity, using the capabilities of blockchains to track and trace transactions in order to solve the issues that have been raised (Li, 2020). In this strategy, they are able to assess the financial profitability that may be realised by resolving customer concerns about the legitimacy and safety of the product bought online (Zhu et al., 2019).

BLOCKCHAIN TECHNOLOGY (BCT)

As most of us are aware, blockchain is the technology directing the world-famous Bitcoin and other cryptocurrencies. However, as technology advances, there are more inventive methods to utilise it (Kim & Kim, 2020). Blockchain has been brought to the e-commerce sector in the form of a payments processor, where it can make online payments safe, transparent, and efficient. The blockchain is a decentralised, continuously updated database of transactions (Liu et al. 2018). This implies that a payment made on Amazon, for instance, does not need to go via a bank or other financial institution. The transaction will be recorded on the blockchain, where it will be accessible to everyone (Frey et al., 2016). The blockchain is a technology that enables the safe and trustworthy movement of data and information. It is a decentralised and distributed ledger capable of recording all types of transactions and all types of assets. The blockchain technology may be used by a variety of industries and marketplaces, including e-commerce. Liao & Shao (2021) in their discussion propagate the potential of blockchain to alter how individuals perceive and engage with online purchasing, as well as how business is conducted.

Figure 1. E-commerce model
Source: Liao and Shao (2021)

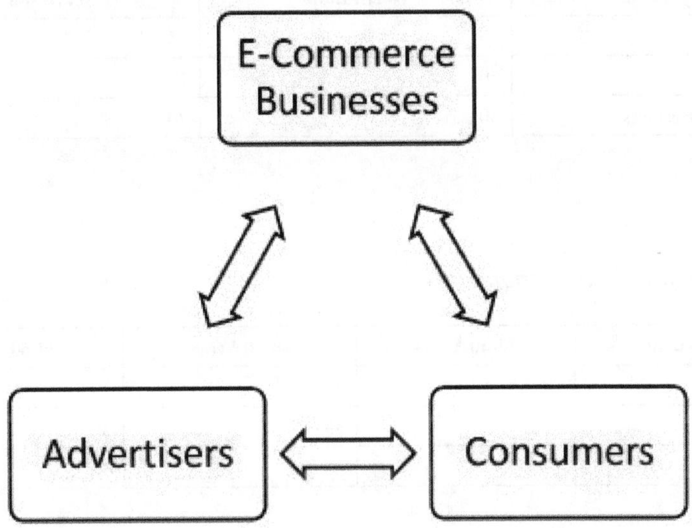

RESEARCH METHODOLOGY

This research explored the experience of online shopping among 400 randomly selected respondents who were online consumers, online advertisers, or e-commerce businesses. Consumers are subjected to a questionnaire where they scale their experience right from the time they log in to make a purchase to the time they actually make the purchase to the time it gets delivered up to expectations.

Table 1. Percentage of consumers, advertisers, and businesses who use online platform

Respondents	Number	Percentage
Consumers	150	37.5%
Advertisers	100	25%
E-Commerce Business	150	37.5%

Table 2. Number of respondents from North and South India

Respondents	North India	South India
Consumers	75	75
Advertisers	60	40
E-Commerce Business	80	70

Table 3. Age profile of respondents

Respondents	30-40 Years	40-50 Years	50-60 Years
Consumers	90	30	30
Advertisers	35	35	30
E-Commerce Business	70	40	40

OBSERVATIONS

Recent decentralised blockchain e-commerce solutions have facilitated the growth of e-commerce enterprises with enhanced security, traceability, and transparency, according to more than 93% of all respondents.

Even though the sector is already operating at a high level of efficiency, there are methods to improve it further, which is feasible with blockchain technology (65%).

The respondents, representing 95%, agreed with the observation that blockchain assists e-commerce enterprises in successfully managing data. They were of the opinion that in a blockchain network, the platforms may arrange information about users, items, orders, delivery, producers, sellers, and much more. Thus, 56% of all respondents also advocated the fact that blockchain is renowned for its security characteristics, which offer the e-commerce industry additional protection levels.

It eliminates middlemen and facilitates peer-to-peer transactions. Interestingly, 80% of consumers reported getting numerous more advantages, like rapid transactions, decreased chargeback fraud, verification of user evaluations, and tailored product offers. With traceability, blockchain ensures clients end-to-end product tracking. (40% advertisers). 75% of respondents informed me that people were now able to ultimately trace their orders in real-time and verify the validity of the merchandise themselves. 90% of respondents suggested that as blockchain technology becomes a major force in the global economy, it will benefit the e-commerce sector tremendously. E-commerce is one of the sectors using blockchain technology to ease financial transactions more often. 98% of advertisers said that the distributed ledger technology used by blockchains was now essential in resolving the problems plaguing the e-commerce industry. Regarding its relevance to e-commerce, blockchains have so much potential.

The most fascinating aspect of blockchain technology reported by 87% of respondents was that in e-commerce, it benefited both businesses and customers and this affirms the findings of Li et. (2020). It provided practical answers for cyber dangers and financial security issues. Additionally, it decreased costs associated with inventory management and payment processing.

Using blockchain technology, e-commerce enterprises were able to connect inventory management, payment processing, product descriptions, and photos with other company operations (66%). In exchange, businesses mostly incur fewer costs for the maintenance of operations and for paying IT support personnel to periodically monitor the systems. Bitcoin and other cryptocurrencies effectively lead to a reduction in the service costs charged by financial institutions to facilitate transactions (reported by 87% of advertisers and e-commerce businesses). The majority of e-commerce merchants (78%) struggled to stay up with their competitors and customers' escalating expectations especially in the last two years. In addition to these obstacles, they also ran the risk of losing crucial data pertaining to their business clients and losing millions of dollars due to cyber hacking and proxy transactions (reported by 56% e-commerce businesses).

Blockchain technology was advocated as ideal by 87% of e-commerce businesses (especially from North India), who responded by resolving these issues faced by online sellers. They agreed that, in the form of distributed ledgers, the technology provided the maximum levels of protection and security for e-commerce database management systems. Customers of e-commerce websites were also able to make quick online payments using blockchain technology such as Waves. (78%). As has been the situation for many decades, online shoppers needed to wait days or sometimes even months to make payments. Blockchains provided the consumers with the time and convenience they needed (89% of consumers). After paying the necessary fees, clients were able to have their shopping items transported immediately from end to end. 92% of e-commerce businesses found it astounding how blockchain technology enabled third-world nations to trade online. Due to Bitcoin's peer-to-peer structure, users in these nations did not need a third party to execute their payment requests. These technologies, however, enabled internet merchants to access consumer marketplaces even in developing markets. Thus, 87% of e-commerce businesses agreed that, though the technology is in its early days, blockchain is proliferating and will undoubtedly become the game changer in the upcoming years. From retail to e-commerce, investment firms, and the health care industry, block chain technology has the potential to revolutionise the way we do business by offering a secure method for transmitting information (87% of all respondents). The respondents were asked to choose the most important issue they thought was being tackled by the blockchain. The results were obtained as follows:

Table 4. Issues tackled by the blockchain

Issues	Consumers (Number)	Advertisers (Number)	E-Commerce Businesses (Number)
Intermediaries	35	15	35
Transparency	45	20	45
Decentralization	40	10	25
Data Security	10	20	15
Trust	10	10	15
Transactional Freedom	10	25	15
Total	**150**	**100**	**150**

The respondents were asked to choose among these uses of block chain, the most important one they experienced in their online transactions. The results were obtained as follows:

Table 5. Uses of blockchain for e-commerce

Uses	Consumers (Number)	Advertisers (Number)	E-Commerce Businesses (Number)
Lower costs overall	10	9	23
B2B transaction ecosystems	15	13	12
Borderless Payments	10	6	10
Crypto Payments	10	4	11
Protection from Chargeback Fraud	8	16	12
Block chain and Crypto Linked Social Payments	6	10	12
Restoring Ownership of Marketing Data	13	10	13
Cutting out dealers and middlemen	16	5	9
Accelerated and Simplified Card/Network payments	17	7	9
Restoring Control over Purchasing Data	10	5	14
Decentralized Cross Border Trade	10	10	10
Better Payment Gateways	25	5	15
Total	**150**	**100**	**150**

How Does Blockchain Work?

1. Mrs. K would like to make a financial contribution to ABC Ltd.
2. The transaction is shown as a block when viewed on the website.
3. The block is then sent out to all of the networks for distribution.
4. The transaction is given the green light by the network.
5. After that, the block is added to the block chain that already exists.
6. The transaction is carried out successfully and is now final.

Most e-commerce businesses (89%) reported encountering functional or operational challenges, such as sluggish transactions, a lack of trust, digital data ownership, and inadequate procedures. The use of blockchain technology does help an e-commerce platform build trust in online transfers (67% of advertisers). Using bitcoin, businesses are able to implement a safe, precise, and speedy payment mechanism in any venture (85% of e-commerce businesses).

Figure 2. Region-wise blockchain usage

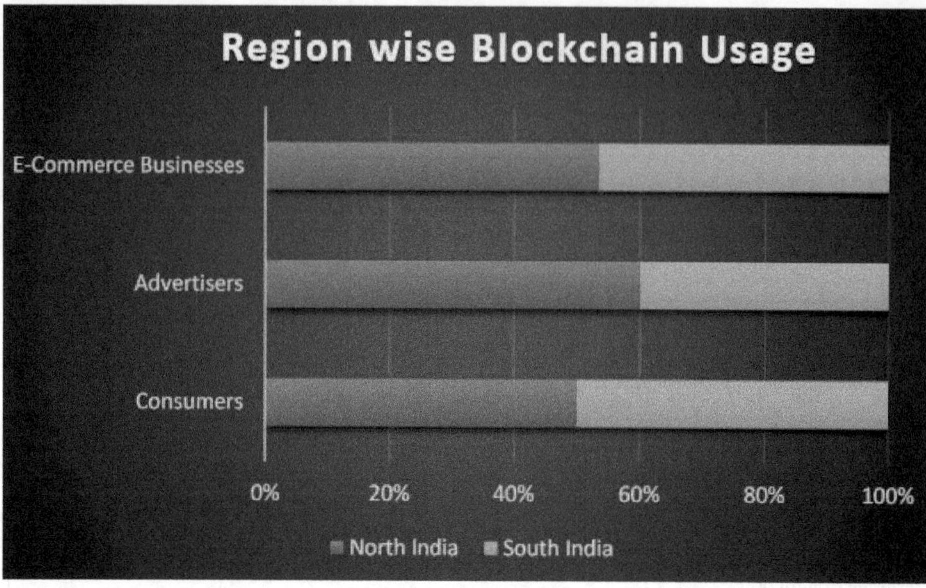

Supply chain management is a problem faced by most e-commerce companies (89% of e-commerce businesses). However, blockchain is solving several supply chain management pain points, including recordkeeping, product tracking, and inventory monitoring (43% of e-commerce businesses). RFID tags and integrated sensors are facilitating recordkeeping and traceability. Any outlier is easily identified. Additionally, many advertisers (78%) reported utilising blockchain technology for marketing and promotional operations online. For instance, incentive points may be added for certain consumers when they hit a certain purchasing threshold. In addition, advertisers often encourage consumers to end up spending much more by offering them customised discounts and special occasion offers (40% advertisers).

THE ROAD AHEAD

Components of blockchain technology, application programming interfaces for blockchain, and blockchain applications are all part of the blockchain network. The applications that are based on distributed ledger technology include procurement finance, e-commerce enabling transactions, product traceability and inventory, user credit systems, wealth management systems, trust systems, clean infrastructure, and many more (Zhou et al., 2021). It does this by constructing an innovative and secure trade settlement system, a payment mechanism, and a robust trust system for online business, all of which are based on blockchain technology.

The following are some of the business scenarios in which we construct a model to implement blockchain technology for e-commerce.

(1) The online platform is realised using blockchain technology for proof certification. To achieve evidence collection from vital documents during the whole process, the essential information is written to the blockchain.
(2) The clearing and settlement of payments using blockchain technology results in increased operational efficiency for all stakeholders.
(3) A realistic application for financing the supply chain based on blockchain technology has been completed by most e-commerce businesses.
(4) A cost-effective model for a blockchain-based trust system has been realised by consumers and advertisers.
(5) E-commerce utilises blockchain technology in the transaction auction process to record the periodic default events concerning both consumers and suppliers, therefore providing a foundation for credit assessment.

It is favourable to boosting social and economic efficiency, maintaining financial security, and strengthening the core competence of the entire system to construct a model based on blockchain technology for e-commerce. The accuracy of credit evaluations is considerably improved by blockchain, as is the clarity of data ownership, the scope of coverage of credit evaluation, guaranteeing the security of records and protecting users' privacy, and other similar services offered by e-commerce. The blockchain approach ensures that the data cannot be altered in any way for all consumers, advertisers, and e-commerce businesses. The effectiveness of synergy is therefore increased manifold. It also creates a brand-new fundamental e-commerce groundwork and offers assistance for the establishment of a trust system. E-commerce transactions, payment clearing, and international payments all benefit from the expediency, accountability, and resiliency offered by blockchain. Transactions and payments made across international borders using blockchain technology take place in real time and are fully automated and seamless, thereby offering consumers a chance to also transact globally online.

REFERENCES

Frey, R., Wörner, D., & Ilic, A. (2016). *Collaborative filtering on the blockchain: a secure recommender system for e-commerce*. Academic Press.

Jiang, J., & Chen, J. (2021). Framework of blockchain-supported e-commerce platform for small and medium enterprises. *Sustainability (Basel)*, *13*(15), 8158. doi:10.3390u13158158

Jiang, Y., Wang, C., Wang, Y., & Gao, L. (2019, February). A privacy-preserving e-commerce system based on the blockchain technology. In *2019 IEEE International Workshop on Blockchain Oriented Software Engineering (IWBOSE)* (pp. 50-55). IEEE. 10.1109/IWBOSE.2019.8666470

Kim, S. I., & Kim, S. H. (2020). E-commerce payment model using blockchain. *Journal of Ambient Intelligence and Humanized Computing*, 1–13.

Kumar, G., Saha, R., Buchanan, W. J., Geetha, G., Thomas, R., Rai, M. K., & Alazab, M. (2020). Decentralized accessibility of e-commerce products through blockchain technology. *Sustainable Cities and Society*, *62*, 102361. doi:10.1016/j.scs.2020.102361

Lahkani, M. J., Wang, S., Urbański, M., & Egorova, M. (2020). Sustainable B2B E-commerce and blockchain-based supply chain finance. *Sustainability (Basel)*, *12*(10), 3968. doi:10.3390u12103968

Li, M., Shao, S., Ye, Q., Xu, G., & Huang, G. Q. (2020). Blockchain-enabled logistics finance execution platform for capital-constrained E-commerce retail. *Robotics and Computer-integrated Manufacturing*, *65*, 101962. doi:10.1016/j.rcim.2020.101962

Li, S. (2020). Structure optimization of e-commerce platform based on artificial intelligence and blockchain technology. *Wireless Communications and Mobile Computing*, *2020*, 2020. doi:10.1155/2020/8825825

Liao, Q., & Shao, M. (2021). Discussion on payment application in cross-border e-commerce platform from the perspective of blockchain. In *E3S Web of Conferences* (Vol. 235, p. 03020). EDP Sciences. doi:10.1051/e3sconf/202123503020

Liu, C., Xiao, Y., Javangula, V., Hu, Q., Wang, S., & Cheng, X. (2018). NormaChain: A blockchain-based normalized autonomous transaction settlement system for IoT-based E-commerce. *IEEE Internet of Things Journal*, *6*(3), 4680–4693. doi:10.1109/JIOT.2018.2877634

Liu, Z., & Li, Z. (2020). A blockchain-based framework of cross-border e-commerce supply chain. *International Journal of Information Management*, *52*, 102059. doi:10.1016/j.ijinfomgt.2019.102059

Ryan, P. A. (2017). Smart contract relations in e-commerce: Legal implications of exchanges conducted on the blockchain. *Technology Innovation Management Review*, *7*(10), 14–21. doi:10.22215/timreview/1110

Treiblmaier, H., & Sillaber, C. (2021). The impact of blockchain on e-commerce: A framework for salient research topics. *Electronic Commerce Research and Applications*, *48*, 101054. doi:10.1016/j.elerap.2021.101054

Zhou, Z., Wang, M., Yang, C. N., Fu, Z., Sun, X., & Wu, Q. J. (2021). Blockchain-based decentralized reputation system in E-commerce environment. *Future Generation Computer Systems*, *124*, 155–167. doi:10.1016/j.future.2021.05.035

Zhu, X., & Wang, D. (2019, April). Research on blockchain application for E-commerce, finance and energy. *IOP Conference Series. Earth and Environmental Science*, *252*(4), 042126. doi:10.1088/1755-1315/252/4/042126

Chapter 7
Initial Coin Offerings as a Form of Alternative Financing for Start-Ups:
A Systematic Literature Review and Bibliometric Analysis

S. Baranidharan
https://orcid.org/0000-0002-7780-4045
School of Business and Management, Christ University, India

ABSTRACT

This chapter aims to provide a comprehensive overview of the field of initial coin offerings ICOs as a form of alternative financing for start-ups. Through a systematic literature review and bibliometric analysis, the study explores the current understanding of ICOs, the potential uses of fractional ownership of digital assets, and the opportunities and challenges associated with this form of fundraising. The study also highlights the importance of study, which provided the first comprehensive explanation of ICOs and their characteristics. The findings of the research suggest that ICOs have the potential to revolutionize the way start-ups raise funds, but they also present significant challenges and risks. The study encourages further research to continue exploring the opportunities and challenges presented by ICOs, as well as the potential impact of regulatory and legal frameworks on the ICO market. Overall, this chapter provides valuable insights into the complex and evolving topic of ICOs and their implications for start-ups, investors, and the broader economy.

DOI: 10.4018/978-1-6684-7649-9.ch007

INTRODUCTION

Start-up firms can face challenges in acquiring funds for their operations and management. The literature indicates that private financial markets, such as peer-to-peer lending, are often used by investors to share assets among different loans, and this can be particularly beneficial with the development of technology. However, it can be difficult for Start-ups to acquire financial support from traditional sources like banks and financial institutions because of asymmetrical information and vague business plans. Many Start-ups turn to alternative financing methods such as venture capital and angel investors, which are supported by governments and public agencies through acceleration programs and research grants, among others. Even with these options, some Start-ups still encounter difficulties in the fundraising stage due to venture capitalists' uncertainty of the Start-up's ability to create value in the future.

However, even with support from various agencies, some Start-ups still encounter difficulties in the fundraising stages. A key issue in this regard is that venture capitalists may have difficulty envisioning how Start-ups will create value in the future. This means that only certain sectors of business may be able to attract private investment.

In light of these challenges, it is suggested in this exploratory discussion that the digital environment can be used to promote and communicate the value of particular businesses, and that a digital asset exchange market can facilitate this possibility. The current study examines how the concept of Initial Coin Offerings (ICOs) can be used by Start-ups to access finance in the digital environment.

This study argues that the digital environment can help overcome these challenges by providing a way for Start-ups to communicate and promote their value to potential investors through a digital asset exchange market. The study examines how Initial Coin Offerings (ICOs) can be used to access finance, as well as the legal and regulatory environment surrounding digital assets that need to be considered. It also looks into the concept of fractional ownership of digital assets as a way for Start-ups to raise funds by sharing ownership of their assets among multiple parties. The study also acknowledges that while majority of the research around ICOs focus on cryptocurrency and its effect on speculation, The concept of tokenization, issuing digital coin/tokens to acquire funds from the public is getting traction as well. The difficulties that Start-up firms may face in obtaining funding for their operations and management. The text references the private financial market, specifically peer-to-peer lending, which is commonly used by investors to share assets among different loans. The advancement of technology in this field can lead to improved investment opportunities. The source cited in the passage, Babaei and Bamdad (2020), likely provides more information on the specific ways in which technology has improved the peer-to-peer lending process for investors.

This passage continues to discuss the challenges Start-up firms may face in acquiring funding. It states that Start-up firms typically acquire financial support for their business operations and management in a similar way, but they may encounter difficulties due to asymmetrical information and vague business plans. Asymmetrical information refers to a situation where one party has more or better information than the other. In the context of Start-up firms seeking funding, it could mean that the investors or funding sources have more information about the industry, market, or the Start-up itself, which might make it difficult for the Start-up to secure funding. The reference to vague business plans refers to an unclear or underdeveloped plan for how the Start-up intends to create value, generate revenue, or achieve profitability, it can also be challenging for them to secure funding from potential investors or funding sources. The source cited in this passage, Awaya and Krishna (2021), likely provides more information about the specific ways in which asymmetrical information and vague business plans can be a barrier for Start-ups in their quest for funding. The issues of asymmetrical information and vague business plans, it's frequently hard for start-up firms to secure financial support from banks and other financial institutions. It references to a study by Chen & Chen, (2020) which likely provides more detailed information about this issue and how it affects the ability of start-up firms to secure funding from traditional financial institutions. The study might have also explained reasons behind it and how frequent this difficulty is.

Many Start-up firms find alternative funding sources, such as venture capital and angel investors, in order to overcome the difficulties of obtaining financial support from traditional banks and financial institutions. The reference to Davila, Foster, & Gupta (2003) likely provides more information on the specific ways in which venture capital and angel investors have become important funding sources for Start-ups, and how it compares to traditional methods. It also gives a background of when this trend started, as the date is 2003.

Venture capital and angel investors are often supported by governments and public agencies through various means, such as acceleration programs that aid in the firms' strategic growth, research grants and national innovation systems. This is mentioned as being true in many countries, and it is backed up by the studies cited, such as Bustamante (2019), Islam, Fremeth, & Marcus (2018), and Richter, Jackson, & Schildhauer (2018). These studies likely provide more information on how and to what extent governments and public agencies are supporting venture capital and angel investment as an alternative funding source for Start-up firms and the specific programs, grants and systems used to do so.

Although some start-up firms may be able to obtain support from various government and public agencies, it may not be enough. Some Start-up founders still encounter difficulties in the fundraising stages. The source cited, Cao, Chen, Fu, & Mao, 202ists, likely provides more information on the difficulties that some

Start-up firms may face even with the support of government and public agencies, and the extent to which this occurs. it may also suggest some potential reasons why they still have difficulties and how frequent the difficulties.

Venture capitalists face when investing in start-ups, which is the difficulty of predicting how the Start-up will create value in the future. This is because of their inability to envision it. This statement is supported by the study by Köseoğlu & Almeany (2020), which likely provides more information on this issue, how common it is and the reasons behind it. It might also give some insights on the venture capital industry's perception and the challenges they face in evaluating start-ups and making investment decisions.

The study of Köhn (2018) is cited as support for this statement, and it provides more information on how the potential value of a Start-up can be effectively communicated through a business model and how it can convince investors. It also implies that if this perception is true, it may limit the sectors of business that can benefit from venture capital investments, since only Start-ups that can effectively communicate their value and potential through a convincing business model would be able to raise money from venture capitalists.

They argue that the digital environment can be used to overcome these challenges, by providing a platform for businesses to promote and communicate their value, and establish and exchange digital assets. This can improve the overall business ecosystem and increase opportunities for related entities. By enabling all entities to communicate their value in this way, the demand and supply for products, services and other intangibles can be met, and a digital asset exchange market could be used to facilitate this process. It is not clear whether the discussion has a clear plan to show how it will happen but the idea is to explore the possibility of using the digital environment to improve the funding process for Start-up firms.

The Internet of Things (IoT) can be used to support Start-up firms to raise funds through the process of Initial Coin Offerings (ICOs). This idea is based on the suggestion of a prior study by O'Leary (2013). The study is considering the potential ways of using digital assets to create value, and acknowledges that in order for this to happen, the legal and regulatory environment surrounding digital assets must be understood and developed. It also notes that recently, some countries have begun revising their regulations to support a digital exchange market. This is likely a key focus of the study, and the authors of this work likely provide more information on how IoT can support start-up firms in the process of ICO and how it can be used to create value. The authors also examine the legal and regulatory environment surrounding digital assets and how it can be developed, as well as the evolution of laws and regulations in some countries to support digital assets' exchange markets.

Adhami, Giudici, & Martinazzi (2018) found that ICOs were a new and innovative way to raise capital, but that they also come with a number of risks. They also found that ICOs are more likely to be successful if they had a clear and concise white paper, a strong team, and a well-defined roadmap. Boreiko & Risteski (2020) found that ICOs were more risky investment than traditional securities, but that they also had the potential to generate higher returns. They also found that ICOs were more likely to be successful if they were conducted by experienced teams and had a strong track record. Schückes & Gutmann (2020) found that ICOs are a disruptive technology that was changing the way that companies raise capital. They also found that ICOs had the potential to democratize access to investment opportunities and to create new markets..

This is an important point as it highlights one of the key features of ICOs, which is that they involve the issuance of digital assets in the form of tokens to raise capital. The paragraph also mentions that a number of studies have examined how digital currency is traded and how blockchain technology is used in the process of ICOs. It also highlights that some studies have looked into determinants of success in ICOs, providing examples of specific studies (Gächter and Gächter (2020); Samieifar and Baur (2020); Moro and Wang (2019); An, Duan, Hou, and Xu (2019); Howell, Niessner, and Yermack (2020); Adhami et al. (2018)) that have looked into this topic. This give an idea of the authors are basing their study on the previous studies done on the topic of ICO.

It states that a review of prior studies about digital assets indicates that the majority of ICO studies focus on cryptocurrency, specifically mentioning research on Bitcoin and Ethereum (Nolan, Dartley, Baker, ReVeal, & Rinearson, 2018). It also highlights that these studies tend to discuss the effects of cryptocurrency on speculation (Kyriazis, 2019). This is an important point as it gives a sense of the context in which this research is being conducted and what kind of research on digital assets and ICOs has been done in the past. This also points out that majority of the studies done on ICOs focus on cryptocurrency and its effects which gives indication that the field is quite new and not much research has been done on the topic.

The literature review will summarize prior research on ICOs and digital assets and review pertinent laws and regulations in different countries. The paper will also propose potential examples of how fractional ownership of digital assets could work and consider the possibility of a digital asset exchange market. The findings will provide significant insights into the opportunities and challenges of ICOs, as well as the types of ICOs and their impacts on Start-ups. Based on this exploratory discussion, the paper will raise a number of questions for investigation in future research. This contribution to the field is important as it aims to understand better the potential of ICOs in providing alternative funding for start-ups and its potential in creating a digital exchange market which can enhance the business ecosystem and increase opportunities for related entities.

Initial Coin Offerings (ICOs) as an alternative form of financing for Start-up firms. It undertakes a systematic literature review in combination with bibliometric analysis to contribute to this somewhat novel field. Prior research on ICOs and digital assets is summarized and pertinent laws and regulations in different countries are reviewed. The article then proposes potential examples of how fractional ownership of digital assets could work and considers the possibility of a digital asset exchange market. The findings provide significant insights into the opportunities and challenges of ICOs, as well as the types of ICOs and their impacts on Start-ups. Based on this exploratory discussion, this paper raises a number of questions for investigation in future research.

The article then proposes potential examples of how fractional ownership of digital assets could work and considers the possibility of a digital asset exchange market. The findings provide significant insights into the opportunities and challenges of ICOs, as well as the types of ICOs and their impacts on Start-ups. Based on this exploratory discussion, this paper raises a number of questions for investigation in future research (Adhami et al., 2018).

It allows multiple parties to access and update the same information simultaneously, providing transparency and security to the transactions made on the network (Adhami et al., 2018). This is the reason why the blockchain technology is being used as the underlying infrastructure for initial coin offerings (ICOs). The use of blockchain technology in ICOs allows for the creation of digital assets, known as tokens, that can be bought and sold on a digital asset exchange market (O'Leary, 2018). This opens up new opportunities for Start-ups to raise funds by selling tokens that represent a stake in their business, rather than traditional forms of fundraising such as venture capital and angel investment (Adhami et al., 2018). In conclusion, the combination of blockchain technology and ICOs provide a new and innovative way for Start-ups to access funds and navigate the challenges they often face in the traditional financing market.

Additionally, section six provides recommendations for future research in the area of ICOs. Overall, this paper aims to provide a comprehensive understanding of the current state of ICOs in commerce and business, and to identify potential opportunities and challenges for both companies and investors. By highlighting the need for further research in specific areas, this paper aims to contribute to the development of the ICO field and to help shape the future of cryptocurrency markets.

INITIAL COIN OFFERINGS

ICOs have been widely used in various industries such as fintech, e-commerce, and gaming (Toma & Cerchiello, 2020). According to a study by KPMG (2018), the fintech industry is the most active sector in terms of ICOs, with 31% of total ICOs taking place in this industry. However, other industries such as e-commerce and gaming are also increasingly turning to ICOs as a fundraising mechanism.

Despite the growing popularity of ICOs, there are also concerns about their risks and regulatory challenges. For example, some ICOs have been found to be fraudulent or have failed to deliver on their promises (KPMG, 2018). Additionally, the lack of regulatory oversight has raised concerns about the potential for financial crime and money laundering (Boreiko & Sahdev, 2018).

Overall, ICOs have the potential to revolutionize the way businesses raise funds, particularly for early-stage Start-ups and SMEs. However, there are also important risks and challenges that need to be addressed to ensure the long-term success of this fundraising mechanism. Further research is needed to better understand the specific opportunities and challenges of ICOs in different industries, as well as the potential regulatory solutions to mitigate risks.

Adhami et al. (2018) explain the importance of ICOs to business activity for at least three reasons. First, by adopting innovative blockchain based technologies it is possible to lower capital raising costs and to avoid intermediaries. Furthermore, ICOs encourage open-source project development and decentralized business, as well as providing a built-in customer base and favorable network effects. Finally, unlike conventional financing contracts that are essentially illiquid, ICOs allow funders to build a secondary market for their investments. Fisch et al. (2021) surveyed 517 investors about their reasons for investing in ICOs and found that they are motivated by ideological, technological, and investment incentives. They discovered that risk attitude, opinions on regulation and the white paper's relevance differ significantly among investors. Hall & Lerner (2009) claim that, in comparison to traditional financing instruments, the benefits of well-designed ICOs are greater security, liquidity and transparency. However, there are certain issues with ICOs including asymmetric information, absence of investor protection, and the lack of regulation. The essential legal concern with ICO tokens is whether they have the status of securities, which would trigger various regulatory requirements and delays for issuers.

Overall, it is clear that ICOs have the potential to revolutionize the way businesses raise funds, but also come with a set of risks and challenges. The success of an ICO depends on various factors such as the type of token being issued, the project's potential, and the investors' motivations. Furthermore, the regulatory environment is a critical aspect to be considered when assessing the potential of an ICO. Overall, the literature suggests that further research is needed to better understand the potential and challenges of ICOs as a fundraising mechanism for businesses. In the real estate industry, ICOs can be used to raise funds for the development of new projects. Instead of traditional methods of raising capital such as bank loans or private equity, companies can use ICOs to raise funds from a global investor base.

The ICO process allows investors to purchase tokens that represent a stake in the development project, and these tokens can be traded on cryptocurrency exchanges after the ICO is completed. This can provide liquidity for investors and allows them to exit their investment at any time.

Furthermore, blockchain technology can be used to create a decentralized platform for the management and ownership of real estate assets, allowing for a more transparent and efficient process for buying, selling and renting properties.

Moreover, having a blockchain-based system for property transactions can also decrease the cost of intermediaries, such as real estate agents and lawyers, thus reducing the overall cost of transactions and making it more accessible for small investors.

However, the real estate industry is still in the early stages of understanding and implementing the use of ICOs and blockchain technology. Further research is needed to identify the opportunities and challenges of using ICOs in the real estate industry, and to develop practical solutions that can be used to implement these technologies in the market. as explained in the discussion in Money and Bank Thailand (2020) and Open-Tec (2019).

Table 1. Information regarding digital asset and ICO laws and regulation in different countries

Country	Laws & Regulations	Digital Asset Sold	Related laws for Digital Asset Exchange	Different Phases of Token Development	Related Agency	References
Switzerland	FINMA Guidance 04/2017 Regulatory Treatment of Initial Coin Offering Guideline for Enquiries Regarding the Regulatory Framework for Initial Coin Offering	Cryptocurrency Payment token Utility token Asset token	Financial Market Infrastructure Act (FMIA) Stock Exchange Act (SESTA) Banking Act (BA) Anti-Money Laundering Act (AMLA)	Pre-financing Pre- sale/ voucher phase Pre-operating phase Operating phase	The Swiss Financial Market Supervisor Authority (FINMA)	FINMA (2017) Mckenzie (2018) Wenger&Vieli (2019)
United States of America	Federal securities law	Cryptocurrency	Securities Exchange Act of 1934	Howey test	The US Securities and Exchange Commission (SEC) Financial Crimes Enforcement Network (FinCEN)	CFTC (2015) CFCT (2017)

Table 1: The laws and regulations for ICOs vary greatly between countries. Switzerland, for example, has a clear regulatory framework in place with guidelines

set out by the Swiss Financial Market Supervisor Authority (FINMA). The FINMA guidance 04/2017 classifies ICOs into three categories: cryptocurrency, payment token, and utility token and asset token, and regulates them accordingly under existing laws such as the Financial Market Infrastructure Act (FMIA) and the Anti-Money Laundering Act (AMLA).

In contrast, the United States does not have a specific set of regulations for ICOs, but rather relies on federal securities laws and the Howey test to determine whether an ICO should be regulated as a security. The US Securities and Exchange Commission (SEC) and the Financial Crimes Enforcement Network (FinCEN) are responsible for enforcing these laws. It's worth noting that regulations for ICOs are changing and evolving rapidly. The above-mentioned countries are just an example, it's crucial for companies and investors to be aware of the laws and regulations in their own country and to consult with a legal professional before launching an ICO.

In addition to traditional financial markets, such as stocks and bonds, digital assets have the potential to open up new opportunities for fundraising and investment. Countries that have developed laws and regulations related to digital assets, such as the United States and Thailand, have recognized the potential of digital assets to create value and generate money in the private financial market.

However, it is important to note that the development of laws and regulations for digital assets is still in its early stages, and there is still much to be done to ensure that these markets are safe and secure for investors. Additionally, there is a need for further research to identify other types of digital assets that could be used to raise funds in different areas, such as real estate, art, and other forms of tangible assets.

Overall, the development of digital asset laws and regulations is crucial for the growth and stability of these markets. It is important for businesses and investors to stay informed about the laws and regulations in their own country and to consult with legal professionals before engaging in any digital asset transactions.

RESEARCH METHODOLOGY

The data collected from the bibliometric analysis was analyzed using various tools such as VOSviewer, and Excel. These tools were used to create visual representations of the data, such as network maps, cluster maps, and histograms. These visualizations were used to identify patterns and trends in the literature, such as the most frequently cited papers, the most productive authors and institutions, and the main research themes.

The systematic review process included the following steps:

- Identifying the research question and objectives of the study

- Defining the inclusion and exclusion criteria for the literature search
- Searching for relevant literature in databases such as Web of Science and Scopus
- Screening the literature for relevance and eligibility
- Extracting and synthesizing data from the selected literature
- Assessing the quality of the literature based on the criteria established in the inclusion and exclusion criteria

The results of the bibliometric analysis were then combined with the systematic literature review to provide a comprehensive understanding of the current state of the research on ICOs. The results were used to answer the research questions and to identify potential areas for future research. The methodology used in this study is a suitable approach for analyzing the research on ICOs as it allows for a comprehensive and systematic examination of the literature. The use of bibliometric analysis in combination with a systematic literature review provides a valuable tool for identifying patterns and trends in the literature and for identifying areas for further investigation.

Overall, the methodology used in this study allows for a comprehensive and systematic examination of the research on ICOs, providing valuable insights into the current state of the field and identifying areas for future research.

In The Initial Stage of This Study, a variety of computerized databases were utilized to conduct a comprehensive review of the concept of Initial Coin Offerings (ICOs). These databases included ABI/INFORM Complete, Emerald, Science Direct (Elsevier), Scopus, ProQuest Management, Google Scholar, and JSTOR. The search process included dissertations, theses, and conference papers that were related to the focus of the study. A combination of keywords associated with ICO and Start-ups was used to find relevant studies. The total number of studies found was 335.

Stage 2: Study Selection, the next step was to assess the relevance of the studies found in stage 1. This was done by reviewing the abstracts and titles of the articles, and excluding those that were not relevant to the focus of this study. The studies that were excluded include those that did not have a clear connection to ICO and its business relevance, those that were not in English, and those that were not peer-reviewed articles. This process resulted in a total of 272 articles that were selected for further analysis.

Keywords; Start-ups, Barriers, Accessing financing, Traditional sources of financing, Initial coin offerings (ICOs), Alternative financing mechanisms, Synthetized overview, Research on ICOs, Systematic literature review, Bibliometric analysis, Digital assets, Laws and regulations, Fractional ownership of digital assets, Digital asset exchange market, Opportunities and challenges, Types of ICOs, Impact on Start-ups, Future research

Stage 3: Data Extraction, the data from the selected articles was extracted and analyzed. This included information such as the authors, publication date, keywords, and the main findings and conclusions of the studies. This data was then organized in a spreadsheet for further analysis.

Stage 4: Quality Assessment, the final step was to assess the quality of the studies that were selected. This was done by reviewing the methodology and sample size of the studies, as well as their conclusions and findings. The studies that met the criteria established in the inclusion and exclusion criteria were deemed to be of high quality and were included in the final analysis.

Overall, this study used a systematic and rigorous methodology to review the literature on the concept of ICO and its business relevance. By using a variety of databases and combination keywords, a large number of relevant studies were found and analyzed, ensuring the validity and reliability of the results.

The analysis process in this study consisted of four stages:

Database Selection And Initial Search: Various computerized databases were used to search for relevant studies related to the concept of Initial Coin Offerings (ICOs) and their relevance to business areas. A combination of keywords was used, and 334 studies were found.

Performing a scoping search: The scoping search was important to select the articles that match the aims of the current study, which focuses on the benefits of ICOs to business. Inclusion criteria were established, including papers that focus on topics such as ICOs, tokens, digital assets, tokenization, fractional ownership, Start-ups, decentralization, whitepapers, blockchain, and smart contracts. Exclusion criteria were also established, including papers that focus on centralized systems and large-sized firms.

Selecting full-text papers: After analysing the abstracts of the studies, only 45 studies were reviewed systematically. Only 33 studies were identified as applicable after reading the full texts.

Analysis: The selected articles were organized in consecutive order, and a structured approach was used to analyse the data. The analysis consisted of three main sections: the classification of the area analysed in the studies, the discussion of the opportunities and challenges of ICOs from a financial perspective, and the review of the impacts of ICO

RESULTS

Network Analysis

Citation analysis is a bibliometric method that measures the impact of a publication by counting the number of times it is cited by other publications (Ding & Cronin, 2011). In this study, a citation analysis is applied to perform a network analysis of the existing literature on ICOs. This approach allows us to identify the most influential papers and authors in the field, and to understand the relationships between different papers and authors.

The network analysis is based on the co-citation relationships between publications. Co-citation is a measure of the similarity between two publications based on the overlap of their citing articles (Small, 1973). The co-citation relationships are represented as links between nodes, where the nodes represent the publications and the links represent the co-citation relationships. The resulting network can be visualized and analyzed to identify patterns and structures in the literature. This approach allows us to identify the most influential papers and authors in the field of ICOs, and to understand the relationships between different papers and authors. Furthermore, network analysis can be used to identify clusters of closely related papers, which can help to identify the main topics and research areas in the field.

Overall, the application of a citation and network analysis allows us to gain a deeper understanding of the existing literature on ICOs and to identify the most influential papers and authors in the field.

A co-citation network is a visualization tool used to analyze the relationships between publications in a field of research. It consists of a set of nodes representing journal articles and a set of edges or linkages representing the co-occurrence of the nodes, that is articles in other papers (Leydesdorff, 2011). This means that two publications are considered to be co-cited when they appear together in the reference lists of other documents. Papers that are more frequently cited together are more likely to be linked or to study the same subject.

The co-citation network can be used to explore the structure of the data, and to identify patterns and trends in the literature. For example, in the context of this study, it can be used to identify the most frequently cited papers and authors in the field of ICOs.

As illustrated in Fig. 1, authors Fisch and Adhami are authors that are most often cited together, indicating that their research is closely related. Additionally, as shown in Fig. 2, authors Fisch and Momtaz are among the most cited authors, indicating that their research has had a significant impact on the field of ICOs.

Overall, the co-citation network is a useful tool for analyzing the relationships between publications in a field of research, and for identifying the most influential papers and authors in the field. By analyzing the co-citation network, it is possible to gain a deeper understanding of the structure of the data and to identify the main research areas and topics in the field.

Figure 1. Co-citation network
Source: ABI/INFORM Complete, Emerald, Science Direct (Elsevier), Scopus, ProQuest Management, Google Scholar, and JSTOR and Computed in VOSviewer.

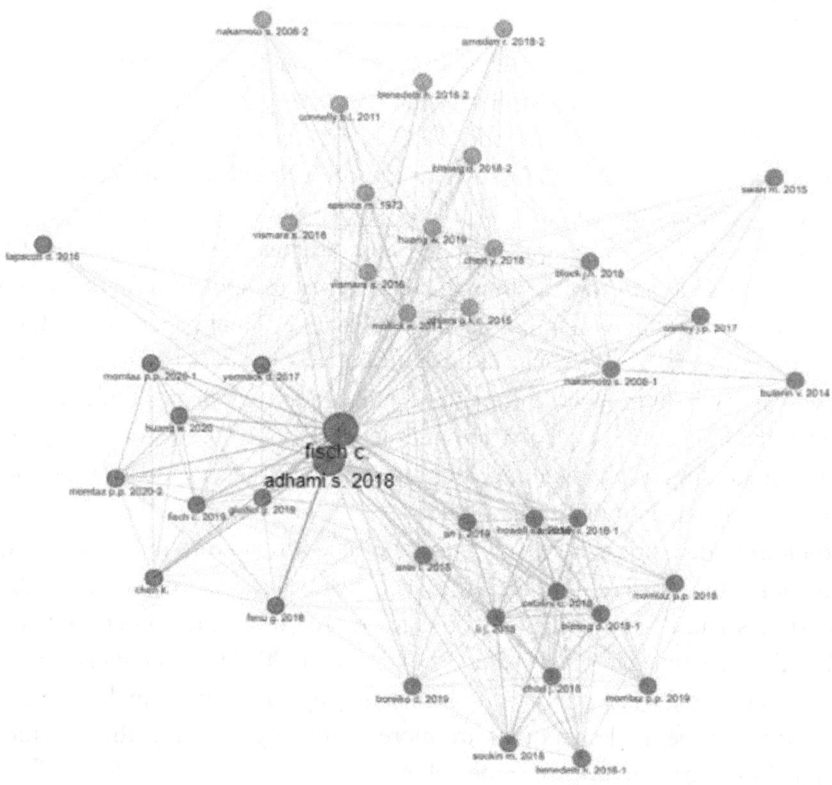

Figure 2. Historical direct citation network
Source: ABI/INFORM Complete, Emerald, Science Direct (Elsevier), Scopus, ProQuest Management, Google Scholar, and JSTOR and Computed in VOSviewer

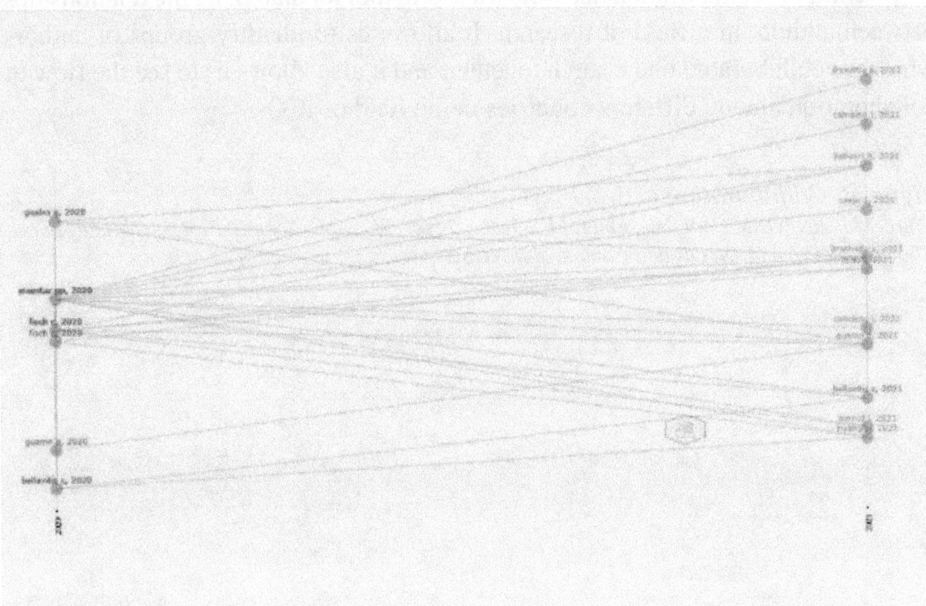

The collaboration network is a visualization tool used to analyze the relationships between authors in a field of research. It indicates the presence of 11 clusters, as shown in Figure 3. These clusters represent groups of authors who have collaborated on research papers together.

In cluster 1 (3 authors, blue), the most productive and strongly collaborative authors include Thompson, Swammy and Loh. They have collaborated on multiple papers together and have a strong connection in the research field. In cluster 2 (4 authors, orange), the most productive authors include Urbach, Regner, Schweizer and G. Fridgen, who have also collaborated on multiple papers together.

Furthermore, in cluster 3 (red) there are 3 authors who emerge as strong contributors, and in cluster 4 (violet) there are also 3 most productive authors. These clusters demonstrate that there are groups of authors who have worked together on research and have a strong connection in the field of ICOs.

The country collaboration map shows the collaboration path in the world, indicating the presence of networks of study among different countries. Figure 3 represents the flow of collaboration between countries, showing an intense level of collaboration between the United States, Europe, and China. These countries have the most number of authors who are actively collaborating on research papers in the field of ICOs.

Overall, the collaboration network is a useful tool for analyzing the relationships between authors in a field of research. It allows us to identify groups of authors who have collaborated on research together, and it also allows us to see the flow of collaboration among different countries in the field of ICOs.

Figure 3. Collaboration network

Source: ABI/INFORM Complete, Emerald, Science Direct (Elsevier), Scopus, ProQuest Management, Google Scholar, and JSTOR and Computed in VOSviewer

Word cloud suggests that the majority of the literature focuses on the topic of blockchain technology, specifically in the context of initial coin offerings and investments. There is also a significant focus on the intersection of blockchain technology and information systems, as well as its use in finance. Other topics mentioned in the literature include electronic money, cryptocurrency, smart contracts, and the economic and social implications of blockchain technology. Overall, this word cloud highlights the wide range of topics and applications that are being explored in the field of blockchain research.

Figure 4. Word cloud
Source: ABI/INFORM Complete, Emerald, Science Direct (Elsevier), Scopus, ProQuest Management, Google Scholar, and JSTOR and Computed in VOSviewer

The co-occurrence analysis in Figure 5 provides a visual representation of the relationships between different keywords found in the literature. The large blue cluster in the center of the graph represents the main topic of blockchain technology, which is surrounded by smaller clusters of related keywords. The first red cluster on the left of the graph represents the keywords related to initial coin offerings (ICO), indicating that there is a strong connection between blockchain technology and ICOs in the literature. The second red cluster on the top of the graph represents the keywords related to information systems, suggesting that blockchain technology has a significant impact on the field of information systems. The third red cluster on the right of the graph represents the keywords related to information use, indicating that blockchain technology has a significant impact on how information is used and shared in various industries. This co-occurrence analysis helps to identify the main themes and relationships between different keywords in the literature, providing a deeper understanding of the topics that are being explored in the field of blockchain research.

Figure 5. Co-occurrence network
Source: ABI/INFORM Complete, Emerald, Science Direct (Elsevier), Scopus, ProQuest Management, Google Scholar, and JSTOR and Computed in VOSviewer

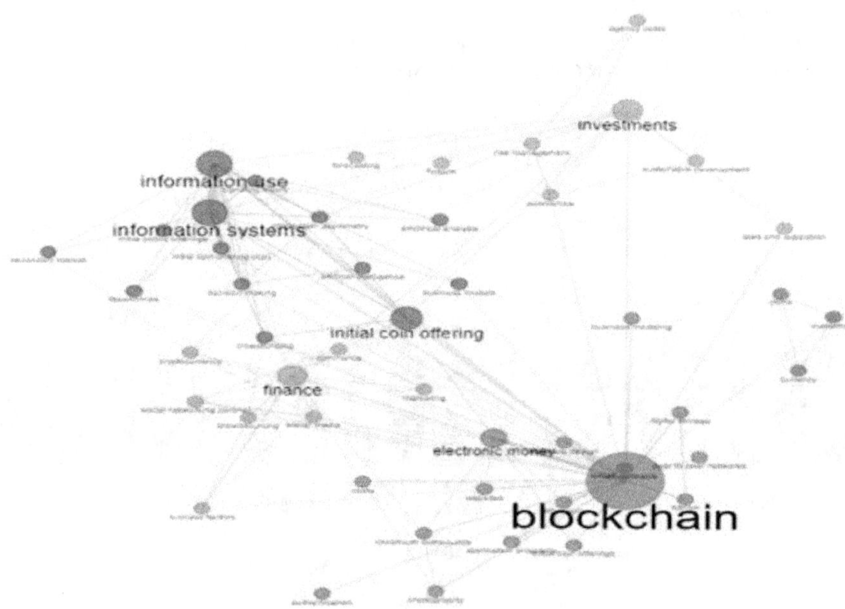

Keywords Analysis

The trend topic analysis is a tool used to identify the most frequently discussed topics in the literature on ICOs. It is based on the frequency of occurrence of specific terms in the literature. The analysis of trend topics in this study indicates that the blockchain is the most represented term in the relevant literature, while the term “initial coin offering” is also one of the most frequently represented terms, as shown in Figure 6.

Figure 6. Trend topics
Source: ABI/INFORM Complete, Emerald, Science Direct (Elsevier), Scopus, ProQuest Management, Google Scholar, and JSTOR and Computed in VOSviewer

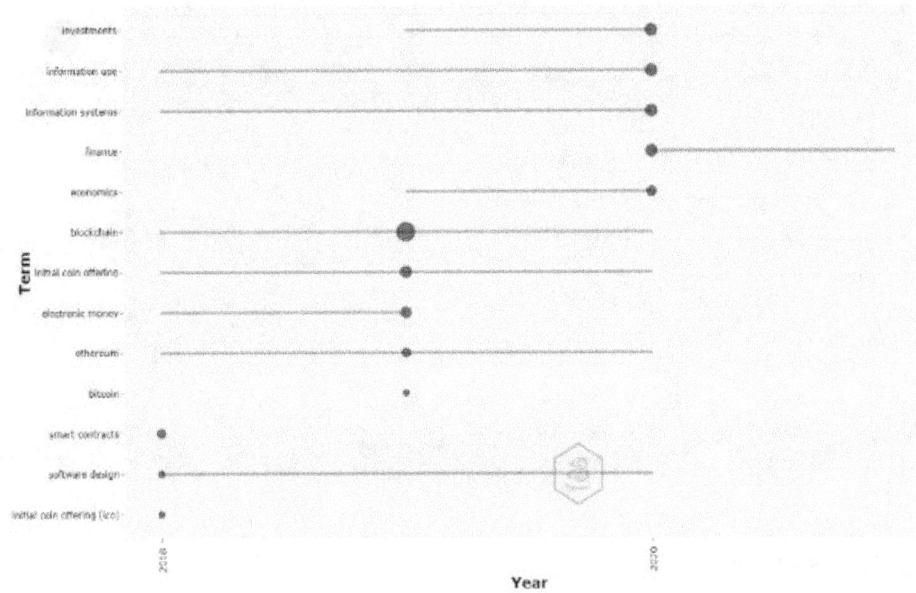

The analysis of the most relevant words shows that blockchain is the term with the highest frequency of occurrence in literature, with 53 times, followed by the terms information systems, information use and investments with an occurrence of 15 times each. Additionally, the word finance occurred 14 times while initial coin offering has an occurrence of 13 times, as shown in Fig. 7.

This analysis reveals that blockchain technology is the most widely discussed topic in the literature on ICOs, followed by information systems, information use, and investments. The word finance is also frequently discussed in relation to ICOs.

Overall, the trend topic analysis is a useful tool for identifying the main topics and themes in the literature on ICOs. It allows us to see which terms are most frequently discussed and to gain a better understanding of the key areas of research in the field.

Figure 7. Most relevant words
Source: ABI/INFORM Complete, Emerald, Science Direct (Elsevier), Scopus, ProQuest Management, Google Scholar, and JSTOR and Computed in VOSviewer

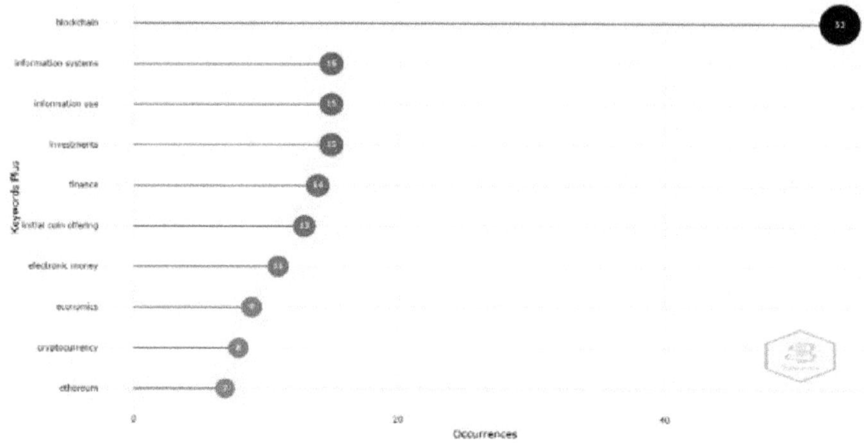

DISCUSSION

The bibliometric analysis conducted in this study aimed to identify key trends and patterns in the literature on ICOs. One of the key findings of this analysis was the importance of Adhami et al.'s (2018) study, which provided the first comprehensive explanation of ICOs and their characteristics. They found that by the end of 2017, Start-ups were able to collect over $5.3 billion through ICOs. Their research, which analyzed a sample of 253 ICOs from 2014 to August 2017, showed that the probability of an ICO's success is higher if certain requirements are met. Specifically, if the code source is available, if a token presale is organized, and if tokens enable investors to access a specific service or share in the profits, the chance of success is higher.

Their study is among the first to address the specific characteristics of ICOs and the factors that have an impact on fundraising success. They argue that ICOs are highly successful (80.0%), and that they are mostly performed in the United States, Russia, the United Kingdom, and Canada. This study is significant as it provides a detailed understanding of the ICOs phenomenon and the factors that contribute to their success.

ICO In Commerce and Business

In summary, the main types of ICOs used in commerce and business areas are private and public ICOs. Additionally, there are two main categories of tokens sold on ICOs: utility tokens and security tokens. Utility tokens are similar to donation-based crowdfunding, reward-based crowdfunding, and sales of APIs, while security tokens are similar to equity crowdfunding, lending crowdfunding, and venture capital funding. Utility tokens are used as digital currency to purchase a product or use a service provided by the developer company, while security tokens represent ownership rights to an asset. Currency tokens, equity tokens, and utility tokens are also three categories of tokens that are used in the blockchain market. Overall, ICOs have become a popular fundraising technique for blockchain technology businesses and Start-ups to raise funds, and have the potential to revolutionize the way SMEs acquire money in their early stages (Howell et al., 2020; Chod et al., 2018; Amsden et al., 2019; Fisch, 2019).

ICOs: A Financial Perspective

Schückes and Gutmann (2021) found that ICOs are a simple and efficient way to raise funds for Start-ups. They argue that the market for ICOs has established an excellent opportunity for Start-ups and that the ICO is a great approach to generate enthusiasm for a new project's launch. However, they also note that the legal status of ICOs is still unclear and that Start-ups may need to comply with certain regulations depending on how the tokens are used.

Conley (2017) also pointed out that the legal status of ICOs is unclear and that Start-ups must adhere to certain regulations to avoid potential repercussions. Adhami et al. (2018) found that the market for ICOs and crowdfunding have some characteristics in common, such as low investor protection and limited information for investors. They also note that there is no supervision by authorities and no adequate track record for investors. Giudici et al. (2018) found that ICO investors are mostly led by intrinsic motives, similar to crowdfunding. They also note that ICOs are blockchain-based and offer cryptocurrency and are not under any kind of authorities' supervision.

Schückes & Gutmann (2021) describe ICOs as a simple and efficient way to raise funds, but with lower barriers to entry, this could lead to a lack of understanding from traditional financial institutions. Conley (2017) argues that the legal status of ICOs is still unclear and that Start-ups may need to comply with certain regulations. Adhami et al. (2018) suggest that the market for ICOs has low investors' protection and a lack of supervision by authorities. Giudici et al. (2018) find that ICO investors are mostly led by intrinsic motives. Amsden et al., 2019 argue that there is a need for regulation to protect investors while allowing entrepreneurs to continue using this fundraising mechanism. Momtaz (2021) suggests that there could be moral hazards in ICOs due to the low entry barriers, the ability for founders to easily implement exit strategies, and the high level of uncertainty in the industry.

Cause and Effect of ICO on Start-Ups Firms

In summary, Chod et al. (2018) found that there are both benefits and costs to financing an entrepreneurial venture through issuing crypto tokens. They identified an agency problem related to ICOs that does not exist under equity financing, but also noted that token financing can mitigate an agency problem connected to equity financing. They found that tokens can be a preferred financing mechanism for certain ventures, particularly those that involve innovation-driven information goods. However, they also noted that the trajectory of the ICO market is uncertain and that financing with tokens could become more mainstream if proper regulation is put in place to protect token investors.

Arnold et al. (2019) found that ICOs offer unique benefits to both investors and Start-ups compared to traditional forms of financing. Start-ups benefit from the ability to collect funds anonymously from anywhere in the world, participate in decision making, and avoid dealing with financial institutions and fees. Investors can also benefit from the ability to impact the success of the Start-up and underlying cryptocurrency, and invest in Start-ups without intermediaries. However, Amsden et al. (2019) also noted that the ICO market is not yet fully transparent due to misrepresentation, lack of technological understanding, and examples of fraud. The market is still in its infancy, but has great potential to transform the way funds are collected and challenge traditional industries.

Huang et al. (2019) also found that countries with a developed and stable financial system have a higher chance of attracting more ICOs. They argue that a stable financial system and a clear regulatory framework can provide a better environment for ICOs to thrive and attract more investors. Additionally, they suggest that governments should take a proactive approach in regulating ICOs to ensure investor protection and promote the growth of the ICO market. Overall, Huang et al. (2019) highlight the importance of considering the financial system and regulatory environment in the analysis of ICOs and its potential impact on economic growth and productivity.

In summary, Dutra, Tumasjan, and Welpe (2018) propose the concept of tokenization in the entertainment industry, where influencers, YouTubers or celebrities can use their fame and reputation to raise money through the sale of digital coins or social tokens. Fans can then use these tokens to participate in unique activities or experiences with the entertainers. Similarly, in the art industry, Tapscott & Tapscott (2017) and Wang, Zhu, Ni, Gu, & Zhu (2020) suggest that tokenization can be applied to digital art and intellectual property, allowing artists to sell their work as digital coins and potentially adding value through social responsibility initiatives. Dosso & Vezzani (2020) and Hutter & Shusterman (2006) also highlight the potential for tokenization in various other industries, including branding, trademarks, skills, and business strategies. However, they note that in certain industries, such as the art industry, it may be difficult to demonstrate value to others and ways of adding aesthetic or social value may need to be considered.

In relation to fan tokens, an avenue for future research could be to investigate different types of social media, then explore how investors can access the intrinsic values of a celebrity or influencer. More token types are likely to emerge in the future, particularly utility tokens (Hill, 2017), and increase transaction opportunities for both issuers and sellers. It is interesting to study whether human capital is actually less important to investors in ICOs compared to crowdfunding or venture capital settings (Fisch, 2019). Consideration may also need to be given to the moral perspective, as ethical concerns regarding using the fame and reputation of someone for fund raising might be seen as a problem by critics. Furthermore, future research could also explore the regulatory challenges and opportunities related to ICOs and how they can be addressed to ensure the protection of investors while also promoting innovation and growth. This could include examining the effectiveness of current regulations, identifying gaps in the regulatory framework, and proposing new regulatory measures to address these gaps. Overall, there is a need for further research to fully understand the potential and challenges of ICOs, and how they can be used to benefit both investors and businesses in various sectors.

According to Balafoutas & Kerschbamer (2020) and Dostov, Shust, Leonova, & Krivoruchko (2019), future research would also need to consider the nature of regulatory and legal frameworks that are needed to protect investors. They suggest that a well-defined legal and regulatory framework is necessary for these transactions, and that the development of a digital intermediary, such as a KYC service, could be considered to verify token developers and buyers. Cong, Li, & Wang (2021) and Hargrave, Sahdev, & Feldmeier (2019) also note the importance of evaluating digital assets in the process of valuation, and suggest that further research is needed to develop new valuation models that incorporate the characteristics of digital assets and the purposes of tokenization. Overall, the paper highlights the potential of fractional ownership and tokenization in various areas, but emphasizes the need for further research and interdisciplinary perspectives to make these concepts workable and ethical.

Managerial Implications

1. **Understanding ICO Success Factors:** Managers and entrepreneurs in the blockchain and cryptocurrency space should take note of the factors that contribute to the success of ICOs as highlighted in Adhami et al.'s (2018) study. Ensuring that code source availability, token presales, and the offering of specific services or profit-sharing mechanisms are part of the ICO strategy can improve the chances of success.

2. **Compliance and Regulation:** The ambiguous legal status of ICOs emphasized by Conley (2017) and Adhami et al. (2018) requires Start-ups to stay informed about evolving regulatory frameworks. Managers should consider compliance as an essential aspect of their ICO planning to avoid potential legal issues and investor repercussions.
3. **Token Financing for Innovation-Driven Ventures:** Chod et al. (2018) suggested that token financing can be a preferred mechanism for ventures involving innovation-driven information goods. Managers of such ventures should explore the potential benefits of token financing, which might mitigate agency problems associated with traditional equity financing.
4. **Market Transparency:** Start-ups and investors should be aware of the current lack of transparency in the ICO market, as noted by Amsden et al. (2019). Managers and entrepreneurs should aim for transparency in their ICO processes to build trust and credibility with potential investors.
5. **Regulatory Challenges and Opportunities:** Future research on regulatory challenges and opportunities, as suggested, is vital. Managers and entrepreneurs should actively participate in these discussions and collaborate with regulatory bodies to establish clear and effective regulations, ensuring investor protection while promoting innovation and growth in the industry.
6. **Tokenization in Various Industries:** The concept of tokenization, as proposed by various studies, presents opportunities for businesses to leverage the token economy in different sectors, such as entertainment, art, branding, and more. Managers can explore how tokenization can be applied to their specific industries and use cases.

Practical Implications

1. **Diversification of Fundraising:** ICOs offer a unique fundraising method, and Start-ups should consider diversifying their fundraising strategies. ICOs, when used appropriately, can provide advantages over traditional financing methods.
2. **Global Accessibility:** ICOs allow Start-ups to collect funds from around the world. Entrepreneurs should take advantage of this global accessibility to attract a more diverse set of investors.
3. **Educating Investors:** Since the ICO market lacks the same level of investor protection and information as traditional markets, Start-ups should focus on educating potential investors about the ICO process, risks, and rewards.

4. **Legal and Regulatory Compliance:** To protect both Start-ups and investors, a strong emphasis on legal and regulatory compliance is essential. Entrepreneurs should seek legal counsel and follow best practices in terms of compliance.
5. **Transparency and Credibility:** Transparency and credibility are crucial for the success of ICOs. Start-ups should work on building a solid reputation by providing clear information about their projects, teams, and progress.
6. **Market Analysis:** Before launching an ICO, it's crucial to conduct a comprehensive market analysis to understand the competitive landscape, investor preferences, and regulatory requirements.
7. **Collaboration and Research:** Managers, entrepreneurs, and researchers should actively collaborate to bridge the gaps in our understanding of ICOs. Further research should focus on creating effective and ethical models for this fundraising method.
8. **Incorporate Interdisciplinary Perspectives:** Recognize that ICOs and tokenization intersect with various fields and industries. Incorporating interdisciplinary perspectives can lead to innovative and ethical solutions.
9. **Compliance Services:** The development of digital intermediaries, such as Know Your Customer (KYC) services as suggested by Balafoutas & Kerschbamer (2020), can aid in verifying token developers and buyers. Entrepreneurs in this space may consider developing or using such services to enhance security and compliance.
10. **Valuation Models for Digital Assets:** As digital assets play a crucial role in ICOs, developing new valuation models that incorporate the characteristics of digital assets, as mentioned by Cong, Li, & Wang (2021) and Hargrave, Sahdev, & Feldmeier (2019), can help both Start-ups and investors make informed decisions.

Target audience consisting of individuals and groups involved in the blockchain, cryptocurrency, and Start-up ecosystems. This audience includes entrepreneurs, managers, investors, regulatory bodies, researchers, and professionals seeking to understand the intricacies of Initial Coin Offerings (ICOs) and their potential implications.

1. Entrepreneurs and Start-Up Managers: The chapter offers insights into the key success factors of ICOs, compliance requirements, and the benefits of token financing. It guides them on how to plan and execute an ICO effectively while emphasizing the importance of transparency and compliance.
2. Investors: Investors considering participation in ICOs will find valuable information on how to assess potential projects. The chapter highlights the

risks, lack of investor protection, and the need for transparency, equipping them with knowledge to make informed investment decisions.

3. Regulatory Bodies: Regulatory bodies can benefit from the chapter's focus on the legal and regulatory challenges of ICOs. It encourages them to develop clear and effective regulations to protect investors and promote industry growth.
4. Researchers: Researchers interested in the blockchain and cryptocurrency space can gather valuable data and insights from the chapter. It identifies gaps in the existing knowledge and encourages further interdisciplinary research, promoting a deeper understanding of ICOs and their impact.
5. Blockchain and Cryptocurrency Professionals: Professionals in the blockchain and cryptocurrency industries can find practical implications for diversifying fundraising methods, educating investors, and ensuring legal compliance. The chapter provides actionable advice for enhancing ICO success and navigating the unique challenges of the field.
6. Tokenization Enthusiasts: Individuals and groups interested in the concept of tokenization in various industries, such as entertainment, art, branding, and intellectual property, will find inspiration and ideas for potential applications of tokenization. It emphasizes the need for creativity and value demonstration in these domains.
7. Compliance Service Providers: Entities offering compliance services, such as KYC verification, can identify opportunities to support ICOs in ensuring legal compliance and building trust within the investor community.

CONCLUSION

In conclusion, the literature reviewed in this paper suggests that ICOs have the potential to revolutionize the way Start-ups raise funds, but they also present significant challenges and risks. The lack of regulation in the ICO market means that investors need to be especially vigilant in performing due diligence before investing. Additionally, the quality of information available to investors is often poor, making it difficult for them to make informed decisions. Despite these challenges, the success rate of ICOs is high, and Start-ups can benefit from the community building and feedback opportunities that come with an ICO. Future research should continue to explore the opportunities and challenges presented by ICOs, as well as the potential impact of regulatory and legal frameworks on the ICO market. Additionally, research should focus on developing new valuation methods that take into account the unique characteristics of digital assets and the purposes of tokenization. Overall, ICOs are a complex and evolving topic that requires continued attention and research to fully understand its implications for Start-ups, investors, and the broader economy.

REFERENCES

Adhami, S., Giudici, G., & Martinazzi, S. (2018). Why do businesses go crypto? An empirical analysis of initial coin offerings. *Journal of Economics and Business, 100*, 64–75. doi:10.1016/j.jeconbus.2018.04.001

Ahlers, G. K., Cumming, D., Günther, C., & Schweizer, D. (2015). Signaling in equity crowdfunding. *Entrepreneurship Theory and Practice, 39*(4), 955–980. doi:10.1111/etap.12157

Allen, J. G., Rauchs, M., Blandin, A., & Bear, K. (2020). *Legal and regulatory considerations for digital assets*. Retrieved from https://www.jbs.cam.ac.uk/wp-content/uploads/2020/10/2020-ccaf-legal-regulatory-considerations-report.pdf

Allison, T. H., Davis, B. C., Webb, J. W., & Short, J. C. (2017). Persuasion in crowdfunding: An elaboration likelihood model of crowdfunding performance. *Journal of Business Venturing, 32*(6), 707–725. doi:10.1016/j.jbusvent.2017.09.002

Amsden, R., Schweizer, D., Alperovych, Y., Benedetti, H., Blaseg, D., Bollaert, H., Braune, E., Cole, R. A., Cumming, D., Geiler, P., Gianfrate, G., Groh, A., Mezzanotti, F., Li, J., Abou Jaoude, J., Proelss, J., Lopez-de-Silanes, F., & Riding, A. (2019). *Are Blockchain Crowdsales the New "Gold Rush"*. Success Determinants of Initial Coin Offerings.

An, J., Duan, T., Hou, W., & Xu, X. (2019). Initial coin offerings and entrepreneurial finance: The role of founders' characteristics. *Journal of Alternative Investments, 21*(4), 26–40. doi:10.3905/jai.2019.1.068

Arnold, L., Brennecke, M., Camus, P., Fridgen, G., Guggenberger, T., Radszuwill, S., Rieger, A., Schweizer, A., & Urbach, N. (2019). Blockchain and Initial Coin Offerings: Blockchain's Implications for Crowdfunding. In Business Transformation through Blockchain (pp. 233–272). Springer International Publishing. doi:10.1007/978-3-319-98911-2_8

Awaya, Y., & Krishna, V. (2021). Start-ups and upstarts: Disadvantageous information in R&D. *Journal of Political Economy, 129*(2).

Babaei, G., & Bamdad, S. (2020). A neural-network-based decision-making model in the peer-to-peer lending market. *International Journal of Intelligent Systems in Accounting Finance & Management, 27*(3), 142–150. doi:10.1002/isaf.1480

Balafoutas, L., & Kerschbamer, R. (2020). Credence goods in the literature: What the past fifteen years have taught us about fraud, incentives, and the role of institutions. *Journal of Behavioral and Experimental Finance*, *26*(100285), 100285. doi:10.1016/j.jbef.2020.100285

Block, J. H., Colombo, M. G., Cumming, D. J., & Vismara, S. (2018). New players in entrepreneurial finance and why they are there. *Small Business Economics*, *50*(2), 239–250. doi:10.100711187-016-9826-6

Boreiko, D., & Risteski, D. (2020). Serial and large investors in initial coin offerings. *Small Business Economics*, 1–19. doi:10.100711187-020-00338-8

BoreikoD.SahdevN. (2018). *To ICO or not to ICO-Empirical analysis of Initial Coin Offerings and Token Sales*. doi:10.2139/ssrn.3209180

Broadus, R. N. (1987). Toward a definition of "bibliometrics." *Scientometrics*, *12*(5/6), 373–379. doi:10.1007/BF02016680

Bustamante, C. V. (2019). Strategic choices: Accelerated Start-ups' outsourcing decisions. *Journal of Business Research*, *105*, 359–369. doi:10.1016/j.jbusres.2018.06.009

Buterin, V. (2014). *A next generation smart contract & decentralized application platform*. Academic Press.

Campino, J., & Rosa, Á. (2021). Success Factors of Initial Coin Offering (ICO) projects''. *Economic Bulletin*, *41*(2).

Cao, Q., Chen, J., Fu, P., & Mao, Y. (2020). Impact of government guidance modes on fundraising effect. In X. J., D. G., A. S., G. M. F., & H. A. (Eds.), *International conference on management science and engineering management* (pp. 226-240). Springer.

Catalini, C., & Gans, J. S. (2018). *NBER working paper series initial coin offerings and the value of crypto tokens*. https://www.nber.org/papers/w24418

CFCT. (2017). *A CFCT primer on virtual currencies*. Retrieved from https://www.cftc.gov/sites/default/files/idc/groups/public/%40customerprotection/d ocuments/file/labcftc_primercurrencies100417.pdf

CFTC. (2015). *Order instituting proceedings pursuant to section 6(c) and 6(d) of the commodity echange act*. Retrieved from https://www.cftc.gov/sites/default/files/idc/groups/public/@lrenforcementactions/d ocuments/legalpleading/enfcoinfliprorder09172015.pdf

Chen, R. R., & Chen, K. (2020). A 2020 perspective on "Information asymmetry in initial coin offerings (ICOs): Investigating the effects of multiple channel signals". *Electronic Commerce Research and Applications*, *40*, 100936. Advance online publication. doi:10.1016/j.elerap.2020.100936

Chen, Y. (2018). Blockchain tokens and the potential democratization of entrepreneurship and innovation. *Business Horizons*, *61*(4), 567–575. doi:10.1016/j.bushor.2018.03.006

Chod, J., Lyandres, E., Benedetti, H., Cong, W., Chemmanur, T., Goldstein, I., Gromb, D., & Li, J. (2018). Jerusalem Summer Finance Conference. In *Santiago Finance Workshop*. Econometric Society North American Winter Meeting.

Chudasri, D. (2020). *SET builds integrated trading platform with KBTG*. Retrieved from https://www.bangkokpost.com/business/1997255/set-builds-integrated-trading-platform-with-kbtg

Cong, L. W., Li, Y., & Wang, N. (2021). Tokenomics: Dynamic adoption and valuation. *Review of Financial Studies*, *34*(3), 1105–1155. doi:10.1093/rfs/hhaa089

Conley, J. P. (2017). Blockchain and the economics of crypto-tokens and initial coin offerings. *Vanderbilt University Department of economics working papers*, (17-00008).

Davila, A., Foster, G., & Gupta, M. (2003). Venture capital financing and the growth of Start-up firms. *Journal of Business Venturing*, *18*(6), 689–708. doi:10.1016/S0883-9026(02)00127-1

De JongA.RoosenboomP.van der KolkT. (2018). What determines success in Initial Coin Offerings? doi:10.2139/ssrn.3250035

Degryse, H., de Goeij, P., & Kappert, P. (2012). The impact of firm and industry characteristics on small firms' capital structure. *Small Business Economics*, *38*(4), 431–447. doi:10.100711187-010-9281-8

Ding, Y., & Cronin, B. (2011). *Popular and/or Prestigious? Measures of Scholarly Esteem*. Academic Press.

Dosso, M., & Vezzani, A. (2020). Firm market valuation and intellectual property assets. *Industry and Innovation*, *27*(7), 705–729. doi:10.1080/13662716.2019.1685374

Dostov, V., Shust, P., Leonova, A., & Krivoruchko, S. (2019). "Soft law" and innovations: Empirical analysis of ICO-related statements. *Digital Policy. Regulation & Governance*, *21*(5), 476–493. doi:10.1108/DPRG-03-2019-0018

Dutra, A., Tumasjan, A., & Welpe, I. (2018). Blockchain is changing how media and entertainment companies compete. *MIT Sloan Management Review*.

FCA. (2018). *British and australian regulators strengthen cooperation on fintech through enhanced cooperation agreement*. Retrieved from https://www.fca.org.uk/news/press-releases/british-and-australian-regulators-strengthen-cooperation-fintech-through-enhanced-cooperation

FINMA. (2017). *Guideline for enquiries regarding the regulatory framework for initial coin offering (ICOs)*. Retrieved from https://www.finma.ch/en/~/media/finma/dokumente/dokumentecenter/myfinma/1bewilligung/fintech/wegleitung-ico.pdf?la=en

Fisch, C. (2019). Initial coin offerings (ICOs) to finance new ventures. *Journal of Business Venturing*, *34*(1), 1–22. doi:10.1016/j.jbusvent.2018.09.007

Fisch, C., Masiak, C., Vismara, S., & Block, J. (2021). Motives and profiles of ICO investors. *Journal of Business Research*, *125*, 564–576. doi:10.1016/j.jbusres.2019.07.036

Gächter, I., & Gächter, M. (2020). Success factors in ICOs: Individual firm characteristics or lucky timing? *Finance Research Letters*. Advance online publication. doi:10.1016/j.frl.2020.101715

GFSC. (2017a). *Distributed ledger technology regulatory framework (dlt framework)*. Retrieved from https://www.gfsc.gi/dlt

GFSC. (2017b). *Statement on initial coin offerings*. Retrieved from https://www.fsc.gi/news/statement-on-initial-coin-offerings-250

Giudici, G., Guerini, M., & Rossi-Lamastra, C. (2018). Reward-based crowdfunding of entrepreneurial projects: The effect of local altruism and localized social capital on proponents' success. *Small Business Economics*, *50*(2), 307–324. doi:10.100711187-016-9830-x

Hall, B. H., & Lerner, J. (2010). The financing of R&D and innovation. In *Handbook of the Economics of Innovation* (Vol. 1, pp. 609-639). North-Holland. doi:10.3386/w15325

Hargrave, J., Sahdev, N., & Feldmeier, O. (2019). How value is created in tokenized assets. In M. Swan, J. Potts, S. Takagi, F. Witte, & P. Tasca (Eds.), *Blockchain economics: Implications of distributed ledgers-markets, communications networks, and algorithmic reality* (pp. 125–141). doi:10.1142/9781786346391_0007

Hill, B. (2017). *ICOs & token types for dummies: A buyer's guide to crypto-tokens*. Retrieved from https://hackernoon.com/icos-token-types-for-dummies-anbuyers-guide-to crypto-tokens-b6edea16776e doi:10.3386/w15325

Howell, S. T., Niessner, M., & Yermack, D. (2020). Initial coin offerings: Financing growth with cryptocurrency token sales. *Review of Financial Studies, 33*(9), 3925–3974. doi:10.1093/rfs/hhz131

Hrga, A., Benčić, F. M., & Žarko, I. P. (2019). *Technical analysis of an initial coin offering*. Paper presented at the 2019 15th International Conference on Telecommunications (ConTEL). 10.1109/ConTEL.2019.8848532

HuangW.MeoliM.VismaraS. (2019). *The geography of Initial Coin Offerings*. https://ssrn.com/abstract=3206234

Hutter, M., & Shusterman, R. (2006). Value and the valuation of art in economic and aesthetic theory. Handbook of the Economics of Art and Culture, 1, 169-208.

Islam, M., Fremeth, A., & Marcus, A. (2018). Signaling by early-stage Start-ups: US government research grants and venture capital funding. *Journal of Business Venturing, 33*(1), 35–51. doi:10.1016/j.jbusvent.2017.10.001

Köhn, A. (2018). The determinants of Start-up valuation in the venture capital context: A systematic review and avenues for future research. *Management Review Quarterly, 68*(1), 3–36. doi:10.100711301-017-0131-5

Köseoğlu, S. D., & Almeany, S. S. A. (2020). Introduction to business valuation. In M. Akkaya (Ed.), *Start-up valuation: Theories, models, and future*. IGI Global.

Kyriazis, N. A. (2019). A survey on efficiency and profitable trading opportunities in cryptocurrency markets. *Journal of Risk and Financial Management, 12*(2), 67. doi:10.3390/jrfm12020067

Leydesdorff, L. B. L. M. R. O. T., Bornmann, L., Mutz, R., & Opthof, T. (2011). Turning the tables on citation analysis one more time: Principles for comparing sets of documents. *Journal of the American Society for Information Science and Technology, 62*(7), 1370–1381. doi:10.1002/asi.21534

Mckenzie, B. (2018). *Regulatory aspects of initial coin offerings (icos) in Switzerland*. Retrieved from https://www.bakermckenzie.com/en/- /media/files/insight/publications/2018/03/regulatory-aspects-ico switzerland/br_switzerland_regulatoryaspectsico_mar2018.pdf

Momtaz, P. P. (2021). Entrepreneurial Finance and Moral Hazard: Evidence from Token Offerings. *Journal of Business Venturing*, *36*(5), 106001. Advance online publication. doi:10.1016/j.jbusvent.2020.106001

Monetary Authority of Singapore. (2018). *A guide to digital token offerings*. Retrieved from https://www.mas.gov.sg/~/media/MAS/News%20and%20Publications/Monograps% 20and%20Information%20Papers/Guide%20to%20Digital%20Token%20Offerings% 20last%20updated%20on%2030%20Nov.pdf

Monetary Authority of Singapore. (2019). *A guide to digital token offerings*. Retrieved from https://www.mas.gov.sg/-/media/MAS/Sectors/Guidance/Guide-to-Digital-Tokens- Offering 23-Dec-2019.pdf

Money and Bank Thailand. (2020). *Smart money*. Retrieved from https://www.moneyandbanking.co.th/article/the-guru/cryptocurency-smart-money- mb466-feb-2021-110264/

Moro, A., & Wang, D. (2019). Fintech projects and initial coin offerings: A research note. *The Journal of Entrepreneurial Finance*, *21*(1), 24–37. doi:10.57229/2373-1761.1350

Nolan, A. R., Dartley, E. T., Baker, M. B., ReVeal, J., & Rinearson, J. E. (2018). Initial coin offerings: Key US legal considerations for ICO investors and sponsors. *Journal of Investment Compliance*, *19*(1), 1–9. doi:10.1108/JOIC-02-2018-0016

O'Leary, D. E. (2013). 'Big data', the 'internet of things' and the 'internet of signs'. *International Journal of Intelligent Systems in Accounting Finance & Management*, *20*(1), 53–65. doi:10.1002/isaf.1336

O'Leary, D. E. (2018). Open information enterprise transactions: Business intelligence and wash and spoof transactions in blockchain and social commerce. *International Journal of Intelligent Systems in Accounting Finance & Management*, *25*(3), 148–158. doi:10.1002/isaf.1438

Open-Tec. (2019). *Look inside jirayut srupsrisopa: The thai digital currency pioneer*. Retrieved from https://www.open-tec.com/look-inside-jirayut-srupsrisopa-the-thai-digital-currency-pioneer-2/

Ostern, N. K., & Riedel, J. (2020). Know-your-customer (kyc) requirements for initial coin offerings. *Business & Information Systems Engineering*, 1–17. doi:10.100712599-020-00677-6

Pietrewicz, L. (2018). Emerging Trends in Entrepreneurial Finance. *The Rise of ICOs*, 2(27), 65–78. doi:10.7172/1733-9758.2018.27.6

Pritchard, A. (1969). Statistical Bibliography or Bibliometrics. *The Journal of Documentation*, 348–349.

Richter, N., Jackson, P., & Schildhauer, T. (2018). Entrepreneurial behaviour and Start-ups: The case of Germany and the USA. In Entrepreneurial innovation and leadership (pp. 1-14). Palgrave Pivot.

Riley, M., & Szivas, E. (2009). The valuation of skill and the configuration of HRM. *Tourism Economics*, *15*(1), 105–120. doi:10.5367/000000009787536771

Samieifar, S., & Baur, D. G. (2020). Read me if you can! An analysis of ICO white papers. *Finance Research Letters*. Advance online publication. doi:10.1016/j.frl.2020.101427

Schückes, M., & Gutmann, T. (2020). The role of economic drivers and social identity on funding choice. *Small Business Economics*, 1–26. doi:10.100711187-020-00337-9

Schückes, M., & Gutmann, T. (2021). Why do Start-ups pursue initial coin offerings (ICOs)? The role of economic drivers and social identity on funding choice. *Small Business Economics*, *57*(2), 1027–1052. doi:10.100711187-020-00337-9

SEC. (2018). *Emergency decree on digital asset businesses B.E. 2561*. Retrieved from https://www.sec.or.th/EN/Documents/ActandRoyalEnactment/RoyalEnactment/enactment-digitalasset2018.pdf

SET. (2020). *Summary of the emergency decree on digital asset businesses B.E. 2561*. https://www.sec.or.th/TH/Documents/DigitalAsset/enactment_digital_2561_summar y_en.pdf

Tapscott, D., & Tapscott, A. (2017). *Blockchain could help artists profit more from their creative works.*

The Story Thailand. (2020). *SET partners with KBTG to launch end-to-end digital-assets platform.* Retrieved from https://www.thestorythailand.com/en/07/10/2020/6639/

Toma, A. M., & Cerchiello, P. (2020). Initial Coin Offerings: Risk or Opportunity? *Frontiers in Artificial Intelligence*, *3*, 18. Advance online publication. doi:10.3389/frai.2020.00018 PMID:33733137

Wang, Q., Zhu, X., Ni, Y., Gu, L., & Zhu, H. (2020). Blockchain for the IoT and industrial IoT: A review. *Internet of Things*, *10*, 100081. Advance online publication. doi:10.1016/j.iot.2019.100081

Wenger & Vieli. (2019). *Baking/fintech license*. Retrieved from https://www.wengervieli.ch/getattachment/39cbfbd7-5897-4bf2-8b48- e56abede6a39/Bank-Fintech-Bewilligung.aspx

KEY TERMS AND DEFINITIONS

Alternative Financing: Alternative financing refers to methods of raising funds for a business or project outside of traditional bank loans or stock offerings, such as crowdfunding, peer-to-peer lending, or venture capital.

Anti-Money Laundering Act (AMLA): It is a law that aims to prevent money laundering and other financial crimes by requiring financial institutions and other regulated entities to implement strict measures to identify and report suspicious transactions, and to maintain accurate records of customer information.

Digital Assets: Digital assets are non-physical, digital representations of value, such as cryptocurrencies, tokens, and virtual goods, that can be traded and stored electronically.

Financial Crimes Enforcement Network (FinCEN): It is a bureau of the US Department of Treasury that is responsible for implementing and enforcing laws to prevent money laundering, terrorist financing, and other financial crime.

Financial Market Supervisory Authority (FINMA): It is an independent government body in Switzerland that is responsible for regulating and supervising the financial markets and protecting the rights of customers and creditors, in order to ensure the stability and integrity of the financial system.

Fractional Ownership of Digital Assets: It refers to a system where multiple investors can jointly own a piece of a digital asset, such as a cryptocurrency or token, and share in its ownership, value and risk.

Initial Coin Offerings (ICOS): An Initial Coin Offering (ICO) is a fundraising mechanism in which a company issues digital tokens to investors in exchange for cryptocurrency or fiat currency.

Start-Ups: Start-ups are new businesses that are in the process of developing and trying to establish a market for a new product or service.

Traditional Sources of Financing: Traditional sources of financing include bank loans, stock and bond offerings, and borrowing from friends and family.

Chapter 8
Conceptual Blockchain Analysis for Disaster Management

Ashutosh D. Gaur
https://orcid.org/0000-0003-4322-5747
Mangalmay Institution of Management and Technology, India

ABSTRACT

Blockchain is a transparent, encrypted, distributed database. It is utilised effectively by financial instruments, e-government, supply networks, and others. This paper examines emergency uses for the Blockchain. There needs to be a sound information system for managing and controlling disasters, making decisions, and creating a conceptual model from disaster and blockchain literature. This chapter discusses parties exchanging and storing data on one platform. This study proposes a system model for pre-, during-, and post-disaster user scenarios. The methodology asserts holistic disaster resolution.

INTRODUCTION

Disaster management, as an essential component of ensuring the safety and well-being of communities, has seen remarkable advancements in recent years, driven by technological innovations and novel approaches to handling crises (Smith, 2019; Federal Emergency Management Agency, 2022). From early warning systems that provide vital seconds to prepare for impending disasters to artificial intelligence-driven predictive models, the landscape of disaster management has been evolving

DOI: 10.4018/978-1-6684-7649-9.ch008

rapidly. Yet, amidst these advancements, one technology has remained relatively underexplored, with the potential to revolutionize the field: blockchain.

Blockchain, the distributed ledger technology initially devised for cryptocurrencies like Bitcoin, offers a decentralized, transparent, and secure framework that holds significant promise for enhancing the various phases of disaster management (Johnson, 2020; Coco et al., 2017). It presents an opportunity to transform the way disaster risk reduction, preparedness, response, and recovery activities are carried out. By establishing an immutable record of transactions and data, blockchain can bolster the reliability and integrity of information, streamline the allocation of resources, and facilitate efficient communication among stakeholders (Adams, 2022).

While the theoretical groundwork for implementing blockchain technology in disaster management has been established through various conceptual models and frameworks (Blockchain for Disaster Management Consortium, 2021; B. Egeland-Müller et al., 2017), the transition from theory to real-world practice remains an underexplored area. The existing literature offers a valuable foundation for understanding the potential advantages of blockchain in this context. However, a significant research gap persists, particularly in terms of empirical, quantitative assessments of the actual impact of blockchain technology on disaster management.

To date, the discourse surrounding blockchain in disaster management largely consists of theoretical discussions and conceptual proposals. While these discussions are vital for generating ideas and laying the groundwork, the absence of empirical investigations quantifying the technology's real-world influence is conspicuous (Rodriguez, 2017). It remains largely unknown how blockchain, when deployed in disaster-affected regions, affects the speed and efficiency of disaster response, the optimization of resource allocation, and the overall resilience of disaster management systems.

This research gap is a significant obstacle in fully understanding the potential of blockchain technology in disaster management. Theoretical models and conceptual frameworks can provide insightful suggestions, but they often lack the empirical support required to convince stakeholders of the real-world utility of blockchain in disaster-prone areas. Addressing this gap through empirical investigations is imperative to bridge the chasm between theory and practice.

Moreover, deploying blockchain in disaster-prone areas, which often feature limited technical infrastructure and expertise, presents unique challenges. This socio-technical dimension remains an under-explored domain in the existing literature (Nguyen, 2016). Overcoming these challenges is essential, and this article aims to investigate potential solutions to make the adoption of blockchain in such contexts more feasible and effective.

In summary, this article seeks to explore the potential of blockchain technology in disaster management while highlighting the research gap that calls for empirical studies to assess its real-world impact. By conducting quantitative investigations in disaster-affected regions, this research intends to provide tangible insights and bridge the gap between theory and practice. The findings are expected to contribute significantly to more resilient, responsive, and efficient disaster management practices.

OBJECTIVE

This chapter aims to harness the potential of blockchain technology to secure disaster-related data effectively. It postulates that blockchain-based solutions can address this problem by integrating data from multiple sources, establishing transparent decentralized networks, and verifying the authenticity of victim certifications. By enhancing both operational and administrative aspects of disaster management, blockchain facilitates swift decision-making throughout the entire disaster management cycle. It connects various stakeholders, validates their interactions, and employs blockchain for victim verification. Within this secure, decentralized database, information on relief camps, victim demographics, health concerns, and supplies is stored. Additionally, it offers early warnings, communication channels, rescue center information, and mechanisms for volunteer engagement.

This chapter not only scrutinizes the integration of blockchain technology into disaster management but also delves into various facets of this transformative process. It focuses on areas such as blockchain scalability, its use cases, interoperability, adoption challenges, cybersecurity, resource allocation, community engagement, privacy, cost-benefit analysis, and the synergy between blockchain and emerging technologies. Moreover, it concludes by offering essential managerial implications for successfully navigating these challenges.

BLOCKCHAIN SCALABILITY

The scalability of blockchain technology is one of the primary concerns when implementing it into disaster management. As disaster scenarios often lead to a significant increase in transactions and data volumes (Adams, 2022), it is imperative that the underlying blockchain infrastructure can efficiently handle this increased load (Johnson, 2020). Research and development efforts should be concentrated on designing and implementing scalable blockchain solutions capable of accommodating the demands of disaster management scenarios (Smith, 2019). These solutions should incorporate features like sharding (Brown, 2018) and off-chain processing to ensure scalability without compromising performance (Nguyen, 2016).

Scalability is integral to the ability to process a vast number of transactions while maintaining acceptable response times and system efficiency (B. Egeland-Müller et al., 2017). Given the potential influx of data during a disaster (Federal Emergency Management Agency, 2022), blockchain solutions need to be able to handle an increased load seamlessly (Coco, Pinna, & Marchesi, 2017). To ensure effective disaster management, blockchain platforms must be capable of scaling horizontally by adding more nodes to the network to distribute the processing workload (Rodriguez, 2017). Additionally, vertical scaling is also essential, allowing the blockchain network to handle larger data volumes efficiently (Johnson, 2020).

Moreover, a balance must be struck between scalability and decentralization (B. Egeland-Müller et al., 2017). As blockchain networks grow, the computational and storage requirements increase significantly, which may lead to centralization tendencies, eroding one of the key advantages of blockchain technology (Johnson, 2020).

SCALABILITY SOLUTIONS

The challenge of scalability within blockchain technology necessitates the development of innovative solutions. Several subtopics emerge as crucial in addressing this issue.

1. **Sharding**: Sharding involves the partitioning of the blockchain network into smaller shards, with each shard being responsible for processing its transactions. This approach significantly augments the network's capacity (Buterin, 2018).
2. **Off-Chain Processing:** Off-chain processing encompasses the practice of executing transactions outside the primary blockchain, thereby mitigating congestion and enhancing overall network efficiency (Swan, 2015).
3. **Layer-2 Solutions:** Layer-2 scaling solutions, including the Lightning Network and sidechains, have the potential to alleviate scalability issues in blockchain systems. These solutions offer various applications in diverse domains, including disaster management (Poon & Dryja, 2016).

BLOCKCHAIN USE CASES

The utility of blockchain technology extends beyond its conventional applications, particularly in the domain of disaster management. This section elucidates a range of practical use cases that underscore the tangible benefits that blockchain can deliver within disaster management processes.

1. **Decentralized Identity Management:** Blockchain technology provides a robust framework for the establishment of decentralized digital identities, thereby ensuring secure interactions for disaster victims, responders, and relief workers. The technology also assists in verifying the authenticity of these identities, reducing the risk of fraudulent activities and impersonation (Makhdoom et al., 2020).
2. **Smart Contracts for Automated Resource Allocation:** Smart contracts enable the automated allocation of resources based on predefined rules and triggers. These self-executing contracts trigger resource allocation when specific conditions are met, ensuring equitable distribution and minimizing response times (Szabo, 1996).
3. **Supply Chain Tracking:** Blockchain's transparent and immutable ledger is particularly well-suited for tracking the movement of relief materials and supplies. This ensures the efficient distribution of essential items, minimizes fraud, and enhances accountability within the supply chain (Mendling et al., 2018).
4. **Disaster-Resilient Communications:** Implementing blockchain-based communication networks ensures that critical information remains accessible even in the event of infrastructure damage. Decentralized communication systems facilitate effective coordination between responders and affected communities (Müller & Martin, 2019).
5. **Humanitarian Aid Distribution:** Utilizing blockchain for humanitarian aid distribution streamlines the tracking of aid delivery and ensures that resources reach their intended recipients. Additionally, blockchain technology effectively prevents fraud and corruption within the distribution process (Narayanan et al., 2016).
6. **Immutable Documentation:** Storing critical documents and information on the blockchain guarantees their immutability and accessibility, even if traditional record-keeping systems become compromised during a disaster (Swan, 2015).

USE CASES EXPLORATION

This section delves further into the mentioned use cases, offering real-world examples and showcasing the advantages they present in disaster management scenarios.

1. **Blockchain-Based Digital Identity:** This subsection highlights instances where blockchain technology has been deployed to establish digital identities for disaster-affected individuals and responders, emphasizing the security and trustworthiness of these identities (Makhdoom et al., 2020).

2. **Smart Contracts for Resource Allocation:** Case studies within this section provide practical examples of how smart contracts have been employed to automate resource allocation in disaster situations, thereby expediting response and ensuring equitable distribution (Szabo, 1996).
3. **Supply Chain Tracking in Relief Operations:** Real-world examples of how blockchain has been used to ensure the transparent and efficient distribution of relief materials are presented, showcasing the technology's capacity to enhance accountability and minimize fraud within supply chains (Mendling et al., 2018).
4. **Disaster-Resilient Communication Networks:** This section explores the implementation of blockchain-based communication networks in disaster-prone areas and elucidates their advantages in maintaining communication integrity during adverse events (Müller & Martin, 2019).
5. **Humanitarian Aid Distribution via Blockchain:** Instances where blockchain technology has been employed to optimize humanitarian aid distribution are showcased, emphasizing its role in ensuring efficient aid delivery and minimizing fraudulent activities (Narayanan et al., 2016).
6. **Immutable Documentation and Records:** This subsection elaborates on how blockchain can securely store critical documents and records that must remain accessible during and after a disaster, reducing the risks associated with data loss and tampering (Swan, 2015).

INTEROPERABILITY AND STANDARDS

One of the paramount challenges in the realm of blockchain technology is the attainment of interoperability across heterogeneous blockchain systems and the establishment of adherence to standardized practices. In the context of disaster management, the importance of interoperability cannot be overstated. This is particularly crucial due to the varied blockchain platforms utilized by different stakeholders, organizations, and governmental entities. Standardization serves as a foundational element in guaranteeing the seamless exchange of information across these disparate blockchain systems, thus facilitating the creation of a cohesive disaster management network.

The absence of interoperability can precipitate the creation of data silos, which, in the context of disaster management, stands as a significant obstacle to effective information dissemination. In disaster scenarios, the prompt sharing of critical data among diverse agencies is of utmost importance, and a failure to ensure interoperability among their blockchain systems could lead to detrimental delays in data transmission to where it is most urgently needed.

INTEROPERABILITY CHALLENGES

Within the sphere of blockchain technology, a multitude of challenges exist concerning the realization of interoperability and adherence to standardized norms. Several subtopics warrant investigation to illuminate these challenges.

1. **Data Silos:** The absence of interoperability between blockchain systems often results in the creation of data silos. These data silos have the potential to substantially impede the efficient exchange of information, particularly within the domain of disaster management, where the rapid and unobstructed transmission of data is paramount (Petrov et al., 2021).
2. **Standardization Efforts:** Currently, there are concerted efforts underway to formulate and establish standards and protocols specific to blockchain technology in the context of disaster management. This section delves into these ongoing standardization efforts, providing insight into the progress made to date and the forthcoming challenges and milestones that lie ahead (NIST, 2018).
3. **Cross-Chain Communication:** The realm of blockchain technology is witnessing the emergence of innovative solutions that facilitate the effective communication between distinct blockchain networks. These solutions, often referred to as cross-chain communication mechanisms, are of particular relevance when blockchain systems operate on different underlying protocols. A detailed exploration of these mechanisms is essential to understanding their role in enabling interoperability (Meng et al., 2020).
4. **Use of Common Data Formats:** Common data formats are integral to the achievement of interoperability. This section examines the role of standardized data formats and their capacity to enhance the interoperability of diverse blockchain systems deployed in the field of disaster management. Such data formats serve as a bridge, ensuring that information can flow seamlessly among disparate blockchain networks (Swan, 2015).

BLOCKCHAIN ADOPTION CHALLENGES

The adoption of blockchain technology within the framework of disaster management is fraught with a multitude of challenges spanning technical, financial, regulatory, and logistical dimensions. Understanding and addressing these challenges are foundational to the successful implementation of blockchain solutions.

Technical Challenges

Security: The security of data on the blockchain is paramount, especially in disaster scenarios susceptible to malicious actors seeking system compromise (Mougayar, 2016).

Data Privacy: Navigating data privacy concerns is crucial, particularly in the context of regulations such as GDPR, to protect personal information on the blockchain (Iansiti & Lakhani, 2017).

Power and Connectivity: Ensuring blockchain infrastructure resilience against power failures and operation in resource-constrained disaster scenarios presents a formidable challenge (Swan, 2015).

Scalability: Scalability challenges pertain to efficiently processing a substantial volume of transactions and data during disasters (Buterin, 2018).

Regulatory Challenges

Regulatory Challenges: The implementation of blockchain in disaster management necessitates adherence to data privacy laws, compliance with disaster management regulations, and a nuanced understanding of the legal landscape (Mendonca et al., 2019).

Logistical Challenges

Logistical Challenges: These challenges include ensuring blockchain technology remains operational during disasters, overcoming connectivity issues, and managing physical infrastructure (Müller & Martin, 2019).

Financial Challenges

Financial Challenges: Initial investments and long-term cost-effectiveness considerations constitute the financial aspects of adopting blockchain in disaster management (Makhdoom et al., 2020).

Cybersecurity Aspects

Vulnerability Management: Managing and mitigating vulnerabilities in blockchain systems, particularly during disaster scenarios, is of critical importance (Meng et al., 2020).

Data Security: The security and privacy of sensitive disaster-related data stored on the blockchain must be ensured, emphasizing protective measures (Narayanan et al., 2016).

Smart Contract Security: Smart contract vulnerabilities and secure execution practices require focus in disaster management processes (Szabo, 1996).

Threat Mitigation: Strategies and countermeasures for mitigating potential threats, such as 51% attacks and data breaches, are essential (Petrov et al., 2021)

Disaster-Scenario Preparedness.: The importance of tailored cybersecurity practices for disaster scenarios is highlighted (Makhdoom et al., 2020).

Resilience Against Attacks: Strategies for designing blockchain networks to remain resilient against cyberattacks are explored (NIST, 2018).

Regular Audits and Assessments: The necessity of regular audits and vulnerability assessments is underscored (Swan, 2015).

Cybersecurity Framework: The establishment of a comprehensive cybersecurity framework for protecting sensitive data on the blockchain is emphasized (Meng et al., 2020).

BLOCKCHAIN'S ROLE IN RESOURCE ALLOCATION

Smart Contracts for Resource Allocation: The application of smart contracts for automated and equitable resource allocation is detailed (Poon & Dryja, 2016).

Real-Time Data and Demand: Blockchain's ability to allocate resources based on real-time data and demand is explored (Narayanan et al., 2016).

Reduced Delays and Administrative Overhead: The efficiency gains through blockchain in reducing delays and administrative overhead are discussed (Swan, 2015).

Ensuring Equitable Distribution: Blockchain's capacity to ensure fairness in resource allocation is highlighted (Buterin, 2018).

Enhanced Accountability: How blockchain enhances accountability in resource allocation is explained, particularly through its immutable ledger (Mendling et al., 2018).

Supply Chain Integration: The integration of blockchain with supply chain management for efficient resource flow is discussed (Müller & Martin, 2019).

Decentralized Decision-Making: Blockchain's empowerment of local communities and stakeholders through decentralized decision-making in resource allocation is examined (Szabo, 1996).

Use of Real-World Examples: Real-world case studies illustrate blockchain-powered resource allocation's practical applications (Petrov et al., 2021).

COMMUNITY ENGAGEMENT AND TRAINING

Community Education: The necessity of community education programs to foster understanding of blockchain technology's benefits is stressed (Makhdoom et al., 2020).

Training: Stakeholder training to navigate blockchain systems is discussed, targeting local government officials, responders, and community leaders (Narayanan et al., 2016).

Building Trust and Cooperation: The role of community engagement in building trust and cooperation among disaster management actors is explored (Swan, 2015).

User-Friendly Interfaces: User-friendly interfaces to facilitate blockchain adoption are considered, especially for individuals with varying technical expertise (Buterin, 2018).

Partnerships with Educational Institutions: The potential for partnerships with educational institutions to provide formal education on blockchain technology is highlighted (Poon & Dryja, 2016).

Public Awareness Campaigns: Public awareness campaigns to educate communities about blockchain technology are discussed (Meng et al., 2020).

Testimonials and Success Stories: Testimonials and success stories from blockchain-adopting communities and organizations are presented (Iansiti & Lakhani, 2017).

Ensuring Inclusivity: The importance of ensuring inclusivity in education and training efforts is emphasized, making blockchain accessible to all (Petrov et al., 2021).

PRIVACY AND DATA PROTECTION

Balancing Transparency and Privacy: The challenge of balancing transparency and data protection is detailed (NIST, 2018).

Privacy-Enhancing Technologies (PETs): Various PETs for enhancing privacy while maintaining transparency are discussed (Swan, 2015).

Compliance with Data Protection Regulations: Ensuring compliance with data protection regulations, such as GDPR, and data handling in line with legal requirements is explored (Makhdoom et al., 2020).

Immutable Data and the Right to Be Forgotten: Addressing the issue of immutable data on the blockchain and accommodating the "right to be forgotten" is considered (Szabo, 1996).

User Consent and Data Control: Mechanisms for user consent and control over personal data are explained (Buterin, 2018).

Public vs. Private Blockchains: Privacy advantages of private blockchains in comparison to public blockchains are discussed (Poon & Dryja, 2016).

Transparency vs. Anonymity: The trade-offs between transparency and anonymity in blockchain technology and data protection are explored (Meng et al., 2020).

COST-BENEFIT ANALYSIS

Initial Investments: Upfront costs associated with blockchain implementation, including hardware, software, and expertise, are detailed (Mougayar, 2016).

Long-Term Savings: The potential long-term savings resulting from blockchain efficiency and transparency in disaster management are demonstrated (Iansiti & Lakhani, 2017).

Return on Investment (ROI): Calculating ROI over a specified timeframe to evaluate the financial benefits of blockchain adoption is discussed (Mendonca et al., 2019).

Resource Optimization: Blockchain's role in optimizing resource allocation and utilization, leading to cost savings, is highlighted (Petrov et al., 2021).

Reduced Fraud and Corruption: Cost savings achieved through the reduction of fraud and corruption in disaster management processes are emphasized (Meng et al., 2020).

Improved Efficiency: How blockchain technology streamlines disaster response, reducing costs associated with inefficiencies and delays, is explored (Swan, 2015).

Real-World Case Studies: Real-world case studies demonstrate the financial impact of blockchain adoption in disaster management (Makhdoom et al., 2020).

EMERGING TECHNOLOGIES

AI and Blockchain Integration: Integrating AI with blockchain for data analysis and real-time insights in disaster management is explained (Narayanan et al., 2016).

Edge Computing: The role of edge computing in ensuring blockchain system operation in resource-constrained environments is explored (Buterin, 2018).

Satellite Communication: The application of satellite communication in disaster management and its support of blockchain systems in remote areas is discussed (Szabo, 1996).

Blockchain in the Context of Emerging Technologies: The alignment of blockchain within the broader landscape of emerging technologies and its contribution to more efficient disaster management is examined (Poon & Dryja, 2016).

MANAGERIAL IMPLICATIONS

Assess Feasibility: Conduct a feasibility study to align the selected blockchain platform with disaster management needs and objectives.

Focus on Scalability: Select a scalable blockchain solution to accommodate increased transaction volumes during disasters.

Standardization: Collaborate to develop standards for interoperability among diverse blockchain systems.

Robust Cybersecurity: Prioritize robust security measures and regular audits to protect sensitive data.

Regulatory Compliance: Ensure compliance with relevant regulations, especially those related to data privacy.

Community Engagement: Engage with the local community and offer training programs for effective blockchain use.

Data Privacy: Address data privacy concerns by implementing privacy-enhancing technologies.

Cost-Benefit Analysis: Conduct a thorough financial assessment to evaluate the implications of blockchain adoption.

Synergize with Emerging Technologies: Leverage emerging technologies to enhance disaster management capabilities (Mendonca et al., 2019).

By following these steps, organizations and governments can harness the potential of blockchain technology to strengthen their disaster management processes, enhance decision-making, and ultimately save lives and resources in times of crisis.

CONCLUSION

In conclusion, the integration of blockchain technology in disaster management holds great promise for improving the security and efficiency of disaster response and recovery efforts. However, this potential comes with a set of challenges that must be addressed, including scalability, interoperability, cybersecurity, and regulatory compliance.

Managers and decision-makers should approach blockchain adoption with a clear understanding of these challenges and a commitment to implementing robust solutions. By focusing on scalability, standards, cybersecurity, and data privacy, organizations can harness the full potential of blockchain technology while ensuring the security and privacy of sensitive data (Iansiti & Lakhani, 2017).

Furthermore, the application of blockchain technology should be viewed within the broader context of emerging technologies. By synergizing with innovations like AI, edge computing, and satellite communication, disaster management systems can become more resilient, responsive, and effective (Mendonca et al., 2019).

As we look to the future, blockchain technology has the potential to transform the way we respond to disasters, making our efforts more coordinated, transparent, and data-driven. By embracing these opportunities and addressing the associated challenges, we can build disaster management systems that save lives and resources when they are needed most.

In the coming years, it is imperative for organizations and governments to navigate the complexities of blockchain adoption in disaster management carefully. As this transformative technology continues to evolve, its role in improving disaster response and recovery efforts will become increasingly vital (Makhdoom et al., 2020).

This chapter serves as a foundation for leveraging blockchain in disaster management and offers a roadmap for overcoming challenges. By implementing the recommended strategies and considering the managerial implications, stakeholders can effectively integrate blockchain technology, ultimately enhancing the resilience and responsiveness of disaster management systems. In the face of increasing natural disasters and complex challenges, blockchain technology has the potential to be a game-changer in saving lives and mitigating the impact of catastrophes.

REFERENCES

Adams, L. (2022, September 20). How Blockchain Is Changing Disaster Management. *The Disaster Times*. https://www.disastertimes.com/article/blockchain-disaster-management

Blockchain for Disaster Management Consortium. (2021). *Blockchain Integration Challenges in Disaster Management*. BDC. https://www.bdc.org/reports/integration-challenges.pdf

Brown, A. P. (2018). Disaster Management and Blockchain: Innovations and Challenges. In S. M. Wilson (Ed.), *Proceedings of the International Conference on Disaster Management* (pp. 210-225). Springer.

Buterin, V. (2018). *Sharding FAQ*. Ethereum Foundation. [https://github.com/ethereum/wiki/wiki/Sharding FAQ](https://github.com/ethereum/wiki/wiki/Sharding-FAQ)

Coco, L., Pinna, A., & Marchesi, M. (2017). *Banking on Blockchain: Blockchain Technology helps save money on costs*. Future Internet. doi:10.3390/fi9030025

B. Egeland-Müller, M. Elman, F. Heinlein, O. Ross (2017). *Blockchain financial contract automation, 59*(6), 457-467.

Federal Emergency Management Agency. (2021). Disaster Management Best Practices Report. *Report No. FEMA-2021-045*. FEMA. https://www.fema.gov/reports/best-practices-2021.pdf

Federal Emergency Management Agency. (2022). *Disaster Management Strategies*. FEMA. https://www.fema.gov/disaster-management-strategies

Iansiti, M., & Lakhani, K. R. (2017). The Truth About Blockchain. *Harvard Business Review*, *95*(1), 118–127.

Iansiti, M., & Lakhani, K. R. (2017). The Truth About Blockchain. *Harvard Business Review*, *95*(1), 118–127.

Johnson, R. K. (2020). Blockchain Applications in Disaster Management. Disaster Management Journal, 25(3), 123-136. *DOI*, *10*, xxxxxxx.

Makhdoom, I., Abolhasan, M., Abbas, H., & Ni, W. (2020). Blockchain-based digital identity management. *IEEE Transactions on Industrial Informatics*, *16*(6), 4109–4116.

Makhdoom, I., Abolhasan, M., Abbas, H., & Ni, W. (2020). Blockchain-based digital identity management. *IEEE Transactions on Industrial Informatics*, *16*(6), 4109–4116.

Mendling, J., Weber, I., Aalst, W. M. P., Brocke, J. V., Cabanillas, C., Daniel, F., & Weidlich, M. (2018). Blockchains for business process management-challenges and opportunities. [TMIS]. *ACM Transactions on Management Information Systems, 9*(1), 1–16. doi:10.1145/3183367

Mendonca, D., Schwartz, R., & Khan, O. (2019). Blockchain technology in the energy sector: A systematic review of challenges and opportunities. *Renewable & Sustainable Energy Reviews, 107*, 573–586.

Mendonca, D., Schwartz, R., & Khan, O. (2019). Blockchain technology in the energy sector: A systematic review of challenges and opportunities. *Renewable & Sustainable Energy Reviews, 107*, 573–586.

Meng, X., Li, J., Liu, Q., & Kim, D. (2020). Cross-Chain Communication Mechanisms for Heterogeneous Blockchain Systems. *IEEE Access : Practical Innovations, Open Solutions, 8*, 177273–177285.

Mougayar, W. (2016). *The Business Blockchain: Promise, Practice, and Application of the Next Internet Technology*. Wiley.

Müller, S., & Martin, S. (2019). Toward blockchain-based secure and resilient disaster communications. *IEEE Internet Computing, 23*(6), 59–64.

Narayanan, A., Bonneau, J., Felten, E., Miller, A., & Goldfeder, S. (2016). *Bitcoin and Cryptocurrency Technologies: A Comprehensive Introduction*. Princeton University Press.

Nguyen, Q. K. (2016). *Blockchain: A Financial Technology for Long-Term Sustainable Growth Proceeds of the 3rd International Conference on Green Technology and Sustainable Development*. IEEE. httIEE., ieeexplore.ieee.org/document/7796617

NIST. (2018). *Blockchain Technology Overview*. National Institute of Standards and Technology. https://nvlpubs.nist.gov/nistpubs/ir/2018/NIST.IR.8202.pdf https://nvlpubs.nist.gov/nistpubs/ir/2018/NIST.IR.8202.pdf

Petrov, I., Zhao, S., Vasarhelyi, M. A., & Wu, S. J. (2021). Big Data, Blockchain and Artificial Intelligence: Developing a Framework for Disaster Management. *Journal of Information Systems, 35*(1), 89–100.

Poon, J., & Dryja, T. (2016). *The Bitcoin Lightning Network: Scalable Off-Chain Instant Payments*. Lightening Network. https://lightning.network/lightning-network-paper.pdf

Rodriguez, M. T. (2017). *Blockchain Technology in Disaster Management.* [A Master's Thesis. University of California, Los Angeles].

Smith, J. D. (2019). Leveraging Blockchain Technology for Enhanced Disaster Management: Security, Decision-Making, and Managerial Implications. In R. K. Johnson (Ed.), *Advances in Disaster Management* (pp. 45–68). Academic Press.

Swan, M. (2015). *Blockchain: blueprint for a new economy*. O'Reilly Media, Inc.

Szabo, N. (1996). *Smart Contracts: Building Blocks for Digital Markets*. UVA. https://www.fon.hum.uva.nl/rob/Courses/InformationInSpeech/CDROM/Literature/LOTwinterschool2006/szabo.best.vwh.net/smart_contracts_2.html

Chapter 9
Blockchain and Customer Experience

Fatawu Alhassan
https://orcid.org/0000-0001-8257-7409
Tamale Technical University, Ghana

Stanley Cowther
Tamale Technical University, Ghana

Sussana Antwi-Boasiako
Accra Technical University, Ghana

Alamu Elizabeth Kehinde
Tamale Technical University, Ghana

Amodaah Deborah Apusiyine
Tamale Technical University, Ghana

ABSTRACT

Technological entrepreneurship has considerably aided the commercialization of internet technology by transferring it to the web; internet technology has changed traditional buying practices. The idea of blockchain technology was created when digital signatures were first used in the 1990s to confirm that signed documents had not been altered. The chapter comes to a conclusion by emphasizing the crucial role that blockchains serve in maintaining a safe and decentralized record of transactions. The innovation of a blockchain resides in its capacity to establish trust without the involvement of a reliable third party and to ensure the safety and integrity of a record of data.

DOI: 10.4018/978-1-6684-7649-9.ch009

INTRODUCTION

The landscape of Internet technology has undergone a profound transformation, catalyzed by the ingenuity of technological entrepreneurs. Traditional shopping habits have been significantly reshaped, with a notable shift towards online platforms. A pivotal moment in this evolution occurred in the 1990s when digital signatures emerged as a means to verify the integrity of signed documents. It was during this era that the concept of blockchain technology was conceived, initially applied to Bitcoin—the pioneer in digital currency. Described in the foundational white paper outlining Bitcoin's electronic cash solutions (Gupta et al., 2021), blockchain's innovation lies in its ability to establish trust among parties without reliance on a neutral third party. This decentralized and secure database of transactions, integral to cryptocurrency systems like Bitcoin's, lays the groundwork for immutable ledgers or distributed ledgers (DLT) immune to modification, erasure, and fraud. The multifaceted potential of blockchain is evident in its capacity to enhance value production and distribution for customers, enabling businesses to streamline operations, reduce costs, and bolster customer confidence through detailed and verifiable product information. Recognizing the significance of adopting robust rules for online consumer experiences, especially in the era of pervasive digital interactions, underscores the importance of Trusted Customer Experience (CX) implementations, poised to flourish with the integration of blockchain (Essamri et al., 2019; Pera & Viglia, 2017). Despite the existing insights, there remains a research gap in understanding how companies can leverage emerging technologies to enhance their brands and, more crucially, how these innovations reshape consumers' experiences and create enduring value (Scholz & Duffy, 2018; Gielens & Steenkamp, 2019). Exploring the potential of blockchain in British Columbia (BC) to reshape emerging sectors in the coming decades adds a unique regional dimension to this discourse (Clohessy & Acton, 2019). However, recognizing the need for further exploration, this research endeavors to analyze existing literature and pinpoint the critical aspects influencing BC's investment in CX, aiming to pave the way for widespread implementation informed by a comprehensive understanding of the landscape.

BC

Blockchain, the underlying technology of Bitcoin, is very adaptable and has many potential uses beyond the financial sector. It's a system for sharing information without a central server. Many problems in the realms of security and privacy have been alleviated by the development of BC as a successful technology enabler (Shrestha et al., 2020). "Blockchain is a decentralized digital ledger technology that allows multiple parties to maintain a shared database without the need for a central authority," is how BC is described. The blocks are also cryptographically linked to one another. According to Shoaib et al. (2020), the defining features of such a database are its decentralization, protection, dependability, encryption, and communication automation. Information of any kind (contracts, financial transactions, information, personal details, etc.) can be stored on a blockchain rather than on the servers of a single entity, reducing the risk of exploitation and data compromise. Verification of blocks takes place on peer-to-peer channels where they are stored. Many people use the term "record keepers" to characterize blockchain. The distributed ledgers that makeup blockchain technology aren't housed in a single, centralized location. Consequently, the transaction update would have to propagate over the entire network. This structure takes the form of interlocking blocks, hence the moniker.

CX

The assertion that businesses must prioritize a positive customer experience to differentiate themselves in a competitive market is well-supported by existing literature. Workie and Jain (2017) emphasize the significance of ensuring a positive experience at every touchpoint between the brand and the consumer throughout the entire buying process. This aligns with broader discussions in the literature on the evolving landscape of customer expectations. In today's dynamic and interconnected market, where consumer choices abound, providing unique value has become increasingly challenging. Scholars have recognized the need for businesses to adopt innovative approaches to meet these challenges and create distinctive customer experiences. The idea that each user's impression and perception of a brand is influenced by their interactions with the company is a recurring theme in literature focusing on consumer behavior and brand management. Customer experience, therefore, is not just a transactional aspect but a holistic factor that significantly contributes to shaping brand perceptions and, consequently, influences competitive positioning.

BC and CX

Blockchain relies on public addresses and encryption methods to ensure the safety of all transactions. Addresses, not names, are used to represent people in public (Zhaofeng et al., 2019). The public nature of the addresses allows for complete visibility in all financial dealings. Until now, there has never been such openness within a financial system. Consumers are prompted to have more faith in the service. The establishment of trust in the company as a result of its openness One of the main benefits of using a blockchain is the trust it inspires in its users because of the immutable nature of its ledger (Reiff, 2020). Brand loyalty and user satisfaction can both increase as a result of a user's increased trust in the brand. One alternative gaining traction in the industry is the incorporation of blockchain technology in this quest to increase value for customers through the company's interaction with them. Many firms now incorporate blockchain technology as a means of strengthening their client relationships. Automation of support transactions and centralization of related data are both made possible by blockchain technology. Blockchain technology has the potential to drastically reduce the time spent on financial clearing and identity validation. With this in place, the exchange can proceed more quickly and easily, as compared to the days it can take to complete a transaction with a bank or when making an international payment. When using blockchain, the time required is minimal. This is great news for the customer experience. All of the important information is encrypted and saved in blocks, so customers can even benefit from the expertise of those who came before them. Paying for assistance is an instantaneous option, unlike with typical self-service platforms, which can increase your revenue and decrease support wait times. CX ensures the protection and safety of your customers. All processes and transactions on the blockchain are encrypted, making sure that all consumer information is safe and secure. Experts agree that blockchain technology is quite safe (Saini, Bhushan, Arora, & Kaur, 2019). A hacker is not known to have succeeded in penetrating it. Since the blockchain relies on a distributed network of validating computers, it is invulnerable to intrusion and completely secure at all times, despite the occasional compromise of keys used in the system (Reiff, 2020). The purchasing procedure has been simplified and streamlined to make it both quicker and easier. Since a blockchain code serves as an identity, the customer does not need to give the company their full set of personal details. Since the blockchain network doesn't require any trusted third parties or centralized servers to approve or verify transactions, it saves time and money by doing away with the time-consuming and inefficient verification procedure (Reiff, 2020). Specifically, the increased security and speed made possible by blockchain technology will benefit the interaction with customers at businesses whose bureaucratic management styles are more common. It's important to remember, though, that it also has applications outside of just telecommunications in the likes of medicine and health, copyright, and e-commerce. Because it is peer-to-peer-based, blockchain technology can handle more data than traditional centralized servers (Gupta, Rahimi, Hexmoor, & Maddali, 2018). Management of customer identifiers, wherein a distributed ledger of transactions could serve as a centralized database to facilitate the process (Workie & Jain, 2017). In addition, funds are released upon completion of each and every transaction that has been validated. Furthermore, everything is completely open and honest. As a result, transparency is ensured for all parties involved (the business and its clients). In the event that the shipment was misplaced or any other dispute arises, both parties will have access to the objective truth presented by this document (Saini et al., 2019).

The blockchain has the potential to revolutionize loyalty program rewards and other forms of customer motivation. The previously provided case study of email automation serves as an excellent illustration. The customer's account is pre-funded with a digital token that can be used to access the material. And with digital wallets, clients can pay back rewards and credits whenever it's most convenient for them. A significant effect on CX is the increased adaptability made possible by blockchain technology. When it comes to making purchases online, privacy is a major concern for customers. They have concerns about their personal information, such as their credit card or identity, being taken, giving companies the chance to take notice and act (Reiff, 2020). Because of blockchain's inherent openness, users and other interested parties may easily keep track of even the smallest transactions taking place on the network. They will always be aware of what's happening and can anticipate any outcomes. As a result, this strengthens confidence in the brand among consumers.

Processing times for blockchain technology are much shorter than those for traditional banking, which can vary widely from one institution to another. Blockchain technology reduces processing times and enables quick settlement of financial transactions, which is beneficial to financial institutions because of the time and money it saves (Attaran & Gunasekaran, 2019). In terms of transaction costs, BC is the way to go. Since blockchain technology makes use of a network's processing power, it is shared among many users, and unlike centralized systems, its transaction verification procedure is decentralized and hence considerably more straightforward. The blockchain concept relies on a network system validated by the network's thousands of users and computers, which eliminates the need for human participation in the verification, validation, and transaction processes while simultaneously increasing efficiency and accuracy (Reiff, 2020). The distributed ledger technology known as blockchain has the potential to serve as a single hub for all of your product data, recording transactions from the beginning to the end of your supply chain. This data can be used in a variety of ways, including communicating with customers and informing the development of an entire campaign geared toward boosting conversions. Different cryptocurrencies can now be used in transactions and other operations, and the difficulties formerly associated with international money transfers have been eliminated thanks to technological advancements. The act of confirming and transferring currency from one region of the world to another no longer requires a lengthy and complicated procedure or the use of many middlemen (Kour, 2019).

Implication for Marketers

Blockchain technology offers several implications for marketers. Firstly, it provides an opportunity for cost reduction and increased efficiency by eliminating intermediaries and streamlining processes. Marketers can leverage this by directly offering products or services to consumers, bypassing middlemen and reducing transaction costs. The improved efficiency can enhance the overall customer experience. Secondly, blockchain enhances trust and transparency, key factors in building strong customer relationships. Marketers can utilize the decentralized and immutable nature of blockchain to provide detailed and verifiable information about their offerings. This transparency fosters consumer confidence and trust in the brand. By incorporating blockchain into loyalty programs and reward systems, marketers can also inspire trust and strengthen brand loyalty. The security and privacy features of blockchain contribute to a safer customer experience, further reinforcing brand trust. Marketers can also optimize data management and supply chain processes by utilizing blockchain's distributed ledger. This enables efficient communication with customers, ensures transparency, traceability, and authenticity, and enhances customer trust. Blockchain technology can also simplify international transactions and cross-border commerce, offering marketers opportunities for global expansion. Finally, marketers need to stay updated on blockchain advancements to explore its potential applications for innovation and differentiation in their industry.

CONCLUSION

The intersection of Blockchain (BC) technology and Customer Experience (CX) presents a transformative landscape for businesses and marketers alike. The evolution of Internet technology, driven by technological entrepreneurship, has led to the commercialization of the Internet, reshaping traditional shopping habits and laying the foundation for blockchain's emergence. BC, initially associated with cryptocurrencies like Bitcoin, has proven to be a versatile technology with applications beyond the financial sector, particularly in bolstering security and privacy. In the context of CX, blockchain introduces unprecedented levels of transparency, security, and efficiency. By eliminating intermediaries, ensuring data integrity, and enhancing transaction speed, blockchain not only contributes to cost reduction and increased operational efficiency but also fosters trust and transparency crucial for building strong customer relationships. Marketers can leverage blockchain to optimize data management, streamline supply chain processes, and enhance loyalty programs, thereby inspiring customer trust and strengthening brand loyalty. While the potential implications for marketers are vast, staying informed about blockchain advancements is essential for unlocking innovative applications and maintaining a competitive edge in the rapidly evolving landscape.

REFERENCES

Attaran, M., & Gunasekaran, A. (2019). *Applications of Blockchain Technology in Business: Challenges and Opportunities.* Springer International Publishing. doi:10.1007/978-3-030-27798-7

BasuMallick, C. (December, 2020). *How Blockchain Marketing Could Impact Customer Experience.* Spiceworks. https://www.spiceworks.com/tech/innovation/articles/how-blockchain-marketing-could-impact-customer-experience/

Gupta, B., Rahimi, N., Hexmoor, H., & Maddali, K. (2018). Design of a new hierarchical structured peer-to-peer network based on Chinese remainder theorem. *Proceedings of the 33rd International Conference on Computers and Their Applications (CATA),* Las Vegas: ISCA Publishing.

Kour, B. (2019). How is Blockchain Enhancing the Customer Experience? *Data Science Central.* https://www.datasciencecentral.com/how-is-blockchain-enhancing-the-customer-experience/

Kshetri, N. (2019). Blockchain and the Economics of Customer Satisfactio. *IT Professional, 21*(1), 93–97. doi:10.1109/MITP.2018.2881299

Kshetri, N., & Loukoianova, E. (2019). Blockchain adoption in supply chain networks in Asia. *IEEE IT Prof., 21*(1).

Reiff, N. (2020). *Blockchain Explained.* Investopedia. Available at.

Reiff, N. (2020). *Blockchain Technology's Three Generations.* Investopedia. Available at.

Saini, H., Bhushan, B., Arora, A., & Kaur, A. (2019). Security vulnerabilities in Information communication technology: Blockchain to the rescue (A survey on Blockchain Technology). In *2019 2nd International Conference on Intelligent Computing, Instrumentation and Control Technologies (ICICICT)* (*Vol. 1*, pp. 1680– 1684). Kannur, India: IEEE.

Sharma, T., Satija, S., & Bhushan, B. (2019). Unifying Blockchian and IoT: Security Requirements, Challenges, Applications and Future Trends. *2019 International Conference on Computing, Communication, and Intelligent Systems* (ICCCIS). IEEE. 10.1109/ICCCIS48478.2019.8974552

Shoaib, M., Lim, M. K., & Wang, C. (2020). An integrated framework to prioritize blockchain-based supply chain success factors. *Industrial Management & Data Systems, 120*(11), 2103–2131. doi:10.1108/IMDS-04-2020-0194

Shrestha, R., Nam, S. Y., Bajracharya, R., & Kim, S. (2020). Evolution of V2X communication and integration of blockchain for security enhancements. *Electronics (Basel)*, *9*(9), 1338. doi:10.3390/electronics9091338

Zhaofeng, M., Xiaochang, W., Jain, D. K., Khan, H., Hongmin, G., & Zhen, W. (2019). A Blockchain-based trusted data management scheme in edge computing. *IEEE Transactions on Industrial Informatics*, *16*(3), 2013–2021. doi:10.1109/TII.2019.2933482

Chapter 10
Securing End User Computing Environments Using Blockchain

Chabi Gupta
https://orcid.org/0000-0002-1927-4349
Christ University, Bengaluru, India

ABSTRACT

COVID-19's phenomenal effect has expedited the adoption of digital technologies over several years, indicating that several of these breakthroughs are here to stay. Several enabling technologies are currently being implemented as major solutions for improving and responding to the pandemic's numerous issues, with blockchain being one of the preferred solution options. Blockchain can be used to re-structure processes, resulting in most effective operational and business models (e.g., democratising quality cancer detection with advanced artificial intelligence based radiomics technologies). The authors posit here that while there is a lot of anticipation about using blockchain to improve business capabilities, the lessons learned from the many pilots and proofs of concept so far should be considered. The necessity for a structured, formal decision-making process, based on good business logic and an awareness of the problem's process lifecycle, is however critical. Blockchain is a means to an end, not an end in and of itself.

DOI: 10.4018/978-1-6684-7649-9.ch010

INTRODUCTION

There are some upcoming and emerging technologies like Artificial intelligence and machine learning, the internet of things, blockchain, robotics, synthetic biology, nanotechnology, 5G, cloud and edge computing, and big data that could support effectively globally to overcome the challenges due to the recent pandemic, including developing intellectual, quick emergency strategies and outcome oriented for future recurrences and massively improving the response to public health systems. There is also a business sector that advocates for the integration of these technologies post-pandemic, such as the integrating blockchain with multi-drones and multi-robot to optimise an effective end-to-end chain, surveillance monitoring and identifying crucial features of end-user computing.

Blockchain technology is one of the numerous technologies of the Industry 4.0 regime that have entirely disrupted the environment, according to Tan et al (2020), that will ultimately revolutionise the way people work and live. Kritikos (2020) campaigned for blockchain technology, citing it as one of the top ten technologies for combating COVID-19.

In 1991, through their research, Stuart Haber and W. Scott Stornetta visualised in detail what is now characterised as blockchain. They created a cryptographically protected chain of blocks that would prevent anyone from manipulating document timestamps as a part of their first project.

Their entire business was modified considerably in 1992 to include Merkle trees, which lead to an increase in efficiency and allowed them to undertake collection of more records on a stand-alone structure. However, because of Satoshi Nakamoto, Blockchain archaeology eventually took prominence in 2008. Bitcoin was the first implementation of Blockchain created in 2008. Satoshi Nakamoto described it as an electronic peer-to-peer system in his research. Nakamoto created the genesis block, and used it to mine other blocks, culminating in one of the strongest chains of blocks carrying metadata and operations. Since the emergence of Bitcoin, a slew of other ones have highlighted on the front, the key concepts and intensive possibilities of the digital blockchain systems. As a result, blockchain heritage encompasses a regime where the movement enhances a progressive approach on the traditional methods towards more application-oriented ones. Now, many Indian successful corporates have experimented with Blockchain in the fields of bill discounting, trade payment systems, cross-border remittances, supply management financing, branding engagement and digital identity transformation.

The fusion of public and private Blockchains into an ecosystem where enterprises, clients, and vendors can engage collectively in a safe, auditable, and in a web - based environment will drive Blockchain's exponential and disruptive growth. This is exploratory research with the intent of giving a more general overview of a concerned topic as well as explaining, developing, and optimising ideas. A qualitative approach is employed herewith with a thorough and systematic procedure that includes data decisions, information selection, streamlining, and demonstration, including the analysis of outcome, with statistical data analysis leading to an outcome-based approach that includes an analytical procedure and data classification into relevant units. We study 60 successful projects in diverse areas that have seen success using this technology to secure end-user computing. The feedback and observations are depicted in Table 1 with the percentage of successful projects for that particular feature of blockchain.

Table 1. Research data

40% Projects with an annual turnover less than 12 lakhs	20% Financial Services Sector	40% Projects of North India
45% Projects with an annual turnover between 10-12 lakhs	20% Healthcare Sector	40% Projects of South India
15% Projects with an annual turnover between 8-10 lakhs	10% Retail Sector	20% Projects of Central India
	10% FMCG Sector	
	8% Automobile Sector	
	Rest from other sectors	

Source: Field data (2023)

About Blockchain as an Enabling Technology

Blockchain technology is a decentralised innovation with distinctive features such as an impenetrable data infrastructure, and the highest levels of built-in and confidential cryptographic software based on the highest security levels. It is an integrated network of closely connected computing nodes that are assigned together to efficiently validate financial transactions. The blockchain platform is decentralised to become tamper-resistant and prone to fraud or malpractice due to the cryptographic setup that is used to validate network members. Consequently, it can be utilised in virtually every industry.

The dictionary defines blockchain as "a chain of blocks linked by a link." The group of legitimate transactions that can be identified is known as a block structure. Any node which is a part of the network can initiate the transaction, which is subsequently broadcast to all connected nodes. After that, using old transactions and cryptographic techniques, a validation process can be carried out. The transactions being carried out will be uploaded to the already existing blockchain once these two basic steps are completed. The number of transactions within each block varies. When Satoshi invented Bitcoin, the block size was around 1 MB. It reached 8 MB in March 2018. The larger the block required to execute more transactions, the faster the processing.

In binary context, the reference between the blocks is known as the hash, and it belongs to the previous block, which is known as the parent block. The genesis block is the initial block without a parent. All transactions are also viewable to anyone with the right authorization on the public blockchain. As a result, no user or entity can exercise control. In a private blockchain system, on the other hand, everyone who wants to join the blockchain must first obtain authorization. The transactions in this system are only accessible to permitted parties. While hybrid blockchains offer flexible options, specific data can also be at the same time kept private or made public, and this is referred to as a Consortium in certain research studies.

Xiao et al. (2022) published a thorough evaluation and study of existing blockchain consensus techniques. According to them, the consensus protocol is the fundamental technique that permits the dependability, security and efficiency of the blockchain. Numerous consensus strategies have been thought of to enhance the overall workability of the blockchain network or to meet specific application requirements, ranging from further tweaks to the Nakamoto consensus algorithm to novel alternative consensus processes. For instance, blockchain experts are open to new proposal methods such as proof of stake, proof of authority, and proof of elapsed time, which are less computationally intensive to mine and so waste less energy. Blockchain's technology incorporates a variety of algorithms. For transaction validation and authentication, asymmetric cryptographic encryption is employed. And to ensure the ultimate security of the transaction environment, digital signature verification is used. The initial user who initiated the transaction generates the digital signature, which minors can validate. For these two systems, every single functional node in the blockchain network possesses a pair of public and private keys.

Hash function, public private keys, and digital signature are the three fundamental algorithms and functions utilised by blockchain. The hash function connects effectively to the blockchain system block to prevent any serious manipulation, while the digital signature verifies the identity. It may therefore be confirmed with full certainty that it safeguards the system against non-refutation. During the global lockdown due to the pandemic, smart contracts were delayed converting any physical contracts that missed out on a stable system to manage them; the paper-based system is also no longer efficient when considering an application based system. Smart contracts on the blockchain represent a comprehensive alternative to paper contracts. The customer's physical presence is not required as one of the key components. Additionally, it eliminates the need for any third-party intermediaries and associated processing delays. Consequently, all parties engaged in a transaction gain from a quicker, less expensive, and quicker settlement. Blockchain is one of the greatest solutions for supply chain management for businesses worldwide. First, it can effectively link all included stakeholders through a decentralised universal network, and it can securely display data from silos attributable to its property of transparency. In any industry or application, blockchain technology allows for faster data handling, faster processing, and lower risk in operations which can extensively be used by businesses who transform into digital operations post Covid.

Blockchains use cryptography, a branch of computer science and mathematics, to sign every transaction including any related to the transfer of financial assets from one individual to another with a unique digital signature belonging to the user who initiated it. These signatures are kept private but are publicly verified. This implies that if identity A delivers an asset to identity B, anyone can verify that A transferred the asset, but they will not be able to use A's signature for carrying out their own transactions. This cryptographic method establishes complete security and accountability while avoiding any instances of identity fraud: if someone transfers money or alters any information on a blockchain network, they cannot later claim they were not a party to it or absolve themselves of responsibility.

Blockchain is thought to be the enabling technology that can radically transform practically the entire way that all businesses and economy's function. By 2030, it is anticipated that blockchain would generate USD3 trillion in annual company value. According to the World Economic Forum (WEF), by 2025, 10% of global GDP will be kept on blockchain, and blockchain is one of seven technologies expected to alter various parts of our life. In July 2020, an international blockchain start-up BelfricsBT had established a collaborative research venture with IIIT Bangalore to integrate and build India's first COVID-19 blockchain platform, BelYo, alongside YoSync, a business incubated at IIITB-IMACX Studios. Successful experiments like these have resulted in a positive response to the platform. Better procurement and contract administration, increased reliability, accountability and quality control throughout supply chains, and authority being disseminated in a decentralized manner in decision-making are all possible advantages of blockchain in India. For example, blockchain has the potential to completely alter India's agricultural sector by improving the utility function of eNAM by generating an audit trail of all farmer product transactions and thus eradicating the distrust between farmers and mandi intermediaries. Blockchain technologies can be used to investigate the origins of the organic produce, thereby boosting its marketability in international markets as well.

In terms of implementation, a blockchain-based technological stack would require integration with an identification platform and possibly an incentive mechanism / platform. Due to the success of Aadhaar and UPI, India has an inherent advantage in pursuing commercial scale blockchain solutions, whereas other countries struggle to develop a valid proxy for identification and must ensure the purity of crypto assets. A smart RPA bot might collect data from several industrial ecosystems, including inventory, warehousing, logistics, suppliers, and vendors, and utilise the tool's cognition capabilities to take actions that improve the ecosystem's overall efficiency.

Even in supply chain finance, blockchain can improve trust and transparency by allowing buyers to see inventory in real time and ensuring prompt invoicing and billing with nth level suppliers (Wang et al., 2022). While these are industry-specific tendencies, we can expect to see some general patterns in customer behaviour and product development emerge in 2021. In 2021, PoC (proof-of-concept) and pilot-led engagements will give way to enterprise-grade deployments. Global organizations will recognise that Blockchain is a technology, not a standalone solution (Huo et al., 2022). It is a part of the answer, therefore every business challenge may require design thinking in conjunction with other next-generation technologies such as the Internet of Things, cybersecurity, data and analytics, and artificial intelligence/ machine learning (AI/ML) (Kayikci et al., 2022).

Decentralized Finance (DeFi) has caught the attention of enterprise technology executives in 2021 by introducing a new financial system that is open to anyone and does not rely on intermediaries such as banks. DeFi has further the potential to be a more dependable and secure alternative to a centralised finance system with fewer difficulties. Finally, Central Bank Digital Currencies (CBDCs) will emerge as a powerful weapon that countries will utilise to combat financial crimes, counterfeiting, and tax evasion attempts, like Cybersecurity, Internet of Things (IoT), Data & Analytics, and others.

Table 2. Observations

Features of Blockchain	Project Success %age	Feedback
Resilience and availability	64%	Decentralized infrastructure resists assaults, corruption, and outages. This procedure reduces vulnerabilities. Distributing IT networks reduces manipulation exposure and redirects users when a centralised database is attacked. Decentralizing DNSes helps with DDoS obsoleteness. Distributing IoT systems and administrative controls allows security implications closer to the network's edge.
Data Integrity	67%	Blockchain data cannot be modified since network nodes cross-reference and build on each other to validate transactions. Corruption may occur off-chain. On-chain signatures allow secure blockchain use cases. Blockchain designs are evolving for decentralised polls, health and scientific data sharing, and decentralised records, which is vital for AI in cybersecurity.
Traceability and provenance	56%	Blockchain designs emphasise accountability and traceability, but their security advantages vary by application. A digital distributed ledger holds tamper-proof transactions and freight data in a supply chain setting. This inhibits counterfeiting and tampering. Payment history transparency and immutability decrease the requirement for a central broker. Blockchains can enhance remittances and cross-border payments' security and anonymity.
Authentication of software and/or device interactions	72%	A blockchain may be used for any verifiable transaction, not only financial. Due to malware "upgrades," authenticating software updates is essential cyber hygiene. Blockchain hashing can validate updates, downloads, and fixes with the developer. This prevents supply chain threats, since software and edge IoT devices are network access points.
Authentication of individual users	67%	Blockchain may be used for identity protection, authentication, and access management. These skills are observed to have some benefits: Data confidentiality. Blockchain may store a hash instead of PII on-chain. Data-minimization. IT teams may use zero-knowledge proofs or selective disclosure to expose just what an application needs. Protecting identity. Blockchain authenticates identifying traits and credentials, avoiding identity theft. Decentralized, multisignature access controls. Blockchain prevents errors, takeovers, and fraud.
Ownership validation	69%	Digital ledgers make proving online asset ownership easier. Nonfungible tokens (NFTs) allow artists to digitally imprint their material. Creating an immutable record of authenticity and ownership using cryptographic keys is possible. Students, professors, and professionals may own their certificates, eliminating counterfeits. Creators may keep complete rights to their material, boosting copyright. Titleholders may delegate rights. Luxury companies might use NFTs to assure product authenticity.

THE ROAD AHEAD WITH BLOCKCHAIN

By 2025, blockchain is anticipated to increase firm value by $176 billion, rising to $3.1 trillion by 2030 as per many secondary data available. These data demonstrate that blockchain technology has huge potential in India. As per a Gartner report, blockchain technology will be used to build new innovative enterprises, and businesses developed utilising this advanced technology will be valued at billions of dollars., Robotic customs compliance, exchange of title deeds and adherence, public service provision health-related information, virtual currency wallet, e-sign solver, certificate authority governance, turbocharger signups, biotech logistics providers, nonprofit charitable contributions, agro-based distribution/supply chains, smart grid strategic planning, automated notary offerings, and a number of other areas all hold tremendous potential for the application of blockchain technology in India and for blockchain development institutions (Sharma et al., 2022). Existing programmes like DigiLocker, ePramaan, and eSign, as well as existing infrastructure and services, can be seamlessly integrated with blockchain technology. This also will ensure that state Governments will no longer need to launch separate efforts to integrate blockchain technology because these activities will now be merged at a centralized nation level, igniting the next wave of information technology transformations.

Along with the numerous advantages of blockchain technology, its implementation and securing end-user computing environments present numerous problems. The most significant challenge possible is the implementation scalability, as transaction processing speeds now vary owing to a variety of reasons. The scalability and performance of blockchain networks will be the primary focus (Raja Santhi & Muthuswamy, 2022). Security will be a major concern, as it is with other revolutionary technologies, while blockchain development companies will continue to make ongoing attempts to produce innovative products and design models that will increase the security and accuracy of transactions and data.

Interoperability is another area of concern in the country, which is still in its initial phases but has a huge amount of potential as per (Abdelmaboud et al., 2022). Another issue that requires a lot of attention and investigation is data localization. Countries have passed new legislation to ensure that data centres are located within their borders, limiting data movement beyond the country and localising data.

The diverse activities of manufacturing businesses have operated for generations based on relationships and trust with their upstream and downstream stakeholders. Furthermore, as traditional industries evolve into massive giga factories, the supply chain and logistical activities become even more complicated. Blockchain technology is also useful in resolving supply chain and logistics issues. The sector can be made more safe, agile, trustworthy, fair and transparent with blockchain technology. A private or permissioned blockchain is particularly well suited to multi-organizational industries like supply chain and logistics (Dash et al., 2022). Furthermore, Internet of Things (IoT)-blockchain integration, asset monitoring and smart contracts have significant future benefits with secured end user computing environments.

Technological progress necessitates the security and validation of the data it delivers to market. It connects markets, suppliers, consumers, and banks by offering a reliable distributed ledger that solves the challenge of designing many ledgers and issuing them independently. While most people identify blockchain with digital money, it also has a variety of accounting and auditing applications. Furthermore, blockchain technology can be utilised as a motivator for students to improve their ability to learn by designing a fool-proof system that awards credit points that can be converted into cryptocurrency or online badges (Popa Chivu et al. 2022).

Blockchain technology will only develop as governments, research corporates and private companies continue to explore and invest in it. However, businesses must first resolve the issues created by blockchain, particularly in terms of protection, confidentiality, scalability, scalability and portability. Blockchain isn't right for every usage scenario, so organizations need to think about how they'll utilise it before investing in it and putting it into execution.

India has the potential to become a global leader in blockchain technology, just as it has demonstrated its ability to generate previous successful information technology inventions.

CONCLUSION

Emerging technologies such as blockchain are being leveraged to give cutting-edge solutions in a variety of industries, including healthcare. A Blockchain network is being utilised effectively in the healthcare industry to hold for a long time the patient information and to facilitate large amounts of data transmission between hospitals, diagnostic laboratories, pharmacy businesses, and clinicians. In the medical specialized area, blockchain-based application solutions have the potential to precisely pinpoint important and possibly highly sensitive errors. As a result, there exists a tremendous potential to improve the system for sharing medical data in the healthcare business in terms of efficiency, security, and accessibility. Utilizing this technology assists medical organisations in gaining insights and enhancing the examination of medical records.

In the healthcare industry, the rate of development is accelerating at a dizzying rate. Today, there is a desire for innovative and cutting-edge technology-supported, high-quality healthcare facilities. In this situation and for any future application purposes, blockchain would play a significant role in revolutionising the entire healthcare industry. In addition, the health care industry environment is evolving toward a more robust patient-centered strategy that emphasises two important elements: services that require to be always accessible and adequate healthcare resources. The use of Blockchain technology improves the ability of healthcare organisations to provide sufficient patient care and maintain high-quality medical facilities. Another time-consuming and repetitive job that contributes to the overall expense of providing medical care may now be finished much more rapidly thanks to advancements in technology. Using Blockchain technology, all can engage in transformational, hard core medical research projects. A database that is maintained centrally is utilised to administer the whole healthcare industry and its associated stakeholders. Enhanced research and data sharing on public health would also improve therapy for numerous populations.

Within the realm of healthcare, blockchain technology may be used in a wide number of settings to accomplish a variety of tasks. The ledger technology helps researchers in the healthcare business read complicated genetic code by allowing the secure transmission of patients' medical information, which they control, and by regulating the medication supply chain, which they control.

Blockchain technology was developed by Bitcoin developer Satoshi Nakamoto and is used in the cryptocurrency Bitcoin. Some of the technically derived and impressive features that are used in the study and evaluation of Blockchain technology include the coverage of healthcare data, electronic data management, hospital information, various genomics management, system integration, digitally enhanced tracking and issues outbreak, and other features with functions that are analogous to those of the original features. The utilization of blockchain technology allows for the development and implementation of a wide variety of functionality in this domain. The fact that the Blockchain technology may be utilised in applications that are related to healthcare and the fact that it is totally digitised are the key reasons for the broad acceptance of this technology.

In addition, Blockchain is not only transparent but also keeps users' information confidential by concealing users' identities behind a series of intricate and fool proof algorithms that protect the sensitive nature of patient information. Patients, doctors, and other providers of medical services can quickly and securely exchange the same information with one another thanks to the decentralised structure of the system. The acceptance rate in the healthcare industry is steadily increasing thanks to blockchain's arrival. People involved in the health ecosystem often have a positive attitude about the technologies in their early stages. The overarching goal of Blockchain technology's application in the healthcare industry over the next few years will be to solve challenges associated with the industry's current organisational structure. It facilitates easy access to all of the information that is currently available at any given time for medical professionals, patients, and pharmacists alike. Throughout day and night, medical companies are researching, experimenting, and learning more about how Blockchain technologies might be used in the medical profession for health records. Considering the timely delivery of life saving medicines, enhancing payment alternatives, and decentralising any patient health history records, it has established itself as an indispensable technology in the healthcare industry. This study can therefore conclude that Blockchain is becoming increasingly important to all industries, including the very crucial medical industry, which already relies heavily on powerful technologies such as machine learning and artificial intelligence. There are some real-world applications of how Blockchain can revolutionise the healthcare business. This study, which was designed to increase the efficiency of the medical supply chain, is based on the blockchain monitoring technology that was established as the basis.

REFERENCES

Abdelmaboud, A., Ahmed, A. I. A., Abaker, M., Eisa, T. A. E., Albasheer, H., Ghorashi, S. A., & Karim, F. K. (2022). Blockchain for IoT Applications: Taxonomy, Platforms, Recent Advances, Challenges and Future Research Directions. *Electronics (Basel), 11*(4), 630. doi:10.3390/electronics11040630

Dash, M. K., Panda, G., Kumar, A., & Luthra, S. (2022). Applications of blockchain in government education sector: a comprehensive review and future research potentials. *Journal of Global Operations and Strategic Sourcing.*

Huo, R., Zeng, S., Wang, Z., Shang, J., Chen, W., Huang, T., Wang, S., Yu, F. R., & Liu, Y. (2022). A Comprehensive Survey on Blockchain in Industrial Internet of Things: Motivations, Research Progresses, and Future Challenges. *IEEE Communications Surveys and Tutorials*, *24*(1), 88–122. doi:10.1109/COMST.2022.3141490

Kayikci, Y., Subramanian, N., Dora, M., & Bhatia, M. S. (2022). Food supply chain in the era of Industry 4.0: Blockchain technology implementation opportunities and impediments from the perspective of people, process, performance, and technology. *Production Planning and Control*, *33*(2-3), 301–321. doi:10.1080/09537287.2020.1810757

Kritikos, M. (2020). *Ten technologies to fight coronavirus.* Eur Parliam Res Serv. https://www.europarl.europa.eu/RegData/etudes/IDAN/2020/641543/EPRS_IDA(2020)641543_EN.pdf

Popa Chivu, R.-G., Popa, I.-C., Orzan, M.-C., Marinescu, C., Florescu, M. S., & Orzan, A.-O. (2022). The Role of Blockchain Technologies in the Sustainable Development of Students' Learning Process. *Sustainability, 14*(3), 1406. MDPI AG. Retrieved from doi:10.3390/su14031406

Raja Santhi, A., & Muthuswamy, P. (2022). Influence of blockchain technology in manufacturing supply chain and logistics. *Logistics*, *6*(1), 15. doi:10.3390/logistics6010015

Sharma, A. K., Sharma, D. M., Purohit, N., Sharma, S. A., & Khan, A. (2022). Blockchain Technology: Myths, Realities and Future. In Blockchain Technology (pp. 163-180). CRC Press.

Tan, L., Tivey, D., Maddern, G., Kopunic, H., Babidge, W., & Langley, S. (2020). Part 2: Blockchain technology in health care. *ANZ Journal of Surgery*, *90*(12), 2415–2419. doi:10.1111/ans.16455 PMID:33236489

Wang, T., Hua, H., Wei, Z., & Cao, J. (2022). Challenges of blockchain in new generation energy systems and future outlooks. *International Journal of Electrical Power & Energy Systems*, *135*, 107499. doi:10.1016/j.ijepes.2021.107499

Xiao, Y., Zhang, N., Lou, W., & Hou, Y. T. (2020). A Survey of Distributed Consensus Protocols for Blockchain Networks. *IEEE Communications Surveys and Tutorials*, *22*(2), 1432–1465. doi:10.1109/COMST.2020.2969706

Chapter 11
Blockchain for Student Experience

Abdul-Mumin Khalid
https://orcid.org/0009-0002-3873-183X
E.P. College of Education, Bimbilla. Ghana

Mohammed Majeed
https://orcid.org/0000-0001-9804-5335
Tamale Technical University, Ghana

ABSTRACT

The chapter aims to unveil blockchain's impact on student experience. As per the literature, blockchain benefits education through: smart contracts for tasks, curriculum, and documents; affordability and wider access; self-data analysis; safety; improved classroom efficacy; enhanced trust between recruiters and candidates; streamlined payments; clear new requirements; transparent credentials; new digital asset exchange; practical application of class knowledge; added credentials; training delivery; heightened visibility; accountability through smart contracts; lowered degree costs; research publication; innate student information processing; transparent transcripts; and cost-effectiveness. These advantages enhance student (customer) experience. For learners and educators, blockchain offers novel avenues in assessment, activity management, and progress tracking in education.

DOI: 10.4018/978-1-6684-7649-9.ch011

INTRODUCTION

The collection, storage, and analysis of data on every pupil's educational pursuit is a major challenge for today's schools. Student performance in the classroom, as well as other relevant information such as portfolios and learning outcomes, is included (Purohit, 2022). In today's globalized university education system, quality is measured not only by the number of employees on staff, the amount of money, infrastructure, devices, scientific studies and training resources obtainable or obtained, but also by level of technological exposure and the level of technology put in place to drive, facilitate, and support decent education and the entire network. Recently, blockchain has been discussed as a data storage opportunity that can generate significant, beneficial impact in previously unexplored industries like manufacturing (Angrish, et al., 2018), healthcare (Agbo, et al., 2019), and education (Bartolomé, et al., 2017), building on the extensive discussion of blockchain as the foundation technology behind cryptocurrencies shown in Yuan and Wang's (2018) study. Many schools and universities want to improve their students' experiences by providing better online learning tools. Even if the bulk of instruction is still conducted in conventional face-to-face classrooms, supplementing traditional instruction with online resources, activities, courses, and feedback has been shown to boost student progress and satisfaction (Abuhassna et al., 2020). Even while the implementation of blockchain technology in academic settings is still in its infancy, it has opened up new possibilities. Blockchain technology's speed and security will help educators of all levels (Originstamp, 2023). Using the blockchain, students will be able to check the legitimacy of their records and prevent their data from falling into the wrong hands.

At the moment, blockchain is mostly used by universities for archiving and sharing academic credentials and information. Researchers, however, think the technology has the potential to radically alter the educational landscape by, among other things, making lifelong learning more accessible, streamlining the work of teachers through the use of smart contracts, and giving students control over their own transcripts and other academic documents. Despite the exciting potential, widespread implementation of blockchain in the education industry faces obstacles like data security, scalability, and cost (Liu & Ot, 2017). The institution's ability to centrally manage such data across departments is crucial to boosting retention and graduation rates. There is a lot of intriguing experimentation and innovation happening with the usage of blockchain in academic settings, despite the fact that this use of blockchain technology is still in its infancy (Purohit, 2022). Increased security and efficiency in today's classrooms are just two of the many areas where blockchain technology might be useful. The requirement to accommodate for variations in learner styles (Liu & Ot, 2017) and to conform to the accrediting standards of current educational systems (Rivera-Vargas, Sancho-Gil, & Sánchez, 2017) is the impetus for utilizing Blockchain for the management of educational endeavors.

Benefits of blockchain technology include decentralization, transparency, immutability, and traceability (Kulkarni, & Patil, 2020). Because data may be captured, saved, and updated on the blockchain in a distributed manner rather than by a central node, the system is said to be decentralized (Kulkani & Patil, 2020). As a result, mathematical approaches are utilized to develop trust among the dispersed nodes, rather than relying on centralized institutions. Blockchain is unchangeable because it is a distributed ledger that is constantly updated by thousands of computers. The technology is still in its infancy, and its advantages are only just being recognized. Therefore, more research is needed. Consequently, the primary goal of this chapter is to demonstrate how BC might improve the students' educational experience.

CONTRIBUTIONS

This chapter helps in practice by looking into how students' experiences with BC technology helped them quickly transition to keep records of student, how beneficial BC is and how this change in learning style affected their perceptions of attending university or any educational institution.

LITERATURE

Blockchain Education Sector

A series of "blocks" called "transactions" that hold data, such as transaction dates, durations, amounts, and/or users, make up the decentralized, unchangeable database known as blockchain (Ma & Fang, 2020). Using a peer-to-peer network, a user can start a transaction with another user, and a cryptographic identification process is utilized to uniquely identify the participants. The term "blockchain" comes to mind when security is an issue. In relation to data breaches, education is also not far away. Cybercriminals are in high demand for student information that contains little financial information. A variety of educational data can be conveniently stored in the education system using blockchain. There are limitless student records. Assets like attendance, assignments, payments for tuition if they attend a private school, grades, and coursework can all be recorded using blockchain technology (Anand, 2022). Additionally, their diploma may be added to their individual blockchain record. At the same time, student verification is growing to be a significant issue at educational facilities that are breached to produce false identities and records. Therefore, as student information becomes more digital, there is increased worry about protecting student privacy (Cheng et al., 2018). There are additional usage besides school or college, where the verification process is restricted. Defending employers, for instance, from those who falsely claim to hold degrees. Blockchain can be a powerful tool for combating phony credentials and degrees in the job. Benefits of Blockchain in Education Data security and data protection even in the event of a compromised node are two advantages of using blockchain in education. During the epidemic, the education industry quickly reacted to digitalisation. Blockchain technology has the power to transform this industry. The collaboration and management of academic records between students and teachers can be substantially changed by blockchain, first and foremost. Blockchain's distributed ledger technology has the potential to have a positive, major impact on the openness and accountability of the education sector. This chapter looks at the potential impact of blockchain on education.

Smart Contracts for Assignments and Courses

On BC, smart contracts are frequently employed. This can help teachers create blockchain-based courses and classes. The course will automatically start teaching once the prerequisite requirements have been met and can then proceed at its own speed. A smart contract detailing the parameters of an assignment, along with the due date and the grading deadline, might be signed by students and teachers.

Curriculum

College curriculum administration is another area where BC may make a significant impact. Blockchain, for example, can be used to safely keep digital course materials like syllabi and assignments. The prospect of the drives being damaged or compromised is a worry for institutions because they rely on them. Blockchains, through the use of smart contracts, may potentially make teachers' lives easier. Whenever predetermined criteria are met, a blockchain will execute the lines of code that make up a smart contract. As an illustration, a teacher could create a blockchain-based course or lesson plan, assigning pupils assignments; the blockchain's smart contract will instead autonomously validate the execution of each work, assigning the next one, and so on. The certification procedure for online courses is another area where blockchain technology might help enhance quality. Because of the widespread adoption of online education, certain organizations that are not properly authorized or approved have been able to compete with legitimate ones by offering online courses. Blockchain-based certification records are verifiable and secure. To aid other students in finding legitimate online courses and programs, blockchain technology can be utilized as a decentralized platform by educational institutions to disseminate information about online courses and programs, and by students to rate these offers.

Certificates, Transcripts, and Other Documentation

By recording transactions in an unalterable ledger, blockchain technology can provide a time-stamped account of events as they occur. Displaying transcripts, displaying a detailed report card, keeping track of attendance, and informing students and stakeholders about their progress can all be accomplished using this method. Using blockchain, students may submit their work without worrying about their submissions getting lost in the mail. Diplomas and degrees can also be delivered to students online, eliminating the need for fragile paper versions. The convenience, orderliness, and lack of bulk associated with digital diplomas and certificates make them the best option.

Lowered Prices and Greater Availability

Open educational resources, including as books, podcasts, and videos in the public domain, are supported by blockchain technology and can be made available to everyone for free use and redistribution. Blockchain technology makes it possible to securely and cheaply pool these assets in a distributed network. And teachers can use blockchain to record student grades, so even pupils in far-flung locations have access to digital courses and exams.

Learners' Ability to Collect and Analyze Their Own Data for Learning Purposes

If a student's credentials, talents, and other data are saved on the Blockchain and not held by an institution like a university, the student retains ownership and control over their data in perpetuity. Conversely, this demonstrates to potential employers that they may trust the facts presented on their CV.

Improvements in Safety and Effectiveness in the Classroom

Using blockchain technology may help protect students' anonymity, confidentiality, and security of their personal information. Blockchain ensures security and authenticity via its immutability and hash function. Because of this, unlike with paper records, students cannot change information about their past academic performance that has been recorded on the Blockchain. Avoiding storage in favor of a hash can protect sensitive information. Alternately, you may encrypt the information before adding it to the Blockchain.

Recruiters and Potential Employees Trust One Another and Communicate Openly

By preventing students from falsifying credentials like degrees and certifications, Blockchain ensures that companies may hire with confidence. With this information, hiring managers can determine if a candidate is a good fit for the position they are trying to fill. In particular, distributed ledger technologies facilitate this.

Reformation of Payments

Making payments for a student's tuition can be a tedious and time-consuming process. Many people are involved in this process, including students, parents, banks, foundations, government agencies, lenders, and different offices at the institution. However, blockchain technology has the potential to streamline this process, resulting in reduced administrative costs and potentially even lower tuition rates. The procedure of paying students has also benefited from the use of blockchain technology (Daley, 2021). The student, the parent, the bank, the scholarship provider, the government, and the school all need to work together to streamline the payment process. Cryptocurrencies are often viewed as a promising payment option for college students (Selwyn, 2016; Rivera-Vargas & Cobo, 2018). One of the most important applications of blockchain technology is the tokenization and crypto-incentivising of educational institutions (Raman & Varshney, 2018). The use of tokens has rapidly become essential to the functioning of blockchain systems. Professors will soon be able to motivate students by rewarding them with cryptocurrencies if they perform well or complete a specific major, and educational institutions will soon be able to incentivize students to repay student debts on time. The use of tokenization's gamification features in the classroom has shown promising results (Daley, 2021). Soon, teachers will be able to incentivize good performance and major completion with cryptocurrency rewards. Incentives for timely loan repayment can be provided to students by educational institutions. To top it all off, the gamification features of tokenization's instructional approach can revolutionize the way we educate and learn.

Information Is Simple for Learners/Students

The Blockchain can be used to record a variety of student data, including certificates, talents, and other information. This eliminates the need for a coordinating body, like a school, to oversee the system. This gives the student permanent access to the material and makes them the exclusive owner and custodian of the knowledge gained. Credibility with potential employers is boosted in this way. Having this verifies that the applicant's resume information is correct.

Trust and Transparency

Using Blockchain, they will be unable to change the results of their academic endeavors or the credentials they have earned. This provides assurance to hiring managers that candidates have the requisite abilities for the position. This can help companies locate candidates who are a better fit for the open roles. Particularly so for DLTs (Daley, 2021). By preventing students from falsifying their academic credentials, blockchain can provide companies confidence that their prospective hires have the knowledge and abilities to do the job well. Thus, blockchain can be seen as a "trust anchor of one truth for credentials" (Tapscott & Kaplan, 2019). In addition, this anchor provides a chance to improve compatibility between prospective employees and companies. In addition to improving "colleges, universities, employers, and their linkages to society," confidence and transparency in the skills transaction and sharing processes are bolstered by distributed ledger technologies' support for learning and the security of academic records. Decentralized ledgers and the BC network serve as the new trust bearers. These registers are distributed throughout a network of unhackable nodes (Underwood 2016).

New Exchange for Digital Assets

The method by which students are compensated is another crucial area where blockchain is finding use. Streamlining the payment procedure is another time-consuming endeavor. Everyone from students and their parents to banks and scholarship foundations to governments and universities must work together on this. Future use as a preferred means of payment for college students may well involve cryptocurrency.

Make New Requirements Clear

Student records might be limited by more than just a student's level of education or certification. Students might also have a wide range of other talents and knowledge. These might include linguistic fluency, interpersonal proficiency, specialized technical expertise, or something else entirely (Daley, 2021). Schools can keep data on a distributed ledger and then provide a link to verify a student's credentials. Since it's hard to validate these skills, the records kept in the Blockchain are inarguable.

Blockchain-Based File Storage

Data such as digital curricula, degrees, and other documents are among the many that an institution must manage. There is a significant amount of data storage required for all this. Storing it on a local device could indicate a need for centralized data storage. As a second benefit, users can simply store it online. This may result in additional costs. Decentralized data storage is an area where Blockchain may prove useful. Solutions such as Filecoin, a blockchain-based cloud storage service, may be one way to go. There are a lot of files that need to be stored because an institution deals with things like digital curricula, degrees, and other information. It may be a matter of data centralization if they keep something on a local drive. In addition, they can put it in the cloud, which may incur additional fees. Blockchain, which may be used as decentralized file storage, may be a viable option in this case. Filecoin and similar blockchain-based cloud storage services could be the answer.

Enhanced Performance of Current Educational Operations

University degrees issued via the blockchain would be digital transcripts or records of a person's educational pursuits and completions during their entire life. Thayer (2018) cites a variety of blockchain-powered efficiency applications, including digital credentials and intellectual property management, streamlined diploma verification, and rapid, trustworthy student payments. Financial and time savings are realized by educational institutions, businesses, and students alike, thanks to these applications. All information is processed automatically according to established protocols. As a result, the use of blockchain technology can not only greatly lessen the expense of labor but also increase productivity. Distributed ledger automation for Blockchain 1.0 digital money focuses primarily on streamlining the settlement process. By removing the need for middlemen and speeding up the reconciliation process, blockchain technology may soon be used to expedite the clearing and settlement of some financial transactions (Wang et al. 2016). This lifetime value variable transcript lessens CV forgery and the burden of verifying credentials across all sectors. Blockchain-based degrees are similar to digital transcripts in their practical application. Education transcripts document a person's whole academic career. This is the single greatest benefit of Blockchain technology for classroom use. This adaptable transcript facilitates more verification of credentials while decreasing CV forgery.

Applying Knowledge Acquired in Classes

BC that is compatible with smart contracts can facilitate the automation of training and assignments. As a result, educational content like courses and lessons can be stored in the Blockchain. Once conditions are met, they can begin running automatically. If a teacher wanted to give their students homework, that's one example. A smart contract on the Blockchain might be used to ensure that all tasks have been completed satisfactorily (Rivera-Vargas et al., 2017).

Add to Your Existing Credentials

The completion of a degree program or the acquisition of a certification is not the sole criterion for access to student information. You can also establish a student's credentials by linking to your Blockchain-stored knowledge of a variety of other topics, such as languages, soft skills, technical expertise, and so on (Rivera-Vargas & Cobo, 2018). Given the difficulty in independently verifying such abilities, the records kept in a distributed ledger like the Blockchain are inarguable. Open Badge Passport and similar services are the pioneering effort in this direction.

Delivering Training and Education

The use of BC that is smart-contract enabled allows for the automatic execution of courses and assignments in educational institutions. In other words, courses and lessons can be pre-programmed into the Blockchain and then completed automatically when certain criteria are met. A teacher, for instance, might assign homework. Smart contracts on the Blockchain could instantly confirm when tasks are finished. Teachers might be compensated in crypto tokens, and pupils could earn credits, if all assignments are complete. Courses in their entirety could be mapped out in this fashion (Anand, 2021).

Increased Visibility

Blockchain's distributed ledger keeps track of time-stamped transactions in near real-time (Daley, 2021). This is a great way to keep tabs on a student's academic standing, display a comprehensive report card, and verify transcripts. Neither the student nor the teacher can claim to have misplaced a blockchain-submitted assignment (Anand, 2022).

Smart Contracts for Accountability

Instructors, administration, and students will soon have access to smart contracts (Daley, 2021). For instance, if there were a digital agreement between students and instructors specifying the parameters of an assignment, together with the due date and grading schedule, this would be a win-win situation for all parties involved. One possible application of smart contracts is the repayment of student loans (Anand, 2021).

Reducing the Price of a College Degree

Implementing Blockchain will allow EIs to automate mundane processes. Using automated processes results in savings for universities. As a result, students will be able to save money (Daley, 2021). . New, more inexpensive avenues of education could be made possible thanks to blockchain technology, which has the ability to upend the traditional dynamic between schools and students. Students, parents, scholarship organizations, private loan providers, government agencies, and universities' own large bureaucracies all play a role in the arduous task of managing tuition payments. Blockchain technology can speed this procedure, cutting down on unnecessary administrative expenditures and possibly resulting in lower tuition fees (Smith, 2021). The elimination of intermediaries in many processes could potentially result in cost savings for educational institutions. In addition, they'd have less need to pay for more space to store documents. In addition to promoting lifelong education, blockchain technology might be implemented to provide everyone with access to public domain materials like books, podcasts, and movies (Anand, 2021). Blockchain technology enables the safe and low-cost distribution of such resources across a public network.

Publishing Findings From Your Study

Each day, the field of study produces a large quantity of high-quality materials. But getting them out on time is a huge challenge. However, publishing on a blockchain could pave the way for up-and-coming writers, academics, and other professionals. Property rights and anti-piracy measures are two other areas where BC could be useful.

The one-way hash function is used in the BC Security network; it is a mathematical function that takes a string of arbitrary length as input and returns a binary sequence of defined length. There is no obvious correlation between the input and the output. Because of this inability to backtrack from the output, the procedure is notoriously difficult to reverse (Yli-Huumo et al. 2016). In addition, the time sequence of events is maintained in the newly produced block.

Students' Innate Ability to Gather and Process Information

In recent years, blockchain technology has risen to prominence in the IT industry due to the many advantages it offers. It protects information in the digital realm by making it auditable and unchangeable. A community or other network of participants is required for the verification of any changes or updates. Besides these primary uses, BC can also be implemented for user authentication, data verification, and ownership auditing. As a result, BC can potentially alter the educational landscape.

Smart Contracts for Accountability

Teachers, administrators, and students at educational institutions will soon have access to smart contracts. For instance, if there were a digital agreement between students and instructors specifying the parameters of an assignment, together with the due date and grading schedule, this would be a win-win situation for all parties involved. One possible application of smart contracts is the repayment of student loans (Anand, 2022).

Student Transcripts

Blockchain is also being used for student records, which is a huge deal in the classroom. There is an inconceivably large volume of student data, and checking their academic credentials is laborious. By letting schools directly code their courses and lessons into the blockchain, blockchain has the potential to streamline the verification process. With blockchain, students can keep their own records and determine their own academic persona. Graduates looking for work can more easily demonstrate the veracity of the credentials listed on their resumes and exert greater control over the information that is made available to potential employers. Alternatively, students might use computers to take the tests, with their results being securely recorded on a distributed ledger system. As an added bonus, blockchain technology has the potential to elevate the standard of distance learning. Recording accreditations on the blockchain gives openness and security, yet some unaccredited online institutions may be enticing.

Inexpensive

Incorporating Blockchain into the academic sector has the potential to reduce expenses considerably. As a result of the technology's ability to promote record sharing, costs associated with education have been reduced. But with Blockchain, we can make them fully automated. Because of this, schools have fewer expenses, which may be passed on to students in the form of reduced tuition. By eliminating the need for physical filing cabinets and other middlemen, educational institutions might save money (Rivera-Vargas et al., 2017). By eliminating the need for so many paper transcripts, blockchain technology can also contribute to cost savings in the educational sector. Blockchain technology has the potential to significantly cut down on educational costs and data storage needs.

CONCEPT OF BLOCKCHAIN AND ITS USE CASES

Maryville Begins Issuing Student-Owned Digital Diplomas

Feng Hou, Maryville's chief digital transformation advocate, is leading the charge on this BC project. Hou supervised a blockchain initiative at Central New Mexico Community College in his prior roles as chief information officer and Chief Learning Officer.

With the introduction of digital certificates in 2020, Maryville gave its students and alums the freedom to control the dissemination of their academic credentials. Maryville has been a pioneer in the use of blockchain technology in higher education. Digital diplomas can be managed by students on their smartphones using a dedicated software. Using blockchain technology, the app generates a verifiable, unchangeable copy of the student's diploma that can be instantaneously shared with prospective employers, other schools, and anybody else the student specifies. Without having to get in touch with Maryville's student services department, an employer or educational institution can instantly authenticate a digital diploma by clicking a link that takes them to the blockchain.

Maryville will also provide students with digital transcripts that are protected by the blockchain technology. Students will be able to transfer their records across institutions, apply for graduate programs, and enter the workforce with confidence thanks to this service. In the future, digital badges will be used to offer in-depth descriptions of abilities learned.

DISCUSSIONS

Thanks to Blockchain technology, cryptocurrencies are already causing a profound shift in the global financial system. With the ability to improve data security and trust, streamline record keeping and sharing, and provide students permanent access to their academic records, this technology has the power to revolutionize the education industry for the better (Anand, 2022). When Blockchain technology is implemented in the classroom, it improves the overall functioning of the educational system and makes better use of available resources. Data privacy, cost, scalability, and backwards compatibility with legacy systems are only some of the issues that must be resolved. These advantages are recognized by both Anand (2022) and Oeiginstamp (2023). There is a pressing need to accommodate for variations in learner styles (Liu & Ot, 2017) and to ensure that Blockchain-based management of educational endeavors is consistent with existing accrediting methods (Rivera-Vargas, Sancho-Gil, & Sánchez, 2017).

Mainettis et al. (2022) state that schools value digital technologies for many reasons, including the opportunities they present for instantaneous feedback on student work, the provision of continuous assessment environments, and the facilitation of the dissemination of students' academic accomplishments via both non-formal (such as social media) and formal channels (such as certificates). Teachers must proceed with caution while implementing these adjustments, though. The fact that innovations like BC can be successful in one area of study but not another demonstrates the complexity of the problem and the need for additional study. In order to be effective, innovations must be guided by pedagogy as well as technology.

IMPLICATIONS

Despite the clear advantages of implementing blockchain technology in the classroom, both administrators and teachers are slow to embrace this new technology. The general public's view of blockchain has shifted from that of a technology used mostly in cryptocurrency transactions to one of a technology with applications in fields as diverse as healthcare and education. Although the technology has been used successfully in areas like supply chain, it is still in its early, "prototyping" stage in the field of education. For blockchain-based education solutions to have a widespread positive impact, both the private sector (global employers) and the public sector (educational institutions, government) will need to work together and, ideally, coordinate their efforts to test, research, develop, implement, and fund such innovations. As a technology, blockchain has far-reaching potential in the realm of education, far beyond the traditional uses of tracking academic progress and issuing diplomas. For both students and educators, blockchain technology holds promising new avenues for use in areas like as formative assessment, the creation and management of learning activities, and the monitoring of progress throughout the educational process.

CONCLUSION

This chapter explored how blockchain technology can be used to enhance educational outcomes for both students and schools. The use of cryptocurrency by BC has already altered the financial environment. Let's take a critical look at the potential effects of BC on schools in 2021 and beyond. To this end, distributed ledger technology and smart contracts will undoubtedly produce a brand-new picture. The blog post's focus on a few key advantages of Blockchain technology in academia merely skims the surface of the many possible applications of this technology. Given that the required technology exists, it is feasible in the near future. Paper certificates will become obsolete as a result of blockchain technology. The certificates that schools issue are permanent and protected from tampering. The distribution and archiving of awards could also be automated. Credits can be transferred and recognized with ease. The blockchain can be used to record and verify a person's full academic transcript. BC have already changed the economic scene with their cryptocurrency. The aforementioned only scratch the surface of the potential of Blockchain technology in the classroom. In the near future, Blockchain could be used in schools because the essential technology currently exists. Blockchain can facilitate necessary shifts in the business, operational, and technological models of higher education by drastically lowering data management costs by automating numerous previously manual operations, such as credential verification. Educators will be aided by the development of a blockchain for education in the creation of more interesting and interactive lessons.

Many students and educators find today's instructional technologies to be unpleasant. Incorporating blockchain technology into the classroom will allow teachers to create more engaging learning resources, thereby improving the quality of distance education. In a similar vein, there will be more platforms than ever for students to showcase their talents to prospective employers, and a permanent record of their credentials will back them up in times of strife.

FUTURE OF BC IN EDUCATION

The aforementioned benefits of blockchain technology in the field of education may represent only the beginning of the technology's potential. The potential uses of blockchain technology in the classroom are intriguing. Blockchain's capabilities and enormous unrealized potential to revolutionize the educational landscape by establishing novel, more convenient avenues for instruction and profoundly changing the traditional dynamic between schools and their students is undeniable. Future generations would greatly benefit from implementing blockchain technology in the academic setting.

It can help in the areas of contract formation, bargaining, simplification of terms, execution, and verification of the compliance state. It digitally attests to the one-of-a-kindness of the transacting parties (the contract subjects) and codifies the rights and obligations of the parties involved (the contract terms). The "third party costs" associated with conventional transactions are much reduced thanks to the smart contract, and the dependability and security of the transaction are greatly increased. When financing a vehicle, for instance, rather than getting a loan from the bank, the buyer negotiates the terms of the installment payment directly with the dealer to avoid paying any additional fees associated with the loan's processing. In the event that the purchaser commits a violation of the terms and conditions, the corresponding code will be run, thus ending the smart contract. Executive power and justice are both considerably enhanced by the smart contract compared to the conventional one. So, some of the problems in education could be resolved if classrooms were to implement teaching and learning activities based on a smart contract.

REFERENCES

Abuhassna, H., Al-Rahmi, W. M., Yahya, N., Zakaria, M. A., Kosnin, A. B. M., & Darwish, M. (2020). Development of a new model on utilizing online learning platforms to improve students' academic achievements and satisfaction. *International Journal of Educational Technology in Higher Education, 17*(1), 38. doi:10.118641239-020-00216-z

Alammary, A., Alhazmi, S., Almasri, M., & Gillani, S. (2019). Blockchain-based applications in education: A systematic review. *Applied Sciences (Basel, Switzerland), 9*(12), 2400. doi:10.3390/app9122400

Anand, A. (February 22, 2022). Blockchain in Education Sector: Advantages and Disadvantages. *Analytical Steps.* https://www.analyticssteps.com/blogs/blockchain-education-sector-advantages-and-disadvantages

Ark, T. V. (2018). 20 ways blockchain will Transform (Okay, May IMPROVE) EDUCATION. *Forbes*. https:// www.forbes.com/sites/tomvanderark/2018/08/20/26-ways-blockchain-will-transform-ok-may-improveeducation/?sh=cb87fff4ac91

Chen, G., Xu, B., Lu, M., & Chen, N. S. (2018). Exploring blockchain technology and its potential applications for education. *Smart Learn. Environ.*, *5*(1), 1–10. doi:10.118640561-017-0050-x

Gomez, D. (2021). Blockchain in education, a large and global encrypted database. *eLearn Center Blog*. https:// elearncenter.blogs.uoc.edu/blockchain-in-education/

Iredale, G. (2021). 6 key blockchain features you need to know now. *101 Blockchains*. https://101blockchains.com/introduction-to-blockchain-features/

Kulkarni, M., & Patil, K. (2020). Blockchain technology adoption using toe framework. *Int. J. Sci. Technol. Res.*, *9*, 1109–1117.

Liu, M., Kang, J., Zou, W., Lee, H., Pan, Z., & Corliss, S. (2017). Using Data to Understand How to Better Design Adaptive Learning. *Technology, Knowledge and Learning, 22*(3), 271-298. https://link.springer.com/article/10.1007/s10758-017-9326-z

Ma, Y.& Fang, Y. (2020). Current status, issues, and challenges of blockchain applications in education. Int. J. Emerg. Technol. Learn. *iJET, 15,* 20–31.

Mainetti, L., Paiano, R., Pedone, M., Quarta, M., & Dervishi, E. (2022). Digital Brick: Enhancing the Student Experience Using Blockchain, Open Badges and Recommendations. *Education Sciences*, *12*(8), 567. doi:10.3390/educsci12080567

Originstamp. (2023). *Benefits and Challenges of Blockchain in Education*. Orginstamp. https://originstamp.com/blog/benefits-and-challenges-of-blockchain-in-education/

Purohit, A. (2022). *The Impact of Blockchain on the Education Industry*. eLearning Industry. https://elearningindustry.com/ways-blockchain-impacts-education-industry-in-2022-and-beyond

Raman, R. K., & Varshney, L. R. (2018). Distributed storage meets secret sharing on the blockchain. *2018 Information Theory and Applications Workshop (ITA)*. IEEE. 10.1109/ITA.2018.8503089

Rivera-Vargas, P., & Cobo, C. (2018). Plan Ceibal en Uruguay: una política que conecta inclusión e innovación. In P. Rivera-Vargas, J. Muñoz-Saavedra, R. Morales Olivares, & S. Butendieck-Hijerra (Eds.), *Políticas Públicas para la Equidad Social* (pp. 4–29). Colección Políticas Públicas, Universidad de Santiago de Chile., Recuperado de https://digital.fundacionceibal.edu.uy/jspui/handle/123456789/266

Rivera-Vargas, P., & Miño-Puigcercós, R. (2018). Young people and virtual communities.: New ways of learning and of social participation in the digital society. *Páginas de Educación*, *11*(1), 67–82. doi:10.22235/pe.v11i1.1554

Rivera-Vargas, P., Sancho-Gil, J. M., & Sánchez, J. A. (2017). Los límites de la disrupción en el orden académico. La cultura DIY en la universidad. *Páginas de Educación*, *10*(2), 127–142. doi:10.22235/pe.v10i2.1428

Selwyn, N. (2015). Data entry: Towards the critical study of digital data and education. *Learning, Media and Technology*, *40*(1), 64–82. https://www.tandfonline.com/doi/abs/10.1080/17439884.2014.921628. doi:10.1080/17439884.2014.921628

Selwyn, N. (2016). *Is technology good for education?* John Wiley & Sons.

Selwyn, N. (2018). Data points: Exploring data-driven reforms of education. *British Journal of Sociology of Education*, *39*(5), 1–9. doi:10.1080/01425692.2018.1469255

Thayer, T. L. (2018). 4 promising and ambitious blockchain initiatives for higher education. *Gartner Research.* https://www.gartner.com/en/documents/3893582/4-promising-and-ambitious-blockchain-initiatives-for-hig.

Thayer, T. L., & Yanckello, R. (2019). Education administrative systems innovation primer for 2019. *Gartner Research.* https://www.gartner.com/en/documents/3901065/education-administrative-systems-innovation-primer-for-2, accessed 28 April 2020.

Tribis, Y., El Bouchti, A., & Bouayad, H. (2018). Supply chain management based on blockchain: A systematic mapping study. *International Workshop on Transportation and Supply Chain Engineering 200*(20). 10.1051/matecconf/201820000020

Zheng, Z., Xie, S., Dai, H., Chen, X., & Wang, H. (2017). An overview of blockchain technology: Architecture, consensus, and future trends. *2017 IEEE International Congress on Big Data (BigData Congress).* IEEE. 10.1109/BigDataCongress.2017.85

Chapter 12
Security Social Networking and Cybersecurity Technology Challenges

Ashutosh D. Gaur
https://orcid.org/0000-0003-4322-5747
Mangalmay Institution of Management and Technology, India

ABSTRACT

Cyber-ethics, cyber-safety, and cyber-security problems must be incorporated into schooling beginning at a young age. Cyber ethics, safety, and security tendencies threaten security and necessitate increased government security and public awareness to protect individual information on the world wide web. This study focuses on social media and social network difficulties and risks due to increasing social network users. The chapter also includes a guideline for protecting individual personal information.

INTRODUCTION

The Internet has caused a significant shift in the way individuals express their opinions and share information. With the rise of Web 3.0, users now have the ability to communicate directly with companies, sharing their thoughts, feelings, and views through social networking sites such as Google Plus, Twitter, and Facebook (Sofaer et al., 2012). Social networking platforms generate an array of content, including tweets, reviews, comments, chats, and blog entries. This user-generated content plays a vital role in influencing purchasing decisions, making it challenging for users to sift through the vast amount of information available.

DOI: 10.4018/978-1-6684-7649-9.ch012

Data security is among the most crucial challenges posed by modern information technology (Sharma, 2012). As the Internet becomes increasingly integral to corporate development across various sectors, ranging from government organizations to private enterprises, the protection of sensitive data is paramount (Sofaer et al., 2012). Social media platforms offer a unique space for users to engage with companies, driving marketing goals, but they also introduce inherent security risks.

OBJECTIVES

This study has two primary objectives:

1. To assess and analyze the evolving security and cybersecurity challenges associated with the growing use of social networking sites, with a focus on identifying potential risks and threats.
2. To develop and recommend practical safety measures and guidelines for social media users, aimed at safeguarding personal information and enhancing online security awareness in order to mitigate the identified risks.

Social Media Difficulties and Dangers

In contemporary society, the emergence of social media platforms has transformed the way people communicate and share information. Blogs, Facebook, Twitter, microblogs, forums, and a plethora of digital forums have become primary channels of interaction, enabling users to engage with content and one another as never before (Garg et al., 2015). However, the ubiquity of these platforms has brought forth a myriad of unique security challenges and vulnerabilities.

Exponential User Growth

The exponential increase in social media users underlines a central security challenge. Social networking sites have experienced an unprecedented surge in user engagement, as an ever-growing number of individuals join these platforms. This expanding user base contributes to the proliferation of data and information exchange. While this connectivity fosters communication, it also creates an expansive digital landscape where user privacy and data security are increasingly at risk.

Impersonation and Identity Misuse

Impersonation stands as a prevalent security concern within social media. Cyber attackers frequently resort to impersonating legitimate users to gain unauthorized access to sensitive information. This deceptive tactic allows the attacker to navigate the platform while masquerading as someone else, thus obtaining access to private data and presenting a substantial threat to personal and organizational security.

Third-Party Applications

The integration of third-party applications introduces another layer of security vulnerability in social networking sites. Many users unwittingly grant these applications access to their personal information during installation. While some applications may have benign purposes, others may harbor malicious intent, downloading malware or surreptitiously collecting sensitive data without the user's consent. Users often underestimate the extent to which third-party applications can compromise their digital privacy.

Data Retention by Operators

Social media platforms routinely retain user data for various purposes, including analytics and targeted advertising. Even when users delete their accounts or associated content, platform operators may persist in storing their data. This enduring retention of user information can culminate in potential privacy breaches and data misuse.

Malware, Phishing Attacks, and Viruses

Social media platforms are not impervious to the threat of malware, phishing attacks, and viruses. Cybercriminals adeptly exploit the digital landscape to disseminate malicious software or deceive users into sharing sensitive information. Users may inadvertently encounter deceptive links or clickbait, thus compromising the security of their devices and the confidentiality of their personal data.

Legal Risks

While social media platforms have evolved into integral communication channels, they concurrently expose users to legal hazards. The posting of offensive content or engagement in cyberbullying can culminate in legal repercussions. Additionally, the unauthorized exposure of personal information can lead to privacy infringements and legal entanglements.

Privacy and Data Security

The core essence of social media lies in the exchange of data. Users voluntarily or inadvertently divulge personal information, giving rise to concerns regarding data privacy and security. When users configure their profiles to "public," they render their personal information accessible to anyone, including potential malicious actors. Accepting connection requests from unknown parties also exposes users to security vulnerabilities.

Geolocation and Physical Security

The incorporation of geolocation features within many social media platforms has heralded a new dimension of security concerns. While these features can enhance social interaction and location-based sharing, they simultaneously introduce significant issues related to physical security. Users must exercise caution when sharing their real-time location data, as it can be exploited by malicious entities for nefarious purposes.

Considering the multifaceted challenges and security risks inherent in social media, it is imperative to adopt a proactive stance toward safeguarding personal and organizational information. This endeavor also necessitates a robust focus on user education and security awareness. To mitigate these risks effectively, it is crucial to garner a comprehensive comprehension of the intricacies of social media security, accompanied by the implementation of practical measures that empower users to protect their data and privacy proficiently.

As we embark on a more profound exploration of the complex realm of social media security, it is imperative to recognize that addressing these challenges extends beyond the responsibility of individual users. It requires a collective effort involving social media platform operators, cybersecurity experts, governmental authorities, and educational institutions. The continuously evolving landscape of social media underscores the need for an ongoing discourse centering on privacy, security, and the ethical use of these influential communication tools. Armed with a multifaceted understanding of these dynamics, we can navigate toward a safer and more secure digital future where the benefits of social media are harnessed without compromising individual and collective security.

In today's digital age, social media platforms have ushered in a transformative revolution in the realm of communication, offering users unprecedented ways to connect, share, and interact. While the rise of platforms like blogs, Facebook, Twitter, microblogs, and forums has enriched global communication, it has also introduced a multitude of security challenges and vulnerabilities that demand a comprehensive understanding. As the proliferation of social media usage surges, it is critical to explore these challenges in depth, their impact on users, and the associated solutions. This extended discussion will delve into the security challenges associated with social media in greater detail, along with the pertinent citations and references.

Misusing Identity

One of the prominent security challenges in the realm of social media is the misuse of identity, which represents a profound risk for users (Garg et al., 2015). The digital realm offers a perfect breeding ground for identity impersonation. Cyber attackers often resort to impersonating legitimate users to gain unauthorized access to sensitive information. They can employ various deceptive tactics, from creating fake profiles to hacking into existing ones, and this deceptive guise enables them to navigate the platform while posing as someone else. This technique provides attackers with access to private data, which can have grave implications for the victim's personal and organizational security.

The scale of this challenge is exacerbated by the sheer number of users on social media platforms. The more users these platforms attract, the more data is generated and shared, creating an expansive digital landscape that is ripe for identity misuse and data breaches. Addressing this issue requires not only individual vigilance but also enhanced security mechanisms on the part of social media companies, including robust authentication and monitoring processes.

Dangers Posed by Utilizing Third-Party Applications

Another pressing security challenge arises from the utilization of third-party applications on social networking sites (Garg et al., 2015). These applications often request extensive access to personal information during installation. While some third-party applications serve benign purposes, others may harbor malicious intent, such as downloading malware or surreptitiously collecting sensitive data without the user's informed consent. Users frequently underestimate the extent to which these third-party applications can compromise their digital privacy, and this naivety is perilous.

To mitigate this risk, users must exercise caution when granting permissions to third-party applications and ensure that these applications come from reputable sources. Moreover, social media platforms should adopt stringent policies and practices to scrutinize and regulate the third-party applications allowed on their platforms, thereby enhancing the overall security posture.

Trusting the Operators of Social Networking Sites

A critical aspect of the security landscape on social networking sites pertains to the level of trust placed in the operators of these platforms (Garg et al., 2015). These operators have unfettered access to user-generated content, even after users delete their accounts or associated data. The perpetual retention of user information by these operators raises concerns related to data privacy and security.

Users often operate under the assumption that when they delete content or their accounts, their data will be erased. However, this is not always the case. The data retained by operators can potentially be accessed by unauthorized parties or utilized for undisclosed purposes. As a result, users should be aware of the data retention policies of the platforms they use, and social media companies should be more transparent about their data management practices to establish trust.

Malware, Phishing Attacks, and Viruses

The sharing of information on social networking sites exposes users to the perils of malware, phishing attacks, and viruses (Garg et al., 2015). Cybercriminals actively exploit the digital environment to propagate malicious software or deceive users into sharing sensitive information. Users may encounter deceptive links, clickbait, or seemingly harmless downloads that ultimately compromise the security of their devices and the confidentiality of their personal data.

Addressing this challenge necessitates robust cybersecurity measures. Users should be educated about recognizing and avoiding potentially harmful content, while social media platforms must implement stringent security measures to detect and remove such content before it reaches users.

Legal Issues

The legal landscape of social networking sites introduces yet another layer of complexity and potential risk (Garg et al., 2015). Posting offensive content or engaging in cyberbullying can result in legal consequences. Moreover, the unauthorized exposure of personal information without consent can lead to privacy violations and legal complications.

It is essential for users to be cognizant of the legal implications of their online activities. They must understand the laws and regulations applicable to their actions on social media and adhere to ethical standards. Furthermore, social media platforms should adopt robust moderation and content removal policies to address offensive or harmful content promptly.

In conclusion, the security challenges associated with social media are multi-faceted and continuously evolving. The widespread use of social networking sites has brought forth vulnerabilities that range from identity misuse to legal issues, underscoring the complexity of this digital landscape. To address these challenges effectively, it is paramount to educate users, enhance security measures, and foster trust between users and social media platforms. A collaborative effort involving individuals, platform operators, cybersecurity experts, and regulatory authorities is essential to navigate this digital realm safely and securely.

Social media platforms have irrevocably reshaped the landscape of human interaction, offering a unique and transformative space for individuals to communicate, share information, and connect in unprecedented ways. However, this rapid proliferation of social media usage has been accompanied by an array of complex security challenges and vulnerabilities (Garg et al., 2015). These challenges have expanded as the number of users continues to grow, creating a digital ecosystem that demands constant vigilance and adaptation to ensure the safety and security of users. In this comprehensive discussion, we will delve into the intricate facets of these challenges and the associated risks while providing solutions and insights into fostering cybersecurity in an era dominated by social networking.

Observing Users

One of the most intriguing and concerning aspects of social media platforms is the capability to observe users in real time, primarily through geolocation features (Garg et al., 2015). While this feature can enhance social interaction and sharing, it also raises significant concerns related to physical security. Users who opt to share their location data may inadvertently expose themselves to potentially malicious entities.

In the context of personal security, it's crucial for users to be discerning about when and with whom they share their real-time location. Social media platforms must simultaneously implement rigorous privacy controls and user education to ensure that this powerful feature is used safely.

Security of Data

Data exchange is at the heart of social networking platforms, as users willingly or inadvertently share personal information with the world (Das et al., 2017). The fundamental nature of these platforms raises concerns regarding data security. Users have the discretion to configure their profiles as "public," allowing virtually anyone, including malicious actors, to access their personal information. Moreover, accepting connection requests from unknown parties can expose users to a wide array of potential security threats.

To counteract these security concerns, it is imperative for social media companies to provide users with comprehensive privacy controls and guidelines to help them secure their data. Additionally, user education plays a pivotal role in inculcating a sense of digital vigilance, urging users to exercise caution when sharing sensitive information.

RISKS AND CHALLENGES

The expanding user base of social media platforms has led to the proliferation of risks and challenges associated with these platforms (Garg et al., 2015). These encompass a range of concerns, including but not limited to:

Phishing Attacks

Phishing attacks are a pervasive threat in the digital realm. Cybercriminals employ deceptive tactics to impersonate trustworthy entities, ultimately leading users to divulge sensitive personal information such as login credentials, banking details, or other private data (Garg et al., 2015). To mitigate this risk, users must be educated about recognizing phishing attempts and encouraged to verify the authenticity of any information requests.

Identity Federation Challenges

Sharing personal information with third-party applications is a common practice on social networking sites (Garg et al., 2015). However, this practice may inadvertently lead to the exposure of sensitive data. To address this challenge, users should exercise caution when authorizing third-party applications and understand the extent of data access they grant.

Malware

Malware is a formidable adversary in the digital realm. Cybercriminals exploit various channels to propagate malicious software that can infiltrate devices and software (Garg et al., 2015). To counteract this threat, users should be vigilant about downloading content from reputable sources, regularly update their antivirus software, and avoid suspicious links or downloads.

Clickjacking Attacks

Clickjacking attacks are deceptive tactics used by attackers to prompt users into clicking on seemingly harmless links, which can, in fact, plant malware on their devices (Garg et al., 2015). Users should exercise caution and be aware of clickbait and potentially dangerous links.

Cyber Security in India

India, like many other countries, has been witness to a surge in cybercrimes in recent years. Between 2011 and 2015, thousands of cybercrime cases were reported, necessitating a concerted effort to tackle this growing menace (Das et al., 2017). In India, these crimes are prosecuted under the Indian Penal Code (IPC) and the Information Technology Act, among other state-level laws.

The Information Technology Act encompasses a wide range of cybercrimes, including but not limited to the modification of computer source materials, damage to computer resources, hacking, and more (Das et al., 2017). This comprehensive legal framework provides authorities with the necessary tools to combat cybercrimes and bring offenders to justice.

SUGGESTIONS TO KEEP SAFE

In the digital age, individuals are becoming increasingly reliant on mobile solutions for online transactions, making them attractive targets for cybercriminals (Dwivedi, 2018). To protect personal information and enhance digital security, users can consider the following measures:

1. **Allow Only Authorized Users Access to Wi-Fi Networks:** Securing Wi-Fi networks with strong, unique passwords and restricting access to authorized users can prevent unauthorized intrusion.
2. **Create Strong, Complex Passwords for Personal Accounts:** Robust passwords that include a combination of letters, numbers, and symbols are crucial for account security.
3. **Keep Antivirus Software Up-to-Date:** Regularly updating antivirus software ensures that the system is protected against the latest threats and vulnerabilities.
4. **Avoid Clicking on Unknown URLs:** Users should exercise caution when encountering unknown links, as they might lead to malicious websites or phishing attempts.

5. **Share Personal Information Only with Reputable Websites:** Users should be cautious when sharing personal information online and should do so only on trusted and reputable websites.
6. **Adjust Social Media Privacy Settings According to Preferences:** Utilizing the privacy settings of social media platforms allows users to control who can access their information and provides an additional layer of protection.
7. **Exercise Caution When Engaging with Online Communities:** Users should be mindful of the information they share in online forums, groups, or communities and should avoid disclosing sensitive personal information.
8. **Implement Multi-Level Authentication for Added Security:** Enabling multi-factor authentication adds an extra layer of security by requiring multiple forms of verification for access to accounts.

In conclusion, the expanding world of social media is brimming with opportunities and challenges, many of which revolve around security and privacy concerns. As the number of users on these platforms continues to soar, it is imperative for users to be vigilant and informed about the evolving threat landscape. Cybersecurity measures should be robust, and user education programs are pivotal in creating a safe digital environment. It is only through these combined efforts that individuals can enjoy the benefits of the digital age while safeguarding their personal and collective security.

SUMMARY AND CONCLUSION

The evolution of the Internet, ushered in by the era of Web 3.0, has transformed the way individuals communicate and share information through social networking platforms. This article has explored the security and cybersecurity challenges that have accompanied the widespread use of social networking sites. The discussion has covered a wide array of risks and threats that have emerged in this digital age, and it has offered practical guidance for enhancing online security awareness and protecting sensitive data.

Web 3.0's impact and the surge in user-generated content via platforms like Twitter, Facebook, and Google Plus have raised critical concerns regarding data privacy and cybersecurity. As users continue to share personal information, engage with content, and participate in online discourse, they expose themselves to a multitude of online threats, including hacking, phishing, and data breaches. The sheer volume of digital interactions has made it increasingly challenging for individuals to scrutinize the content they encounter.

These challenges call for a proactive approach to safeguarding personal information and mitigating these threats. This article's primary objectives have been to examine the multifaceted challenges presented by social networking sites, propose safety measures, and raise awareness about cybersecurity in the digital age. It serves as a comprehensive guide for individuals, businesses, and policymakers, offering valuable insights into strengthening defenses against the dynamic landscape of online risks.

In conclusion, the impact of social media on society is undeniable, offering new avenues for expression and connection. However, it also introduces intricate security challenges. The responsibility for addressing these challenges does not fall solely on individual users. It requires a concerted effort from social media platform operators, cybersecurity experts, governmental authorities, and educational institutions. The ever-evolving landscape of social media emphasizes the need for an ongoing dialogue on privacy, security, and the ethical use of these influential communication tools. With a multifaceted understanding of these dynamics, we can work toward a safer and more secure digital future where the benefits of social media are harnessed without compromising individual and collective security.

LIMITATIONS OF STUDY

While this article has provided a comprehensive overview of the security and cybersecurity challenges associated with social networking sites, it is essential to acknowledge some limitations. The complexities of this subject matter mean that it is impossible to cover every nuance and emerging threat comprehensively within the scope of a single article.

Firstly, the rapidly evolving nature of the digital landscape means that new threats and vulnerabilities may emerge between the time of writing and publication. Therefore, readers are encouraged to stay informed about the latest developments in cybersecurity and adapt their practices accordingly.

Secondly, the focus of this article has been largely on the challenges and risks associated with social networking sites, with a greater emphasis on user practices and platform operators. While these aspects are critical, a more in-depth exploration of technical security measures, encryption technologies, and evolving security frameworks would provide a more holistic view of the subject.

Lastly, the article has provided general recommendations and guidelines for enhancing online security, but specific circumstances and individual needs can vary widely. Readers are encouraged to seek more detailed guidance and consult cybersecurity experts or organizations for tailored advice.

Despite these limitations, this article offers valuable insights and a solid foundation for understanding the multifaceted landscape of social media security, making it a valuable resource for individuals, organizations, and policymakers aiming to navigate this digital realm safely and securely.

REFERENCES

Burtescu, E. (2009). Database Security-attack and control methods. *Journal of Applied Quantitative Methods*, *4*(4).

Das, R., & Patel, M. (2017). *Cyber Security for Social Networking Sites: Issues.* Challenges, and Solutions.

Das, S., Kapoor, M., & Raj, P. (2017). Cyber Security in India: An Emerging Domain of Research and Development. *Advances in Computer Science and Ubiquitous Computing*, *2*(3), 17–26.

Dwivedi, Y. K. (2018). Developing Security Measures for Mobile Commerce (M-commerce). *International Journal of Information Management*, *38*(1), 20–28.

Garg, R., Veerubhotla, R. S., & Saxena, A. (2015). Security, Privacy and Trust in Social Networking Sites. *CSI Communications*, *39*(2).

Rajaretnam, T. (2012). The Society of Digital Information and Wireless Communications (SDIWC). *International Journal of Cyber-Security and Digital Forensics*, *1*(3), 232–240.

Sofaer, D., Clark, D., & Diffie, W. (2012). *Cyber Security and International Agreements*. Internet Corporation for Assigned Names and Numbers.

Chapter 13
Challenges of Blockchain Usage in the Education Sector

Abdul-Mumin Khalid
https://orcid.org/0009-0002-3873-183X
E.P. College of Education, Bimbilla, Ghana

Mohammed Majeed
Tamale Technical University, Ghana

Ahmed Tijani
Minerals Commission, Ghana

ABSTRACT

The blockchain (BC) is the next technologically mediated socioeconomic megatrend in the age of technological revolution. In this chapter, the authors look at some of the obstacles that BC technology faces in the classroom. It is stated that the education sector cannot take for granted that the digital transformation. BC has many potential uses in education, including improving teacher and student agency, streamlining the rollout of educational projects, and establishing a transparent, decentralized system for accrediting and certifying students' proficiency. Educational BC with its distributed ledger offers innovative norms of crypto-learning and crypto-administration that are acceptable across companies and nations, strengthening thus the objectivity, authenticity, and control of information without being compromised by socio-economic instabilities. BC technology's delayed acceptance in the education sector mirrors that in the teaching and learning sectors, but it also presents several major hurdles, including a lack of funding, security, cost, scalability, and awareness.

DOI: 10.4018/978-1-6684-7649-9.ch013

INTRODUCTION

Online learning has becoming increasingly popular, and BC technology has the potential to help keep students secure while also fostering expansion of this promising new field. BC's mixture of data protection and the capacity to distribute this facts among a vast network of stakeholders, all in a purely virtual manner, appears nearly tailor-made to assist safeguard and protect this new model of education. In particular, there are a few things teachers teaching online, schools providing online education, and private sector BC businesses may do to enhance the quality of their teaching and the courses they offer (Smith, 2021). Through the use of cryptocurrency, BC technology is already influencing the banking sector. Furthermore, this technology has the potential to revolutionize the educational system by making it easier to store and share information, more secure, speeding the employment process, and allowing students permanent access to their academic transcripts (Gilda, & Mehrotra, 2018). BC could revolutionize the educational system by introducing novel, low-cost methods of teaching and challenging the traditional dynamic between institutions of higher learning and their students. Tuition management is a time-consuming process that involves numerous stakeholders, including students, parents, scholarship foundations, private lending businesses, federal and state agencies, and the frequently bloated bureaucracy of university financial departments. BC technology can speed this procedure, cutting down on administrative costs and hence potentially lowering tuition rates. Researchers and industry professionals alike have recently shown a lot of interest in BC technology. Its distinguishing characteristics—among them decentralization, security, reliability, and data integrity—are largely responsible for this popularity. Lastly, from the standpoint of potential employers, there is a lack of trust because of inconsistencies in students' descriptions of their abilities and qualifications on resumes (Awaji et al., 2020). As a result, there is a pressing requirement for a deeper understanding of BC and its complexities in order to shed light on the primary benefits of BC for students and HEIs, which frequently employ insufficient education and coordinating systems for preparing professional staff working via outdated, inflexible pedagogical practices that have little to do with the latest developments in information technology (Abdeldayem, & Al Dulaimi, 2020).. While academics have addressed BC's potential economic applications (Swan 2015). Despite this increased curiosity, information about the current level of obstacles associated with implementing BC technology in the classroom is scant. Hence, the chapter discusses the challenges confronting students and educational institutions usage of BC.

CONTRIBUTION

Overall, this work presents a comprehensive analysis of the current research on BC's potential uses and limitations in higher education. Researchers will benefit from these understandings since they will better be able to focus their efforts. Using a literature review approach, this chapter explores how BC technology might be used in the classroom. This is one of the first studies to provide a comprehensive overview of BC technology, discussing its history, potential future uses, and existing limitations.

LITERATURE

BC

Bitcoin's BC technology is based on a proposal from Satoshi Nakamoto in 2008 to establish immutable distributed ledgers across thousands of computers (Nakamoto 2008). According to Zheng et al. (2017), a comprehensive overview of BC technologies, BC is a decentralized, immutable database consisting of a chain of "blocks" that contain data such as the dates, times, amounts, and/or parties involved in transactions (participants on the BC are usually not personally identifiable). Public, private, hybrid, and consortium BCs are just some of the variants out there. In a public BC, anyone may view and verify a transaction, as well as take part in the consensus-building procedure. Public BCs like Bitcoin and Ethereum are shared by everyone. With private BC, a network is either operating in a private setting (such as a limited network) or is under the management of a single individual (Parizo, 2021). Rather than being accessible to anybody with a computer, they are usually restricted to a closed network within a company or organization. Some other names for these systems include permissioned BCs and commercial BCs. A hybrid BC includes aspects of both private and public BCs, appealing to organizations who want the best of both worlds. Alongside a public, permissionless system, businesses can build a private, permission-based one, giving them control over which BC data is made public and which is kept private. Consortium BCs, also known as federated BCs, are the fourth form of BC and are similar to hybrid BCs in that they combine aspects of both private and public BCs. But the fact that many diverse people from the same organization work together on a decentralized network makes all the difference. The hazards associated with having a single party run the network in a private BC are mitigated in a consortium BC because access is restricted to a certain group (Parizo, 2021).

There was talk of a massive, distributed, encrypted, open book of records where many specialists control the accuracy of the data and certify that it is morally sound.

It can be used to store and transfer cryptographic currencies, charge accounts, and transaction histories over lengthy periods of time. (Gomez, 2021). Along with the steam engine, electricity, and computer technology, it has been dubbed part of the Fourth Industrial Revolution (Schwab 2017). BC is essentially a network of computers (nodes) used to manage a shared database. Each node keeps a full set of ledgers of previous transactions in order to ensure the security and integrity of the data. To construct a new block, a miner must first verify all of the transactions within it, and then use the hash function to create a digital signature for the block that satisfies a set of rules. All nodes in the BC will have access to the same authoritative copy of the ledger thanks to the newly produced block being broadcast to the entire network (Tschorsch & Scheuermann 2016). BC's distributed ledger architectures have been adopted in a wide range of industries due to their robust cybersecurity features. BC's potential in the classroom is still in its infancy. Additionally, BC is a system used for issuing, confirming, and exchanging certificates in educational settings (Gräther et al., 2018). Technology in the classroom allows students to keep track of their own formal education records in a digital, decentralized, and open ledger of all cryptographic data transactions, which can then be easily shared with anybody who shows interest (Han et al., 2018). Industrial sectors such as construction logbooks, engineering works such as aviation, and trades including, for example, tracking commodities such as diamonds, drugs, and leisure event tickets all use BC technology, which was originally developed for personal data management applications like identity verification and information sharing (Gatteschi et al., 2020).

FEATURES OF BC

Decentralization

The BC operates decentralized, without a single controlling node or authority. All nodes share the same rights and responsibilities. Each node contributes to the upkeep of the entire chain. There is no need for a trusted third party or central authority to verify transactions in a BC network. Since no central authority is required, users need only access it via the web in order to store their assets there. Bitcoins, along with other valuable digital assets such as important documents and contracts, can be saved. Additionally, the user will have complete authority over them by virtue of the private key via BC (Iredale, 2021). Because of the potential for decentralization to increase fragmentation and ambiguity, as well as create major differences in rights, educational service availability, and educational service quality, parties may need to engage in protracted negotiations. Decentralization may work better than centralization since it decreases the buildup of labor at centralized service points for education, increases overall efficiency, and decreases bureaucracy. Because of BC's distributed structure, users can take charge of their own assets and data. Because the BC is decentralized, each database is spread out across several nodes, ensuring that there is no single point of failure. So, the BC will still be safe even if a single computer is attacked. This fundamental aspect of BC also offers users full transparency. Since BC operations are automated and do not require much human control, there is a lower chance of failures or errors, which is one of the many advantages of using a decentralized network like BC.

Disintermediation

BC technology helps maintain confidence because it eliminates the need for intermediaries and replaces them with mathematical calculations (Piscini et al. 2016). Participants on a BC are connected in a shared market where they can buy and sell goods and assets without the need for a central authority to verify the legitimacy of the trades or verify the transfers of ownership. There is no single controlling entity in a value network.

Immutable

Being immutable means never changing or evolving. Among the most important aspects of BC technology, this is undoubtedly a standout. The BC's unalterability and reliability as a network feature is one of its greatest strengths (Shardeum, 2023). On the one hand, blocks are used to hold all transactions, with one hash key leading to the next block and the other linking to the previous block. Changes to a transaction would produce new hash values, which would be picked up by all the other nodes using the same validation procedure. The BC, on the other hand, is a public ledger that can be accessed by anyone and is distributed among thousands of nodes, all of which are in constant sync with one another. 51% of the network's ledgers would need to be modified for tampering to be successful (Tschorsch & Scheuermann 2016). This paper employs the concept of immutable mobile to show that whereas digital mapping of interfaces in higher education learning systems is obviously unchangeable, mobile has been undergoing a subtle but substantial change with regards to eternity. As a result, BC's immutability attribute is ideally suited for this use in the academic sector, where formerly malleable data can be transformed into useful insights.

Security

All of the transactions in the ledger are protected. Using encrypted communications strengthens the safety of the entire BC network. One of the most appealing aspects of the BC as it currently exists is that it makes the internet a more secure place for its users (Web 2.0). The following are three ways in which BC ensures the security of data. The data is first stored in highly redundant storage to guarantee consensus. The networks can only be updated if a majority of them are in agreement. In addition, the encrypted data is checked by the algorithm to prevent tampering (Shardeum, 2023). The BC network validates and updates itself every few minutes, which helps to create a self-reviewing mechanism, further enhancing the security provided by BC technology. It contributes to providing an extremely reliable system. Since the data is already part of the network, it may be accessed by anybody. Therefore, it helps promote openness (Shardeum, 2023). In conclusion, the multi-private keys are used to regulate access permissions. Users' anonymity can be preserved without compromising the BC's immutability or auditability.

Openness/Transparency

Transactions on the BC were governed by trustworthy computational models. It's easy to understand and abide by the system's regulations and operational protocols. With the exception of protected private data, all BC-stored data is public and does not require any special permissions to access. On top of that, numerous copies of the data are kept in various nodes across the network. The information is publicly accessible via the block header hash value. The data is hard to conceal, making the system open and honest.

Teachers who have done a good job will be well-protected by this aspect of openness. There also needs to be a shift in mindset from school administration with regards to how teachers are evaluated in order to fully embrace this new technology. When it comes to trust, BC technology is becoming the new gold standard. This is due to the fact that one of the key advantages and benefits of BC technology is the unprecedented level of data openness and transparency it brings to financial systems. Network users can view the balances and transactions of public addresses by using a block explorer. You can use a block explorer to go through a BC's blocks, their data, and other pertinent information. Each BC consists of blocks, and within each block is data that serves as a log of previous transactions. One of the most important aspects of this network is that it does not belong to any one company or person.

Crytocurrency

To put it another way, any BC network possesses some type of cryptocurrency property because of the inherent nature of BC technology. Because BC transactions are conducted directly between users, intermediaries are unnecessary (Shardeum, 2023).

Persistency

Validating a transaction is fast, and honest miners will not accept ones that are invalid. Once a transaction is recorded in the BC, it cannot be easily removed or undone. Incorrect transactions chunks might be quickly uncovered (Shardeum, 2023).

Anonymity

Every participant can use an anonymous address created by the BC client to connect with the network. Keep in mind that due to an inherent constraint, BC cannot ensure 100% privacy. It's true that everyone can see every purchase, but the actual people's identities are hidden behind their addresses. Because public BCs are decentralized, all participants in the network must be able to reach a consensus on the BC's shared state (Shardeum, 2023). A major component of BC technology is the consensus reached by all nodes in the network, which results in a single BC holding data (transactions) that has been verified and is, the network claims, correct (Shardeum, 2023).

BARRIERS OF USING BC IN EDUCATION SECTOR

BC has many promising applications, but its widespread use has yet to materialize. Problems with security, scalability, adoption, and cost may all contribute to people's reluctance.

Security and Privacy

Security is the safeguarding of important assets and data. Intellectual property issues are just one example of modern problems with property ownership that cannot be proven. Despite being a key differentiator, BC's security is not foolproof. Institutions need to be careful about what data they save and how they choose to store it on the BC because to the sensitive nature of the information being stored there, which includes students' academic records and credentials (Gilda, & Mehrotra, 2018). Alammary et al. (2019) point out how challenging it is to secure privacy and security on the BC, but how important it is when a student's future is at stake (educational credentials and certificates). Furthermore, it may be difficult to comply with local, state, and federal regulations pertaining to the privacy of personal information. Private or permissioned BC, or BC encryption, are two potential additional privacy safeguards that universities may need to employ. Since data of each public key is publicly exposed (Farah et al., 2018), users' transactions can be linked to reveal their information, making it impossible for BC to ensure transactional privacy. Likewise, all members' private keys should be safely stored and protected, which is another security problem that may and should be settled peacefully (Turkanovic et al., 2018). A security risk that must be taken into account is data leakage, which can occur when data is updated frequently.

Scalability

Zheng et al. point out that one issue that could develop with scaling is that the most common consensus algorithm, Proof of Work (PoW), consumes a great deal of electricity (2017). As a result of the massive amounts of information that educational institutions have about their students and alums, scalability can be a difficulty for BC adoption in this sector. One potential concern with implementing BC in educational institutions is the slow speed of BC transactions, also known as the BC's scalability problem. The vast majority of written works address this topic. As the BC's record of transactions grows in size, the transaction confirmation time for large blocks can take a long time. Due to the need for peer-to-peer verification of each transaction, the BC's transaction throughput suffers as the volume of data involved grows, necessitating more blocks. This may become a major barrier if widespread implementation occurs. Permissioned BCs, in contrast to permissionless ones, process more transactions per second.

Financial Barriers

BC is gaining traction as a potential answer to the technological challenges faced by today's educational institutions. However, the paucity of available funds remains the primary obstacle to widespread adoption of such technologies. Until more schools make the investment in technology, staff, and knowledge necessary to implement it, its broad use in classrooms is doubtful. BC technology in the classroom is a potent answer to this issue, but its implementation will take time.

The Rate of Adoptions

Graduates may only reap the benefits of owning their credentials if the schools or industries they are applying to recognize their legitimacy, just as with previous technologies (Gilda, & Mehrotra, 2018). BC credentials are now the exception rather than the rule; nonetheless, hundreds of institutions are already issuing and accepting them, and a network of employment portals like Upwork and ZipRecruiter are advocating their acceptance.

Lack of Awareness

Due to the potential lack of familiarity with BC, arguing for its use in educational settings can be challenging. Educators and other institutions need to prioritize developing a business case for BC's value.

Cost

Although there may be cost reductions in other areas, introducing new technology is rarely cheap. BC is a new technology that must be incorporated into the current infrastructure. It's important to note that the expenses associated with adoption and implementation can be substantial. In addition to the high price of implementation, several BC solutions have prohibitively expensive transaction or computing costs (Farah et al., 2018). As was previously indicated, the expense of managing and storing such massive amounts of student data would increase as block size increases in tandem with the number of users (Han et al., 2018). It will be impossible to use this method in conventional schooling without first handling the associated development and operating costs (Bore et al., 2017; Purdon & Erturk, 2017). Investing in more computing power or updating an existing infrastructure can be pricey. Institutions may also need to spend time and money training school administrators to use the technology (Gilda, & Mehrotra, 2018) because many of them lack the knowledge and skills essential to manage student data on a BC platform.

Examples of Student Experience

It can be difficult for employers and colleges and universities to verify the legitimacy of college diplomas, degrees, and other qualifications, but blockchain technology for academia can give them a secure and tamper-proof method of confirming and maintaining academic credentials.

To guarantee that the appropriate parties are being reimbursed for their work and that all students have access to adequate instructional materials, blockchain technology can be applied in the field of education to monitor and verify the ownership of digital learning assets.

Distributing anything from textbooks and digital learning materials to laboratory apparatus and supplies might be made more transparent and efficient with the use of blockchain-based systems.

BLOCKCERTS: MANAGEMENT OF ACADEMIC QUALIFICATIONS USING BLOCKCHAIN TECHNOLOGY

To securely store and verify digital certificates, such as transcripts and credentials, Blockcerts was developed as an open-standard platform. Diplomas, transfer records, and grade point averages are just some of the data that might be stored on its blockchain network. This establishes a standard environment in which academic records can be created, issued, viewed, and validated by any interested party. Universities may verify the accuracy of student records using the system, and future employers can learn more about a candidate's skills and expertise by viewing their complete profile, which includes honors and awards (Blockchain Education Applications & Use Cases pixelplex.io).

Online Distribution and Exchange for Educational Materials

ODEM is a blockchain-based online learning platform that provides flexible, student-tailored education at low costs. The best possible educational experience can be determined through collaborative discussion between students and faculty. Educators and students alike can benefit from the platform's use of blockchain-enabled payment systems and smart contracts for incentive and reward. The blockchain serves as a secure repository for all student certifications. As a result, they can be quickly retrieved and distributed via social media or included as supporting evidence in electronic resumes (Blockchain Education Applications & Use Cases pixelplex.io).

Sony International Education's Electronic Graduation Record System

Sony Global Education facilitates the distributed ledger-based sharing of student accomplishments across numerous educational institutions. Each student's permanent digital transcript that can be used for transferring between schools is stored on the blockchain network. Sony plans to expand the service and provide supporting infrastructure so that the future generation of educators can work together for the benefit of their pupils and be compensated in bitcoin.

Implication

As BC technology has progressed and been applied, new technical bases and practical models for educational reform have emerged. Education is a relatively new area of application for BC technology, with most current studies focusing on its potential to disrupt established financial sectors. Inadequate policy protection and lack of practical expertise are two obstacles to further development. To begin, the decentralization will have a major effect on conventional educational institutions because of the absence of governmental supervision and protection. After suffering enormous losses, the traditional education platform has become increasingly hostile to new applications. Second, there aren't enough use cases for professionals and academics to get excited about spreading the word. This chapter lays the basis for universities, governments, and researchers to investigate further use cases for BC technology with little to no resistance. Security, trustworthiness, and the ability to track and trace the dissemination of knowledge are of primary importance in the context of BC technology in the educational sector. Subsequently, the ledger serves as a safe repository for the information that has been collected from the various educational institutions involved in the field of education, including the teaching and learning process, which includes accreditation and validation of educational achievements. BC technology has been shown to facilitate a setting in which students can maintain and control their own academic records independently of outside parties. The widespread certificate fraud can be reduced if educational institutions began issuing, validating, and exchanging certificates utilizing BC technology, a form of cryptographic data exchange.

CONCLUSION

This chapter delves into the intersection of BC technology and the difficulties encountered by students and educational institutions in its usage. Researchers and academics as well as international organizations with responsibility for education monitoring contribute to this work by drawing on their previous publications and studies on the topic. When it comes to education, BC technology is one of the newest inventions that is gaining widespread interest from a wide range of interested parties. This is largely attributable to its several positive characteristics, which include decentralization, transparency, traceability, security, and dependability. BC technology has some promising applications, but it also has a ways to go before it gains widespread use. To produce its decentralized, traceable, immutable, and monetary properties, BC technology employs cryptograph techniques and distributed consensus algorithms. The intrinsic value of its currency could inspire a plethora of creative pedagogical uses. It's easy to see how the "learning is earning" mentality may be bolstered by BC technology in the classroom. It may keep track of all the details, both good and bad, of a student's educational journey, from their first steps into the classroom through their final assessments in both formal and informal settings. Additionally, it can keep track of how and when teachers do things in the classroom, providing a benchmark for evaluating their effectiveness. Simply put, BC has vast promise in the realms of instructional design, behavior recording and analysis, and formative assessment, for both students and educators. Equally, it presents researchers, developers, and educators with new difficulties and opportunities.

REFERENCES

Abdeldayem, M. M., & Al Dulaimi, S. H. (2020). Trends ofglobal fintech education practices and the gcc perspective. *Int. J. Adv. Sci. Technol.*, *29*, 7150–7163.

Awaji, B., Solaiman, E., & Marshall, L. (2020). Blockchain-based trusted achievement record system design. In Proceedings of the *ICIEI 2020: 5th International Conference on Information and Education Innovations*, London, UK. 10.1145/3411681.3411689

Bore, N., Karumba, S., Mutahi, J., Darnell, S. S., Wayua, C., & Weldemariam, K. (2017). Towards Blockchain-enabled school information hub. In *Proceedings of the 9th International Conference on Information and Communication Technologies and Development*, Lahore, Pakistan.

Farah, J. C., Vozniuk, A., Rodríguez-Triana, M. J., & Gillet, D. (2018). *A Blueprint for a Blockchain-Based Architecture to Power a Distributed Network of Tamper-Evident Learning Trace Repositories*. In *Proceedings of the 2018 IEEE 18th International Conference on Advanced Learning Technologies (ICALT)*, Mumbai, India. 10.1109/ICALT.2018.00059

Gatteschi, V., Lamberti, F., & Demartini, C. (2020). Blockchaintechnology use cases. In S. Kim & G. C. Deka (Eds.), *Advanced applications of BC technology* (pp. 91–114). Springer.

Gilda, S., & Mehrotra, M. (2018). *BC for Student Data Privacy and Consent*. In *Proceedings of the 2018 International Conference on Computer Communication and Informatics (ICCCI)*, Coimbatore, India.

Gräther, W., Kolvenbach, S., Ruland, R., Schütte, J., Torres, C., & Wendland, F. (2018), Blockchainfor education: lifelong learning passport. In *Proceedings of 1st ERCIM BC Workshop 2018, European Society for Socially Embedded Technologies (EUSSET)*. ERIC.

Han, M., Li, Z., He, J., Wu, D., Xie, Y., & Baba, A. (2018). A novel Blockchain-based education records verification solution. *Proceedings of the 19th Annual SIG Conference on Information Technology Education*, (pp. 178-183). ACM. 10.1145/3241815.3241870

Iredale, G. (2021). *6 key Blockchainfeatures you need to know now*. 101 Blockchain. https://101BCs.com/introduction-to-Blockchain-features/

Ma, Y.; Fang, Y. (2020). Current status, issues, and challenges of Blockchainapplications in education. *Int. J. Emerg. Technol. Learn. iJET, 15*, 20–31.

Maryvilla University. (2023). *How BlockchainIs Used in Education*. Maryvilla University. https://online.maryville.edu/blog/Blockchain-in-education/

Parizo, C. (2021). *What are the 4 different types ofblockchain technology?* TechTarget. https://www.techtarget.com/searchcio/feature/What-are-the-4-different-types-of-blockchain-technology

Piscini, E., Guastella, J., Rozman, A., & Nassim, T. (2016). *Blockchain: Democratized trust. Distributed ledgers and the future of value*. Deloitte University Press. https://www2.deloitte.com/content/dam/Deloitte/uk/Documents/technology/deloitte-uktech-trends-2016-BC.pdf

Purdon, I., & Erturk, E. (2017). Perspectives of BC Technology, its Relation to the Cloud and its Potential Role in Computer Science Education. *Eng. Technol. Appl. Sci. Res.*, *7*(6), 2340–2344. doi:10.48084/etasr.1629

Purohit, A. (2022). *The Impact of Blockchainon the Education Industry*. eLearning Industry. https://elearningindustry.com/ways-BC-impacts-education-industry-in-2022-and-beyond

Smith, S. S. (2021). Blockchain and Online Learning Are A Powerful Combination. *Forbes*. https://www.forbes.com/sites/seansteinsmith/2020/08/31/BC-and-online-learning-are-a-powerful-combination/?sh=5c52b665718d

Swan, M. (2015). *BC: Blueprint for a New Economy* (1st ed.). O'Reilly Media.

Tschorsch, F., & Scheuermann, B. (2016). Bitcoin and beyond: A technical survey on decentralized digital currencies. *IEEE Communications Surveys and Tutorials*, *18*(3), 2084–2123. doi:10.1109/COMST.2016.2535718

Underwood, S. (2016). Blockchainbeyond Bitcoin. *Communications of the ACM*, *59*(11), 15–17. doi:10.1145/2994581

Wang, H., Chen, K., & Xu, D. (2016). A maturity model for Blockchainadoption. [J]. *Financial Innovation*, *2*(1), 12. doi:10.118640854-016-0031-z

Yli-Huumo, D., Ko, D., Choi, S., Park, S., & Smolander, K. (2016). Where is current research on BC technology?—A systematic review. *PLoS One*, *11*(10), e0163477. doi:10.1371/journal.pone.0163477 PMID:27695049

Zheng. (2017). An Overview of Blockchain Technology: Architecture, Consensus, and Future Trends. *6th IEEE International Congress on Big Data*. IEEE. https://www.researchgate.net/publication/318131748_An_Overview_of_BC_Tec hnology_Architecture_Consensus_and_Future_Trends, accessed June 6 2020.

Chapter 14
Challenges of Blockchain Implementation for Patient Services

Mohammed Abdul-Basit Fuseini
Tamale Technical University, Ghana

Mohammed Majeed
https://orcid.org/0000-0001-9804-5335
Tamale Technical University, Ghana

ABSTRACT

Today, technology dominates businesses across all scales and sectors, including healthcare. Blockchain (BC) is a pivotal technology in this transformation. It securely stores medical data, updates clinics seamlessly, enhances workflows, and thwarts hacking threats. However, research on BC's implementation challenges for patient services remains limited. This chapter investigates these challenges, categorizing BC into public, private, hybrid, and consortium forms. Major obstacles encompass interconnectivity, security, standardization absence, storage limits, hospital hesitancy, patient mistrust, cost, limited medical proficiency, and data governance. Overcoming these hurdles is crucial for widespread healthcare BC adoption, despite the abundant opportunities. In comparison to other technologies, BC's unique issues require deeper exploration. Researchers can scrutinize BC comprehensively for its business potential. This chapter stands as a prominent effort in pinpointing and analyzing BC's integration in healthcare.

DOI: 10.4018/978-1-6684-7649-9.ch014

INTRODUCTION

When it comes to the delivery of treatment, health informatics (HI) is an offshoot of medical informatics that puts an emphasis on the clinical setting and the use of technology. Medical facilities and their staffs are using a variety of methods and technologies to share their patients' medical records (Esmaeilzadeh & Mirzaei, 2019). For a variety of reasons, people frequently change their residence, necessitating the use of a variety of new doctors and hospitals. Disjointed and out-of-date health data can weaken the bond between healthcare practitioners and their patients, making it difficult for them to share vital information. If properly implemented, BC has the potential to revolutionize healthcare data management. Health care informatics is developing as a result of developments in both medical technology and medical practice. Using today's cutting-edge tools, HI equips medical practitioners and healthcare institutions with comprehensive bodies of knowledge that improve the standard of care delivered to patients (Norris, 2016). A blockchain (BC) is a distributed digital ledger of transactions that can't be easily hacked or altered. This technology facilitates safe transactions between people without the need for a central authority, financial institution, or other middleman. By utilizing a decentralized ledger spread over multiple sites as opposed to one centralized one, BC can support electronic business transactions (i.e. information sharing) in a decentralized context. Patients can have control over their data by deciding what information is shared and with whom (Esmaeilzadeh & Mirzaei, 2019).

Decentralized systems, distributed ledgers, and immutable and cryptographically secure BC technologies are all examples of the emerging Internet of Things applications that are part of Industry 4.0. In this system, many entities store and use identical copies of a set of transaction lists. Due to a more patient-centric approach to the health care system and BC's capacity to integrate disparate systems and boost the accuracy of electronic health data, healthcare is one industry where BC technology has significant potential. Because of its disruptive nature, blockchain technology (BC) has the potential to radically alter the way healthcare providers interact with their customers. Using their own credentials and encryption key, users can grant others access to their health data in a transparent, auditable manner with the help of BC. This includes authorizing health professionals, service providers, and relevant actors (such as researchers and social care providers) to access their medical records and other information for the purposes of direct health care delivery or to permit research, statistical, or other secondary uses of their data (Organization for Economic Co-operation and Development, 2020). Although Bitcoin and Ethereum are examples of digital currencies, BC is often thought as its underlying technology. Healthcare, supply chain management, digital rights management, energy, and government are just few of the many industries that might benefit from BC (Hughes et al., 2019). In its capacity as a tool for managing electronic data, BC has the potential to promote openness and responsibility. A BC is a shared database where all participants can view the same set of transaction records at the same time. Data entered into the ledger are verified by the network before they become permanent (OECD, 2020). For cryptocurrencies, BC was initially designed to safeguard against fraud and theft while also removing the need for intermediaries like banks. Researchers are focused on BC techniques to bring security to healthcare applications as this new technology becomes more widespread. However, due to the differing needs of BC technologies, such integration in healthcare, is exceptionally difficult and challenging. Hence, this chapter focuses on the implementation challenges of BC in the healthcare sector from patience data management.

CONTRIBUTION

The content outlined in this chapter for ensuring the challenges such security and privacy of the people engaged even as the technology continues to expand wider usage and implementation in healthcare settings are critical for both the developers of BC technologies, patients and the common users. This is one of the few main studies to specifically target the identification and analysis of BC uptake in the healthcare sector. The literature of this chapter has real-world applications because they will help developers and healthcare administrators anticipate and address these types of challenges when they plan, build, and implement systems that are headquartered in BC.

LITERATURE

Blockchain

Blockchain (BC) is a distributed, unchangeable ledger that can be used to record transactions and keep tabs on assets in a corporate network. A property, vehicle, money, or piece of land are all examples of tangible assets (intellectual property, patents, copyrights, branding). Using BC as a security approach has many benefits, as stated by Esposito et al. (2018), including reducing the need for a trusted third party to reach an agreement and eliminating a bottleneck, and having comprehensive and coherent antecedent medical data as a result of the chaining. However, the price tag for this technology is quite high. It's also important to remember that the BC uses a lot of CPU, which is problematic for e-health systems. It offers several useful properties without the need for intermediaries, such as being tamper-proof, immutable, traceable, having data integrity, being confidential, and being private. Where visibility and data integrity are valued, as in low-volume digital transactions, BC excels. Identity verification, pharmaceuticals supply chain management, and the administration of variable patient permission and data sharing and access permissions are all potential areas of application for blockchain technology in the healthcare industry (OECD, 2020).

BC, also called as distributed ledger technology, can be understood by looking at the Bitcoin system as an example: Nodes in a network of powerful computers receive and process the transaction data for buying and selling Bitcoin. Using complex mathematical calculations, thousands of nodes all over the world compete to verify the transaction. Bitcoin mining refers to this process. The miner that finishes a new block first receives Bitcoin as payment for their efforts. These bonuses are covered by newly minted Bitcoin and shared network costs with the buyer and seller. Fees are variable and may increase or decrease based on the number of transactions made. The transaction is added to the distributed ledger as a new block once the cryptographic confirmation of the purchase has been received. Following this, the sale needs approval from the vast majority of the system's nodes. A cryptographic fingerprint called a hash is used to link the block to all prior blocks of Bitcoin transactions, and the transaction is completed.

TYPES OF BLOCKCHAIN

Private Blockchain

A private business Blockchain is used to monitor the flow of information between employees or departments within a single company. Once a member of the network has given their permission, they are a recognized member of the network (Ray et al., 2020). In a closed Blockchain network, only a predetermined number of users can verify transactions or data. Whenever confidentiality and safety are of paramount importance in a network, these are deployed. The organization's stated mission serves as the basis for its openness. Limited access means there is no anatomy to speak about. When comparing public and private Blockchain, transactions in the latter happen much quicker. This is due to the fact that, unlike a public network, a private network has a finite number of nodes. This speeds up the time it takes for all nodes in a network to reach agreement or verify a transaction. Further, additional transactions are quickly added to a block.

Public BC

Public (also called Permissionless or trustless) BC allows anyone to take part in the verification of transactions and data. Wherever stringent openness standards are called for in a network, these are deployed. Bitcoin and Ethereum are two examples of public BC that offer a truly decentralized network in which every user has full access to all blockchain data and may participate in the network's consensus procedure (Ray et al., 2020). Such CBs are not at all resistant to the concept of decentralization. All that is required to join this public BC is access to the internet and a reasonably powerful computer. Each computer in the network stores an exact replica of every node and block in the system. Verifying deals or documents is another service we may use this public BC for. To this day, trading and mining cryptocurrencies are the two most common uses for public BC (Wegrzyn & Wang, 2021). Public BC allow users to "mine" cryptocurrency by solving cryptographic equations in order to create blocks for the network's desired transactions. Because of all their efforts, the miner nodes receive a token amount of cryptocurrency (Wegrzyn & Wang, 2021).

A public network is a safe network since it does not restrict the number of users or nodes. The greater the size of the network, the more widely spread out the records will be, making it more difficult for hackers to compromise the entire network. Moreover, all nodes will perform transaction and proof-of-work verification, ensuring the validity of each and every transaction and block (Dataflaire Team, 2023). As a result of these precautions and well-considered cryptogenic encrypting methods, a public BC is far more secure than a private one.

Hybrid

The advantages of both private and public health care systems are merged in hybrid BC. As a result, a public BC is used to ensure that everyone has access to the ledger, while a private BC operates in the background to regulate who has access to the ledger's evolving records (Ray et al., 2020). Hybrid BC are privately operated BC that yet fall under the watchful eye of the public BC in order to validate certain types of transactions. IBM Food Trust, a hybrid BC created to increase productivity all along the food supply chain, is one example (Wegrzyn & Wang, 2021). Consortium BCs are a form of semi-decentralized BCs in which multiple entities share network management responsibilities. The private BC we visited was controlled by a single entity, so this finding stands in stark contrast (Dataflair Team, 2023). In this form of BC, multiple entities can participate as nodes to do tasks like information exchange and data mining. Banks, government agencies, and other establishments frequently use Consortium BC.

Consortium BC

Those who are invited to join a consortium BC have access to a private network. As a distributed database that can be trusted to stay in sync and record all of the data transfers between its users, it serves as a transparent audit trail. The difference between a private business corporation and a consortium BC is that the latter is governed by a number of different organizations rather than just one. Consortium BC therefore benefits from greater decentralization than private BC, increasing safety. However, forming a consortium can be difficult due to the fact that it necessitates the cooperation of multiple organizations, which poses both logistical obstacles and potential antitrust risk (which we shall discuss in a subsequent piece) (Wegrzyn & Wang, 2021). Consortium BCs are a form of semi-decentralized BCs in which multiple entities share network management responsibilities. And this is in stark contrast to what we observed in a private BC, where there was only one authority figure in charge of everything. In this form of BC, multiple entities can participate as nodes to do tasks like information exchange and data mining. Banks, government agencies, and other establishments frequently use Consortium BC.

BC IN HEALTH CARE INDUSTRY

Because it deals with highly private and secret information, the healthcare sector has specific data management requirements. Unfortunately, this information is frequently held and distributed among a number of different facilities and providers, which can make accessing it a time-consuming and inefficient procedure, especially in the event of an emergency (Zajc, 2018). Accordingly, BC technology is perfect for overcoming these difficulties. It can safely store sensitive information like medical records, automatically update that information across all of your clinics, improve your workflow, and safeguard your patients' information from hackers.

Patient and BC

Global healthcare significantly underutilizes BC technologies. For all parties involved in the healthcare industry, it can provide an accessible, open, secure, and effective method of information and facts communication. It provides the chance to scale back or do away with the pre-authorization process in the healthcare industry through tokenization and the usage of smart contracts. When connecting with other parties, BC technologies for healthcare records include secure encryption methods that protect the confidentiality of individuals' personal information. Pre-authorization will be drastically reduced by tokenization, smart contracts, and the encryption methods used in BC network transactions, allowing patients to receive the necessary and informed care more quickly (Philip, 2021). When previously relying on the patients or on documents manually delivered or emailed from many sources, such as local doctors, labs, etc., the healthcare professional is now able to get the pertinent information promptly. BC has the potential to significantly alter the healthcare industry and provide patients access to their data. Medical Records, which provides patients and physicians with a permanent record of their medical history, is one particularly intriguing step in this direction (Zajc, 2018). By granting access to anonymized healthcare data in return for maintaining the network, it adopts a different strategy for rewarding miners. The introduction of a decentralized platform into the world's healthcare system will assist the patient in various ways. One benefit is that it will enable patients to own their medical records rather than the healthcare provider (Bamakan et al., 2021). Decentralization will also free patients from restrictions and enable them to give their medical records to any doctor, anywhere in the world, making healthcare more accessible to all.

CHALLENGES OF BC ADOPTION

Interconnection, security, absence of standardization, storage capacity, hospitals' reluctance to start sharing patient information, lack of trust among sick people, lack of skills among doctors and medical professionals, and finally, culpability and data governance are among the most significant obstacles to the widespread adoption of BC technology in the healthcare sector.

Secured Storage

The safe keeping and sharing of patient data is one of the healthcare industry's biggest obstacles. Due to the nature of compartmentalized record-keeping systems, data may be inconsistent, unclear, or missing. In addition, when doctors refer patients to other doctors, patients typically have to transport their medical records themselves. Particularly if medical professionals are using antiquated and unprotected technologies that are not integrated with modern healthcare systems and apps, this leads to improper data handling, increased security risks, and accidental exposures (Philip, 2021). Problems like this lead to lost time, money, and legal risk.

Inadequate Criteria

One of the biggest challenges in creating an interoperable healthcare information exchange (HIE) that bridges numerous data silos is the lack of common healthcare data standards. The introduction of incentives through BC-based data exchange, however, could help drive the establishment of open data standards. An intriguing use case that will test the balance of privacy, transparency, and efficiency is the creation of HIE based on BC.BC has an image problem

BC's Image Issues

Unfortunately, many people still associate BC with crypto, contributing to a negative reputation. And it's thought of as a place full of criminals, hackers, con artists, and speculators. In the minds of many, Bitcoin Cash is inextricably intertwined with cryptocurrencies. In particular, crypto has a bad reputation because of all the scammers and hackers that use it for illegal purposes (Zajc, 2018). All of BC technology is getting a terrible rap because of one incident, and its widespread adoption is being seriously questioned as a result. The people at large must be educated on the distinctions between Bitcoin, other cryptocurrencies, and BC before widespread use can occur. You should know that cryptos are just one use case of BC technology. As a result, people will be more likely to embrace the technology and stop worrying about the potential downsides.

Time Consuming

Getting paid is a major, frustrating, and time-consuming problem for healthcare professionals. Micropayments settled via centralized third-party services are commonly used in today's healthcare system. However, it is not transparent, can be hacked, has significant fees over time, and takes a long time (Philip, 2021).

Lack of Scalability

To complicate matters, particularly for public BC, the technical scalability of the network is a big technological problem. The speed with which traditional transaction networks can execute thousands of transactions per second is legendary. The problems of handling, storage, and scalability are further highlighted by Nagasubramanian (2020). It is impractical to keep records for every patient in a secure manner. Laboratory reports, pictures, and papers are the normal components of the medical record. Large amounts of data storage may be required for digital medical records that cover several patient populations. The healthcare system may be profoundly affected if every medical transaction is recorded in a decentralized manner, with the same kind of record stored in different locations. As an example, Visa can handle over 2000 transactions per second. Bitcoin and Ethereum, the two main BC networks, lag significantly behind in transaction speeds. Ethereum can process around 20 transactions per second, while the Bitcoin BC can only process three to seven transactions. Since private BC network nodes are built to conduct transactions in a trusted environment, this lack of scalability is not as much of a problem for private BC networks (Zajc, 2018).

Vulnerability

Privacy violations cost the pharmaceutical industry billions of dollars every year, undermine patient confidence in the system, and tarnish the reputation of the affected companies and professionals. Furthermore, such violations can be in violation of a wide range of statutes and regulations depending on the specifics of the infraction (Philip, 2021). Data breaches, like those caused by ransomware, are a constant threat to businesses, and hackers can make off with a lot of money by gaining access to sensitive information stored in electronic health records.

Data Governance

The envisioned BC-based hospital system must allow for data exchange between public and private BCs. This highlights the importance of internationally coordinated norms and agreements that apply across country boundaries and legal systems.

Lack of BC Developers

Although there has been a tremendous rise in the need for certified BC workers, there is now a severe lack of personnel who have the necessary training and experience to build and manage sophisticated person to person (P2P) networks. However, using BC technology properly requires more education and experience (Zajc, 2018). The need for workers in the BC sector is expected to grow by about 2000% between 2017 and 2020, according to some estimates. There is significant worry about the lack of available skilled developers. Emerging and developing, BC technologies is still in its infancy. Time is needed for its adoption by the development community and the introduction of necessary BC-related curriculum in schools and universities. Despite the fact that this will reduce pressure on the market, the benefits won't be seen until students have completed their education, which could take a while.

The BC Process Can Be Ponderous and Tedious at Times

BC can be sluggish and inconvenient because of its complexity and encrypted, decentralized nature. Compared to "conventional" payment methods like cash or debit cards, processing times for transactions can be quite long (Zajc, 2018). It takes more time to handle transitions when there are more users on the network. The whole transaction could take several days to complete. So, the transaction fees are larger than usual, and more people can't use the network. This concept, at least in theory, can be applied to BC networks that serve some other purpose than simply storing currency (for example logging transactions or interactions in and IoT environment). Technical progress and faster computers may eventually be able to remedy this issue.

Lack of Trust

Attaran (2020) argues that a lack of confidence among patients and other key stakeholders is another significant barrier to BC's widespread adoption in healthcare devices. Most patients might be reluctant to make their EHRs public and accessible to third parties. As a result, it is crucial to build confidence amongst individual patients regarding the privacy and security benefits of BC technology in the healthcare sector.

Lack of Education and Knowledge

Companies involved with BC, particularly smaller and medium-sized ones, face a significant barrier in the form of a general public's ignorance about the technologies and its capabilities. A lot of businesses have no idea what BC is or how it may help them. The prevalence of technicians and an overreliance on technology play significant roles in this phenomenon in the BC region. Because of this, investment and the pursuit of new ideas are being hampered. Rather, what is required is a strategy that is more business-like. A better user experience for non-technical users is requested. In order to keep up with this new development, businesses need to learn more about it. They need to broaden their horizons and learn more about everything. Consequently, enhanced educational programs are required to disseminate this information to the broadest possible audience.

Conflict in Productivity

Then there's the 'BC paradox,' as it's commonly known. While BC networks can perform peer-to-peer transactions quickly and efficiently, this efficiency comes with a high aggregate cost that is higher for some types of BC than others (Zajc, 2018). This inefficiency results from each node competing with the others to solve the problem first by processing its own copy of the data in the exact same way. Because of this, businesses should use caution when deciding whether or not to adopt BC apps. As a network expands, the benefits of doing your own processing could decrease. That's why BC apps need to take advantage of network effects to benefit businesses and consumers alike.

Cost

Although it is currently unknown how much it will cost to implement and maintain such a system, as well as to migrate from existing health information management platforms, the decentralized and open-source nature of BC and other similar technologies may help mitigate these costs. To keep the proposed BC-based integrated health system running smoothly, it will be necessary to have access to a steady stream of resources for things like bug fixing, software upgrades, data backups, and status reports (Justinia., 2019).

Problems With Security and Privacy

In addition to how to evaluate the many threats to users' safety and privacy. Important problems concerning privacy and the security of the data kept and accessible on the shared ledger arise since many prospective uses of the BC require smart transactions and contracts to be conclusively tied to known individuals, but cryptocurrencies enable pseudonymity. Many businesses in the modern day adhere to legally mandated privacy policies (Zajc, 2018). While BC technology has many potential benefits, its emphasis on openness may not always be desirable in the health industry. Although encryption helps keep sensitive information safe, the fact that a database exists at all—even in an encrypted form—remains a major concern for many involved in the healthcare system. Their clients are comfortable sharing their most private data with them. However, if all of this data is recorded in a shared ledger, its confidentiality will be compromised. It's possible that BC, either privately or in a consortium, may be useful here. Another important consideration is safety. However, only a select few cases have well-developed protocols to handle this. Even though apps, systems, and businesses created on BC are safer than those based on traditional computers, hackers can still break in.

Insufficiently Clear Regulations and Poor Administration

Another major barrier to widespread use is the ambiguity of current regulations about the technology at the heart of BC. It has always been difficult for rules and laws to keep up with technological development. In the case of BC, this is also true. The lack of oversight is a problem with the BC method, but it was also one of the reasons it was developed. If an HIE is to connect various regulatory regions, it will face additional challenges from country-specific rules. A BC-enabled patient-centric healthcare data model may be a suitable means of avoiding such legislative hurdles, given that patients hold complete ownership of their healthcare data in many countries. Multiple businesses are adopting BC technology as a payment method.

But there are still no hard and fast rules about it. Thus, there is still no safety in the BC because no one observes any particular regulations (Justinia, 2019). Despite the difficulties and constraints, centralized systems might "serve as shock absorbers in times of crisis," especially in the banking sector. Without proper planning, decentralized networks may be highly vulnerable to disturbances that directly affect their constituents (Zajc, 2018).

Implication

Challenges of implementing BC in healthcare settings are highlighted in this research. The research looks into the important questions concerning the necessary aid, the obstacles to adoption, and the primary advantages of adoption preparation and action. Applications like patient-centric systems and distributed, secure medical and clinical data are anticipated to emerge as a result of the widespread adoption of new technologies in the healthcare sector. The patient will get new benefits from integrating a decentralized platform into the world's healthcare system. As one benefit, patients, rather than healthcare providers, will have legal title to their own medical records. By breaking down barriers and letting people share their health records with any doctor in the world, decentralization will make healthcare more available to everyone.

DISCUSSIONS

As a relatively new technological solution, BC technology is finding early adopters. However, it is still a difficulty to ensure that solutions built on top of BC technology adhere to all applicable rules and regulations. Private BC are better suited to serve corporate objectives since they are more energy-efficient, give more privacy to safeguard trade secrets, and have fewer security risks. Thus, it is argued that BC apps should conform to preexisting rules rather than trying to create their own. Government and highly regulated industries may need to establish rules for Blockchain in order to help the province overcome these obstacles. However, this necessitates that regulators everywhere learn about the technology and its effects on the businesses and customers in their respective fields. Trust problems in a cloud infrastructure were one of the main topics discussed by Rahmani et al. (2022), who also discussed possible applications of BC technology. Centralization, tremendous cost, trust evidence, less adaptability, and inaccuracy are just few of the problems with cloud computing that were discovered in the study.

Because public BC doesn't rely on a central authority and may be used to replace conventional monetary systems with "proof of effort" or "proof of stake," it is a disruptive innovation in the financial sector. This BC's smart contract, which allowed it to support decentralization, is its cutting edge. Bitcoin and Ethereum are two popular forms of public BC. If properly protected and maintained, this BC can be an excellent tool for keeping sensitive data out of the wrong hands. As a result, they are utilized in internal auditing, voting, and asset management. Hyperledger and Corda are two private BC examples. The healthcare sector, government, real estate, and financial institutions all benefit from this enhanced solution. It's a solution for situations where people need public access to protected information. Ripple and its XRP token are two working examples of Hybrid BC. There is a great deal of potential for it in financial institutions, commercial enterprises, and other payment systems. The organizations' food tracking frequently collaborates with their sectors, so a federated solution is ideal for their use. consortium BC is used by projects like Tendermint and Multichain.

PREDICTING THE FUTURE

In most cases, the development and refinement of a new technology takes years before it is ready for commercial release. BC adoption will resemble that of other technological advances over the next few years. There are lots of opportunities, but it will take work to overcome the obstacles and start reaping the rewards. The difficulties associated with widespread adoption of BC highlighted above highlight the urgent need for technological advancements. In fact, businesses are extremely active in addressing them. Once we've addressed these issues and taken away the numerous roadblocks, things will undoubtedly improve and spark widespread adoption.

CONCLUSION

Although proofs of concept incorporating BC technologies into the healthcare sector have been established, widespread adoption remains hampered by a number of obstacles. The intrinsic unwillingness of the healthcare business to change its current practices, especially those 40 pertaining to organizational, structural, technological, and human aspects, will be one of the most significant obstacles. Individual problems (lack of expertise), organizational problems (implementation issues), technological problems (different types of BC models), and regulatory concerns all suggest that BC-based applications in healthcare remain a developing topic. Removing these hurdles would boost the adoption of BC-based HIEs across a variety of healthcare settings and improve regional and community health information networks' interoperability and connectedness. There is no doubt that BC will significantly alter the healthcare business in the future, and that its applications will grow much beyond those listed above. However, there are still many open questions concerning privacy and operational concerns. Public, private, hybrid, and consortium BC are all mentioned in the research.

A BC is a distributed ledger that holds data in blocks that are cryptographically linked together. A new block is created for each influx of data. As each block is updated with new information, it is linked to the one before it in a chain that represents the progression of time. A BC can be used to record many different kinds of data, but thus far, financial transactions have been its most prevalent application. To ensure that no single entity or group of individuals has monopolized Bitcoin's BC, the technology is employed in a decentralized manner in which the users themselves retain governance over the currency. Since the information submitted into a decentralized BC cannot be changed, any actions taken based on the information contained therein are permanent. Bitcoin transactions are publicly accessible and will remain so indefinitely.

RECOMMENDATIONS

Harmonization of governance with regulations. Certain aspects of BC-based solutions must be assessed for compliance with relevant statutes, rules, and data governance frameworks. Blockchain technology (BC) is an enabling, general-purpose digital technology. After comparing it to other possible remedies, it should be used when it is shown to be the most effective. The government should prioritize the creation of infrastructure in different regions of the country to host BC platforms. A native BC platform has the potential to lower the barrier to entry for healthcare organizations looking to embrace BC by making the technology more affordable.

Recommendation for Future Research

For the sake of patient confidentiality and safety, new research should examine the effects of BC in the healthcare and biological sectors. Similarly, another paper suggests a health information exchange (HIE) system headquartered on Blockchain to track patients. Later research may be able to confirm the BC acceptance model empirically. When compared to other technologies, the difficulties that have been associated with BC technology need to be investigated further. There is potential for researchers to examine all facets of the BC and the opportunities it presents for businesses.

REFERENCES

Attaran, M. (2020). Digital technology enablers and their implications for supply chain management. *Supply Chain Forum 21*(1). 10.1080/16258312.2020.1751568

Bamakan, S. M. H., Moghaddam, S. G., & Manshadi, S. D. (2021). BC-enabled pharmaceutical cold chain: Applications, key challenges, and future trends. *Journal of Cleaner Production*, *302*, 127021. doi:10.1016/j.jclepro.2021.127021

DataFlaire Team. (2023). *Types of BC – Decide which one is better for your Investment Needs*. Data Flair. https://data-flair.training/blogs/types-of-BC

Esmaeilzadeh, P., & Mirzaei, T. (2019). The potential of BC technology for health information exchange: Experimental study from patients' perspectives. *Journal of Medical Internet Research*, *21*(6), e14184. http://www.jmir.org/2019/6/e14184/. doi:10.2196/14184 PMID:31223119

Esposito, C., de Santis, A., Tortora, G., Chang, H., & Choo, K.-K. R. (2018). BC: A panacea for healthcare cloud-based data security and privacy? *IEEE Cloud Comput.*, *5*(1), 31–37. doi:10.1109/MCC.2018.011791712

Hughes, A., Park, A., Kietzmann, J., & Archer-Brown, C. (2019). Beyond Bitcoin: What BC and distributed ledger technologies mean for firms. *Business Horizons*, *62*(3), 273–281. doi:10.1016/j.bushor.2019.01.002

Justinia, T. (2019). BC technologies: Opportunities for solving real-world problems in healthcare and biomedical sciences. *Acta Informatica Medica*, *27*(4), 284. doi:10.5455/aim.2019.27.284-291 PMID:32055097

Norris A. C. (2016). Current trends and challenges in health informatics. *Health Informatics J Jul 25, 8*(4), 205-213. [] doi:10.1177/146045820200800407

OECD. (2020). *Opportunities and Challenges of BC Technologies in Health Care.* OECD BC Policy Series. https://www.oecd.org/finance/Opportunities-and-Challenges-of-BC-Technologies-in-Health-Care.pdf

Philip, F. (2021). 3 Ways That BC Can Help the Healthcare Industry Focus More on Patient Care and Less on Administrative Headaches. *Insights*. https://www.fisherphillips.com/news-insights/3-ways-that-BC-help-healthcare-industry.html

Rahmani, M. K. I., Shuaib, M., Alam, S., Siddiqui, S. T., Ahmad, S., Bhatia, S., & Mashat, A. (2022). BC-Based Trust Management Framework for Cloud Computing-Based Internet of Medical Things (IoMT): A Systematic Review. *Computational Intelligence and Neuroscience*, *2022*, 9766844. doi:10.1155/2022/9766844 PMID:35634070

Ray, P. P., Dash, D., Salah, K., & Kumar, N. (2020). BC for IoT-based healthcare: Background, consensus, platforms, and use cases. *IEEE Systems Journal.*

Wegzyn, K. E., & Wang, W. E. (2021). *Types of BC: Public, Private, or Something in Between.* Foley & Larner LLP. https://www.foley.com/en/insights/publications/2021/08/types-of-BC-public-private-between

Zajc, T. (2018). F020 BC, value of data, and the role of legislation with adoption. *Medium.* https://medium.com/faces-of-digital-health/f020-BC-value-of-data-and-the-role-of-legislation-withadoption-ray-dogum-health-80919d909e97

Chapter 15
Customer Experience in the Web 3.0 Era:
The Meeting of Blockchain and the Metaverse

Lubza Nihar Khaliq
GITAM University (Deemed), India

Vijaya Kittu Manda
https://orcid.org/0000-0002-1680-8210
Independent Researcher, India

ABSTRACT

Modern disruption technologies such as the Blockchain and the Metaverse have promising features that can help businesses offer their products and services to customers in a better format. The Metaverse creates a virtual environment and a new communication path between the customer and the business. As a new marketing channel, it helps customers appear as virtual avatars and have a 3D preview/experience of goods and services before adding them to the shopping cart or signing up subscriptions. Blockchain-based systems allow making payments using wallet money, CDBC, or even cryptocurrencies and securely store personal data in a public immutable ledger transaction, which others will verify easily. Marketers have to address specific issues that come with deploying these systems – such as data privacy, amongst others - to give the best consumer experience powered by the confluence of various technologies. The book chapter will have managerial and practical implications for businesses during customer interactions.

DOI: 10.4018/978-1-6684-7649-9.ch015

INTRODUCTION

Improving and giving out delightful levels of customer experience is a priority for marketers. Customer experience and ensuring customers are locked into the products and services, such as by building barriers to exit, have become essential to enhance customer retention (Gao et al., 2022). Several studies acknowledged that information technology and its various tools improve customer experience. No wonder corporates spend heavily on technology infrastructure and their upgrades to automate tasks to the extent possible, thereby reducing costs and having happy and loyal customers. Ample use cases, particularly from finance and retail, demonstrate how these technologies can take customer management to the next level.

Early disruption technologies of the Industry 4.0 era, such as Artificial Intelligence (Jangra & Jangra, 2022) and Machine Learning, have already improved customer purchasing behavior and decision-making in areas such as e-commerce. With the Internet moving into a different form, the remaining technologies in the stack, such as Blockchain and Metaverse, promise a vital role in connecting to the next industrial revolution – Industry 5.0. Globalization and the Internet transition from Web 1.0 to Web 2.0 are two critical developments that happened in recent times. With Web 3.0 evolving, companies have to prioritize their metaverse investments in order to gain a foothold in the market (Mercanoğlu Erín & Dİnçşahİn, 2021).

This chapter consists of four sections. The first section explores the role of technology in shaping the contemporary customer experience, with a specific focus on the Metaverse and how it gets benefited with the technology backing of Metaverse. The second section delves into the evolution of the Metaverse as a novel marketing channel. It also presents four case studies that examine the intersection of the Metaverse and customer experience, featuring Microsoft Mesh, Accenture Nth Floor, Seoul's transformation into a Metaverse City, and the impact of the Metaverse on banking. Following this, the chapter addresses the convergence of various technologies, including the Metaverse, Blockchain, Artificial Intelligence (AI), 5G communications, and others. The final section discusses the barriers that hinder market adoption. The concluding section provides a summary of the chapter's key findings.

MODERN CUSTOMER EXPERIENCE

Customer experience defines what customers feel and think about the brand. The delights and disappointments and the overall feel of the product or service are accounted for. Customer experience has evolved into a new dimension, focusing on the current state of technology, consumer behavior, and market trends. Existing research identified three critical factors linking innovative technologies and customer shopping: channel choice, value dimensions related to convenience and enjoyment, and social interaction (Ylilehto et al., 2021). Modern customer experience can be evaluated in several ways, by way of new technology adoption, increased loyalty, cost savings, and - most crucially - value co-creation. Customers are moving from traditional physical stores to hybrid or fully online stores; hence, customer experience measurements should be hybrid and digital. No matter how strong an offline brand is, the retail organization needs an online presence to maximize customer interaction. Information technology can be used in mapping, enabling, and monitoring the customer journey (Helouani, 2021). Retail companies have already embraced technological innovations in the retailing industry, such as smart mirrors, checkout-free stores, chatbots, and facial recognition-based shopping. However, with Metaverse, the customer experience will be taken up to whole newer interactive level, thanks to its immersive shopping features. For example, chatbots are getting integrated with the Metaverse (Xie et al., 2023). Virtual avatar characters/personalities will now interact with the customer instead of the boring text-only interaction mode that was used earlier. However, marketers should ensure that the availability and usage of multiple touchpoints do not lead to customer irritation. Customers must be facilitated with a smooth passage from one touchpoint to another to create fluidity between them (Vanheems, 2019).

The Metaverse transfers the retail drama stage from a traditional two-dimensional web to a three-dimensional virtual one (Papagiannidis & Bourlakis, 2010). Electronic Commerce (e-commerce) has already met certain consumer expectations and made customers ready to transact in a non-physical area. However, modern technologies such as the Metaverse will become the platforms where the next primary medium of interaction with the Internet will take place. The platform promises to take the customer experience to a higher level. While traditional online environments often lead to impulsive buying, metaverse environments offer interaction within the virtual space, giving more impetus to perceiving value before buying. So, the sale does not end up as an impulsive buy but as one where the customer perceives value. After all, research has already shown that perceived value is more robust and valuable than impulsive buying when it comes to making customers intend to buy, stick, and be loyal and repurchase (Damanik, 2022). Furthermore, when incorporated into the Metaverse, various Augmented reality characteristics enhance the online customer experience (OCE) (Habil et al., 2023). Metaverse and Non-fungible tokens can help marketers issue digital assets like tokens and coins to loyal customers (Olaleye et al., 2024).

Customer experience differs from customer to customer, and markets constantly pursue developing new and innovative customer experiences (Inge Furseth & Cuthbertson, 2016). Hence, increased personalization in marketing and improved

Customer Relationship Management (CRM) is necessary. Companies have to integrate in-store, online, and mobile (smartphone/tablet) platforms to create an expanded shopping experience for new buyers, as seen in the case of cars (just - auto, 2022). In addition, Customer Online Brand Experience (COBE) directly impacts the intention of an existing customer to become an influencer by forwarding online company-generated content (CGC) within his network and thereby helping companies extend their brand reach (Yasin et al., 2020).

Contextualization has come to Churches and religious places, and studies confirmed a positive relationship between worship experience and parishioners' commitment, meaning a positive experience for all stakeholders (Ojiaku et al., 2022). Celebrities are moving to the Metaverse, and so are their fans. With endless interconnected virtual communities, the Metaverse appears to give a parallel digital life to individuals, making marketers use it for brand extension. Metaverse has been the perfect place for property investment, travel planners, performances, ceremonies, simulated laboratories, and meetings (Bushell, 2022).

Reinventing customer experience became necessary because of rapid digital transformation because the space (or location) where customers are located, the time they spend (such as attention span), and the mode of purchase (switching to online mode) are all changing. Most shops these days are happening from desktop computers and sophisticated smartphones. QR codes have replaced the need to type website addresses or mobile phone numbers when making payments. Digital payments from wallets are already popular, while the latest trend is to use cryptocurrencies or Central Bank Digital Currencies (CBDCs) to replace the age-old fiat currencies (and currency notes).

Traditional banks are spending more money on technology and hiring more technology professionals. Citi, for example, increased its budget allocation for technology from US$ 10 billion in 2020 to US$ 11 billion in 2021. It increased its software engineer headcount by 30% to 30,000. In addition, Citi partnered with Alibaba and the Ant group to create an instant, 24/7, blockchain-powered cross-border payment solution using accounts in Singapore, Hong Kong, and the US (The Banker, 2022).

Security features – both for money value and user personal privacy are built into the devices that help us access the network. Space effectiveness and less baggage improve customer experience, especially for financial transactions. Increased investments are happening in NFT and digital asset formats instead of traditional wall paintings.

Product returns by dissatisfied customers are happening easily and quickly. Product return requests are made online and picked up at the customer's doorstep. Refunds are processed without judging the reason. Customer response at the return time is considered feedback rather than a complaint. By responding faster despite the product return and the loss, marketers try not to lose customers forever or to afford to damage their brand reputation. Business analytics are helping store owners and product manufacturers to find patterns leading to the defects/product returns, helping them to improve the product or to discard it, giving way to a different product. Blockchain has numerous supply chain use cases that can help companies trace the source of the mistake or the erring part/component and alert the component manufacturer to make necessary changes. Systems like these can help reduce corporates in product recalls by only recalling very specifically chosen units instead of a whole batch of units. Reverse logistics can help in improved sustainability of products. Reverse logistics is a set of activities conducted after a product's sale to recapture value and end the product's lifecycle. It typically involves returning a product to the manufacturer or distributor or forwarding it for servicing, refurbishment, or recycling. Organizations transform digitally by changing their structures, processes, functions, and business models, keeping the customer at the center (Hess et al., 2020). The critical success factors of the digital transformation in improving customer experience are well explained in the ABCD Framework. There are four components in the framework, with sub-components in each component - Analytics (data analytics, process analytics, and trend analytics), Business (Strategic execution, Business model, and Value proposition), Customer (Process, Collaboration, Services, and Engagement), and Digital (Integration, Capability, and Capacity) (Neeraj et al., 2018).

The role of augmented and virtual reality as a part of the Customer eXperience Management (CXM) process is explained in research circles with the help of a strategic CXM framework based on the value co-creation theory and experience economy (Tom Dieck & Han, 2022). Traditional Customer Relationship Management (CRM) platforms and Blockchain technologies can give new and improved customer experiences (Ghazaleh & Zabadi, 2021). About 70% of business customers are not involved with service providers regarding service co-design. Research already stated that Interfuctional coordination (IC), customer engagement (CE), and service design have a positive influence on business customer experience (BCX) (Ruiz-Alba et al., 2023). Web technologies can help in these three areas, making businesses closer to their customers.

A six-dimensional, eighteen-item customer experience (CX) scale measure can be applied to the omnichannel environments' different experience partners, touchpoints, and journey stages. The same can also be used in a virtual environment to a large extent.

Table 1. Dimensions and items in measuring customer experience (CX)

Affective (CR)
1. The contact with the experience partner induced good emotions.
2. I had positive feelings during the contact with the experience partner.
3. The contact with the experience partner put me in a good mood.
Cognitive (CR)
1. The contact with the experience partner piqued my curiosity.
2. I learned something beneficial during the contact with the experience partner.
3. I got positive insights during the contact with the experience partner.
Physical (CR)
1. My physical responses during the contact with the experience partner were pleasant.
2. During the contact with the experience partner, I actively moved in a way I liked.
3. During the contact with the experience partner, I was active in a way I liked.
Relational (CR)
1. I established a personal relationship with the experience partner.
2. I felt positively connected with the experience partner.
3. The contact with the experience partner made me feel like I belonged to a community.
Sensorial (CR)
1. The contact with the experience partner had a positive sensory appeal.
2. The contact with the experience partner had a positive impact on my senses.
3. The contact with the experience partner positively engaged my senses in a variety of ways.
Symbolic (CR)
1. The contact with the experience partner was in line with my personal values.
2. My personal beliefs were confirmed during the contact with the experience partner.
3. The contact with the experience partner was in line with my self-image.

Source: (Gahler et al., 2022)

Blockchain has several use cases on supply chain management that help organizations link with supply chain networks to quickly process customer orders with backend integration. Products procurement time is reduced, and shipment speeds have increased. Customers will be able to receive their orders quickly. Customer experiences and feedback go back to the suppliers and even designers more quickly so that product changes and enhancements are made faster than before. In case of dissatisfied customers, the dispute resolution process will be faster. All interaction between the parties is stored in an immutable ledger. The product co-creation process goes a step forward because of the communication/interaction time cut between the end-user and the product designer. All these processes help build products and services that fit customer requirements, leading to overall customer satisfaction. Not just this, the technologies help map employees' journey in serving the customer (orders). Employee journey mapping was documented to be an excellent tool for improving organizational communication and optimizing business processes (Belli, 2022).

METAVERSE AS A NEW CHANNEL

While the Internet is a network of networks, a Metaverse is an immersive network of 3D virtual worlds comprising virtual realms focused on social connection. COVID-led lockdowns have accelerated the push for digital forms of conducting classes, meetings, and conferences. While the online platforms were able to take the experience to the next level, the Metaverse is disruptive. It has the potential to take customer experience to a whole higher level.

Features of the Metaverse make it an ideal platform for corporates offering products and services to use as a whole new world of marketing and selling opportunities. It is agreed that the Metaverse is in its early evolutionary stage, and those real-life adoptions will take some time. However, some leading giants have already started experimenting to see how well it fits into corporate marketing strategies. The rebranding of Facebook to Meta in October 2021 and Microsoft's acquisition of Activision Blizzard show the seriousness of some of the giants in using the platform as the future commonplace. Though Metaverse is intended to be not owned by any single institution, some corporates are ensuring they have an early presence to become a common word in this virtual reality world.

Metaverse engages all five senses to create engaging and immersive experiences, so spatial audio, haptics (touch), and olfactory (smell) inputs are necessary. Marketers can use auditory marketing, such as music and light in a Metaverse environment, to improve the customer's mood (Nwachukwu & Maudlinepac, 2022). Metaverse can bring in delight (and not just *pleasure*) because it can bring in two ingredients that make the delight – the joyful surprise element and captivation (Sosa-Tzec, 2022).

Decentraland and The Sandbox are amongst the first and by far the most successful Metaverse that created a virtual world in themselves. These Metaverse environments have virtual lands (such as landmark buildings and diverse backdrops) where goods and services can be purchased. The best part is that corporate companies rush to open their offices in these virtual metaverses and provide offline goods and services for orders placed within the environment. The whole ecosystem is becoming an emerging sales channel and new medium (after-store or office-based offline and internet-based online). Multiple delivery channels have become more necessary for marketers now than before, thanks to the COVID-19 pandemic (Karadkar, 2022). Metaverse offers shopping for which payments can be made using fiat currency, Central Bank Digital Currency (CBDCs), or cryptocurrencies.

Metaverse promises to change the way services are performed and rendered. The service industry does not have any ownership transfer. It is intangible, variable, and perishable, giving more importance to customer experience. Telemedicine, clinical care, education, mental health, physical fitness, veterinary medicine, and pharmaceuticals are a few conventional sectors of healthcare services where metaverse applications have already been investigated (Bansal et al., 2022).

Healthcare communication, for example, can move from information-based to experience-based. Office meetings and industrial labor can use IoT-enabled Metaverse for remote manufacturing, repairs/maintenance, starting new manufacturing lines, remote monitoring/troubleshooting, remote control, and new user/manager training through simulation. Unlike other screen addiction tools, the Metaverse makes users actively participate in physical movements. EduMetaverse brings profound changes in education and empowers the future of education. The current vocal podcasts we hear can transform into a metaverse podcast in which a VRM 3D Model renders the content with facial expressions and body language. The model will look very realistic because of the real-time import of face capture and motion capture. Hotels can offer a 3D-rendered preview of how the whole ambiance will look, thereby addressing two of the nine key factors – "area" and "location" even before the customer checks in (Olorunsola et al., 2023). So, the Metaverse has the potential to start delighting customers and setting the right expectations even before they sign up.

Microsoft Mesh for Teams

As a progression to the Metaverse, Microsoft released Mesh for Teams to make collaboration in the Metaverse personal and fun in the mixed-reality environment (John, 2021). Their internal research showed that while meetings will be interesting when all participants turn on their cameras, it was evident that few do not prefer to do so. Hence, the concept of virtual avatars has stepped in and become a new feature in Mesh. Participants can join from different physical locations, appear as virtual characters, collaborate with shared files, work, and chat, giving a close-to-reality experience of working in a typical office environment. While Mesh for Teams is available for smartphones and laptops, the "real" virtual experience can best be experienced from a mixed-reality headset.

Accenture Nth Floor

Accenture Nanolabs worked closely with Microsoft and AltspaceVR and has experimented with an Immersive Collaboration Platform (ICP) during the 2020 COVID pandemic times called "The Nth Floor" (Jason, 2020). The platform features multi-user, cross-platform meeting solutions with public and private meeting rooms and fits well with large corporates with a very distributed workforce. The broad idea is to move as many physical meetings to virtual meeting rooms yet not lose the experience to the extent possible.

Seoul: First Major Metaverse City

Citizens and Residents are the most significant users of public administration services offered by Municipal, State, and Federal Governments. Civic technology or civic tech enhances the relationship between the people and government with software for communications, decision-making, service delivery, and political process (Wikipedia, 2022). Digital platforms are built by these Governments to provide interfaces for these users to report issues, pay taxes, and get updates on various programs and events. However, these digital spaces come with issues and challenges, such as data privacy, service orientation, federated operations, and synergetic operations, to name a few (Spillner, 2021). Further, various stakeholders will have different conceptions and expectations of data, design, and civics (users of a civic tech system) (Boehner & DiSalvo, 2016). We must overcome these challenges to build smart cities and regions.

True, the digital transformation journey will have many ups and downs. For example, there was a first-generation failure but a second-generation improvement when U.S. President Barack Obama heralded the open data movement in 2009, during which Government datasets were made open for civic to understand and use (Lee et al., 2015). However, users could not understand how to use the openly available Government data and gain insights. As a result, governments had to return to their system design teams to make the data easier to understand and give analytical insights. Nevertheless, Metaverse attempts to address several challenges typically encountered in civic tech and appears to be a promising technology that can improve the civic service experience.

In November 2021, Seoul, the capital city of South Korea, announced that various public services and cultural events would soon be available in the Metaverse. The announcement officially made Seoul the first major city to offer civil services in a virtual environment.

An investment plan of KRW 3.9 billion ($3.3 million) is earmarked to raise the city's global competitiveness and make it "a city of coexistence, a global leader, a safe city, and a future emotional city." The plan is part of a broader national plan called Digital New Deal that aims to embrace digital and AI tools to improve healthcare, central infrastructure, and the economy in its recovery from the economic crisis caused by COVID-19. The Seoul Metropolitan Government (SGM) began building the virtual infrastructure, and the project is expected to be complete by 2026. The project is titled "Metaverse Seoul" and is expected to create a virtual communications ecosystem under its jurisdiction. By then, public functions will be on the Metaverse, including a virtual mayor's office, spaces serving the business sector, a fintech incubator, and a public investment organization. The "Metaverse 120 Center" is expected to be ready by 2023, with virtual public services where avatars will handle citizen concerns that could only be addressed by physically going to city hall. Seoul has a much broader vision as part of its Seoul Vision 2030 plan.

Metaverse Banking

Metaverse allows people to go places that they cannot otherwise go. While video conferencing-based banking confirms the physical presence of a bank customer, Metaverse Banking can allow safe and secure transactions without going to the bank. Integrated with Blockchain, Metaverse Banking can protect customer data and prevent digital frauds from happening, which in turn helps gain customer trust and confidence. As a result, digital spaces are more lifelike and can be experienced to the next level. So, one of the expectations from Metaverse is that it improves the quality of engagement between the relationship manager and the bank customer.

Many banks across the world have started opening virtual branches in the Metaverse. Global banks like JPMorgan and HSBC have virtual representative offices in the Metaverse. As a further step, these banks have opened virtual lounges where walk-ins from the Metaverse could obtain information on bank services and goods.

The target audience, at least at this point, is the millennials. Their banking requirements will be different, too. Perhaps the walk-in visitor would ask for a crypto-to-dollar exchange if a game user has won prize money in Mana (Decentraland cryptocurrency) and wants to convert it to dollars. Similarly, they could seek funding to purchase Non-Fungible Tokens in the Metaverse or provide investment banking support for cryptocurrency NFOs.

Banks have a fiduciary duty to know their customers before offering any service. Hence, a Know Your Customer (KYC) via the Metaverse (for in-person verification) and with One Time Password (OTP), and payments with existing wallets (or internet banking) can be initiated. However, since customers do not wish to remove their VR headset when being present in a Metaverse, it needs to be checked how far an OTP on a smartphone is feasible. Hence, banks will have to experiment with some newer forms of verification - voice prints or unique cyber tokens.

Sygnum Bank recently announced it would open its first Metaverse branch at New York's virtual Times Square in the Decentraland hub. The bank will welcome visitors with a crypto punk and showcase Sygnum's Web3 product innovations. Banks understand the limitations of offering services using offline branches. However, considering climate change and other such sustainability practices, moving to a Metaverse environment gets them better sustainability rankings and a new medium through which the services can be offered.

CONVERGENCE OF TECHNOLOGIES

A convergence and confluence of various disruptive technologies such as Metaverse, Blockchain (Mishra et al., 2022), Artificial Intelligence (AI) (Goundar et al., 2022), Big Data, Cloud Computing, and Internet-of-Things (IoT) will result in giving a new delightful experience for customers. Coupled with AI as a service, customer experience management and personalization can be higher. Customer experience in Metaverse can be enhanced by using features of Blockchain – such as security and trust, smart contracts to automate activities (such as refunds), decentralized identity (which increases privacy and security), supply chain transparency, and tokenization. The optimization process can begin right from sensing customer intentions till adaptively improving and offering loopback into prior design stages (Blümel & Jha, 2023).

Several countries in the world are on the cusp of starting to adopt 5G technology for communications. The timing is also perfect to put emerging technologies like Blockchain and IoT into practice. 5G, with these technologies, can overcome legacy issues such as latency and density that hampered the pairing of the emerging technologies with 4G earlier. Blockchain eliminates intermediaries to the extent possible and ensures international, cross-border telecommunication and internet services be offered at low cost. Domestically, cars communicate with other commuting cars, sharing weather, traffic updates, and safety levels, thereby improving the alert systems.

Web 3 comprises several technologies that will shape the next generation of the web, called the decentralized web. From a customer experience perspective, it focuses on the following:

1. **Data Ownership and Privacy,** in which the customer has more control over their personal information and content, and it is the customer who decides which market will have access to their information.
2. **Monetization and Incentives**, in which loyalty and reward points are given in the form of NFTs or cryptocurrencies automatically.
3. **Decentralized Applications (DApps)** that run on decentralized networks and can provide new and innovative customer experiences, often with greater transparency, security, and resistance to censorship.
4. **Interoperability features** make it easier for customers to move seamlessly between various online services, enhancing their overall experience.
5. **Smart Contracts** are self-executing agreements with the terms of the contract directly written into code. Smart contracts can automate various aspects of customer interactions, such as purchases, subscriptions, and payments, streamlining the customer experience.

6. **Middlemen and intermediaries** are eliminated (or at least minimized) by Blockchain, leading to lower transaction fees and faster, more cost-effective customer experiences.
7. **Community and Governance** are strongly built. Customers can have a more direct role in shaping their services, ensuring their needs and preferences are considered.

BARRIERS IN ADOPTION

Metaverse is still in its early stages, but the concepts appear revolutionary – especially service marketing. The technology will revolutionize service marketing and management by disrupting existing business strategies, consumer norms, and marketing practices (Gursoy et al., 2023). Increased research is now documenting the customer journey from reality to an immersive world (Neves et al., 2024). Every new technology comes with some boon and some bane, and it is no wonder Metaverse has some issues that marketers must address. Privacy issues, potential threats in virtual worlds, and being unfamiliar with the technology are found to delay or hamper the mass adoption of the Metaverse. Understanding country-level aspects (such as cultural differences) that can emerge in virtual environments is also essential. Blockchain offers excellent control over personal data, preventing data breaches and improving customer privacy. Setting permission levels limits data access to authorized agencies only, giving a higher degree of individual control over personal data privacy. However, several privacy-related issues remain, particularly when blockchain and Metaverse are integrated.

A wide range of personal data (such as demographics and preferences) can be captured within a few minutes of interaction in a VR environment. The scale and scope of the data captured in the Metaverse often exceed the traditional mobile and web environments, posing an unprecedented risk (Nair et al., 2022a).

Together with AI, the data can be a treasure trove of understanding and deep insights into the participants. However, considering the increasing importance (and awareness) of data privacy laws globally, marketers and VR participants must consider the extent to which personal data is captured, retained, and used.

There is a clear and definite need for an "incognito mode for VR" that quantifiably obfuscates various sensitive user data attributes, much like the traditional privacy tools available in our web browser software (Nair et al., 2022b).

Customers love when their interactions with the systems are smoother, faster, more efficiently done, and yet available at low or affordable costs. Unfortunately, blockchain networks are initially slow, and when integrated with metaverse environments, the network lag only worsens and eventually hampers customer experience. However, as technology evolves, network nags reduce, and transactions proceed faster.

CONCLUSION

The congruence of Blockchain technologies (cryptocurrencies, NFTs, DeFi, DAO, and other forms) and Metaverse aided with disruptive technologies such as Artificial Intelligence, Machine Learning, Edge Computing, and others can bring in a profound positive change in the way customers experience products and services. Moreover, it creates a new virtual medium and marketing channel for businesses to reach out to customers. The technologies offer a delightful preview experience before the customer makes a formal transaction. Payments become seamless, and businesses can deliver the product faster than before because of supply chain integrations. The products are better targeted, thanks to the co-creation process. The customer feedback cycle becomes shorter, and disputes get resolved faster. While it is too early to speak of emerging technologies' impact, it can be said that they will have more positives than negatives. Businesses will have to address specific challenges (barriers), such as data privacy issues and network lags.

REFERENCES

Bansal, G., Rajgopal, K., Chamola, V., Xiong, Z., & Niyato, D. (2022). Healthcare in Metaverse: A Survey on Current Metaverse Applications in Healthcare. *IEEE Access : Practical Innovations, Open Solutions*, *10*, 119914–119946. doi:10.1109/ACCESS.2022.3219845

Belli, A. (2022). *Creating journey mapping from employee experience in communicating to enhance communication inside a business' internal environment* [Bachelor's dissertation, L-Universita ta' Malta]. https://www.um.edu.mt/library/oar/handle/123456789/104619

Blümel, J., & Jha, G. (2023, January 3). Designing a Conversational AI Agent: Framework Combining Customer Experience Management, Personalization, and AI in Service Techniques. *Proceedings of the 56th Hawaii International Conference on System Sciences*. HDL. https://hdl.handle.net/10125/102805

Boehner, K., & DiSalvo, C. (2016). Data, Design and Civics: An Exploratory Study of Civic Tech. *Proceedings of the 2016 CHI Conference on Human Factors in Computing Systems*, (pp. 2970–2981). ACM. 10.1145/2858036.2858326

Bushell, C. (2022). The Impact of Metaverse on Branding and Marketing—A Study of How Individuals and Celebrities Use Metaverse as a Brand Extension, and the Implications for Marketing. SSRN *Electronic Journal*. doi:10.2139/ssrn.4144688

Damanik, M. K. (2022). The Effect of Impulsive Buying and Perceived Value on Repurchase Intention: The Mediating Role of Customer Loyalty Program and Moderating Role of Satisfying Customer Experience. *Journal of Economics. Finance and Management Studies*, *05*(12). doi:10.47191/jefms/v5-i12-51

Gahler, M., Klein, J. F., & Paul, M. (2022). Customer Experience: Conceptualization, Measurement, and Application in Omnichannel Environments. *Journal of Service Research, 109467052211265*. doi:10.1177/10946705221126590

Gao, L., de Haan, E., Melero-Polo, I., & Sese, F. J. (2022). Winning your customers' minds and hearts: Disentangling the effects of lock-in and affective customer experience on retention. *Journal of the Academy of Marketing Science*. doi:10.100711747-022-00898-z

Ghazaleh, M. A., & Zabadi, A. M. (2021). BlockChain (BC) Upending Customer Experience: Promoting a New Customer Relationship Management (CRM) Structure Using Blockchain Technology (BCT). *Journal of Management and Sustainability*, *11*(1), 203. doi:10.5539/jms.v11n1p203

Goundar, S., Suseendran, G., & Anandan, R. (Eds.). (2022). *The convergence of artificial intelligence and blockchain technologies: Challenges and opportunities*. World Scientific. doi:10.1142/11959

Gursoy, D., Lu, L., Nunkoo, R., & Deng, D. (2023). Metaverse in services marketing: An overview and future research directions. *Service Industries Journal*, *43*(15-16), 1–33. doi:10.1080/02642069.2023.2252750

Habil, S. G. M., El-Deeb, S., & El-Bassiouny, N. (2023). The metaverse era: Leveraging augmented reality in the creation of novel customer experience. *Management & Sustainability: An Arab Review*. doi:10.1108/MSAR-10-2022-0051

Helouani, W. B. (2021). How Can Firms Effectively Use Technology in Customer Journey Management. *Technology Innovation Management Review*, *11*(7/8), 33–47. doi:10.22215/timreview/1455

Hess, T., Matt, C., Benlian, A., & Wiesböck, F. (2020). Options for Formulating a Digital Transformation Strategy. In R. D. Galliers, D. E. Leidner, & B. Simeonova (Eds.), *Strategic Information Management* (5th ed., pp. 151–173). Routledge. doi:10.4324/9780429286797-7

Inge Furseth, P., & Cuthbertson, R. (2016). *Innovation in an Advanced Consumer Society: Value-Driven Service Innovation.* Oxford University Press., doi:10.1093/acprof:oso/9780198705116.001.0001

Jangra, G., & Jangra, M. (2022). Role of Artificial Intelligence in Online Shopping and its Impact on Consumer purchasing behaviour and Decision. *2022 Second International Conference on Computer Science, Engineering and Applications (ICCSEA)*, (pp. 1–7). IEEE. 10.1109/ICCSEA54677.2022.9936374

Jason, W. (2020, November 30). *Are you ready for close encounters of the virtual kind?* Accenture. https://www.accenture.com/us-en/blogs/how-accenture-does-it/are-you-ready-for-close-encounters-of-the-virtual-kind

John, R. (2021, November 2). *Mesh for Microsoft Teams aims to make collaboration in the "metaverse" personal and fun.* Microsoft. https://news.microsoft.com/innovation-stories/mesh-for-microsoft-teams/

Karadkar, M. P. (2022). A critical understanding of multi delivery channel for Customer Relationship in Restaurant business. *Seybold Report.*

Lee, M., Almirall, E., & Wareham, J. (2015). Open data and civic apps: First-generation failures, second-generation improvements. *Communications of the ACM, 59*(1), 82–89. doi:10.1145/2756542

Mercanoğlu Erin, S. & Dİnçşahİn, A. (2021). Barriers to Global Branding and The Metaverse. *International Aegean Scientific Research Symposium.* AMA.

Mishra, S., Arora, H., Parakh, G., & Khandelwal, J. (2022). Contribution of Blockchain in Development of Metaverse. *2022 7th International Conference on Communication and Electronics Systems (ICCES)*, (pp. 845–850). IEEE. 10.1109/ICCES54183.2022.9835986

Neeraj, S., Hepu, D., & Alemyehu, M. (2018, May). Investigating the Critical Success Factors of Digital Transformation for Improving Customer Experience. *International Conference on Information Resources Management (CONF-IRM).* AISEL. https://aisel.aisnet.org/cgi/viewcontent.cgi?article=1020&context=confirm2018

Neves, J., Bacalhau, L. M., & Santos, V. (2024). A Systematic Review on the Customer Journey Between Two Worlds: Reality and Immersive World. In J. L. Reis, M. Del Rio Araujo, L. P. Reis, & J. P. M. Dos Santos (Eds.), *Marketing and Smart Technologies* (Vol. 344, pp. 401–416). Springer Nature Singapore. doi:10.1007/978-981-99-0333-7_29

Nwachukwu, D., & Maudlinepac, B. E. (2022). Auditory Marketing Strategy and Customers Experience in Bar & Restaurant Businesses in Port Harcourt. *International Journal of Business, Economics and Entrepreneurship Development in Africa, 10*(5).

Ojiaku, O. C., Euphemia, M. I., & Chike, N. K. (2022). Customer Experience Management and Customers'. *Commitment: Evidence from the Church Parishioners in Nigeria, 4*(10), 19.

Olaleye, S. A., Kwafo, D., Atobatele, A. J., & Olaoye, O. P. (2024). The Bibliometric Commingling of Metaverse and Non-fungible Tokens in Marketing. In J. L. Reis, M. Del Rio Araujo, L. P. Reis, & J. P. M. Dos Santos (Eds.), *Marketing and Smart Technologies* (Vol. 344, pp. 387–399). Springer Nature Singapore. doi:10.1007/978-981-99-0333-7_28

Olorunsola, V. O., Saydam, M. B., Lasisi, T. T., & Eluwole, K. K. (2023). Customer experience management in capsule hotels: A content analysis of guest online review. *Journal of Hospitality and Tourism Insights*. doi:10.1108/JHTI-03-2022-0113

Papagiannidis, S., & Bourlakis, M. A. (2010). Staging the New Retail Drama: At a Metaverse near you! *Journal of Virtual Worlds Research, 2*(5), 425–446. doi:10.4101/jvwr.v2i5.808

Ruiz-Alba, J. L., Quero, M. J., & López-Tenorio, P. J. (2023). Institutions and business customer experience: The role of interfunctional coordination and service co-design. *European Research on Management and Business Economics, 29*(1), 100213. doi:10.1016/j.iedeen.2022.100213

Sosa-Tzec, O. (2022). Delight in the User Experience: Form and Place. In G. Bruyns & H. Wei (Eds.), [ ] With Design: Reinventing Design Modes (pp. 111–120). Springer Nature Singapore. doi:10.1007/978-981-19-4472-7_8

Spillner, J. (2021). FixMyStadtmelder: Challenges and Solutions in Civic Services for Smart Cities and Regions. *CEUR Workshop Proceedings, 9*. https://ceur-ws.org/Vol-3116/Paper_10.pdf

The Banker. (2022, August 1). INNOVATION IN DIGITAL BANKING AWARDS 2022. *The Banker*. https://www.proquest.com/trade-journals/banker-innovation-digital-banking-awards-2022/docview/2696958117

Tom Dieck, M. C., & Han, D. D. (2022). The role of immersive technology in Customer Experience Management. *Journal of Marketing Theory and Practice, 30*(1), 108–119. doi:10.1080/10696679.2021.1891939

Vanheems, R. (2019). The Augmented Customer Experience: Between Humanity and Robotization? In G. N'Goala, V. Pez-Pérard, & I. Prim-Allaz (Eds.), *Augmented Customer Strategy* (1st ed., pp. 117–132). Wiley. doi:10.1002/9781119618324.ch7

Vivek, N., Gonzalo, M.G., Dawn, S. (2022a). *Exploring the Unprecedented Privacy Risks of the Metaverse*. doi:10.48550/ARXIV.2207.13176

Vivek, N., Gonzalo, M.G., Dawn, S. (2022b). *Going Incognito in the Metaverse: Achieving Theoretically Optimal Privacy-Usability Tradeoffs in VR*. doi:10.48550/ARXIV.2208.05604

Wikipedia. (2022). *Civic technology*. https://en.wikipedia.org/wiki/Civic_technology

Xie, Q., Lu, W., Zhang, Q., Zhang, L., Zhu, T., & Wang, J. (2023). Chatbot Integration for Metaverse—A University Platform Prototype. *2023 IEEE International Conference on Omni-Layer Intelligent Systems (COINS)*, (pp. 1–6). IEEE. 10.1109/COINS57856.2023.10189232

Yasin, M., Liébana-Cabanillas, F., Porcu, L., & Kayed, R. N. (2020). The role of customer online brand experience in customers' intention to forward online company-generated content: The case of the Islamic online banking sector in Palestine. *Journal of Retailing and Consumer Services*, *52*, 101902. doi:10.1016/j.jretconser.2019.101902

Ylilehto, M., Komulainen, H., & Ulkuniemi, P. (2021). The critical factors shaping customer shopping experiences with innovative technologies. *Baltic Journal of Management*, *16*(5), 661–680. doi:10.1108/BJM-02-2021-0049

Compilation of References

Abdeldayem, M. M., & Al Dulaimi, S. H. (2020). Trends ofglobal fintech education practices and the gcc perspective. *Int. J. Adv. Sci. Technol.*, *29*, 7150–7163.

Abdelmaboud, A., Ahmed, A. I. A., Abaker, M., Eisa, T. A. E., Albasheer, H., Ghorashi, S. A., & Karim, F. K. (2022). Blockchain for IoT Applications: Taxonomy, Platforms, Recent Advances, Challenges and Future Research Directions. *Electronics (Basel)*, *11*(4), 630. doi:10.3390/electronics11040630

Abuhassna, H., Al-Rahmi, W. M., Yahya, N., Zakaria, M. A., Kosnin, A. B. M., & Darwish, M. (2020). Development of a new model on utilizing online learning platforms to improve students' academic achievements and satisfaction. *International Journal of Educational Technology in Higher Education*, *17*(1), 38. doi:10.118641239-020-00216-z

Adams, L. (2022, September 20). How Blockchain Is Changing Disaster Management. *The Disaster Times*. https://www.disastertimes.com/article/blockchain-disaster-management

Adhami, S., Giudici, G., & Martinazzi, S. (2018). Why do businesses go crypto? An empirical analysis of initial coin offerings. *Journal of Economics and Business*, *100*, 64–75. doi:10.1016/j.jeconbus.2018.04.001

Ahlers, G. K., Cumming, D., Günther, C., & Schweizer, D. (2015). Signaling in equity crowdfunding. *Entrepreneurship Theory and Practice*, *39*(4), 955–980. doi:10.1111/etap.12157

Alammary, A., Alhazmi, S., Almasri, M., & Gillani, S. (2019). Blockchain-based applications in education: A systematic review. *Applied Sciences (Basel, Switzerland)*, *9*(12), 2400. doi:10.3390/app9122400

Allen, J. G., Rauchs, M., Blandin, A., & Bear, K. (2020). *Legal and regulatory considerations for digital assets*. Retrieved from https://www.jbs.cam.ac.uk/wp- content/uploads/2020/10/2020-ccaf-legal-regulatory-considerations-report.pdf

Allison, T. H., Davis, B. C., Webb, J. W., & Short, J. C. (2017). Persuasion in crowdfunding: An elaboration likelihood model of crowdfunding performance. *Journal of Business Venturing*, *32*(6), 707–725. doi:10.1016/j.jbusvent.2017.09.002

Amsden, R., Schweizer, D., Alperovych, Y., Benedetti, H., Blaseg, D., Bollaert, H., Braune, E., Cole, R. A., Cumming, D., Geiler, P., Gianfrate, G., Groh, A., Mezzanotti, F., Li, J., Abou Jaoude, J., Proelss, J., Lopez-de-Silanes, F., & Riding, A. (2019). *Are Blockchain Crowdsales the New "Gold Rush"*. Success Determinants of Initial Coin Offerings.

Anand, A. (February 22, 2022). Blockchain in Education Sector: Advantages and Disadvantages. *Analytical Steps*. https://www.analyticssteps.com/blogs/blockchain-education-sector-advantages-and-disadvantages

An, J., Duan, T., Hou, W., & Xu, X. (2019). Initial coin offerings and entrepreneurial finance: The role of founders' characteristics. *Journal of Alternative Investments*, *21*(4), 26–40. doi:10.3905/jai.2019.1.068

Ark, T. V. (2018). 20 ways blockchain will Transform (Okay, May IMPROVE) EDUCATION. *Forbes*. https:// www.forbes.com/sites/tomvanderark/2018/08/20/26-ways-blockchain-will-transform-ok-may-improveeducation/?sh=cb87fff4ac91

Arnold, L., Brennecke, M., Camus, P., Fridgen, G., Guggenberger, T., Radszuwill, S., Rieger, A., Schweizer, A., & Urbach, N. (2019). Blockchain and Initial Coin Offerings: Blockchain's Implications for Crowdfunding. In Business Transformation through Blockchain (pp. 233–272). Springer International Publishing. doi:10.1007/978-3-319-98911-2_8

Attaran, M. (2020). Digital technology enablers and their implications for supply chain management. *Supply Chain Forum 21*(1). 10.1080/16258312.2020.1751568

Attaran, M., & Gunasekaran, A. (2019). *Applications of Blockchain Technology in Business: Challenges and Opportunities*. Springer International Publishing. doi:10.1007/978-3-030-27798-7

Awaji, B., Solaiman, E., & Marshall, L. (2020). Blockchain-based trusted achievement record system design. In Proceedings of the *ICIEI 2020: 5th International Conference on Information and Education Innovations*, London, UK. 10.1145/3411681.3411689

Awaya, Y., & Krishna, V. (2021). Start-ups and upstarts: Disadvantageous information in R&D. *Journal of Political Economy, 129*(2).

B. Egeland-Müller, M. Elman, F. Heinlein, O. Ross (2017). *Blockchain financial contract automation, 59*(6), 457-467.

Babaei, G., & Bamdad, S. (2020). A neural-network-based decision-making model in the peer-to-peer lending market. *International Journal of Intelligent Systems in Accounting Finance & Management*, *27*(3), 142–150. doi:10.1002/isaf.1480

Balafoutas, L., & Kerschbamer, R. (2020). Credence goods in the literature: What the past fifteen years have taught us about fraud, incentives, and the role of institutions. *Journal of Behavioral and Experimental Finance*, *26*(100285), 100285. doi:10.1016/j.jbef.2020.100285

Bamakan, S. M. H., Moghaddam, S. G., & Manshadi, S. D. (2021). BC-enabled pharmaceutical cold chain: Applications, key challenges, and future trends. *Journal of Cleaner Production*, *302*, 127021. doi:10.1016/j.jclepro.2021.127021

Bansal, G., Rajgopal, K., Chamola, V., Xiong, Z., & Niyato, D. (2022). Healthcare in Metaverse: A Survey on Current Metaverse Applications in Healthcare. *IEEE Access : Practical Innovations, Open Solutions*, *10*, 119914–119946. doi:10.1109/ACCESS.2022.3219845

BasuMallick, C. (December, 2020). *How Blockchain Marketing Could Impact Customer Experience*. Spiceworks. https://www.spiceworks.com/tech/innovation/articles/how-blockchain-marketing-could-impact-customer-experience/

Belli, A. (2022). *Creating journey mapping from employee experience in communicating to enhance communication inside a business' internal environment* [Bachelor's dissertation, L-Universita ta' Malta]. https://www.um.edu.mt/library/oar/handle/123456789/104619

Blockchain for Disaster Management Consortium. (2021). *Blockchain Integration Challenges in Disaster Management*. BDC. https://www.bdc.org/reports/integration-challenges.pdf

Block, J. H., Colombo, M. G., Cumming, D. J., & Vismara, S. (2018). New players in entrepreneurial finance and why they are there. *Small Business Economics*, *50*(2), 239–250. doi:10.100711187-016-9826-6

Blümel, J., & Jha, G. (2023, January 3). Designing a Conversational AI Agent: Framework Combining Customer Experience Management, Personalization, and AI in Service Techniques. *Proceedings of the 56th Hawaii International Conference on System Sciences*. HDL. https://hdl.handle.net/10125/102805

Boehner, K., & DiSalvo, C. (2016). Data, Design and Civics: An Exploratory Study of Civic Tech. *Proceedings of the 2016 CHI Conference on Human Factors in Computing Systems*, (pp. 2970–2981). ACM. 10.1145/2858036.2858326

Boreiko, D., & Risteski, D. (2020). Serial and large investors in initial coin offerings. *Small Business Economics*, 1–19. doi:10.100711187-020-00338-8

BoreikoD.SahdevN. (2018). *To ICO or not to ICO-Empirical analysis of Initial Coin Offerings and Token Sales*. doi:10.2139/ssrn.3209180

Bore, N., Karumba, S., Mutahi, J., Darnell, S. S., Wayua, C., & Weldemariam, K. (2017). Towards Blockchain-enabled school information hub. In *Proceedings of the 9th International Conference on Information and Communication Technologies and Development*, Lahore, Pakistan.

Broadus, R. N. (1987). Toward a definition of "bibliometrics." *Scientometrics*, *12*(5/6), 373–379. doi:10.1007/BF02016680

Brown, A. P. (2018). Disaster Management and Blockchain: Innovations and Challenges. In S. M. Wilson (Ed.), *Proceedings of the International Conference on Disaster Management* (pp. 210-225). Springer.

Burtescu, E. (2009). Database Security-attack and control methods. *Journal of Applied Quantitative Methods*, *4*(4).

Bushell, C. (2022). The Impact of Metaverse on Branding and Marketing—A Study of How Individuals and Celebrities Use Metaverse as a Brand Extension, and the Implications for Marketing. SSRN *Electronic Journal*. doi:10.2139/ssrn.4144688

Bustamante, C. V. (2019). Strategic choices: Accelerated Start-ups' outsourcing decisions. *Journal of Business Research*, *105*, 359–369. doi:10.1016/j.jbusres.2018.06.009

Buterin, V. (2014). *A next generation smart contract & decentralized application platform*. Academic Press.

Buterin, V. (2018). *Sharding FAQ*. Ethereum Foundation. [https://github.com/ethereum/wiki/wiki/Sharding FAQ](https://github.com/ethereum/wiki/wiki/Sharding-FAQ)

Campino, J., & Rosa, Á. (2021). Success Factors of Initial Coin Offering (ICO) projects''. *Economic Bulletin*, *41*(2).

Cao, Q., Chen, J., Fu, P., & Mao, Y. (2020). Impact of government guidance modes on fundraising effect. In X. J., D. G., A. S., G. M. F., & H. A. (Eds.), *International conference on management science and engineering management* (pp. 226-240). Springer.

Catalini, C., & Gans, J. S. (2018). *NBER working paper series initial coin offerings and the value of crypto tokens*. https://www.nber.org/papers/w24418

CFCT. (2017). *A CFCT primer on virtual currencies*. Retrieved from https://www.cftc.gov/sites/default/files/idc/groups/public/%40customerprotection/d ocuments/file/labcftc_primercurrencies100417.pdf

CFTC. (2015). *Order instituting proceedings pursuant to section 6(c) and 6(d) of the commodity echange act*. Retrieved from https://www.cftc.gov/sites/default/files/idc/groups/public/@lrenforcementactions/d ocuments/legalpleading/enfcoinfliprorder09172015.pdf

Chen, G., Xu, B., Lu, M., & Chen, N. S. (2018). Exploring blockchain technology and its potential applications for education. *Smart Learn. Environ.*, *5*(1), 1–10. doi:10.118640561-017-0050-x

Chen, L., Zhao, N., Chen, Y., Yu, F. R., & Wei, G. (2018). Over-the-air computation for IoT networks: Computing multiple functions with antenna arrays. *IEEE Internet of Things Journal*, *5*(6), 5296–5306. doi:10.1109/JIOT.2018.2843321

Chen, R. R., & Chen, K. (2020). A 2020 perspective on "Information asymmetry in initial coin offerings (ICOs): Investigating the effects of multiple channel signals". *Electronic Commerce Research and Applications*, *40*, 100936. Advance online publication. doi:10.1016/j.elerap.2020.100936

Chen, Y. (2018). Blockchain tokens and the potential democratization of entrepreneurship and innovation. *Business Horizons*, *61*(4), 567–575. doi:10.1016/j.bushor.2018.03.006

Chod, J., Lyandres, E., Benedetti, H., Cong, W., Chemmanur, T., Goldstein, I., Gromb, D., & Li, J. (2018). Jerusalem Summer Finance Conference. In *Santiago Finance Workshop*. Econometric Society North American Winter Meeting.

Chudasri, D. (2020). *SET builds integrated trading platform with KBTG*. Retrieved from https://www.bangkokpost.com/business/1997255/set-builds-integrated-trading-platform-with-kbtg

Coco, L., Pinna, A., & Marchesi, M. (2017). *Banking on Blockchain: Blockchain Technology helps save money on costs*. Future Internet. doi:10.3390/fi9030025

Cong, L. W., Li, Y., & Wang, N. (2021). Tokenomics: Dynamic adoption and valuation. *Review of Financial Studies*, *34*(3), 1105–1155. doi:10.1093/rfs/hhaa089

Conley, J. P. (2017). Blockchain and the economics of crypto-tokens and initial coin offerings. *Vanderbilt University Department of economics working papers*, (17-00008).

Corcoran, P., & Datta, S. K. (2016). Mobile-edge computing and the Internet of Things for consumers: Extending cloud computing and services to the edge of the network. *IEEE Consumer Electronics Magazine*, *5*(4), 73–74. doi:10.1109/MCE.2016.2590099

Crosby, M., Nachiappan, P., Verma, S., & Kalyanaraman, V. (2016). BlockChain Technology: Beyond Bitcoin. *Applied Innovation Review Issue*, (2), 6–19.

Cvitanovic, P. L. (2018). New technologies in marketing as competitive advantage. *2018 ENTRENOVA Conference Proceedings (Split: ECONSTOR),* (pp. 294–302). EconStor.

Dai, H. N., Zheng, Z., & Zhang, Y. (2019). Blockchain for Internet of Things: A survey. *IEEE Internet of Things Journal*, *6*(5), 8076–8094. doi:10.1109/JIOT.2019.2920987

Damanik, M. K. (2022). The Effect of Impulsive Buying and Perceived Value on Repurchase Intention: The Mediating Role of Customer Loyalty Program and Moderating Role of Satisfying Customer Experience. *Journal of Economics. Finance and Management Studies*, *05*(12). doi:10.47191/jefms/v5-i12-51

Dash, M. K., Panda, G., Kumar, A., & Luthra, S. (2022). Applications of blockchain in government education sector: a comprehensive review and future research potentials. *Journal of Global Operations and Strategic Sourcing*.

Das, R., & Patel, M. (2017). *Cyber Security for Social Networking Sites: Issues*. Challenges, and Solutions.

Das, S., Kapoor, M., & Raj, P. (2017). Cyber Security in India: An Emerging Domain of Research and Development. *Advances in Computer Science and Ubiquitous Computing*, *2*(3), 17–26.

DataFlaire Team. (2023). *Types of BC – Decide which one is better for your Investment Needs*. Data Flair. https://data-flair.training/blogs/types-of-BC

Davila, A., Foster, G., & Gupta, M. (2003). Venture capital financing and the growth of Start-up firms. *Journal of Business Venturing*, *18*(6), 689–708. doi:10.1016/S0883-9026(02)00127-1

De JongA.RoosenboomP.van der KolkT. (2018). What determines success in Initial Coin Offerings? doi:10.2139/ssrn.3250035

Degryse, H., de Goeij, P., & Kappert, P. (2012). The impact of firm and industry characteristics on small firms' capital structure. *Small Business Economics, 38*(4), 431–447. doi:10.100711187-010-9281-8

Deighton, J., & Kornfeld, L. (2008). *Digital Interactivity: Unanticipated Consequences for Markets, Marketing, and Consumers*. Harvard Business School. http://weigend.com/files/teaching/tsinghua/readings/DeightonKornfeldHBS2007.pdf

Ding, Y., & Cronin, B. (2011). *Popular and/or Prestigious? Measures of Scholarly Esteem.* Academic Press.

Dosso, M., & Vezzani, A. (2020). Firm market valuation and intellectual property assets. *Industry and Innovation, 27*(7), 705–729. doi:10.1080/13662716.2019.1685374

Dostov, V., Shust, P., Leonova, A., & Krivoruchko, S. (2019). "Soft law" and innovations: Empirical analysis of ICO-related statements. *Digital Policy. Regulation & Governance, 21*(5), 476–493. doi:10.1108/DPRG-03-2019-0018

Dutra, A., Tumasjan, A., & Welpe, I. (2018). Blockchain is changing how media and entertainment companies compete. *MIT Sloan Management Review.*

Dutta, P., Choi, T.-M., Somani, S., & Butala, R. (2020). Blockchain technology in supply chain operations: Applications, challenges and research opportunities. *Transportation Research Part E, Logistics and Transportation Review, 142*, 102067. doi:10.1016/j.tre.2020.102067 PMID:33013183

Dwivedi, Y. K. (2018). Developing Security Measures for Mobile Commerce (M-commerce). *International Journal of Information Management, 38*(1), 20–28.

Esmaeilzadeh, P., & Mirzaei, T. (2019). The potential of BC technology for health information exchange: Experimental study from patients' perspectives. *Journal of Medical Internet Research, 21*(6), e14184. http://www.jmir.org/2019/6/e14184/. doi:10.2196/14184 PMID:31223119

Esposito, C., de Santis, A., Tortora, G., Chang, H., & Choo, K.-K. R. (2018). BC: A panacea for healthcare cloud-based data security and privacy? *IEEE Cloud Comput., 5*(1), 31–37. doi:10.1109/MCC.2018.011791712

Farah, J. C., Vozniuk, A., Rodríguez-Triana, M. J., & Gillet, D. (2018). *A Blueprint for a Blockchain-Based Architecture to Power a Distributed Network of Tamper-Evident Learning Trace Repositories*. In *Proceedings of the 2018 IEEE 18th International Conference on Advanced Learning Technologies (ICALT)*, Mumbai, India. 10.1109/ICALT.2018.00059

FCA. (2018). *British and australian regulators strengthen cooperation on fintech through enhanced cooperation agreement.* Retrieved from https://www.fca.org.uk/news/press-releases/british-and-australian-regulators-strengthen-cooperation-fintech-through-enhanced-cooperation

Federal Emergency Management Agency. (2021). Disaster Management Best Practices Report. *Report No. FEMA-2021-045*. FEMA. https://www.fema.gov/reports/best-practices-2021.pdf

Federal Emergency Management Agency. (2022). *Disaster Management Strategies*. FEMA. https://www.fema.gov/disaster-management-strategies

FINMA. (2017). *Guideline for enquiries regarding the regulatory framework for initial coin offering (ICOs)*. Retrieved from https://www.finma.ch/en/~/media/finma/dokumente/dokumentecenter/myfinma/1bewilligung/fintech/wegleitung-ico.pdf?la=en

Fisch, C. (2019). Initial coin offerings (ICOs) to finance new ventures. *Journal of Business Venturing, 34*(1), 1–22. doi:10.1016/j.jbusvent.2018.09.007

Fisch, C., Masiak, C., Vismara, S., & Block, J. (2021). Motives and profiles of ICO investors. *Journal of Business Research, 125*, 564–576. doi:10.1016/j.jbusres.2019.07.036

Frey, R., Wörner, D., & Ilic, A. (2016). *Collaborative filtering on the blockchain: a secure recommender system for e-commerce*. Academic Press.

Frizzo-Barker, J., Chow-White, P. A., Adams, P. R., Mentanko, J., Ha, D., & Green, S. (2020). Blockchain as a disruptive technology for business: A systematic review. *International Journal of Information Management, 51*, 102029. doi:10.1016/j.ijinfomgt.2019.10.014

Gächter, I., & Gächter, M. (2020). Success factors in ICOs: Individual firm characteristics or lucky timing? *Finance Research Letters*. Advance online publication. doi:10.1016/j.frl.2020.101715

Gahler, M., Klein, J. F., & Paul, M. (2022). Customer Experience: Conceptualization, Measurement, and Application in Omnichannel Environments. *Journal of Service Research, 109467052211265*. doi:10.1177/10946705221126590

Gao, L., de Haan, E., Melero-Polo, I., & Sese, F. J. (2022). Winning your customers' minds and hearts: Disentangling the effects of lock-in and affective customer experience on retention. *Journal of the Academy of Marketing Science*. doi:10.100711747-022-00898-z

Garg, R., Veerubhotla, R. S., & Saxena, A. (2015). Security, Privacy and Trust in Social Networking Sites. *CSI Communications, 39*(2).

Gartner. (2020, July 13). *Hype Cycle for Blockchain Technologies, 2020*. Gartner. https://www.gartner.com/en/documents/3987450/hype-cycle-for-blockchaintechnologies-2020

Gatteschi, V., Lamberti, F., & Demartini, C. (2020). Blockchaintechnology use cases. In S. Kim & G. C. Deka (Eds.), *Advanced applications of BC technology* (pp. 91–114). Springer.

GFSC. (2017a). *Distributed ledger technology regulatory framework (dlt framework)*. Retrieved from https://www.gfsc.gi/dlt

GFSC. (2017b). *Statement on initial coin offerings*. Retrieved from https://www.fsc.gi/news/statement-on-initial-coin-offerings-250

Ghazaleh, M. A., & Zabadi, A. M. (2021). BlockChain (BC) Upending Customer Experience: Promoting a New Customer Relationship Management (CRM) Structure Using Blockchain Technology (BCT). *Journal of Management and Sustainability*, *11*(1), 203. doi:10.5539/jms.v11n1p203

Gilda, S., & Mehrotra, M. (2018). *BC for Student Data Privacy and Consent.* In *Proceedings of the 2018 International Conference on Computer Communication and Informatics (ICCCI)*, Coimbatore, India.

Giudici, G., Guerini, M., & Rossi-Lamastra, C. (2018). Reward-based crowdfunding of entrepreneurial projects: The effect of local altruism and localized social capital on proponents' success. *Small Business Economics*, *50*(2), 307–324. doi:10.100711187-016-9830-x

Gomez, D. (2021). Blockchain in education, a large and global encrypted database. *eLearn Center Blog*. https:// elearncenter.blogs.uoc.edu/blockchain-in-education/

Goundar, S., Suseendran, G., & Anandan, R. (Eds.). (2022). *The convergence of artificial intelligence and blockchain technologies: Challenges and opportunities*. World Scientific. doi:10.1142/11959

Gräther, W., Kolvenbach, S., Ruland, R., Schütte, J., Torres, C., & Wendland, F. (2018), Blockchainfor education: lifelong learning passport. In *Proceedings of 1st ERCIM BC Workshop 2018, European Society for Socially Embedded Technologies (EUSSET)*. ERIC.

Gupta, A., & Gupta, S. (2018). Blockchain technology: Application in Indian banking sector. *Delhi Business Review, 19*(2), 75-84. https://search.proquest.com/docview/2247499893?accountid=10007

Gupta, B., Rahimi, N., Hexmoor, H., & Maddali, K. (2018). Design of a new hierarchical structured peer-to-peer network based on Chinese remainder theorem. *Proceedings of the 33rd International Conference on Computers and Their Applications (CATA),* Las Vegas: ISCA Publishing.

Gupta, M. (2018). *Blockchain for dummies* (3rd ed.). John Wiley & Sons.

Gursoy, D., Lu, L., Nunkoo, R., & Deng, D. (2023). Metaverse in services marketing: An overview and future research directions. *Service Industries Journal*, *43*(15-16), 1–33. doi:10.1080/02642069.2023.2252750

Habil, S. G. M., El-Deeb, S., & El-Bassiouny, N. (2023). The metaverse era: Leveraging augmented reality in the creation of novel customer experience. *Management & Sustainability: An Arab Review*. doi:10.1108/MSAR-10-2022-0051

Hall, B. H., & Lerner, J. (2010). The financing of R&D and innovation. In *Handbook of the Economics of Innovation* (Vol. 1, pp. 609-639). North-Holland. doi:10.3386/w15325

Han, M., Li, Z., He, J., Wu, D., Xie, Y., & Baba, A. (2018). A novel Blockchain-based education records verification solution. *Proceedings of the 19th Annual SIG Conference on Information Technology Education*, (pp. 178-183). ACM. 10.1145/3241815.3241870

Hargrave, J., Sahdev, N., & Feldmeier, O. (2019). How value is created in tokenized assets. In M. Swan, J. Potts, S. Takagi, F. Witte, & P. Tasca (Eds.), *Blockchain economics: Implications of distributed ledgers-markets, communications networks, and algorithmic reality* (pp. 125–141). doi:10.1142/9781786346391_0007

He, J., Wei, J., Chen, K., Tang, Z., Zhou, Y., & Zhang, Y. (2017). Multitier fog computing with large-scale IoT data analytics for smart cities. *IEEE Internet of Things Journal*, *5*(2), 677–686. doi:10.1109/JIOT.2017.2724845

Helouani, W. B. (2021). How Can Firms Effectively Use Technology in Customer Journey Management. *Technology Innovation Management Review*, *11*(7/8), 33–47. doi:10.22215/timreview/1455

Hess, T., Matt, C., Benlian, A., & Wiesböck, F. (2020). Options for Formulating a Digital Transformation Strategy. In R. D. Galliers, D. E. Leidner, & B. Simeonova (Eds.), *Strategic Information Management* (5th ed., pp. 151–173). Routledge. doi:10.4324/9780429286797-7

Hollebeek, L. D., Sharma, T. G., Pandey, R., Sanyal, P., & Clark, M. K. (2021) Fifteen years of customer engagement research: a bibliometric and network analysis. *Journal of Product & Brand Management*. https://centaur.reading.ac.uk/98973/ doi:10.1108/JPBM-01-2021-3301

Howell, S. T., Niessner, M., & Yermack, D. (2020). Initial coin offerings: Financing growth with cryptocurrency token sales. *Review of Financial Studies*, *33*(9), 3925–3974. doi:10.1093/rfs/hhz131

Hrga, A., Benčić, F. M., & Žarko, I. P. (2019). *Technical analysis of an initial coin offering*. Paper presented at the 2019 15th International Conference on Telecommunications (ConTEL). 10.1109/ConTEL.2019.8848532

HuangW.MeoliM.VismaraS. (2019). *The geography of Initial Coin Offerings*. https://ssrn.com/abstract=3206234

Hughes, A., Park, A., Kietzmann, J., & Archer-Brown, C. (2019). Beyond Bitcoin: What BC and distributed ledger technologies mean for firms. *Business Horizons*, *62*(3), 273–281. doi:10.1016/j.bushor.2019.01.002

Huo, R., Zeng, S., Wang, Z., Shang, J., Chen, W., Huang, T., Wang, S., Yu, F. R., & Liu, Y. (2022). A Comprehensive Survey on Blockchain in Industrial Internet of Things: Motivations, Research Progresses, and Future Challenges. *IEEE Communications Surveys and Tutorials*, *24*(1), 88–122. doi:10.1109/COMST.2022.3141490

Hutter, M., & Shusterman, R. (2006). Value and the valuation of art in economic and aesthetic theory. Handbook of the Economics of Art and Culture, 1, 169-208.

Iansiti, M., & Lakhani, K. R. (2017). The Truth About Blockchain. *Harvard Business Review*, *95*(1), 118–127.

Inge Furseth, P., & Cuthbertson, R. (2016). *Innovation in an Advanced Consumer Society: Value-Driven Service Innovation*. Oxford University Press., doi:10.1093/acprof:oso/9780198705116.001.0001

Iredale, G. (2021). 6 key blockchain features you need to know now. *101 Blockchains*. https://101blockchains.com/introduction-to-blockchain-features/

Iredale, G. (2021). *6 key Blockchainfeatures you need to know now*. 101 Blockchain. https://101BCs.com/introduction-to-Blockchain-features/

Islam, M., Fremeth, A., & Marcus, A. (2018). Signaling by early-stage Start-ups: US government research grants and venture capital funding. *Journal of Business Venturing*, *33*(1), 35–51. doi:10.1016/j.jbusvent.2017.10.001

Jangra, G., & Jangra, M. (2022). Role of Artificial Intelligence in Online Shopping and its Impact on Consumer purchasing behaviour and Decision. *2022 Second International Conference on Computer Science, Engineering and Applications (ICCSEA)*, (pp. 1–7). IEEE. 10.1109/ICCSEA54677.2022.9936374

Jason, W. (2020, November 30). *Are you ready for close encounters of the virtual kind?* Accenture. https://www.accenture.com/us-en/blogs/how-accenture-does-it/are-you-ready-for-close-encounters-of-the-virtual-kind

Jiang, J., & Chen, J. (2021). Framework of blockchain-supported e-commerce platform for small and medium enterprises. *Sustainability (Basel)*, *13*(15), 8158. doi:10.3390u13158158

Jiang, Y., Wang, C., Wang, Y., & Gao, L. (2019, February). A privacy-preserving e-commerce system based on the blockchain technology. In *2019 IEEE International Workshop on Blockchain Oriented Software Engineering (IWBOSE)* (pp. 50-55). IEEE. 10.1109/IWBOSE.2019.8666470

John, R. (2021, November 2). *Mesh for Microsoft Teams aims to make collaboration in the "metaverse" personal and fun*. Microsoft. https://news.microsoft.com/innovation-stories/mesh-for-microsoft-teams/

Johnson, R. K. (2020). Blockchain Applications in Disaster Management. Disaster Management Journal, 25(3), 123-136. *DOI*, *10*, xxxxxxx.

Justinia, T. (2019). BC technologies: Opportunities for solving real-world problems in healthcare and biomedical sciences. *Acta Informatica Medica*, *27*(4), 284. doi:10.5455/aim.2019.27.284-291 PMID:32055097

Kamble, S., Gunasekaran, A., & Arha, H. (2019). Understanding the Blockchain technology adoption in supply chains-Indian context. *International Journal of Production Research*, *57*(7), 2009–2033. doi:10.1080/00207543.2018.1518610

Kamble, S., Gunasekaran, A., & Sharma, R. (2020). Modeling the blockchain enabled traceability in agriculture supply chain. *International Journal of Information Management*, *52*, 101967. doi:10.1016/j.ijinfomgt.2019.05.023

Karadkar, M. P. (2022). A critical understanding of multi delivery channel for Customer Relationship in Restaurant business. *Seybold Report*.

Kaushik, N., & Bagga, T. (2020, March). Internet of Things (IOT): Implications in Society. *Proceedings of the International Conference on Innovative Computing & Communications (ICICC)*. SSRN. 10.2139srn.3563104

Kayikci, Y., Subramanian, N., Dora, M., & Bhatia, M. S. (2022). Food supply chain in the era of Industry 4.0: Blockchain technology implementation opportunities and impediments from the perspective of people, process, performance, and technology. *Production Planning and Control*, *33*(2-3), 301–321. doi:10.1080/09537287.2020.1810757

Kim, S. I., & Kim, S. H. (2020). E-commerce payment model using blockchain. *Journal of Ambient Intelligence and Humanized Computing*, 1–13.

Köhn, A. (2018). The determinants of Start-up valuation in the venture capital context: A systematic review and avenues for future research. *Management Review Quarterly*, *68*(1), 3–36. doi:10.100711301-017-0131-5

Köseoğlu, S. D., & Almeany, S. S. A. (2020). Introduction to business valuation. In M. Akkaya (Ed.), *Start-up valuation: Theories, models, and future*. IGI Global.

Kouhizadeh, M., Saberi, S., & Sarkis, J. (2021). Blockchain technology and the sustainable supply chain: Theoretically exploring adoption barriers. *International Journal of Production Economics*, *231*, 107831. doi:10.1016/j.ijpe.2020.107831

Kour, B. (2019). How is Blockchain Enhancing the Customer Experience? *Data Science Central*. https://www.datasciencecentral.com/how-is-blockchain-enhancing-the-customer-experience/

Kritikos, M. (2020). *Ten technologies to fight coronavirus*. Eur Parliam Res Serv. https://www.europarl.europa.eu/RegData/etudes/IDAN/2020/641543/EPRS_IDA(2020)641543_EN.pdf

Kshetri, N., & Loukoianova, E. (2019). Blockchain adoption in supply chain networks in Asia. *IEEE IT Prof.*, *21*(1).

Kshetri, N. (2018). 1 Blockchain's roles in meeting key supply chain management objectives. *International Journal of Information Management*, *39*, 80–89. doi:10.1016/j.ijinfomgt.2017.12.005

Kshetri, N. (2019). Blockchain and the Economics of Customer Satisfactio. *IT Professional*, *21*(1), 93–97. doi:10.1109/MITP.2018.2881299

Kulkarni, M., & Patil, K. (2020). Blockchain technology adoption using toe framework. *Int. J. Sci. Technol. Res.*, *9*, 1109–1117.

Kumar, G., Saha, R., Buchanan, W. J., Geetha, G., Thomas, R., Rai, M. K., & Alazab, M. (2020). Decentralized accessibility of e-commerce products through blockchain technology. *Sustainable Cities and Society*, *62*, 102361. doi:10.1016/j.scs.2020.102361

Kumar, V., & Pansari, A. (2016). Competitive advantage through engagement. *JMR, Journal of Marketing Research*, *53*(4), 497–514. doi:10.1509/jmr.15.0044

Kumar, V., Rajan, B., Gupta, S., & Dalla Pozza, I. (2019). Customer engagement in service. *Journal of the Academy of Marketing Science*, *47*(1), 138–160. doi:10.100711747-017-0565-2

Kumar, V., & Ramachandran, D. (2020). (in press). Developing firms' growth approaches as a multidimensional decision to enhance key stakeholders' wellbeing. *International Journal of Research in Marketing*. doi:10.1016/j.ijresmar.2020.09.004

Kyriazis, N. A. (2019). A survey on efficiency and profitable trading opportunities in cryptocurrency markets. *Journal of Risk and Financial Management*, *12*(2), 67. doi:10.3390/jrfm12020067

Lahkani, M. J., Wang, S., Urbański, M., & Egorova, M. (2020). Sustainable B2B E-commerce and blockchain-based supply chain finance. *Sustainability (Basel)*, *12*(10), 3968. doi:10.3390u12103968

Lee, M., Almirall, E., & Wareham, J. (2015). Open data and civic apps: First-generation failures, second-generation improvements. *Communications of the ACM*, *59*(1), 82–89. doi:10.1145/2756542

Leydesdorff, L. B. L. M. R. O. T., Bornmann, L., Mutz, R., & Opthof, T. (2011). Turning the tables on citation analysis one more time: Principles for comparing sets of documents. *Journal of the American Society for Information Science and Technology*, *62*(7), 1370–1381. doi:10.1002/asi.21534

Liao, Q., & Shao, M. (2021). Discussion on payment application in cross-border e-commerce platform from the perspective of blockchain. In *E3S Web of Conferences* (Vol. 235, p. 03020). EDP Sciences. doi:10.1051/e3sconf/202123503020

Li, M., Shao, S., Ye, Q., Xu, G., & Huang, G. Q. (2020). Blockchain-enabled logistics finance execution platform for capital-constrained E-commerce retail. *Robotics and Computer-integrated Manufacturing*, *65*, 101962. doi:10.1016/j.rcim.2020.101962

Li, S. (2020). Structure optimization of e-commerce platform based on artificial intelligence and blockchain technology. *Wireless Communications and Mobile Computing*, *2020*, 2020. doi:10.1155/2020/8825825

Liu, M., Kang, J., Zou, W., Lee, H., Pan, Z., & Corliss, S. (2017). Using Data to Understand How to Better Design Adaptive Learning. *Technology, Knowledge and Learning*, *22*(3), 271-298. https://link.springer.com/article/10.1007/s10758-017-9326-z

Liu, C., Xiao, Y., Javangula, V., Hu, Q., Wang, S., & Cheng, X. (2018). NormaChain: A blockchain-based normalized autonomous transaction settlement system for IoT-based E-commerce. *IEEE Internet of Things Journal*, *6*(3), 4680–4693. doi:10.1109/JIOT.2018.2877634

Liu, Z., & Li, Z. (2020). A blockchain-based framework of cross-border e-commerce supply chain. *International Journal of Information Management*, *52*, 102059. doi:10.1016/j.ijinfomgt.2019.102059

Li, X., Li, D., Wan, J., Liu, C., & Imran, M. (2018). Adaptive transmission optimization in SDN-based industrial Internet of Things with edge computing. *IEEE Internet of Things Journal*, *5*(3), 1351–1360. doi:10.1109/JIOT.2018.2797187

Lu, X., Niyato, D., Jiang, H., Kim, D. I., Xiao, Y., & Han, Z. (2018). Ambient backscatter assisted wireless powered communications. *IEEE Wireless Communications*, *25*(2), 170–177. doi:10.1109/MWC.2017.1600398

Ma, Y.& Fang, Y. (2020). Current status, issues, and challenges of blockchain applications in education. Int. J. Emerg. Technol. Learn. *iJET, 15,* 20–31.

Ma, Y.; Fang, Y. (2020). Current status, issues, and challenges of Blockchainapplications in education. *Int. J. Emerg. Technol. Learn. iJET, 15*, 20–31.

Mainetti, L., Paiano, R., Pedone, M., Quarta, M., & Dervishi, E. (2022). Digital Brick: Enhancing the Student Experience Using Blockchain, Open Badges and Recommendations. *Education Sciences*, *12*(8), 567. doi:10.3390/educsci12080567

Makhdoom, I., Abolhasan, M., Abbas, H., & Ni, W. (2020). Blockchain-based digital identity management. *IEEE Transactions on Industrial Informatics*, *16*(6), 4109–4116.

Maryvilla University. (2023). *How BlockchainIs Used in Education*. Maryvilla University. https://online.maryville.edu/blog/Blockchain-in-education/

Mckenzie, B. (2018). *Regulatory aspects of initial coin offerings (icos) in Switzerland.* Retrieved from https://www.bakermckenzie.com/en/-/media/files/insight/publications/2018/03/regulatory-aspects-ico switzerland/br_switzerland_regulatoryaspectsico_mar2018.pdf

Mendling, J., Weber, I., Aalst, W. M. P., Brocke, J. V., Cabanillas, C., Daniel, F., & Weidlich, M. (2018). Blockchains for business process management-challenges and opportunities. [TMIS]. *ACM Transactions on Management Information Systems*, *9*(1), 1–16. doi:10.1145/3183367

Mendonca, D., Schwartz, R., & Khan, O. (2019). Blockchain technology in the energy sector: A systematic review of challenges and opportunities. *Renewable & Sustainable Energy Reviews*, *107*, 573–586.

Meng, X., Li, J., Liu, Q., & Kim, D. (2020). Cross-Chain Communication Mechanisms for Heterogeneous Blockchain Systems. *IEEE Access : Practical Innovations, Open Solutions*, *8*, 177273–177285.

Mercanoğlu Erín, S. & Dİnçşahİn, A. (2021). Barriers to Global Branding and The Metaverse. *International Aegean Scientific Research Symposium.* AMA.

Mishra, S., Arora, H., Parakh, G., & Khandelwal, J. (2022). Contribution of Blockchain in Development of Metaverse. *2022 7th International Conference on Communication and Electronics Systems (ICCES)*, (pp. 845–850). IEEE. 10.1109/ICCES54183.2022.9835986

Momtaz, P. P. (2021). Entrepreneurial Finance and Moral Hazard: Evidence from Token Offerings. *Journal of Business Venturing*, *36*(5), 106001. Advance online publication. doi:10.1016/j.jbusvent.2020.106001

Monetary Authority of Singapore. (2018). *A guide to digital token offerings*. Retrieved from https://www.mas.gov.sg/~/media/MAS/News%20and%20Publications/Monograps% 20and%20 Information%20Papers/Guide%20to%20Digital%20Token%20Offerings% 20last%20updated%20 on%2030%20Nov.pdf

Monetary Authority of Singapore. (2019). *A guide to digital token offerings*. Retrieved from https://www.mas.gov.sg/-/media/MAS/Sectors/Guidance/Guide-to-Digital-Tokens- Offering 23-Dec-2019.pdf

Money and Bank Thailand. (2020). *Smart money*. Retrieved from https://www.moneyandbanking.co.th/article/the-guru/cryptocurency-smart-money- mb466-feb-2021-110264/

Moro, A., & Wang, D. (2019). Fintech projects and initial coin offerings: A research note. *The Journal of Entrepreneurial Finance*, *21*(1), 24–37. doi:10.57229/2373-1761.1350

Mougayar, W. (2016). *The Business Blockchain: Promise, Practice, and Application of the Next Internet Technology*. Wiley.

Müller, S., & Martin, S. (2019). Toward blockchain-based secure and resilient disaster communications. *IEEE Internet Computing*, *23*(6), 59–64.

Murray, C. (2020). *What is Customer Engagement? Definition, Benefits, and Strategies for Success*. Outreach. https://www.outreach.io/blog/what-is-customer-engagement

Nakamoto, S. (2008). *Bitcoin: A Peer-to-Peer Electronic Cash System*. Bitcoin. https://bitcoin.org/bitcoin.pdf

NanoMatriX. (2022). *The Future of Customer Engagement with Blockchain*. NanoMatriX. https://www.nanomatrixsecure.com/the-future-of-customer-engagement-with-blockchain/

Narayanan, A., Bonneau, J., Felten, E., Miller, A., & Goldfeder, S. (2016). *Bitcoin and Cryptocurrency Technologies: A Comprehensive Introduction*. Princeton University Press.

Neeraj, S., Hepu, D., & Alemyehu, M. (2018, May). Investigating the Critical Success Factors of Digital Transformation for Improving Customer Experience. *International Conference on Information Resources Management (CONF-IRM)*. AISEL. https://aisel.aisnet.org/cgi/viewcontent.cgi?article=1020&context=confirm2018

Neves, J., Bacalhau, L. M., & Santos, V. (2024). A Systematic Review on the Customer Journey Between Two Worlds: Reality and Immersive World. In J. L. Reis, M. Del Rio Araujo, L. P. Reis, & J. P. M. Dos Santos (Eds.), *Marketing and Smart Technologies* (Vol. 344, pp. 401–416). Springer Nature Singapore. doi:10.1007/978-981-99-0333-7_29

Nguyen, Q. K. (2016). *Blockchain: A Financial Technology for Long-Term Sustainable Growth Proceeds of the 3rd International Conference on Green Technology and Sustainable Development*. IEEE. httIEE., ieeexplore.ieee.org/document/7796617

NIST. (2018). *Blockchain Technology Overview*. National Institute of Standards and Technology. https://nvlpubs.nist.gov/nistpubs/ir/2018/NIST.IR.8202.pdf https://nvlpubs.nist.gov/nistpubs/ir/2018/NIST.IR.8202.pdf

Nolan, A. R., Dartley, E. T., Baker, M. B., ReVeal, J., & Rinearson, J. E. (2018). Initial coin offerings: Key US legal considerations for ICO investors and sponsors. *Journal of Investment Compliance*, *19*(1), 1–9. doi:10.1108/JOIC-02-2018-0016

Norris A. C. (2016). Current trends and challenges in health informatics. *Health Informatics J Jul 25, 8*(4), 205-213. [] doi:10.1177/146045820200800407

Novo, O. (2018). Blockchain meets IoT: An architecture for scalable access management in IoT. *IEEE Internet of Things Journal*, *5*(2), 1184–1195. doi:10.1109/JIOT.2018.2812239

Nwachukwu, D., & Maudlinepac, B. E. (2022). Auditory Marketing Strategy and Customers Experience in Bar & Restaurant Businesses in Port Harcourt. *International Journal of Business, Economics and Entrepreneurship Development in Africa, 10*(5).

O'Leary, D. E. (2013). 'Big data', the 'internet of things' and the 'internet of signs'. *International Journal of Intelligent Systems in Accounting Finance & Management*, *20*(1), 53–65. doi:10.1002/isaf.1336

O'Leary, D. E. (2018). Open information enterprise transactions: Business intelligence and wash and spoof transactions in blockchain and social commerce. *International Journal of Intelligent Systems in Accounting Finance & Management*, *25*(3), 148–158. doi:10.1002/isaf.1438

OECD. (2020). *Opportunities and Challenges of BC Technologies in Health Care*. OECD BC Policy Series. https://www.oecd.org/finance/Opportunities-and-Challenges-of-BC-Technologies-in-Health-Care.pdf

Ojiaku, O. C., Euphemia, M. I., & Chike, N. K. (2022). Customer Experience Management and Customers'. *Commitment:Evidence from the Church Parishioners in Nigeria*, *4*(10), 19.

Olaleye, S. A., Kwafo, D., Atobatele, A. J., & Olaoye, O. P. (2024). The Bibliometric Commingling of Metaverse and Non-fungible Tokens in Marketing. In J. L. Reis, M. Del Rio Araujo, L. P. Reis, & J. P. M. Dos Santos (Eds.), *Marketing and Smart Technologies* (Vol. 344, pp. 387–399). Springer Nature Singapore. doi:10.1007/978-981-99-0333-7_28

Olorunsola, V. O., Saydam, M. B., Lasisi, T. T., & Eluwole, K. K. (2023). Customer experience management in capsule hotels: A content analysis of guest online review. *Journal of Hospitality and Tourism Insights*. doi:10.1108/JHTI-03-2022-0113

Open-Tec. (2019). *Look inside jirayut srupsrisopa: The thai digital currency pioneer*. Retrieved from https://www.open-tec.com/look-inside-jirayut-srupsrisopa-the-thai- digital-currency-pioneer-2/

Originstamp. (2023). *Benefits and Challenges of Blockchain in Education*. Orginstamp. https://originstamp.com/blog/benefits-and-challenges-of-blockchain-in-education/

Ostern, N. K., & Riedel, J. (2020). Know-your-customer (kyc) requirements for initial coin offerings. *Business & Information Systems Engineering*, 1–17. doi:10.100712599-020-00677-6

Pansari, A., & Kumar, V. (2018). Customer engagement marketing. In R. Palmatier, V. Kumar, & C. Harmeling (Eds.), *Customer Engagement Marketing* (pp. 1–27). Springer. doi:10.1007/978-3-319-61985-9_1

Papagiannidis, S., & Bourlakis, M. A. (2010). Staging the New Retail Drama: At a Metaverse near you! *Journal of Virtual Worlds Research*, *2*(5), 425–446. doi:10.4101/jvwr.v2i5.808

Parizo, C. (2021). *What are the 4 different types of blockchain technology?* TechTarget. https://www.techtarget.com/searchcio/feature/What-are-the-4-different-types-of-blockchain-technology

Petrov, I., Zhao, S., Vasarhelyi, M. A., & Wu, S. J. (2021). Big Data, Blockchain and Artificial Intelligence: Developing a Framework for Disaster Management. *Journal of Information Systems*, *35*(1), 89–100.

Philip, F. (2021). 3 Ways That BC Can Help the Healthcare Industry Focus More on Patient Care and Less on Administrative Headaches. *Insights*. https://www.fisherphillips.com/news-insights/3-ways-that-BC-help-healthcare-industry.html

Pietrewicz, L. (2018). Emerging Trends in Entrepreneurial Finance. *The Rise of ICOs*, *2*(27), 65–78. doi:10.7172/1733-9758.2018.27.6

Piscini, E., Guastella, J., Rozman, A., & Nassim, T. (2016). *Blockchain: Democratized trust. Distributed ledgers and the future of value.* Deloitte University Press. https://www2.deloitte.com/content/dam/Deloitte/uk/Documents/technology/deloitte-uktech-trends-2016-BC.pdf

Poon, J., & Dryja, T. (2016). *The Bitcoin Lightning Network: Scalable Off-Chain Instant Payments*. Lightening Network. https://lightning.network/lightning-network-paper.pdf

Popa Chivu, R.-G., Popa, I.-C., Orzan, M.-C., Marinescu, C., Florescu, M. S., & Orzan, A.-O. (2022). The Role of Blockchain Technologies in the Sustainable Development of Students' Learning Process. *Sustainability, 14*(3), 1406. MDPI AG. Retrieved from doi:10.3390/su14031406

Pritchard, A. (1969). Statistical Bibliography or Bibliometrics. *The Journal of Documentation*, 348–349.

Purdon, I., & Erturk, E. (2017). Perspectives of BC Technology, its Relation to the Cloud and its Potential Role in Computer Science Education. *Eng. Technol. Appl. Sci. Res.*, *7*(6), 2340–2344. doi:10.48084/etasr.1629

Purohit, A. (2022). *The Impact of Blockchain on the Education Industry*. eLearning Industry. https://elearningindustry.com/ways-blockchain-impacts-education-industry-in-2022-and-beyond

Purohit, A. (2022). *The Impact of Blockchainon the Education Industry*. eLearning Industry. https://elearningindustry.com/ways-BC-impacts-education-industry-in-2022-and-beyond

Qiu, C., Yao, H., Yu, F. R., Jiang, C., & Guo, S. (2019). A service-oriented permissioned blockchain for the Internet of Things. *IEEE Transactions on Services Computing*, *13*(2), 203–215. doi:10.1109/TSC.2019.2948870

Rahmani, M. K. I., Shuaib, M., Alam, S., Siddiqui, S. T., Ahmad, S., Bhatia, S., & Mashat, A. (2022). BC-Based Trust Management Framework for Cloud Computing-Based Internet of Medical Things (IoMT): A Systematic Review. *Computational Intelligence and Neuroscience*, *2022*, 9766844. doi:10.1155/2022/9766844 PMID:35634070

Raja Santhi, A., & Muthuswamy, P. (2022). Influence of blockchain technology in manufacturing supply chain and logistics. *Logistics*, *6*(1), 15. doi:10.3390/logistics6010015

Rajaretnam, T. (2012). The Society of Digital Information and Wireless Communications (SDIWC). *International Journal of Cyber-Security and Digital Forensics*, *1*(3), 232–240.

Raman, R. K., & Varshney, L. R. (2018). Distributed storage meets secret sharing on the blockchain. *2018 Information Theory and Applications Workshop (ITA)*. IEEE. 10.1109/ITA.2018.8503089

Ray, P. P., Dash, D., Salah, K., & Kumar, N. (2020). BC for IoT-based healthcare: Background, consensus, platforms, and use cases. *IEEE Systems Journal*.

Reiff, N. (2020). *Blockchain Explained*. Investopedia. Available at.

Reiff, N. (2020). *Blockchain Technology's Three Generations*. Investopedia. Available at.

Rejeb, A., Keogh, J. G., & Treiblmaier, H. (2020). How Blockchain Technology Can Benefit Marketing. *Six Pending Research Areas. Front. Blockchain*, *3*, 3. doi:10.3389/fbloc.2020.00003

Richter, N., Jackson, P., & Schildhauer, T. (2018). Entrepreneurial behaviour and Start-ups: The case of Germany and the USA. In Entrepreneurial innovation and leadership (pp. 1-14). Palgrave Pivot.

Riley, M., & Szivas, E. (2009). The valuation of skill and the configuration of HRM. *Tourism Economics*, *15*(1), 105–120. doi:10.5367/000000009787536771

Rivera-Vargas, P., & Cobo, C. (2018). Plan Ceibal en Uruguay: una política que conecta inclusión e innovación. In P. Rivera-Vargas, J. Muñoz-Saavedra, R. Morales Olivares, & S. Butendieck-Hijerra (Eds.), *Políticas Públicas para la Equidad Social* (pp. 4–29). Colección Políticas Públicas, Universidad de Santiago de Chile., Recuperado de https://digital.fundacionceibal.edu.uy/jspui/handle/123456789/266

Rivera-Vargas, P., & Miño-Puigcercós, R. (2018). Young people and virtual communities.: New ways of learning and of social participation in the digital society. *Páginas de Educación*, *11*(1), 67–82. doi:10.22235/pe.v11i1.1554

Rivera-Vargas, P., Sancho-Gil, J. M., & Sánchez, J. A. (2017). Los límites de la disrupción en el orden académico. La cultura DIY en la universidad. *Páginas de Educación*, *10*(2), 127–142. doi:10.22235/pe.v10i2.1428

Rodriguez, M. T. (2017). *Blockchain Technology in Disaster Management.* [A Master's Thesis. University of California, Los Angeles].

Ruiz-Alba, J. L., Quero, M. J., & López-Tenorio, P. J. (2023). Institutions and business customer experience: The role of interfunctional coordination and service co-design. *European Research on Management and Business Economics*, *29*(1), 100213. doi:10.1016/j.iedeen.2022.100213

Ryan, P. A. (2017). Smart contract relations in e-commerce: Legal implications of exchanges conducted on the blockchain. *Technology Innovation Management Review*, *7*(10), 14–21. doi:10.22215/timreview/1110

Saini, H., Bhushan, B., Arora, A., & Kaur, A. (2019). Security vulnerabilities in Information communication technology: Blockchain to the rescue (A survey on Blockchain Technology). In *2019 2nd International Conference on Intelligent Computing, Instrumentation and Control Technologies (ICICICT)* (*Vol. 1*, pp. 1680– 1684). Kannur, India: IEEE.

Samieifar, S., & Baur, D. G. (2020). Read me if you can! An analysis of ICO white papers. *Finance Research Letters*. Advance online publication. doi:10.1016/j.frl.2020.101427

Schmidt, C. G., & Wagner, S. M. (2019). Blockchain and supply chain relations: A transaction cost theory perspective. *Journal of Purchasing and Supply Management*, *25*(4), 100552. doi:10.1016/j.pursup.2019.100552

Schückes, M., & Gutmann, T. (2020). The role of economic drivers and social identity on funding choice. *Small Business Economics*, 1–26. doi:10.100711187-020-00337-9

SEC. (2018). *Emergency decree on digital asset businesses B.E. 2561*. Retrieved from https://www.sec.or.th/EN/Documents/ActandRoyalEnactment/RoyalEnactment/enac tment-digitalasset2018.pdf

Selwyn, N. (2015). Data entry: Towards the critical study of digital data and education. *Learning, Media and Technology*, *40*(1), 64–82. https://www.tandfonline.com/doi/abs/10.1080/17439884.2014.921628. doi:10.1080/17439884.2014.921628

Selwyn, N. (2016). *Is technology good for education?* John Wiley & Sons.

Selwyn, N. (2018). Data points: Exploring data-driven reforms of education. *British Journal of Sociology of Education*, *39*(5), 1–9. doi:10.1080/01425692.2018.1469255

SET. (2020). *Summary of the emergency decree on digital asset businesses B.E. 2561*. https://www.sec.or.th/TH/Documents/DigitalAsset/enactment_digital_2561_summar y_en.pdf

Sharma, A. K., Sharma, D. M., Purohit, N., Sharma, S. A., & Khan, A. (2022). Blockchain Technology: Myths, Realities and Future. In Blockchain Technology (pp. 163-180). CRC Press.

Sharma, T., Satija, S., & Bhushan, B. (2019). Unifying Blockchian and IoT: Security Requirements, Challenges, Applications and Future Trends. *2019 International Conference on Computing, Communication, and Intelligent Systems* (ICCCIS). IEEE. 10.1109/ICCCIS48478.2019.8974552

Shoaib, M., Lim, M. K., & Wang, C. (2020). An integrated framework to prioritize blockchain-based supply chain success factors. *Industrial Management & Data Systems, 120*(11), 2103–2131. doi:10.1108/IMDS-04-2020-0194

Shrestha, R., Nam, S. Y., Bajracharya, R., & Kim, S. (2020). Evolution of V2X communication and integration of blockchain for security enhancements. *Electronics (Basel), 9*(9), 1338. doi:10.3390/electronics9091338

Smith, S. S. (2021). Blockchain and Online Learning Are A Powerful Combination. *Forbes.* https://www.forbes.com/sites/seansteinsmith/2020/08/31/BC-and-online-learning-are-a-powerful-combination/?sh=5c52b665718d

Smith, J. D. (2019). Leveraging Blockchain Technology for Enhanced Disaster Management: Security, Decision-Making, and Managerial Implications. In R. K. Johnson (Ed.), *Advances in Disaster Management* (pp. 45–68). Academic Press.

Sofaer, D., Clark, D., & Diffie, W. (2012). *Cyber Security and International Agreements.* Internet Corporation for Assigned Names and Numbers.

So, K., King, C., & Sparks, B. (2015). Customer Engagement with Tourism Brands: Scale Development and Validation. *Journal of Hospitality & Tourism Research (Washington, D.C.)*, 304–329.

Sosa-Tzec, O. (2022). Delight in the User Experience: Form and Place. In G. Bruyns & H. Wei (Eds.), [ ] With Design: Reinventing Design Modes (pp. 111–120). Springer Nature Singapore. doi:10.1007/978-981-19-4472-7_8

Spillner, J. (2021). FixMyStadtmelder: Challenges and Solutions in Civic Services for Smart Cities and Regions. *CEUR Workshop Proceedings, 9.* https://ceur-ws.org/Vol-3116/Paper_10.pdf

Swan, M. (2015). *BC: Blueprint for a New Economy* (1st ed.). O'Reilly Media.

Swan, M. (2015). *Blockchain: blueprint for a new economy.* O'Reilly Media, Inc.

Szabo, N. (1996). *Smart Contracts: Building Blocks for Digital Markets.* UVA. https://www.fon.hum.uva.nl/rob/Courses/InformationInSpeech/CDROM/Literature/LOTwinterschool2006/szabo.best.vwh.net/smart_contracts_2.html

Tan, L., Tivey, D., Maddern, G., Kopunic, H., Babidge, W., & Langley, S. (2020). Part 2: Blockchain technology in health care. *ANZ Journal of Surgery, 90*(12), 2415–2419. doi:10.1111/ans.16455 PMID:33236489

Tapscott, D., & Tapscott, A. (2017). *Blockchain could help artists profit more from their creative works.*

Tapscott, D., & Tapscott, A. (2016). *Blockchain Revolution: How the technology behind Bitcoin is changing money, business, and the world.* Penguin.

Tapscott, D., & Tapscott, A. (2017). How Blockchain Will Change Organizations. *MIT Sloan Management Review*, *58*(2), 10–13.

Thayer, T. L. (2018). 4 promising and ambitious blockchain initiatives for higher education. *Gartner Research*. https://www.gartner.com/en/documents/3893582/4-promising-and-ambitious-blockchain-initiatives-for-hig.

Thayer, T. L., & Yanckello, R. (2019). Education administrative systems innovation primer for 2019. *Gartner Research*. https://www.gartner.com/en/documents/3901065/education-administrative-systems-innovation-primer-for-2, accessed 28 April 2020.

The Banker. (2022, August 1). INNOVATION IN DIGITAL BANKING AWARDS 2022. *The Banker*. https://www.proquest.com/trade-journals/banker-innovation-digital-banking-awards-2022/docview/2696958117

The Story Thailand. (2020). *SET partners with KBTG to launch end-to-end digital-assets platform*. Retrieved from https://www.thestorythailand.com/en/07/10/2020/6639/

Tom Dieck, M. C., & Han, D. D. (2022). The role of immersive technology in Customer Experience Management. *Journal of Marketing Theory and Practice*, *30*(1), 108–119. doi:10.1080/10696679.2021.1891939

Toma, A. M., & Cerchiello, P. (2020). Initial Coin Offerings: Risk or Opportunity? *Frontiers in Artificial Intelligence*, *3*, 18. Advance online publication. doi:10.3389/frai.2020.00018 PMID:33733137

Treiblmaier, H., & Sillaber, C. (2021). The impact of blockchain on e-commerce: A framework for salient research topics. *Electronic Commerce Research and Applications*, *48*, 101054. doi:10.1016/j.elerap.2021.101054

Tribis, Y., El Bouchti, A., & Bouayad, H. (2018). Supply chain management based on blockchain: A systematic mapping study. *International Workshop on Transportation and Supply Chain Engineering 200*(20). 10.1051/matecconf/201820000020

Tschorsch, F., & Scheuermann, B. (2016). Bitcoin and beyond: A technical survey on decentralized digital currencies. *IEEE Communications Surveys and Tutorials*, *18*(3), 2084–2123. doi:10.1109/COMST.2016.2535718

Uncles, M. D., Dowling, G. R., & Hammond, K. (2003). Customer loyalty and customer loyalty programs. *Journal of Consumer Marketing*, *20*(4), 294–316. doi:10.1108/07363760310483676

Underwood, S. (2016). Blockchainbeyond Bitcoin. *Communications of the ACM*, *59*(11), 15–17. doi:10.1145/2994581

Vanheems, R. (2019). The Augmented Customer Experience: Between Humanity and Robotization? In G. N'Goala, V. Pez-Pérard, & I. Prim-Allaz (Eds.), *Augmented Customer Strategy* (1st ed., pp. 117–132). Wiley. doi:10.1002/9781119618324.ch7

Vivek, N., Gonzalo, M.G., Dawn, S. (2022a). *Exploring the Unprecedented Privacy Risks of the Metaverse*. doi:10.48550/ARXIV.2207.13176

Vivek, N., Gonzalo, M.G., Dawn, S. (2022b). *Going Incognito in the Metaverse: Achieving Theoretically Optimal Privacy-Usability Tradeoffs in VR*. doi:10.48550/ARXIV.2208.05604

Wang, H., Chen, K., & Xu, D. (2016). A maturity model for Blockchainadoption. [J]. *Financial Innovation*, *2*(1), 12. doi:10.118640854-016-0031-z

Wang, Q., Zhu, X., Ni, Y., Gu, L., & Zhu, H. (2020). Blockchain for the IoT and industrial IoT: A review. *Internet of Things*, *10*, 100081. Advance online publication. doi:10.1016/j.iot.2019.100081

Wang, T., Hua, H., Wei, Z., & Cao, J. (2022). Challenges of blockchain in new generation energy systems and future outlooks. *International Journal of Electrical Power & Energy Systems*, *135*, 107499. doi:10.1016/j.ijepes.2021.107499

Wegzyn, K. E., & Wang, W. E. (2021). *Types of BC: Public, Private, or Something in Between.* Foley & Larner LLP. https://www.foley.com/en/insights/publications/2021/08/types-of-BC-public-private-between

Wenger & Vieli. (2019). *Baking/fintech license*. Retrieved from https://www.wengervieli.ch/getattachment/39cbfbd7-5897-4bf2-8b48- e56abede6a39/Bank-Fintech-Bewilligung.aspx

Wikipedia. (2022). *Civic technology*. https://en.wikipedia.org/wiki/Civic_technology

Xiao, Y., Zhang, N., Lou, W., & Hou, Y. T. (2020). A Survey of Distributed Consensus Protocols for Blockchain Networks. *IEEE Communications Surveys and Tutorials*, *22*(2), 1432–1465. doi:10.1109/COMST.2020.2969706

Xie, Q., Lu, W., Zhang, Q., Zhang, L., Zhu, T., & Wang, J. (2023). Chatbot Integration for Metaverse—A University Platform Prototype. *2023 IEEE International Conference on Omni-Layer Intelligent Systems (COINS)*, (pp. 1–6). IEEE. 10.1109/COINS57856.2023.10189232

Yao, H., Mai, T., Wang, J., Ji, Z., Jiang, C., & Qian, Y. (2019). Resource trading in blockchain-based industrial Internet of Things. *IEEE Transactions on Industrial Informatics*, *15*(6), 3602–3609. doi:10.1109/TII.2019.2902563

Yasin, M., Liébana-Cabanillas, F., Porcu, L., & Kayed, R. N. (2020). The role of customer online brand experience in customers' intention to forward online company-generated content: The case of the Islamic online banking sector in Palestine. *Journal of Retailing and Consumer Services*, *52*, 101902. doi:10.1016/j.jretconser.2019.101902

Yli-Huumo, J., Ko, D., Choi, S., Park, S., & Smolander, K. (2016). Where Is Current Research on Blockchain Technology?-A Systematic Review. *PLoS One*, *11*(10), e0163477–e0163477. doi:10.1371/journal.pone.0163477 PMID:27695049

Ylilehto, M., Komulainen, H., & Ulkuniemi, P. (2021). The critical factors shaping customer shopping experiences with innovative technologies. *Baltic Journal of Management*, *16*(5), 661–680. doi:10.1108/BJM-02-2021-0049

Zachariadis, M., Hileman, G., & Scott, S. V. (2019). Governance and control in distributed ledgers: Understanding the challenges facing blockchain technology in financial services. *Information and Organization*, *29*(2), 105–117. doi:10.1016/j.infoandorg.2019.03.001

Zajc, T. (2018). F020 BC, value of data, and the role of legislation with adoption. *Medium*. https://medium.com/faces-of-digital-health/f020-BC-value-of-data-and-the-role-of-legislation-withadoption-ray-dogum-health-80919d909e97

Zhaofeng, M., Xiaochang, W., Jain, D. K., Khan, H., Hongmin, G., & Zhen, W. (2019). A Blockchain-based trusted data management scheme in edge computing. *IEEE Transactions on Industrial Informatics*, *16*(3), 2013–2021. doi:10.1109/TII.2019.2933482

Zheng, Z., Xie, S., Dai, H., Chen, X., & Wang, H. (2017). An overview of blockchain technology: Architecture, consensus, and future trends. *2017 IEEE International Congress on Big Data (BigData Congress)*. IEEE. 10.1109/BigDataCongress.2017.85

Zheng. (2017). An Overview of Blockchain Technology: Architecture, Consensus, and Future Trends. *6th IEEE International Congress on Big Data*. IEEE. https://www.researchgate.net/publication/318131748_An_Overview_of_BC_Tec hnology_Architecture_Consensus_and_Future_Trends, accessed June 6 2020.

Zheng, Z., Xie, S., Dai, H. N., Chen, X., & Wang, H. (2018). Blockchain challenges and opportunities: A survey. *International Journal of Web and Grid Services*, *14*(4), 352–375. doi:10.1504/IJWGS.2018.095647

Zhou, Z., Wang, M., Yang, C. N., Fu, Z., Sun, X., & Wu, Q. J. (2021). Blockchain-based decentralized reputation system in E-commerce environment. *Future Generation Computer Systems*, *124*, 155–167. doi:10.1016/j.future.2021.05.035

Zhu, X., & Wang, D. (2019, April). Research on blockchain application for E-commerce, finance and energy. *IOP Conference Series. Earth and Environmental Science*, *252*(4), 042126. doi:10.1088/1755-1315/252/4/042126

About the Contributors

|Kwame Ofori - Editor| **Kwame Simpe Ofori** is currently a PhD student at the Department of Operations and Management Information Systems at the University of Ghana Business School. He has taught courses in areas of Finance and Telecommunications Engineering. He holds a Doctorate Degree in Finance. His research interests are in the areas of consumer behaviour, technology adoption, trust in online systems and PLS path modelling. His papers have appeared in Marketing Intelligence and Planning, International Journal of Bank Marketing, Total Quality Management and Business Excellence and African Journal of Economic and Management Studies.

|George Amoako - Editor| **George Kofi Amoako** BSc (Hons, KNUST); MBA (Marketing, UG); PhD (LondonMet) Chartered Marketer-CIM-UK Profile George Kofi Amoako, is a senior lecturer of department at Marketing Department of University of Professional Studies in Accra Ghana, an academic and a practicing Chartered Marketer (CIM_UK) with specialization in, Sustainability, Branding, CSR and Strategic Marketing. He was educated in Kwame Nkrumah University of Science and Technology in Kumasi Ghana and at the University of Ghana and the London School of Marketing (UK).. He has considerable research, teaching, consulting and practice experience in the application of Marketing Theory and principles to everyday marketing challenges and management and Organizational issues .He is a Chartered Marketer with The Chartered Institute of Marketing-UK . He has consulted for Public Sector and Private organizations both in Ghana and UK. George has published extensively in internationally peer-reviewed academic journals and presented many papers at international conferences

|Fatawu Alhassan - Contributing Author| **Alhassan Fatawu** is a PhD candidate at KNUST, Ghana. He is a Senior Lecturer at Tamale Technical Universityt. Fatawu holds an MBA and MA Marketing.He also holds an Msc Hospitality and Tourism Management. His research interests include strategic marketing, hospitality and tourism marketing in emerging economies. Fatawu is the curreent Head of depart-

met for the Hospitality and Tourism Management Department in Tamale Technical University in Ghana

|Abdul-Rasheed Alhassan Alolo - Contributing Author| **Alhassan Alolo Abdul-Rasheed Akeji** is a senior lecturer in the School of Business attached to the Department of Logistics and Procurement Management at the Tamale Technical University (TaTu), Ghana. He received his doctorate degree in Management Science and Engineering from Jiangsu University in the People's Republic of China. He also obtained Masters in Business Administration (MBA) in strategic management and consulting, Master of Arts in Human Resource Development (HRD), MSc in Logistics and Supply Chain management, and an MSc in Organisational Development from KNUST, UCC, KNUST, and UDS respectively. His research interest include application of Big Data analytics and supply-Chain Management, IOT and supply chain management, supply-Chain ecosystem, shared value creation.

|Sussana Antwi-Boasiako - Contributing Author| **Sussana Antwi-Boasiako** is a lecturer with Accra Technical University Department of Hotel Catering and Institutional Management.

|Amodaah Apusiyine - Contributing Author| **Amodah Deborah Apusiyine** is an aspiring Masters candidate, She is a Teaching Assistant at Tamale Technical University. Amodaah Deborah holds a Bachelor of Technology in Hospitality Management and HND in Hotel Catering and Institutional Management. Her research interests include strategic marketing, hospitality and tourism marketing in emerging economies and comparing market orientation and product innovation on restaurant new product performance and the mediation role of generic strategies. Amodaah Deborah is currently a Teaching Assistant in Tamale Technical University, Ghana.

|Gideon Awini - Contributing Author| **Gideon Awini** is a PhD candidate at the University of Ghana Business School, and a lecturer at Tamale Technical University, Department of Marketing. He holds a Master of Philosophy degree in Marketing. He is a reviewer to Journal of Sport Management and inderscience publishers. His research interests include digital marketing, blockchain, financial services marketing, sports marketing and branding. His recent publications are on "Internet of Things and Retail Performance in an Emerging Market: A Qualitative Analysis", "The Impact of Social Media on Consumer Purchase Behaviour", and "Internet of Things (IoTs) in the Hospitality Sector: Challenges and Opportunities."

|Stanley Cowther - Contributing Author| **Stanley Cowther** is a Lecturer at Tamale Technical University Deaprtment of Hospitality and Tourism Management.

|Mohammed Abdul-Basit Fuseini - Contributing Author| **Mohammed Abdul-Basit Fuseini** is a lecturer with Tamale Technical University in the marketing department. Interest in high academic research and Entrepreneurship. Believes in collaboration with experienced and innovative thinking in resolving social and economic challenges in highly deprived society through research and education.

|Chabi Gupta - Contributing Author| **Chabi Gupta**, Dr., is affiliated with Christ University, India. She has numerous international publications to her credit in reputed globally indexed journals. Her area of interest includes finance, banking and analytics.

|Ruchi Gupta - Contributing Author| **Ruchi Gupta** is a Professor of Marketing at Shaheed Bhagat Singh College, University of Delhi. An educationist, researcher and author. Her interest areas include marketing, digital marketing and advertising.

|Sardar Islam - Contributing Author| **Sardar Islam** is a Professor, ISILC, Victoria University, Melbourne, Australia. Distinguished Visiting Professor of Artificial Intelligence, UnSri. Adjunct Professor of IT and Business, Armstrong Institute, Melbourne. Editor-in-Chief of "International Transactions on Artificial Intelligence".

|Alamu Kehinde - Contributing Author| **Alamu Kehinde** is a Technologist at Tamale Technical University

|Abdul-Mumin Khalid - Contributing Author| **Abdul-Mumin Khalid** (DBE, B.Ed. Mathematics, MPhil Applied Mathematics) The author started his circular education quite late, in 2000/2001 academic year at Jilo Primary School in Bimbilla. This was as a result of his crave for Islamic knowledge. He successfully completed basic school and Junior High and proceeded to Business Senior High in Tamale for secondary education by dint of hard work, determination and perseverance. Abdul-Mumin Khalid's current academic qualifications include M.Phil. Applied Mathematics, a Bachelor's degree in Education in Mathematics, and a Diploma of Education in Science and Mathematics. Abdul-Mumin Khalid had the opportunity of teaching at the Junior High level, Senior High level and currently he is a tutor at E. P. College of Education, Bimbilla in the Northern part of Ghana. Currently, he is the Seminary Presentation Coordinator and Academic Counselor in the College. His research interests include, modeling, integration of technology in Mathematics education, prediction and forecasting, optimizations as well as educational research in the teaching and learning process. Abdul-Mumin Khalid is a part-time lecturer in one of the public universities in Ghana which is the University for Development Studies, (UDS). He is of royal lineage and currently the chief of Yalzoli Yaashenaa in the suburb of Yalzoli, Zabzugu in the Northern part of Ghana. He is currently one

of the renowned Islamic scholars in the Northern part of Ghana. As he is keen in the interest of publications, he has since published a paper on Modeling, the impact and effects of the climatic variable on electricity energy consumption in the Yendi Municipality of Ghana. He has another paper titled, The Benefits and Challenges of social media in Higher Education. He is the proprietor of Al-Khalidiya Technical Islamic School in Bimbilla, the Northern part of Ghana.

|Lubza Nihar Khaliq - Contributing Author| **Lubza Nihar** is an Associate Professor at GITAM School of Business, Gandhi Institute of Technology and Management (Deemed to be University), India. Her research areas include Earnings Management, Islamic finance, Corporate Governance, Financial Inclusion, and Mutual Funds. She is a researcher and case writer. She has published in national and international, Scopus and ABDC-ranked scholarly journals, and presented papers at various national, and international conferences. She is on the editorial board of two reputed national academic journals, and regularly reviews research papers of reputed international journals.(7b5d9c48-4c59-4241-abb2-9e17d913713b)

|Vijaya Kittu Manda - Contributing Author| **Vijaya Kittu Manda** is a multi-dimensional personality, Dr. Vijaya Kittu Manda has nearly 12+ years of experience in capital markets, financial planning, and investing. He is an Advocate, a technocrat, an academician, a book writer, and a stock market enthusiast. He has 10 University Postgraduate Degrees, is NISM Certified in multiple subjects and just submitted his Ph.D. thesis on Mutual Funds. Associated with Smart Investment publications for several years, he contributed over 680 articles to the outlet. He is the Chief Editor for a Management Book Series, writers research papers and case studies, and is a speaker for colleges and universities. He conducts Seminars & Webinars in India and abroad on various trading and investing topics. He is a resource person for various conferences and is a peer reviewer for various research outlets.

|Yuan Miao - Contributing Author| **Yuan Miao** received his MEng and PhD from Tsinghua University's Automation Department and has since held various academic positions, including lecturer and associate professor at the Department of Computer Science and Technologies. He also earned a BSc from Shandong University's Control and System Science Institute. Yuan's recent research focus on AI and digital transformation, particularly cognitive knowledge modelling (FCM), NLP, ehealth, cyber security, and their practical applications. He has published 131 research papers, two of which are among the most highly cited works in FCM from 2000-2010. Yuan's research has been generously supported by industry leaders such as Microsoft, Amazon, Oracle, and Google, as well as government funding bodies like the Australia Research Council ARC, Data61, and Singapore NRF. Currently,

he holds the position of professor and Head of IT Program at the College of Arts, Business, Law, Education, and IT, as well as the Institute for Sustainable Industries and Liveable Cities.

|Noel Nutsugah - Contributing Author| **Noel Nutsugah** is a Lecturer at the Ghana Institute of Journalism, University of Media, Arts and Communication who has previously published in highly ranked peer-reviewed journals such as the Public Relations Review. He holds a Master of Philosophy degree in Communication and Media Studies from the University of Education, Winneba, and a Master of Arts degree in Corporate Communications and Public Relations from the University of Leeds, England. As a former member of the International Association of Business Communicators (IABC) and currently a member of the Communication Educators' Association of Ghana (CEAG) and the Institute of Public Relations (IPR) – Ghana, Noel is passionate about communication and media research.

|Raphael Odoom - Contributing Author| **Raphael Odoom** is a lecturer of Marketing and Entrepreneurship at the University of Ghana Business School. His research interests are in the areas of branding, digital marketing and small business management. He has published in the International Journal of Contemporary Hospitality Management, Journal of Enterprise Information Management, Qualitative Market Research: An International Journal, Journal of Product and Brand Management, among others.

|Ashish Ramlakan - Contributing Author| **Ashish Ramlakan** is a PhD candidate at Victoria University.

|Baranidharan S. - Contributing Author| **Baranidharan S.** is specialized in Finance Economics and Econometrics. Having 5 years research experience, 2 years of Industrial experience and 6 years of teaching experience. Published 6 patent, 45 research articles in international and national journal which are indexed in Scopus, WoS, Proquest, ABDC, etc.,

Index

P

S

T

U

V

W

www.ingramcontent.com/pod-product-compliance
Lightning Source LLC
LaVergne TN
LVHW081336300926
849161LV00008B/1986
* 9 7 8 1 6 6 8 4 7 6 4 9 9 *